Workshop on Discourse Relation Parsing and Treebanking (DISRPT 2019)

Minneapolis, Minnesota, USA
6 June 2019

Editors:

Amir Zeldes
Debopam Das
Erick Galani Maziero

Juliano Desiderato Antonio
Mikel Iruskieta

ISBN: 978-1-5108-8781-7

NAACL HLT 2019

The Workshop on Discourse Relation Parsing and Treebanking

Proceedings of the Workshop

June 6, 2019
Minneapolis, MN

Proceedings of DISRPT 2019 -
The Workshop on Discourse Relation Parsing and Treebanking

Edited by:

Amir Zeldes, Georgetown University
Debopam Das, Humboldt University of Berlin
Erick Galani Maziero, University of São Paulo
Juliano Desiderato Antonio, Universidade Estadual de Maringa
Mikel Iruskieta, University of the Basque Country

Organizers:

Amir Zeldes, Georgetown University
Debopam Das, Humboldt University of Berlin
Erick Galani Maziero, University of São Paulo
Juliano Desiderato Antonio, Universidade Estadual de Maringa
Mikel Iruskieta, University of the Basque Country

Program Committee:

Stergos Afantenos, IRIT - Université Paul Sabatier, France
Farah Benamara, IRIT - Université Paul Sabatier, France
Eduard Hovy, Carnegie Mellon University, USA
Irene Castellon, Universitat de Barcelona, Spain
Johann Christian Chiarcos, Wolfgang Goethe Universität Frankfurt, Germany
Maria Beatriz Nascimento Decat, Universidade Federal de Minas Gerais, Brazil
Iria da Cunha, Universidad Nacional de Educación a Distancia, Spain
Barbara Di Eugenio, University of Illinois at Chicago, USA
Arantza Diaz de Ilarraza, University of the Basque Country, Spain
Flavius Frasincar, Erasmus University Rotterdam, Netherlands
Maria Eduarda Giering, Universidade do Vale do Rio dos Sinos, Brazil
Nancy Green, University of North Carolina, USA
Kerstin Kunz, Universität Heidelberg, Germany
Ekaterina Lapshinova-Koltunski, Universität des Saarlandes, Germany
Jiri Mirovsky, Charles University, Czech Republic
Anna Nedoluzhko, Charles University, Czech Republic
Thiago Pardo, Universidade de São Paulo, Brazil
Lucie Polakova, Charles University, Czech Republic
Gisela Redeker, University of Groningen, Netherlands
Hannah Rohde, University of Edinburgh, UK
Gerardo Sierra, Universidad Nacional Autónoma de México, Mexico
Christian Stab, Technische Universität Darmstadt, Germany
Manfred Stede, Universität Potsdam, Germany
Mihai Surdeanu, University of Arizona, USA
Maite Taboada, Simon Fraser University, Canada
Juan-Manuel Torres, Laboratoire Informatique d'Avignon, France
Nianwen Xue, Brandeis University, USA

Invited Speaker:

Bonnie Webber, University of Edinburgh

Table of Contents

Conference Program

Thursday, June 6, 2019

09:00–12:00 *Session S1: Session 1*

09:00–09:15 *Opening remarks*
Amir Zeldes, Debopam Das, Erick Galani Maziero, Juliano Antonio Desiderato, Mikel Iruskieta

09:15–10:15 *Invited Talk: "Discourse (2009–2019): Recent successes, future challenges"*
Bonnie Webber

10:15–10:30 *Coffee break*

10:30–11:00 *Toward Cross-theory Discourse Relation Annotation*
Peter Bourgonje and Olha Zolotarenko

11:00–11:30 *Acquiring Annotated Data with Cross-lingual Explicitation for Implicit Discourse Relation Classification*
Wei Shi, Frances Yung and Vera Demberg

11:30–12:00 *From News to Medical: Cross-domain Discourse Segmentation*
Elisa Ferracane, Titan Page, Junyi Jessy Li and Katrin Erk

12:00–13:30 *Lunch break*

13:30–15:00 *Session S2: Session 2*

13:30–14:00 *Nuclearity in RST and signals of coherence relations*
Debopam Das

14:00–14:30 *The Rhetorical Structure of Attribution*
Andrew Potter

14:30–15:00 *Annotating Shallow Discourse Relations in Twitter Conversations*
Tatjana Scheffler, Berfin Aktaş, Debopam Das and Manfred Stede

15:00–16:00   *Session P1: Regular posters*

A Discourse Signal Annotation System for RST Trees
Luke Gessler, Yang Liu and Amir Zeldes

EusDisParser: improving an under-resourced discourse parser with cross-lingual data
Mikel Iruskieta and Chloé Braud

Beyond The Wall Street Journal: Anchoring and Comparing Discourse Signals across Genres
Yang Liu

Towards the Data-driven System for Rhetorical Parsing of Russian Texts
Artem Shelmanov, Dina Pisarevskaya, Elena Chistova, Svetlana Toldova, Maria Kobozeva and Ivan Smirnov

RST-Tace A tool for automatic comparison and evaluation of RST trees
Shujun Wan, Tino Kutschbach, Anke Lüdeling and Manfred Stede

15:00–16:00   *Session P2: Shared task posters*

Multi-lingual and Cross-genre Discourse Unit Segmentation
Peter Bourgonje and Robin Schäfer

ToNy: Contextual embeddings for accurate multilingual discourse segmentation of full documents
Philippe Muller, Chloé Braud and Mathieu Morey

Multilingual segmentation based on neural networks and pre-trained word embeddings
Mikel Iruskieta, Kepa Bengoetxea, Aitziber Atutxa Salazar and Arantza Diaz de Ilarraza

GumDrop at the DISRPT2019 Shared Task: A Model Stacking Approach to Discourse Unit Segmentation and Connective Detection
Yue Yu, Yilun Zhu, Yang Liu, Yan Liu, Siyao Peng, Mackenzie Gong and Amir Zeldes

16:00–18:15   *Session S3: Session 3*

Introduction to Discourse Relation Parsing and Treebanking (DISRPT): 7th Workshop on Rhetorical Structure Theory and Related Formalisms [*]

Amir Zeldes
Georgetown University
az364@georgetown.edu

Debopam Das
University of Potsdam
ddas@sfu.ca

Erick Galani Maziero
Federal University of Lavras
erick.maziero@ufla.br

Juliano Desiderato Antonio
Universidade Estadual de Maringa
jdantonio@uem.br

Mikel Iruskieta
University of the Basque Country
mikel.iruskieta@ehu.eus

Abstract

This overview summarizes the main contributions of the accepted papers at the 2019 workshop on Discourse Relation Parsing and Treebanking (DISRPT 2019). Co-located with NAACL 2019 in Minneapolis, the workshop's aim was to bring together researchers working on corpus-based and computational approaches to discourse relations. In addition to an invited talk, eighteen papers outlined below were presented, four of which were submitted as part of a shared task on elementary discourse unit segmentation and connective detection.

1 Introduction

Study of coherence relations in frameworks such as RST (Mann and Thompson, 1988), SDRT (Asher and Lascarides, 2003) and PDTB (Miltsakaki et al., 2004), has experienced a revival in the last few years, in English and many other languages (Matthiessen and Teruya, 2015; da Cunha, 2016; Iruskieta et al., 2016; Zeldes, 2016, 2017). Multiple sites are now actively engaged in the development of discourse parsers (Feng and Hirst, 2014; Joty et al., 2015; Surdeanu et al., 2015; Xue et al., 2016; Braud et al., 2017), as a goal in itself, but also for applications such as sentiment analysis, argumentation mining, summarization, question answering, or machine translation evaluation (Benamara et al. 2017; Gerani et al. 2019; Durrett et al. 2016; Peldszus and Stede 2016; Scarton et al. 2016 among many others). At the same time, evaluation of results in discourse parsing has proven complicated (see Morey et al. 2017), and progress in integrating results across discourse treebanking frameworks has been slow.

DISRPT 2019 follows a series of biennial events on discourse relation studies, which were initially focused especially on RST, first in Brazil (2007, 2009, 2011, 2013) as part of Brazilian NLP conferences, and then in Spain in 2015 and in 2017, as part of the Spanish NLP conference[1] and INLG 2017.[2] The 2019 workshop aims to broaden the scope of discussion to include participants and program committee members from different discourse theories (especially, but not limited to, RST, SDRT and PDTB). We encouraged the submission of papers with a computational orientation, resource papers and work on discourse parsing, as well as papers that advance the field with novel theoretical contributions and promote cross-framework fertilization. A major theme and a related shared task on discourse unit identification across formalisms aimed to promote convergence of resources and a joint evaluation of discourse parsing approaches.

Fourteen theoretical and applied papers plus four papers for the shared task were accepted for the DISRPT 2019 workshop. A summary of these papers is provided below.

2 Workshop papers

In the first paper of the proceedings, Shi, Yung and Demberg (Shi et al., 2019) consider implicit discourse relation classification as one of the most challenging and important tasks in discourse parsing, due to the lack of connectives as strong linguistic cues. A principle bottleneck to further improvement is the shortage of training data (ca. $\approx$18k instances in the Penn Discourse Treebank (PDTB)). Shi et al. (2019) proposed to acquire additional data by exploiting connectives in transla-

---

[*]Website at https://sites.google.com/view/disrpt2019 in conjunction with the Annual Conference of the NAACL 2019 in Minneapolis, MN.

[1]https://sites.google.com/site/workshoprst2015/.
[2]https://sites.google.com/site/workshoprst2017/.

Proceedings of Discourse Relation Parsing and Treebanking (DISRPT2019), pages 1–6
Minneapolis, MN, June 6, 2019. ©2019 Association for Computational Linguistics

tion: human translators mark discourse relations which are implicit in the source language explicitly in the translation. Using back-translations of such explicitated connectives improves discourse relation parsing performance. This paper addresses the open question of whether the choice of the translation language matters, and whether multiple translations into different languages can be effectively used to improve the quality of the additional data.

Scheffler, Aktaş, Das and Stede (Scheffler et al., 2019) introduce their pilot study applying PDTB-style annotation to Twitter conversations. They present their corpus of 185 Twitter threads and their relational annotation, including an inter-annotator agreement study. They discuss their observations as to how Twitter discourses differ from written news text with respect to discourse connectives and relations. They confirm their hypothesis that discourse relations in written social media conversations are expressed differently than in (news) text. They also find that connective arguments in Twitter often do not appear as full syntactic clauses, and that a few general connectives expressing EXPANSION and CONTINGENCY relations make up the majority of the explicit relations in their data.

Jiang, Yang, Suvarna, Cassula, Zhang and Rose (Jiang et al., 2019) present a package of annotation resources that can be used to apply RST to essays written by students. Furthermore, they highlight the great potential of using RST to provide automated feedback for improving writing quality across genres.

Ferracane, Page, Li and Erk (Ferracane et al., 2019) analyze how well news-trained segmenters perform segmentation in a small-scale medical corpus in English. While they find the expected drop in performance, the nature of the segmentation errors suggests that some problems can be addressed earlier in the pipeline, while others would require expanding the corpus to a trainable size to learn the nuances of the medical domain.

Das (2019) investigates the relationship between the notion of nuclearity as proposed in Rhetorical Structure Theory (RST) and the signalling of coherence relations, examining how mononuclear relations (e.g., ANTITHESIS, CONDITION) and multinuclear relations (e.g., CONTRAST, LIST) are indicated by relational signals, more particularly by discourse markers (e.g., 'be-

cause', 'however', 'if', 'therefore'). He conducts a corpus study, examining the distribution of either type of relations in the RST Discourse Treebank (Carlson et al., 2002) and the distribution of discourse markers for those relations in the RST Signalling Corpus (Das and Taboada, 2018). The results show that discourse markers are used more often to signal multinuclear relations than mononuclear relations. The findings also suggest a complex relationship between the relation types and syntactic categories of discourse markers (subordinating and coordinating conjunctions).

Potter (2019) discusses the relational status of ATTRIBUTION in RST, which has been a matter of ongoing debate. Although several researchers have weighed in on the topic, and although numerous studies have relied upon attributional structures for their analyses, nothing approaching consensus has emerged. Potter's paper identifies three basic issues which, he argues, must be resolved to determine the relational status of attributions. These are identified as the Discourse Units Issue, the Nuclearity Issue, and the Relation Identification Issue. These three issues are analyzed from the perspective of classical RST. A finding of this analysis is that the nuclearity and the relational identification of attribution structures are shown to depend on the writer's intended effect, such that attributional relations cannot be considered as a single relation, but rather as attributional instances of other RST relations.

Bourgonje and Zolotarenko (2019) attempt to automatically induce PDTB-style relations from RST trees. They work with a German corpus of news commentary articles, annotated for RST trees and explicit PDTB-style relations, and focus on inducing the implicit relations in an automated way. Preliminary results look promising as a high-precision (but low-recall) way of finding implicit relations where there is no shallow structure annotated at all, but mapping proves more difficult in cases where EDUs and relation arguments overlap, yet do not seem to signal the same relation.

Alkorta, Gojenola and Iruskieta (Alkorta et al., 2019) present the first results on the annotation of the Basque Opinion Corpus using RST, based on the assumption that discourse information is crucial for a better understanding of the text structure. It is also necessary to describe which part of an opinionated text is more relevant to decide how a text span can change the polarity (strengthen or weaken) of other span by means of coherence relations. Their evaluation results and analysis show the main avenues to improve on a future annotation process. They have also extracted the subjectivity of several rhetorical relations and the results show the effect of sentiment words in relations and the influence of each relation in the semantic orientation value.

Wang, Gyawali, Bruno, Molloy, Evanini and Zechner (Wang et al., 2019) present a paper which aims to model the discourse structure of spontaneous spoken responses within the context of an assessment of English speaking proficiency for non-native speakers. Rhetorical Structure Theory (RST) has been commonly used in the analysis of discourse organization of written texts; however, limited research has been conducted to date on RST annotation and parsing of spoken language, in particular, non-native spontaneous speech. Due to the fact that the measurement of discourse coherence is typically a key metric in human scoring rubrics for assessments of spoken language, they conducted research to obtain RST annotations on non-native spoken responses from a standardized assessment of academic English proficiency. Subsequently, automatic parsers were trained on these annotations to process non-native spontaneous speech. Finally, a set of features were extracted from automatically generated RST trees to evaluate the discourse structure of non-native spontaneous speech, which were then employed to further improve the validity of an automated speech scoring system.

Gessler, Liu and Zeldes (Gessler et al., 2019) present a new system for open-ended discourse relation signal annotation in the framework of Rhetorical Structure Theory (RST), implemented on top of an online tool for RST annotation. The authors discuss existing projects annotating textual signals of discourse relations, which have so far not allowed simultaneously structuring and annotating words signaling hierarchical discourse trees, and demonstrate the design and applications of their interface by extending existing RST annotations in the freely available GUM corpus (Zeldes, 2017).

The paper by Liu (2019) points out that recent research on discourse relations has found that such relations are cued not only by discourse markers (DMs) but also by other textual signals, and that signaling information can be genre-specific. However, while several corpora exist with discourse relation signaling information such as the Penn Discourse Treebank (PDTB, Prasad et al. 2008 and the Rhetorical Structure Theory Signalling Corpus (RST-SC, Das and Taboada 2017), they all annotate a single text type, specifically the Wall Street Journal (WSJ) section of the Penn Treebank (PTB, Marcus et al. 1993), which is limited to the news domain. Liu's paper adapts signal identification and a signal anchoring scheme (Liu and Zeldes, 2019) to three more genres beyond news, and examines the distribution of signaling devices across relations and text types, providing a taxonomy of indicative signals found in her dataset.

For Iruskieta and Braud (2019), development of discourse parsers to annotate the relational discourse structure of a text is crucial for many downstream tasks. However, most existing studies focus on English, assuming quite a large dataset. Discourse data have been annotated for Basque, but training a system on these data is challenging since the corpus is very small. In their paper, Iruskieta and Braud create the first parser based on RST for Basque and investigate the use of data in another language to improve the performance of a Basque discourse parser. More precisely, they build a monolingual system using the small set of data available and investigate the use of multilingual word embeddings to train a system for Basque using data annotated for another language.

Wang, Kutschbach, Lüdeling and Stede (Wang et al., 2019) present RST-Tace, a tool for automatic comparison and evaluation of RST trees. RST-Tace serves as an implementation of Iruskieta's comparison method (Iruskieta et al., 2015), which allows trees to be compared and evaluated without the influence of decisions at lower levels in a tree in terms of four factors: constituent, attachment point, nuclearity and relation. RST-Tace can be used regardless of the language or the size of rhetorical trees. This tool aims to measure the agreement between two annotators. The result is reflected by F-measure and inter-annotator agreement. Both the comparison table and the result of the evaluation can be obtained automatically.

Shelmanov, Pisarevskaya, Chistova, Toldova, Kobozeva and Smirnov (Shelmanov et al., 2019) present results of the first experimental evaluation of machine learning models trained on Ru-RSTreebank (the first Russian corpus annotated within the RST framework). Various lexical,

quantitative, morphological, and semantic features
were used. In rhetorical relation classification, an
ensemble CatBoost model with selected features
and a linear SVM model provide the best score
(macro F1 = 54.67 $\pm$ 0.38). The authors discovered that most of the important features for rhetorical relation classification are related to discourse
connectives derived from the lexicon of connectives for Russian and from other sources.

3 Shared task

As mentioned above, four papers addressed the
shared task activity proposed for the workshop.
More detailed information about the DISRPT
2019 shared task, along with quantitative results
and system analyses, is provided in a separate report (Zeldes et al., 2019) accompanying these proceedings.

Yu, Zhu, Liu, Liu, Peng, Gong and Zeldes (Yu
et al., 2019) present GumDrop, Georgetown University's entry at the DISRPT 2019 Shared Task
on automatic discourse unit segmentation and connective detection. The authors' approach relies on
model stacking, creating a heterogeneous ensemble of classifiers, which feed into a meta-learner
for each final task: discourse unit segmentation
and connective detection. The system encompasses three trainable component stacks: one for
sentence splitting, one for discourse unit segmentation and one for connective detection. The flexibility of each ensemble allows the system to generalize well to datasets of different sizes and with
varying levels of homogeneity.

Bourgonje and Schäfer (2019) describe a series
of experiments applied to data sets from different languages and genres annotated for coherence
relations according to different theoretical frameworks. Specifically, they investigate the feasibility
of a unified (theory-neutral) approach to discourse
segmentation. The authors apply a Random Forest
and an LSTM based approach for all datasets and
improve over a simple baseline assuming sentence
or clause-like segmentation. Performance however varies considerably depending on language,
and more importantly genre, with F-scores ranging from 0.73 to 0.944.

For Iruskieta, Bengoetxea, Salazar and Diaz de
Ilarraza (Iruskieta et al., 2019), Elementary Discourse Units (EDUs) are quite similar across different theories. Segmentation is the very first stage
on the way of rhetorical annotation. Still, each

annotation project adopted several decisions with
consequences not only for the annotation of the relational discourse structure but also at the segmentation stage. In this shared task, the authors have
employed pre-trained word embeddings, neural
networks (BiLSTM+CRF) to perform the segmentation. They report F1 results for 6 languages:
Basque (0.853), English (0.919), French (0.907),
German (0.913), Portuguese (0.926) and Spanish
(0.868 and 0.769) (for results on more datasets, see
the report in Zeldes et al. 2019). Finally, they also
pursued an error analysis based on clause typology
for Basque and Spanish, in order to understand the
performance of the segmenter.

According to Muller, Braud and Morey (Muller
et al., 2019), segmentation is the first step in building practical discourse parsers, and is often neglected in discourse parsing studies. The goal
is to identify the minimal spans of text to be
linked by discourse relations, or to isolate explicit
marking of discourse relations. Existing systems
on English report F1 scores as high as 0.95, but
they generally assume gold sentence boundaries
and are restricted to English newswire texts annotated within the RST framework. Their paper
presents a generic approach and a system, ToNy,
a discourse segmenter developed for the DISRPT
shared task where multiple discourse representation schemes, languages and domains are represented. In their experiments, the authors found
that a straightforward sequence prediction architecture with pretrained contextual embeddings is
sufficient to reach performance levels comparable
to existing systems, when separately trained on
each corpus. They report performance between
0.81 and 0.96 in F1 score. They also observed
that discourse segmentation models only display
a moderate generalization capability, even within
the same language and discourse representation
scheme.

References

Jon Alkorta, Koldo Gojenola, and Mikel Iruskieta.
2019. Towards discourse annotation and sentiment
analysis of the Basque Opinion Corpus. In *Proceedings of Discourse Relation Treebanking and Parsing
(DISRPT 2019)*, Minneapolis, MN.

Nicholas Asher and Alex Lascarides. 2003. *Logics of
conversation*. Cambridge University Press.

Farah Benamara, Maite Taboada, and Yannick Mathieu. 2017. Evaluative language beyond bags of

words: Linguistic insights and computational applications. *Computational Linguistics*, 43(1):201–264.

Peter Bourgonje and Robin Schäfer. 2019. Multilingual and cross-genre discourse unit segmentation. In *Proceedings of Discourse Relation Treebanking and Parsing (DISRPT 2019)*, Minneapolis, MN.

Peter Bourgonje and Olha Zolotarenko. 2019. Toward cross-theory discourse relation annotation. In *Proceedings of Discourse Relation Treebanking and Parsing (DISRPT 2019)*, Minneapolis, MN.

Chloé Braud, Maximin Coavoux, and Anders Søgaard. 2017. Cross-lingual RST Discourse Parsing. In *Proceedings of EACL 2017*, pages 292–304, Valencia, Spain.

L Carlson, D Marcu, and ME Okurowski. 2002. RST Discourse Treebank. Linguistic Data Consortium.

Iria da Cunha. 2016. towards discourse parsing in Spanish. In *TextLink–Structuring Discourse in Multilingual Europe Second Action Conference Károli Gáspár University of the Reformed Church in Hungary Budapest, 11–14 April, 2016*, page 40.

Debopam Das. 2019. Nuclearity in RST and signals of coherence relations. In *Proceedings of Discourse Relation Treebanking and Parsing (DISRPT 2019)*, Minneapolis, MN.

Debopam Das and Maite Taboada. 2017. Signalling of coherence relations in discourse, beyond discourse markers. *Discourse Processes*, pages 1–29.

Debopam Das and Maite Taboada. 2018. RST Signalling Corpus: a corpus of signals of coherence relations. *Language Resources and Evaluation*, 52(1):149–184.

Greg Durrett, Taylor Berg-Kirkpatrick, and Dan Klein. 2016. Learning-based single-document summarization with compression and anaphoricity constraints. In *Proceedings of ACL 2016*, pages 1998–2008, Berlin.

Vanessa Wei Feng and Graeme Hirst. 2014. A linear-time bottom-up discourse parser with constraints and post-editing. In *Proceedings of the 52nd Annual Meeting of the Association for Computational Linguistics (Volume 1: Long Papers)*, volume 1, pages 511–521.

Elisa Ferracane, Titan Page, Junyi Jessy Li, and Katrin Erk. 2019. From news to medical: cross-domain discourse segmentation. In *Proceedings of Discourse Relation Treebanking and Parsing (DISRPT 2019)*, Minneapolis, MN.

Shima Gerani, Giuseppe Carenini, and Raymond Ng. 2019. Modeling content and structure for abstractive review summarization. *Computer Speech & Language*, (53):302–331.

Luke Gessler, Yang Liu, and Amir Zeldes. 2019. A discourse signal annotation system for RST trees. In *Proceedings of Discourse Relation Treebanking and Parsing (DISRPT 2019)*, Minneapolis, MN.

Mikel Iruskieta, Kepa Bengoetxea, Aitziber Atutxa, and Arantza Diaz de Ilarraza. 2019. Multilingual segmentation based on neural networks and pretrained word embeddings. In *Proceedings of Discourse Relation Treebanking and Parsing (DISRPT 2019)*, Minneapolis, MN.

Mikel Iruskieta and Chlo Braud. 2019. EusDisParser: improving an under-resourced discourse parser with cross-lingual data. In *Proceedings of Discourse Relation Treebanking and Parsing (DISRPT 2019)*, Minneapolis, MN.

Mikel Iruskieta, Iria Da Cunha, and Maite Taboada. 2015. A qualitative comparison method for rhetorical structures: identifying different discourse structures in multilingual corpora. *Language resources and evaluation*, 49(2):263–309.

Mikel Iruskieta, Gorka Labaka, and Juliano Desiderato Antonio. 2016. Detecting the central units in two different genres and languages: a preliminary study of Brazilian Portuguese and Basque texts. *Procesamiento del Lenguaje Natural*, (56):65–72.

Shiyan Jiang, Kexin Yang, Chandrakumari Suvarna, Pooja Casula, Mingtong Zhang, and Carolyn Rose. 2019. Applying Rhetorical Structure Theory to student essays for providing automated writing feedback. In *Proceedings of Discourse Relation Treebanking and Parsing (DISRPT 2019)*, Minneapolis, MN.

Shafiq Joty, Giuseppe Carenini, and Raymond T Ng. 2015. Codra: A novel discriminative framework for rhetorical analysis. *Computational Linguistics*, 41(3):385–435.

Yang Liu. 2019. Beyond the wall street journal: Anchoring and comparing discourse signals across genres. In *Proceedings of Discourse Relation Treebanking and Parsing (DISRPT 2019)*, Minneapolis, MN.

Yang Liu and Amir Zeldes. 2019. Discourse relations and signaling information: Anchoring discourse signals in RST-DT. In *Proceedings of the Society for Computation in Linguistics*, volume 2, pages 314–317.

William C. Mann and Sandra A. Thompson. 1988. Rhetorical Structure Theory: Toward a functional theory of text organization. *Text*, 8(3):243–281.

Mitchell Marcus, Beatrice Santorini, and Mary Ann Marcinkiewicz. 1993. Building a large annotated corpus of English: The Penn Treebank.

Christian MIM Matthiessen and Kazuhiro Teruya. 2015. Grammatical realizations of rhetorical relations in different registers. *Word*, 61(3):232–281.

Eleni Miltsakaki, Rashmi Prasad, Aravind K. Joshi, and Bonnie L. Webber. 2004. The Penn Discourse Treebank. In *Proceedings of LREC 2004*.

Mathieu Morey, Philippe Muller, and Nicholas Asher. 2017. How much progress have we made on RST discourse parsing? A replication study of recent results on the RST-DT. In *Proceedings of EMNLP 2017*, pages 1319–1324, Copenhagen, Denmark.

Philippe Muller, Chloé Braud, and Mathieu Morey. 2019. ToNy: Contextual embeddings for accurate multilingual discourse segmentation of full documents. In *Proceedings of Discourse Relation Treebanking and Parsing (DISRPT 2019)*, Minneapolis, MN.

Andreas Peldszus and Manfred Stede. 2016. Rhetorical structure and argumentation structure in monologue text. In *Proceedings of the Third Workshop on Argument Mining (ArgMining2016)*, pages 103–112.

Andrew Potter. 2019. The rhetorical structure of attribution. In *Proceedings of Discourse Relation Treebanking and Parsing (DISRPT 2019)*, Minneapolis, MN.

Rashmi Prasad, Nikhil Dinesh, Alan Lee, Eleni Miltsakaki, Livio Robaldo, Aravind Joshi, and Bonnie Webber. 2008. The Penn Discourse Treebank 2.0. In *Proceedings of the 6th International Conference on Language Resources and Evaluation (LREC 2008)*, pages 2961–2968, Marrakesh, Morocco.

Carolina Scarton, Daniel Beck, Kashif Shah, Karin Sim Smith, and Lucia Specia. 2016. Word embeddings and discourse information for quality estimation. In *Proceedings of the First Conference on Machine Translation: Volume 2, Shared Task Papers*, volume 2, pages 831–837.

Tatjana Scheffler, Berfin Akta, Debopam Das, and Manfred Stede. 2019. Annotating shallow discourse relations in Twitter conversations. In *Proceedings of Discourse Relation Treebanking and Parsing (DISRPT 2019)*, Minneapolis, MN.

Artem Shelmanov, Dina Pisarevskaya, Elena Chistova, Svetlana Toldova, Maria Kobozeva, and Ivan Smirnov. 2019. Towards the data-driven system for rhetorical parsing of Russian texts. In *Proceedings of Discourse Relation Treebanking and Parsing (DISRPT 2019)*, Minneapolis, MN.

Wei Shi, Frances Yung, and Vera Demberg. 2019. Acquiring annotated data with cross-lingual explicitation for implicit discourse relation classification. In *Proceedings of Discourse Relation Treebanking and Parsing (DISRPT 2019)*, Minneapolis, MN.

Mihai Surdeanu, Tom Hicks, and Marco Antonio Valenzuela-Escarcega. 2015. Two practical Rhetorical Structure Theory parsers. In *Proceedings of the 2015 conference of the North American chapter of the association for computational linguistics: Demonstrations*, pages 1–5.

Xinhao Wang, Binod Gyawali, James V. Bruno, Hillary R. Molloy, Keelan Evanini, and Klaus Zechner. 2019. Using Rhetorical Structure Theory to assess discourse coherence for non-native spontaneous speech. In *Proceedings of Discourse Relation Treebanking and Parsing (DISRPT 2019)*, Minneapolis, MN.

Nianwen Xue, Hwee Tou Ng, Sameer Pradhan, Attapol Rutherford, Bonnie Webber, Chuan Wang, and Hongmin Wang. 2016. CoNLL 2016 shared task on multilingual shallow discourse parsing. *Proceedings of the CoNLL-16 shared task*, pages 1–19.

Yue Yu, Yilun Zhu, Yang Liu, Yan Liu, Siyao Peng, Mackenzie Gong, and Amir Zeldes. 2019. GumDrop at the DISRPT2019 shared task: A model stacking approach to discourse unit segmentation and connective detection. In *Proceedings of Discourse Relation Treebanking and Parsing (DISRPT 2019)*, Minneapolis, MN.

Amir Zeldes. 2016. rstWeb - a browser-based annotation interface for Rhetorical Structure Theory and discourse relations. In *Proceedings of NAACL-HLT 2016 System Demonstrations*, pages 1–5, San Diego, CA.

Amir Zeldes. 2017. The GUM corpus: Creating multilayer resources in the classroom. *Language Resources and Evaluation*, 51(3):581–612.

Amir Zeldes, Debopam Das, Erick Galani Maziero, Juliano Desiderato Antonio, and Mikel Iruskieta. 2019. The DISRPT 2019 Shared Task on elementary discourse unit segmentation and connective detection. In *Proceedings of Discourse Relation Treebanking and Parsing (DISRPT 2019)*, Minneapolis, MN.

Toward Cross-theory Discourse Relation Annotation

Peter Bourgonje and **Olha Zolotarenko**
Applied Computational Linguistics
University of Potsdam / Germany
`firstname.lastname@uni-potsdam.de`

Abstract

In this exploratory study, we attempt to automatically induce PDTB-style relations from RST trees. We work with a German corpus of news commentary articles, annotated for RST trees and explicit PDTB-style relations and we focus on inducing the implicit relations in an automated way. Preliminary results look promising as a high-precision (but low-recall) way of finding implicit relations where no shallow structure is annotated at all, but mapping proves more difficult in cases where EDUs and relation arguments overlap, yet do not seem to signal the same relation.

1 Introduction

The task of *discourse processing* or *discourse parsing* refers to the extraction of coherence relations between abstract entities (propositions, etc.) from plain text. Within this field, three of the most popular frameworks in terms of influence and available annotated data; the Penn Discourse Treebank (PDTB) (Prasad et al., 2008), Rhetorical Structure Theory (RST) (Mann and Thompson, 1988) and Segmented Discourse Representation Theory (SDRT) (Asher et al., 2003), each have their own characteristics when it comes to representing these coherence relations, both at elementary (segmentation) level, internal structure (global vs. local) and in terms of sense sets used. Generating annotated data for discourse parsing is a costly process (as reflected by the relatively small size of available corpora and the low inter-annotator agreement figures ((Carlson et al., 2001), (Asher et al., 2016))), and available corpora as a result are relatively small compared to corpora annotated for other NLP tasks. Enabling annotations from one framework to enrich annotations in another thus seems a fruitful goal to pursue. For at least two such corpora, annotations on the same source text for two different frameworks

exist; the PDTB and the RST-Discourse Treebank (RST-DT) both use (an overlapping set of) (English) Wall Street Journal articles, and the Potsdam Commentary Corpus has PDTB-style annotations and RST annotations on a set of (German) news commentary articles.

We are working with the Potsdam Commentary Corpus. As a first step toward comparing the relations in both frameworks in independently annotated text, we attempt to map the segments of both frameworks. The main contribution of this paper is to investigate the feasibility of enriching a shallow, PDTB-style annotation layer by exploiting RST-trees for the same text. An overview of similar approaches is listed in Section 2, the corpus we work with is described in Section 3. Results of aligning segments and relations are presented in Section 4 and a brief wrap-up is provided in Section 5.

2 Related Work

There is a large amount of literature on both the RST and PDTB frameworks, but we focus here on the mapping between the two. Earlier work on the same corpus is described in Scheffler and Stede (2016), where PDTB relations are projected onto RST relations (the opposite of what we are doing in this paper) to obtain an overview of sense synergies. The authors note that of the 2,536 RST relations in the corpus, only 932 were marked by an explicit connective, rendering the majority (63%) implicit, which is a promising percentage given our goal of enriching the shallow layer with implicit relations (see Section 3 for more details). Several attempts have been made at unifying the set of senses used in the difference discourse relation frameworks, but most of them do so from a theoretical perspective, i.e. Rehbein et al. (2016), Benamara and Taboada (2015), Bunt and Prasad

7

Proceedings of Discourse Relation Parsing and Treebanking (DISRPT2019), pages 7–11
Minneapolis, MN, June 6, 2019. ©2019 Association for Computational Linguistics

(2016), Chiarcos (2014) and Sanders et al. (2018).

A notable exception is the practical approach based on the PDTB and the RST-DT described by Demberg et al. (2017). The PDTB (Prasad et al., 2008) is annotated on the same set as the RST-DT (Carlson et al., 2002), but the former is considerably larger, with over 1.3m tokens compared to ca. 200k tokens, respectively. This makes the exploitation of shallow annotations to construct RST-trees a potentially more promising (yet probably more complex) venture. Our data however is already annotated for RST-trees and only partly annotated on a shallow level, and also in German (as opposed to English for the PDTB and RST-DT). The general aim of bringing together different discourse frameworks is at the heart of the 2019 DISRPT workshop[1] and hopefully the workshop will inspire more work in this direction.

3   Data & Method

The corpus under investigation is the Potsdam Commentary Corpus (PCC) (Stede and Neumann, 2014), a German collection of news commentary articles from a local German newspaper containing ca. 33k words. The RST layer has been annotated according to the structural constraints defined by Mann and Thompson (1988), using a slightly modified relation set and relations with centrally embedded segments are not annotated in the corpus. The entire corpus contains 176 RST trees (for the 176 articles), containing 3,018 Elementary Discourse Units (EDUs). The shallow (PDTB-style) layer has been annotated only for relations using an explicit connective (using the definition of Pasch et al. (2003)). An explicit relation comprises the connective token(s), the external argument (*arg1*) and the internal argument (*arg2*). There are 1,110 explicit relations in the corpus, meaning that we have twice that number (2,220) of arguments. Both layers have been annotated independently from each other. For further details on annotation procedures, we refer to Stede and Neumann (2014).

Before proceeding with our mapping procedure, it is important to note that the nature of the segments (EDUs in the RST layer, arguments in the shallow layer) are by design of a different type. While in the RST approach, segmentation is a first and essential step in annotating or analysing a text, this is not the case in the PDTB approach. Instead,

the latter first identifies explicit connectives and then locates arguments according to the "minimality principle", which prescribes that only as much material should be included in the argument as is *minimally required* to interpret the relation. Arguments of explicit relations and RST EDUs will be the types of segments we are comparing. Arguments for explicit and implicit relations are of a fundamentally different type (with implicit relation arguments being typically entire sentences, or complete clauses delimited by a (semi-)colon (see Prasad et al. (2017) for more details). However, since we do not have implicit relations in our corpus (in fact, this is exactly what we intend to infer from the RST relations), we can discard this difference during the mapping phase. Section 4 will include more details on the implications of this discrepancy for induced relations.

Additionally, in the RST layer we expect to find many more relations than in the shallow layer. Not only because implicit relations are not included in the latter, but also because RST, in contrast to the shallow approach, includes complex relations, i.e. relations where one or both of the components can be complex units. Because we intend to extract shallow relations, we discard all complex RST relations. The relation between segment 17 and 18 in Figure 1 is taken into account, but the relation involving segment 16 (the conjunction relations 16-18) is not, since one of its nodes is a complex node.

Demberg et al. (2017) implement a more complex, and more complete mapping algorithm, incorporating the Strong Nuclearity hypothesis (Marcu, 2000), which would result in more RST relations (since we could then also consider the relation between a "flat" nucleus and that of a complex structure). Due to the exploratory nature of our approach, we leave this to future work. Our filtering thus results in 2,111 non-complex RST relations in the corpus, compared to the 1,110 relations in the shallow layer. Recall that we have 3,018 EDUs in the RST layer and 2,220 arguments in the shallow layer. Looking at a very general characteristic, the token length, EDUs and *arg1* and *arg2*[2] segments seem relatively comparable. The average length (in tokens) and the standard deviation for the EDUs, *arg1* and *arg2* segments respectively are 11.0/6.1, 13.5/7.3 and 13.0/10.4.

When attempting to map relations, we start

---

[1] https://sites.google.com/view/disrpt2019

[2] Connective tokens are included in *arg2*.

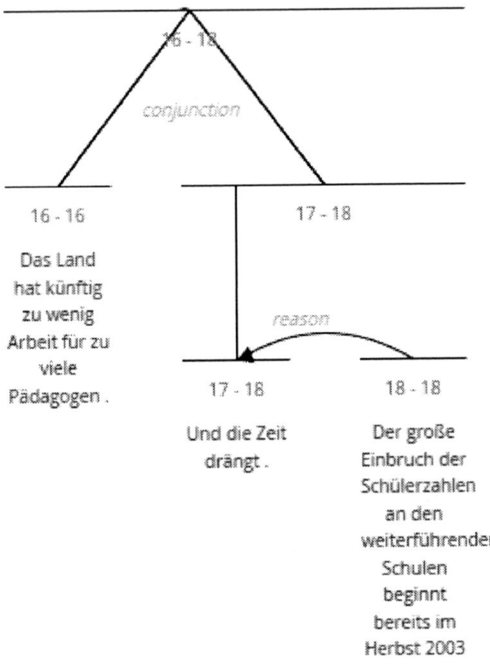

Figure 1: Part of an RST tree

from the RST relation and distinguish three different scenarios:

- There is a complete match, given a small tolerance[3], for the two EDUs and the *arg1* and *arg2*.

- One of the EDUs matches one of the arguments, but the other argument does not match the other EDU(s).

- There is no overlap between the EDU and any argument of any relation.

For the 2,111[4] RST relations, we find 305 complete matches. The second category (where one of the EDUs matches one of the arguments) contains 323 cases, leaving 1,483 cases for the last category. At this point, we leave the further categorisation and investigation of the 323 cases where one EDU matches to future efforts, because the

---

[3]When comparing EDUs and arguments, we assume two segments to match when there is a >75% token overlap, to include cases where the difference is just a punctuation symbol or function word.

[4]Note that this number is smaller than the 2,536 mentioned in Scheffler and Stede (2016) because we use non-complex relations only, also resulting in fewer complete matches (their 452 compared to our 305).

ways in which an existing (explicit) relation interacts with a potential implicit relation induced from the RST layer need careful investigation first. It could be the case that the annotations on both levels refer to the same coherence relation in the text but the arguments are annotated differently. Or they may describe a different relation (as is the case in Example (1) below). We first turn to the remaining 1,483 cases, as these are likely to provide the best candidates for (semi-)automatically adding the RST relations to the shallow layer as implicit relations.

4 Analysis & Results

We manually checked the outcome of the mapping process for 17 documents (ca. 10% of the entire corpus). In these 17 documents, we found 64 RST relations of the third type, i.e. relations for which there was no overlap between the EDU and any argument of any relation (given our tolerance of 75%). Focusing on these cases, we still find many cases (21) where there is partial overlap (but below our threshold) and segmentation differs. An example is shown in (1), where the *arg1* and *arg2* are marked in italics and bold face, respectively. The two EDUs that were recognised in the RST layer however, were "Nun wird der Katastrophenschutz einen neuen Stellenwert bekommen." (*Now disaster prevention will take on a new significance.*) and "Der Landkreis und die Kommunen, vordergründig bedroht oder einfach nur in verständlicher Sorge, sind auf Hilfe angewiesen." (*The administrative district and the municipalities, ostensibly threathened or simply with understandable concern, are dependent on help.*)

(1) "Nun wird der Katastrophenschutz einen neuen Stellenwert bekommen. Der Landkreis und die Kommunen, *vordergründig bedroht* <u>oder</u> **einfach nur in verständlicher Sorge**, sind auf Hilfe angewiesen."

*Now disaster prevention will take on a new significance. The administrative district and the municipalities, ostensibly threatened <u>or</u> **simply with understandable concern**, are dependent on help.*

Before unification at the segmentation level is realised, these cases are difficult to process, as both annotation layers essentially talk about different propositions.

There were several cases where one *arg1* or *arg2* contained two EDUs, meaning that the RST layer made a more fine-grained distinction. This was the case for 7 *arg1*s and 9 *arg2*s. An example is shown in (2), which contains an *arg2* in the PDTB layer (i.e. the first two tokens ("Und so" *And so*) are the connective, and the remaining "muss Landrat ... Folgen angeht." (*district administrator ... its consequences.*) is the entire *arg2*). This argument contains two EDUs: "Und so muss Landrat Christian Gilde jetzt eine gewisse Hilflosigkeit erkennen lassen," (*And so district administrator Christian Gilde must now admit a certain helplessness,*) and "was das Reagieren auf möglichen Terror und seine Folgen angeht." (*when it comes to reacting to possible terror and its consequences.*).

(2) "<u>Und so</u> **muss Landrat Christian Gilde jetzt eine gewisse Hilflosigkeit erkennen lassen, was das Reagieren auf möglichen Terror und seine Folgen angeht.**"

<u>And so</u> *district administrator Christian Gilde must now admit a certain helplessness when it comes to reacting to possible terror and its consequences.*

Example (2) is a good candidate for enriching the shallow layer, as it is introducing structure (an implicit relation) inside an entire argument in the PDTB layer.

This leaves 27 cases where there was no annotation in the PDTB layer at all, marking these as good candidates for (semi-)automated addition as implicit arguments as well. The distribution of senses is quite diverse, with 6 cases annotated (in the RST tree) as e-elaboration, 6 as joint, 5 as span, 3 as sequence and the remaining distributed over conjunction, evaluation-s, contrast, list, elaboration, purpose and reason. Earlier work on sense unification from Scheffler and Stede (2016) can guide in automatically assigning a PDTB sense for these cases. An important note is that there is a fundamental difference between the arguments of explicit and that of implicit relations, as mentioned earlier in Section 3. The arguments of implicit relations typically are sentences and the average sentence length and standard deviation in the PCC is 15.2/8.9 respectively, compared to 11.0/6.1 for EDUs. Using EDUs to populate implicit relations may result in a skewed distribution of implicit arguments. Especially if this semi-automatic step is done first, and then the blanks are filled out by annotating implicit relation in a manner similar to the PDTB one. Arguably, the RST segmentation is more meaningful than the segmentation procedure for implicit PDTB relation stipulation (which links sentences without any further consideration). One way to proceed, after this first semi-automatic step, could therefore be to start out with EDUs from the RST layer and assign them implicit relations if they are not involved in an explicit relation. This effectively puts the segmentation task central to shallow annotations as well, which deviates from the original annotation strategy for shallow discourse relations. As mentioned above, our use case may be somewhat unusual (with the more complex, expensive-to-obtain RST trees available, but only the explicit part of the shallow relations), but first steps indicate that this first phase of our approach is essentially a high-precision, but relatively low-recall means of (semi-)automatically finding implicit relations.

5 Conclusions & Outlook

We explore the feasibility of exploiting discourse annotations following the RST framework to add implicit relations in PDTB-style for a German corpus of news commentary articles annotated for explicit discourse relations (in PDTB-style) only. Our use case may be non-typical, with RST annotations typically being harder and more costly to obtain than shallow PDTB-style annotations, but the first results for adding implicit relations in a semi-automated way look promising. Several issues need more detailed analysis though. Partially overlapping relations (where one of the EDUs matched with one of the arguments) can be about wholly different relations (hence must not be mapped without further investigation), and we focus first on pieces of text for which no PDTB-style annotation exists at all. We consider flat, non-complex RST relations only and our approach can be improved by using the Strong Nuclearity Principle as applied in earlier work on mapping PDTB and RST relations. Segmentation differences between EDUs and implicit relation arguments specifically need more investigation, and generally arriving at a (theory-neutral) standard for discourse segmentation may prove to be very beneficial for the purpose of cross-theory annotation augmentation.

Acknowledgments

Funded by the Deutsche Forschungsgemeinschaft (DFG, German Research Foundation) - 323949969. We would like to thank the anonymous reviewers for their helpful comments on an earlier version of this manuscript.

References

N. Asher, A. Lascarides, S. Bird, B. Boguraev, D. Hindle, M. Kay, D. McDonald, and H. Uszkoreit. 2003. *Logics of Conversation.* Studies in Natural Language Processing. Cambridge University Press.

Nicholas Asher, Julie Hunter, Mathieu Morey, Farah Benamara, and Stergos D. Afantenos. 2016. Discourse structure and dialogue acts in multiparty dialogue: the STAC corpus. In *LREC*. European Language Resources Association (ELRA).

Farah Benamara and Maite Taboada. 2015. Mapping different rhetorical relation annotations: A proposal. In *Proceedings of the Fourth Joint Conference on Lexical and Computational Semantics*, pages 147–152. Association for Computational Linguistics.

Harry Bunt and R. Prasad. 2016. ISO DR-Core (ISO 24617-8): Core Concepts for the Annotation of Discourse Relations. In *Proceedings 10th Joint ACL-ISO Workshop on Interoperable Semantic Annotation*, pages 45–54.

Lynn Carlson, Daniel Marcu, and Mary Ellen Okurowski. 2001. Building a discourse-tagged corpus in the framework of rhetorical structure theory. In *Proceedings of the Second SIGdial Workshop on Discourse and Dialogue - Volume 16*, SIGDIAL '01, pages 1–10, Stroudsburg, PA, USA. Association for Computational Linguistics.

Lynn Carlson, Daniel Marcu, and Mary Ellen Okurowski. 2002. RST Discourse Treebank, ldc2002t07.

Christian Chiarcos. 2014. Towards interoperable discourse annotation. discourse features in the ontologies of linguistic annotation. In *Proceedings of the Ninth International Conference on Language Resources and Evaluation (LREC'14)*, Reykjavik, Iceland. European Language Resources Association (ELRA).

Vera Demberg, Fatemeh Torabi Asr, and Merel Scholman. 2017. How consistent are our discourse annotations? insights from mapping RST-DT and PDTB annotations. *CoRR*, abs/1704.08893.

William Mann and Sandra Thompson. 1988. Rhetorical structure theory: Towards a functional theory of text organization. *Text*, 8:243–281.

Daniel Marcu. 2000. *The Theory and Practice of Discourse Parsing and Summarization.* MIT Press, Cambridge, MA, USA.

Renate Pasch, Ursula Brauße, Eva Breindl, and Ulrich Herrmann Waßner. 2003. *Handbuch der deutschen Konnektoren.* Walter de Gruyter, Berlin/New York.

Rashmi Prasad, Nikhil Dinesh, Alan Lee, Eleni Miltsakaki, Livio Robaldo, Aravind Joshi, and Bonnie Webber. 2008. The Penn Discourse Treebank 2.0. In *In Proceedings of LREC*.

Rashmi Prasad, Katherine Forbes-Riley, and Alan Lee. 2017. Towards full text shallow discourse relation annotation: Experiments with cross-paragraph implicit relations in the pdtb. In *Proceedings of the 18th Annual SIGdial Meeting on Discourse and Dialogue*, pages 7–16. Association for Computational Linguistics.

Ines Rehbein, Merel Scholman, and Vera Demberg. 2016. Annotating Discourse Relations in Spoken Language: A Comparison of the PDTB and CCR Frameworks. In *LREC*.

Ted J.M. Sanders, Vera Demberg, Jet Hoek, Merel C.J. Scholman, Fatemeh Torabi Asr, Sandrine Zufferey, and Jacqueline Evers-Vermeul. 2018. Unifying dimensions in coherence relations: How various annotation frameworks are related. *Corpus Linguistics and Linguistic Theory*, 0(0). Exported from https://app.dimensions.ai on 2019/02/06.

Tatjana Scheffler and Manfred Stede. 2016. Mapping pdtb-style connective annotation to RST-style discourse annotation. In *Proceedings of KONVENS*, Bochum, Germany.

Manfred Stede and Arne Neumann. 2014. Potsdam Commentary Corpus 2.0: Annotation for discourse research. In *Proceedings of the Ninth International Conference on Language Resources and Evaluation (LREC'14)*, Reykjavik, Iceland. European Language Resources Association (ELRA).

Acquiring Annotated Data with Cross-lingual Explicitation
for Implicit Discourse Relation Classification

Wei Shi[†], **Frances Yung**[†] and **Vera Demberg**[†,‡]
[†]Dept. of Language Science and Technology
[‡]Dept. of Mathematics and Computer Science, Saarland University
Saarland Informatic Campus, 66123 Saarbrücken, Germany
{w.shi, frances, vera}@coli.uni-saarland.de

Abstract

Implicit discourse relation classification is one of the most challenging and important tasks in discourse parsing, due to the lack of connectives as strong linguistic cues. A principle bottleneck to further improvement is the shortage of training data (ca. 18k instances in the Penn Discourse Treebank (PDTB)). Shi et al. (2017) proposed to acquire additional data by exploiting connectives in translation: human translators mark discourse relations which are implicit in the source language explicitly in the translation. Using back-translations of such explicitated connectives improves discourse relation parsing performance. This paper addresses the open question of whether the choice of the translation language matters, and whether multiple translations into different languages can be effectively used to improve the quality of the additional data.

1 Introduction

Discourse relations connect two sentences/clauses to each other. The identification of discourse relations is an important step in natural language understanding and is beneficial to various downstream NLP applications such as text summarization (Yoshida et al., 2014; Gerani et al., 2014), question answering (Verberne et al., 2007; Jansen et al., 2014), machine translation (Guzmán et al., 2014; Meyer et al., 2015), and so on.

Discourse relations can be marked explicitly using a discourse connective or discourse adverbial such as "because", "but", "however", see example 1. Explicitly marked relations are relatively easy to classify automatically (Pitler et al., 2008). In example 2, the causal relation is not marked explicitly, and can only be inferred from the texts. This second type of case is empirically even more common than explicitly marked relations (Prasad et al., 2008), but is much harder to classify automatically.

1. *[No one has worked out the players' average age.]*$_{Arg1}$ **But** *[most appear to be in their late 30s.]*$_{Arg2}$
   — Explicit, Comparison.Contrast

2. *[I want to add one more truck.]*$_{Arg1}$ **(Implicit = Because)** *[I sense that the business will continue grow.]*$_{Arg2}$
   — Implicit, Contingency.Cause

The difficulty in classifying implicit discourse relations stems from the lack of strong indicative cues. Early work has already shown that implicit relations cannot be learned from explicit ones by just removing the discourse markers, which may lead to a meaning shift in the examples (Sporleder and Lascarides, 2008), making human-annotated relations currently the only reliable source for training implicit discourse relation classification.

Due to the limited size of available training data, several approaches have been proposed for acquiring additional training data using automatic methods (Wang et al., 2012; Rutherford and Xue, 2015). The most promising approach so far, Shi et al. (2017), exploits the fact that human translators sometimes insert a connective in their translation even when a relation was implicit in the original text. Using a back-translation method, Shi et al. showed that such instances can be used for acquiring additional labeled text.

Shi et al. (2017) however only used a single target langauge (French), and had no control over the quality of the labels extracted from back-translated connectives. In this paper, we therefore systematically compare the contribution of three target translation languages from different language families: French (a Romance language), German (from the Germanic language family) and Czech (a Slavic language). As all three of these languages are part of the EuroParl corpus, this also allows us to directly test whether higher quality

Proceedings of Discourse Relation Parsing and Treebanking (DISRPT2019), pages 12–21
Minneapolis, MN, June 6, 2019. ©2019 Association for Computational Linguistics

can be achieved by using those instances that were consistently explicitated in several languages. We use cross-lingual explicitation to acquire more reliable implicit discourse relation instances with separate arguments that are from adjacent sentences in a document, and conducted experiments on PDTB benchmark with multiple conventional settings including cross validation. The experimental results show that the performance has been improved significantly with the additional training data, compared with the baseline systems.

2 Related Work

Recognizing implicit discourse relation, as one of the most important and challenging part of discourse parser system, has drawn a lot of attention in recent years after the release of PDTB (Prasad et al., 2008), the largest available corpus with annotated implicit examples, including two shared task in CoNLL-2015 and CoNLL-2016 (Xue et al., 2015, 2016).

Early attempts focused on statistical machine learning solutions with sparse linguistic features and linear models. They used several linguistically informed features like polarity tags, Levin verb classes and brown cluster etc. (Pitler et al., 2009; Park and Cardie, 2012; Rutherford and Xue, 2014).

Recent methods for discourse relation classification have increasingly relied on neural network architectures (Ji et al., 2016; Qin et al., 2016, 2017; Shi and Demberg, 2018). However, with the high number of parameters to be trained in more and more complicated deep neural network architectures, the demand for more reliable annotated data has become even more urgent. Data extension has been a longstanding goal in implicit discourse relation classification. Wang et al. (2012) proposed to differentiate typical and atypical examples for each relation and augment training data for implicit only by typical explicits. Rutherford and Xue (2015) designed criteria for selecting explicit samples in which connectives can be omitted without changing the interpretation of the discourse. More recently, Shi et al. (2017) proposed a pipeline to automatically label English implicit discourse samples based on explicitation of discourse connectives during human translating in parallel corpora, and achieve substantial improvements in classification. Our work here directly extends theirs by employing document-aligned cross-lingual parallel corpora and majority votes to get more reliable and in-topic annotated implicit discourse relation instances.

3 Methodology

Our goal here aims at sentence pairs in cross-lingual corpora where connectives have been inserted by human translators during translating from English to several other languages. After back-translating from other languages to English, explicit relations can be easily identified by discourse parser and then original English sentences would be labeled accordingly.

We follow the pipeline proposed in Shi et al. (2017), as illustrated in Figure 1, with the following differences:

- Shi et al. (2017) suffered from the fact that typical sentence-aligned corpora may have some sentences removed and make the sentences no longer coherent to get inter-sentential discourse relation instances. Here we filter and re-paragraph the line-aligned corpus to parallel document-aligned files, which makes it possible to obtain in-topic inter-sentential instances. After preprocessing, we got 532,542 parallel sentence pairs in 6,105 documents.

- Shi et al. (2017) pointed out that having correct translation of explicit discourse connective is more important than having the correct translation of the whole sentence. In this paper we use a statistical machine translation system instead of a neural one for more stable translations of discourse connectives.

- Instead of a single language pair, we use three language pairs and majority votes between them to get annotated implicit discourse relation instances with high confidence.

Figure 1 illustrates the pipeline of our approach. It consists of a few steps including preprocessing, back-translating, discourse parsing and majority voting. For each document, we back-translate its German, French and Czech translation back to English with the MT system and parse them with discourse parser. In this way, we can easily identify those instances that are originally implicit but explicit in German, French or Czech. With majority vote by the explicit examples in those three languages, the original English instance could be labeled with different confidences.

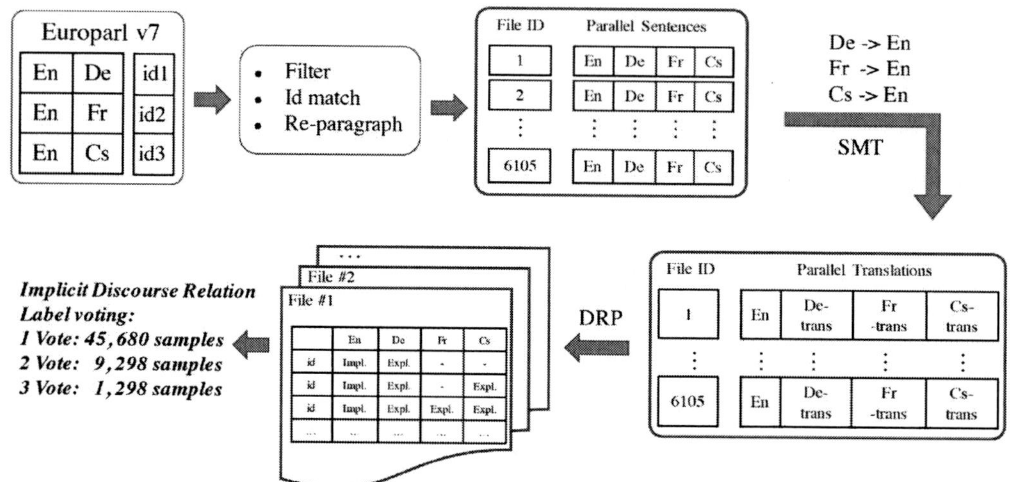

Figure 1: The pipeline of proposed method. "SMT" and "DRP" denote statistical machine translation and discourse relation parser respectively.

3.1 Preprocessing

We use European Parliament Proceedings Parallel Corpus (Europarl[1]) (Koehn, 2005) and choose English-French, German and Czech pairs as our parallel corpora. Each source-target pair consists of source and target sentences along with a sentence ID with which we could easily identify the location of the sentence in certain paragraphs. In order to get document-aligned parallel sentences among all these four languages, we do preprocessing steps as follows:

- Filtering: remove those sentences that don't have all the three translations in French, German or Czech.

- ID matching: re-group each sentence into different documents by the sentence IDs.

- Re-paragraph: rank the sentences in each documents by the ID and re-paragraph them.

3.2 Machine Translation

We train three MT systems to back-translate French, German and Czech to English. To have word alignments, better and stable back-translations, we employ a statistical machine translation system MOSES (Koehn et al., 2007), trained on the same parallel corpora. Source and target sentences are first tokenized, true-cased and then fed into the system for training. In our case,

the translation target texts are identical with the training set of the translation systems; this would not be a problem because our only objective in the translation is to back-translate connectives in the translation into English. On the training set, the translation system achieves BLEU scores of 66.20 (French), 65.30 (German) and 69.05 (Czech).

3.3 Discourse Parser

We employ the PDTB-style parser proposed in (Lin et al., 2014), which achieved about 96% accuracy on explicit connective identification, to pick up those explicit examples in back-translations in each document. Following the definitions of discourse relations in the PDTB that the arguments of the implicit discourse relations should be adjacent sentences but not for the explicit relations, we screen out all those explicit samples from the outputs of the parser that don't have consecutive arguments.

3.4 Majority Vote

After parsing the back-translations of French, German and Czech, we can compare whether they contain explicit relations which connect the same relational arguments. The analysis of this subset then allows us to identify those instances that could be labeled with high confidence, i.e. where back-translations from all three languages allow us to infer the same coherence label. Note that it is not necessarily the case that all back-translations contain an explicitation for the same instance (for

[1]Data is downloaded from http://opus.nlpl.eu/Europarl.php

instance, the French translator may have explicitated a relation, while the German and the Czech translators didn't do so), or that they propose *the same* coherence label: the human translation can introduce "noise" in the sense of the human translators inferring different coherence relations, the machine translation model can introduce errors in back-translation, and the discourse parser can mislabel ambiguous explicit connectives. When we use back-translations of several languages, the idea is that we can eliminate much of this noise by selecting only those instances where all back-translations agree with one another, or the ones where at least two back-translations allow us to infer identical labels.

Figure 2 illustrates the number of automatically labeled implicit discourse relation examples together with the information of how many of the instances that just one, two or all three back-translations provided the same labels.

In the One Vote agreement, every explicit relation has been accepted and the original implicit English sentences have been annotated correspondingly. Likewise, Two Votes agreement needs at least two out of three languages to have the same explicit relation label after back-translation; agreement between all three back-translations is denoted as Three Votes.

4   Experiments and Results

4.1   Data

Europarl Corpora: The parallel corpora used here are from Europarl (Koehn, 2005), it contains about 2.05M English-French, 1.96M English-German and 0.65M English-Czech pairs. After preprocessing, we got about 0.53M parallel sentence pairs in all these four languages.

The Penn Discourse Treebank (PDTB): PDTB (Prasad et al., 2008) is the largest available manually annotated corpus of discourse relations from Wall Street Journal. Each discourse relation has been annotated in three hierarchy levels. In this paper, we follow the previous conventional settings and focus on the second-level 11-ways classification (Lin et al., 2009; Ji and Eisenstein, 2015; Rutherford et al., 2017; Shi et al., 2017), after removing the relations with few instances.

4.2   Implicit discourse relation classification

To evaluate whether the extracted data is helpful to this task, we use a simple and effective

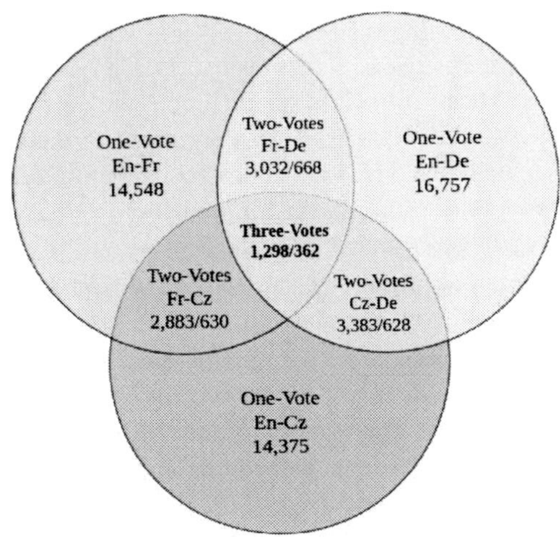

Figure 2: Numbers of implicit discourse relation instances from different agreements of explicit instances in three back-translations. En-Fr denotes instances that are implicit in English but explicit in back-translation of French, same for En-De and En-Cz. The overlap means they share the same relational arguments. The numbers under "Two-Votes" and "Three-Votes" are the numbers of discourse relation agreement / disagreement between explicits in back-translations of two or three languages.

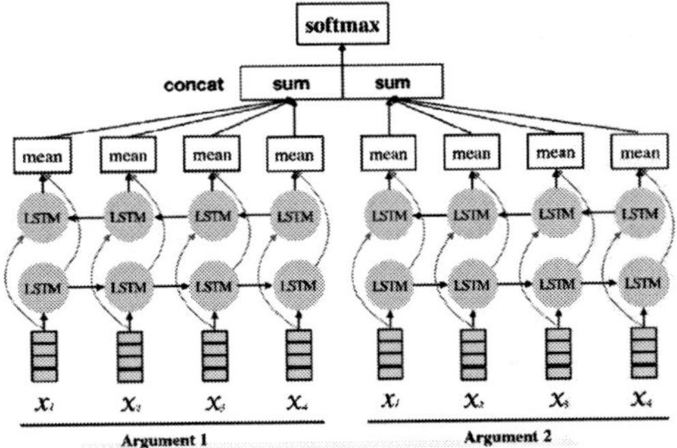

Figure 3: Bi-LSTM network for implicit discoure relation classification.

bidirectional Long Short-Term Memory (LSTM) (Hochreiter and Schmidhuber, 1997) network.

A LSTM recurrent neural network processes a variable-length sequence $x = (x_1, x_2, ..., x_n)$. At time step t, the state of memory cell c_t and hidden h_t are calculated with the Equations 1:

$$\begin{bmatrix} i_t \\ f_t \\ o_t \\ \hat{c}_t \end{bmatrix} = \begin{bmatrix} \sigma \\ \sigma \\ \sigma \\ \tanh \end{bmatrix} W \cdot [h_{t-1}, x_t]$$
$$c_t = f_t \odot c_{t-1} + i_t \odot \hat{c}_t$$
$$h_t = o_t \odot \tanh(c_t)$$
(1)

After being mapped to vectors, words are fed into the network sequentially. Hidden states of LSTM cell from different directions are averaged. The representations of two arguments from two separate bi-LSTMs are concatenated before being fed into a softmax layer for prediction. The architecture is illustrated in Figure 3.

Implementation: The model is implemented in Pytorch[2]. All the parameters are initialized uniformly at random. We employ cross-entropy as our cost function, Adagrad with learning rate of 0.01 as the optimization algorithm and set the dropout layers after embedding and output layer with drop rates of 0.5 and 0.2 respectively. The word vectors are pre-trained word embeddings from Word2Vec[3].

Settings: We follow the previous works and evaluate our data on second-level 11-ways classification on PDTB with 3 settings: Lin et al. (2009) (denotes as PDTB-Lin) uses sections 2-21, 22 and 23 as train, dev and test set; Ji and Eisenstein (2015) uses sections 2-20, 0-1 and 21-22 as train, dev and test set; Moreover, we also use 10-folds cross validation among sections 0-23 (Shi and Demberg, 2017). For each experiment, the additional data is only added into the training set.

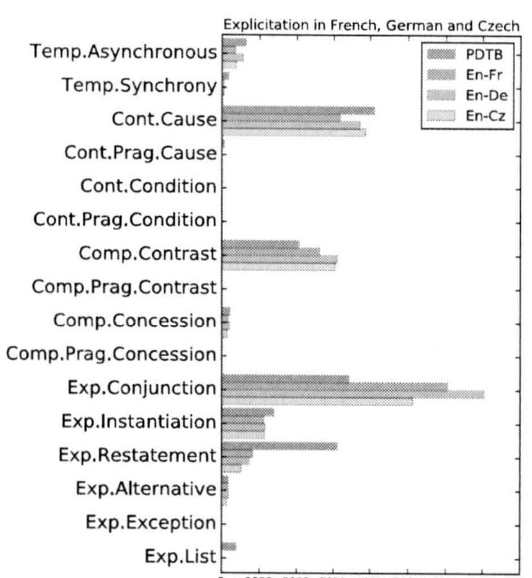

Figure 4: Distributions of PDTB and the extracted data among each discourse relation.

---

[2]https://pytorch.org/
[3]https://code.google.com/archive/p/word2vec/

4.3 Results

4.3.1 Distribution of new instances

Figure 4 shows the distributions of expert-annotated PDTB implicit relations and the implicit discourse examples extracted from the French, German and Czech back-translations. Overall, there is no strong bias – all relations seem to be represented similarly well, in line with their general frequency of occurrence. One interesting exception is the higher number of *Expansion.Conjunction* relation from the German translations. The over-representation of *Expansion.Conjunction* relation in German indicates that German translators tend to use more explicit cues to mark these relations. This is an independently discovered well-known finding from the literature (Kunz and Lapshinova-Koltunski, 2015), which observed that German tends to mark conjunction relations with discourse cues, while English tends to use coreference instead. We also find that *Expansion.Restatement* relations are underrepresented in our back-translation method, indicating that these relations are explicitated particularly rarely in translation. We also find that we can identify more *Contingency.Cause* and *Comparison.Contrast* relations from the German and Czech back-translations compared to the French ones. This provides us with an interesting lead for future work, to investigate whether French tends to explicitate these relations less, expressing them implicitly like in the English original, or whether French connectives for causal and contrastive relations are more ambiguous, causing problems in the back-translations.

Figure 5 shows that the filtering by majority votes (including only two cases where at least two back-translations agree with one another vs. where all three agree) does again not change the distribution of extracted relations.

In summary, we can conclude that the choice of translation language *can* matter: depending on what types of relations are most important to acquire more data for the target task at hand, a language that tends to explicitate that relation frequently can be particularly suitable. On the other hand, if no strong such preferences on labelling specific relations exist, we can see that the choice of translation language only has a minor effect on the overall distribution of additional implicit discourse relation labels.

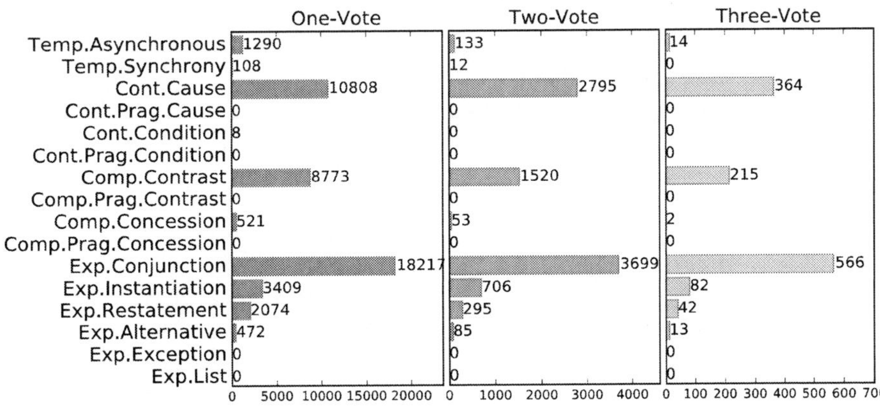

Figure 5: Distributions of discourse relations with different agreements.

	PDTB-Lin	PDTB-Ji	Cross Validation	size of extra data
Majority Class	26.11	26.18	25.59	-
Rutherford et al. (2017)	38.38	-	-	-
Shi et al. (2017)	**45.50**	-	37.84	102,314
PDTB only	37.95(0.59)	40.57(0.67)	37.82(0.14)	-
PDTB + En-Fr	38.96(0.69)	40.14(0.78)	38.32(0.62)	14,548
PDTB + En-De	39.65(0.95)	39.96(0.44)	37.97(0.46)	16,757
PDTB + En-Cz	37.90(1.27)	40.59(0.51)	37.42(0.50)	14,375
PDTB + All	37.73(0.74)	40.41(0.65)	37.16(0.64)	45,680
PDTB + 2-votes	**40.34**(0.75)	**41.95**(0.97)	**38.98**(0.14)	9,298
PDTB + 3-votes	39.88(0.79)	41.19(0.63)	38.33(0.50)	1,298

Table 1: Performances with different sets of additional data. Average accuracy of 10 runs (5 for cross validations) are shown here with standard deviation in the brackets. Numbers in bold are significantly (p<0.05) better than the *PDTB only* baseline with unpaired t-test.

4.3.2 Quantitative Results

Table 1 shows that best results are achieved by adding only those samples for which two back-translations agree with one another. This may represent the best trade-off between reliability of the label and the amount of additional data. The setting where the data from all languages is added performs badly despite the large number of samples, because this method contains different labels for the same argument pairs, for all those instances where the back-translations don't yield the same label, thus introducing noise into the system. The size of the extra data used in Shi et al. (2017) is about 10 times larger than our 2-votes data. The selection of instances differs in their paper from ours, in that they only use French, and in that they, unlike this paper, focus on intra-sentential samples. The model using the few reliable samples ex-

tracted from the back-translations of the three languages here significantly outperforms the results found in Shi et al. (2017) in the cross-validation setting. On the PDTB-Lin test set, we don't match performance, but note that this test set is based only on 800 instances, as opposed to the 16k instances in the cross-validation evaluation.

4.3.3 Qualitative analysis

Finally, we want to provide insight into what kind of instances the system extracts, and why back-translation labels sometimes disagree. We have identified four major cases based on a manual analysis of 100 randomly sampled instances.

Case 1: Sometimes, back-translations from several languages may yield the same connective because the original English sentence actually was not really unmarked, but rather contained an expression which could not be automatically recognized as a discourse relation marker by the automatic discourse parser[4]. This can actually help us to identify new alternative lexicalisation for discourse relations, and thus represents a promising technique for improving discourse relation classification also on texts for which no translations are available.

Original English: I presided over a region crossed by heavy traffic from all over Europe, with significant accidents which gave rise to legal actions. *What is more,* In 2002, two Member States of the European Union appealed to the European Court of Justice to repeal Directive 2002/15/EC because it included self-employed drivers ; the Court rejected their appeal on the grounds of road safety.

French back-translation: I presided over a region crossed by heavy traffic from the whole of Europe, with significant accidents which gave rise to legal actions, **moreover**, (Expansion.Conjunction) in 2002 , two Member States have appeal on the European Court of Justice, which has condemned the rejection of the grounds of road safety.

German back-translation: I presided over a region crossed by heavy traffic from across Europe, with significant accidents which, **moreover** (Expansion.Conjunction) in 2002, two Member States of the European Union appealed to the European Court of Justice to repeal Directive 2002/15/EC , because it included self-employed drivers ; the Court quashed for reasons of road safety.

Czech back-translation: I was in the region with very heavy traffic from all over Europe, with significant accidents which gave rise to legal actions **therefore** (Contingency.Cause) after all, in 2002, two Member States of the European Union appealed to the European Court of Justice to repeal Directive 2002/15/EC that also applies to self-employed drivers; the Court rejected their appeal on the grounds of road safety.

The expression *what is more* is not part of the set of connectives labeled in PDTB and hence was not identified by the discourse parser. Our method is successful because such cues can be automatically identified from the consistent back-translations into two languages. (The case in Czech is more complex because the back-translation contains two signals, *therefore* and *after all*, see case 4.)

We also found some similar expressions in this case like:

"in reality" ("implicit", original English) → "in fact" (explicit, back-translation);

"for that reason" → "therefore";

"this is why" → "therefore";

"be that as it may" → "however / nevertheless";

"for another" → "furthermore / on the other hand";

"in spite of that" → "however / nevertheless" and so on.

Case 2: Majority votes help to reduce noise related to errors introduced by the automatic pipeline, such as argument or connective misidentification: in the below example, *also* in the French translation is actually the translation of *along with*.

Original English: on behalf of the PPE-DE Group. (DE) Madam President, Commissioner, ladies and gentlemen, the public should be able to benefit in two ways from the potential for greater road safety. *For this reason*, along with the report we are discussing today, I call for more research into the safety benefits of driver-assistance systems.

French back-translation: (DE) Madam President, Commissioner, ladies and gentlemen, citizens should be able to benefit in two ways of the possibility of improving road safety. **also** (Expansion.Conjunction) when we are discussing this report today, I appeal to the intensification of research at the level of the benefits of driver-assistance systems in terms of security, as well as the transmission of information about them.

German back-translation: (DE) Madam President, Commissioner, ladies and gentlemen, road safety potentials should citizens in the dual sense **therefore** (Contingency.Cause) I urge, together with the report under discussion today, the prevention and education about the safety benefits of driver-assistance systems.

Czech back-translation: (DE) Madam President, Commissioner, ladies and gentlemen, the public would be the potential for greater road safety should have a two-fold benefit, **therefore** (Contingency.Cause) I call, in addition to the report, which we are debating today , for more research and education in the safety benefits of driver-assistance systems.

Case 3: Discrepancies between connectives in back-translations can also be due to differences in how translators interpreted the original text. Here are cases of genuine ambiguities in the implicit discourse relation.

Original English: with regard, once again, to European Union law, we are dealing in this case with the domestic legal system of the Member States. *That being said*, I cannot answer for the Council of Europe or for the European Court of Human Rights, which have issued a decision that I understand may raise some issues for Parliament.

---

[4]In the following examples, the original English sentence is shown is followed by the back-translations from French, German and Czech along with the connectives and senses.

French back-translation: with regard, once again, the right of the European Union, we are here in the domestic legal system of the Member States. **however,** (Comparison.Contrast) I cannot respond to the place of the Council of Europe or for the European Court of Human Rights, which have issued a decision that I understand may raise questions in this House.
German back-translation: once again on the right of the European Union, we have it in this case with the national legal systems of the Member States. **therefore,** (Contingency.Cause) I cannot, for the Council of Europe and the European Court of Human Rights, which have issued a decision, which I can understand, in Parliament raises some issues.
Czech back-translation: I repeat that, when it comes to the European Union, in this case we are dealing with the domestic legal system of the Member States. **in addition,** (Expansion.Conjunction) I cannot answer for the Council of Europe or for the European Court of Human Rights , which has issued a decision that I understand may cause in Parliament some doubts.

Case 4: Implicit relations can co-occur with marked discourse relations (Rohde et al., 2015), and multiple translations help discover these instances, for example:

Original English: We all understand that nobody can return Russia to the path of freedom and democracy, *(implicit: but)* *what is more*, the situation in our country is not as straightforward as it might appear to the superficial observer.
French back-translation: we all understand that nobody can return Russia on the path of freedom and democracy but Russia itself, its citizens and its civil society **but** (Comparison.Contrast) there is more, the situation in our country is not as simple as it might appear to be a superficial observer.
German back-translation: we are all aware that nobody Russia back on the path of freedom and democracy, as the country itself, its people and its civil society **but** (Comparison.Contrast) the situation in our country is not as straightforward as it might appear to the superficial observer.
Czech back-translation: we all know that Russia cannot return to the path of freedom and democracy there, but Russia itself, its people and civil society. **in addition** (Expansion.Conjunction) the situation in our country is not as straightforward as it might appear to the superficial observer.

5   Conclusion

We compare the explicitations obtained from translations into three different languages, and find that instances where at least two back-translations agree yield the best quality, significantly outperforming a version of the model that does not use additional data, or uses data from just one language.

We also found that specific properties of the translation language affect the distribution of the additionally acquired data across coherence relations: German, for instance, is known to mark conjunction relations using discourse cues more frequently, while English and other languages tend to express these relations rather through lexical cohesion or pronouns. This was reflected in our experiments: we found a larger proportion of explicitations for conjunction relations in German than the other translation languages.

Finally, our qualitative analysis shows that the strength of the method partially stems from being able to learn additional discourse relation signals because these are typically translated consistently. The method thus shows promise for the identification of discourse markers and alternative lexicalisations, which can subsequently be exploited also for discourse relation classification in the absence of translation data. Our analysis also shows that our method is useful for identifying cases where multiple relations holding between two arguments.

6   Acknowledgments

We would like to thank all the anonymous reviewers for their careful reading and insightful comments. This research was funded by the German Research Foundation (DFG) as part of SFB 1102 "Information Density and Linguistic Encoding".

References

Shima Gerani, Yashar Mehdad, Giuseppe Carenini, Raymond T Ng, and Bita Nejat. 2014. Abstractive summarization of product reviews using discourse structure. In *Proceedings of the 2014 Conference on Empirical Methods in Natural Language Processing (EMNLP)*, pages 1602–1613.

Francisco Guzmán, Shafiq Joty, Lluís Màrquez, and Preslav Nakov. 2014. Using discourse structure improves machine translation evaluation. In *Proceedings of the 52nd Annual Meeting of the Association for Computational Linguistics (Volume 1: Long Papers)*, volume 1, pages 687–698.

Sepp Hochreiter and Jürgen Schmidhuber. 1997. Long short-term memory. *Neural computation*, 9(8):1735–1780.

Peter Jansen, Mihai Surdeanu, and Peter Clark. 2014. Discourse complements lexical semantics for non-factoid answer reranking. In *Proceedings of the 52nd Annual Meeting of the Association for Computational Linguistics (Volume 1: Long Papers)*, volume 1, pages 977–986.

Yangfeng Ji and Jacob Eisenstein. 2015. One vector is not enough: Entity-augmented distributed semantics for discourse relations. *Transactions of the Association for Computational Linguistics*, 3:329–344.

Yangfeng Ji, Gholamreza Haffari, and Jacob Eisenstein. 2016. A latent variable recurrent neural network for discourse relation language models. In *Proceedings of the 2016 Conference of the North American Chapter of the Association for Computational Linguistics on Human Language Technology*, pages 332–342. Association for Computational Linguistics.

Philipp Koehn. 2005. Europarl: A parallel corpus for statistical machine translation. In *MT summit*, volume 5, pages 79–86.

Philipp Koehn, Hieu Hoang, Alexandra Birch, Chris Callison-Burch, Marcello Federico, Nicola Bertoldi, Brooke Cowan, Wade Shen, Christine Moran, Richard Zens, et al. 2007. Moses: Open source toolkit for statistical machine translation. In *Proceedings of the 45th annual meeting of the ACL on interactive poster and demonstration sessions*, pages 177–180. Association for Computational Linguistics.

Kerstin Kunz and Ekaterina Lapshinova-Koltunski. 2015. Cross-linguistic analysis of discourse variation across registers. *Nordic Journal of English Studies*, 14(1):258–288.

Ziheng Lin, Min-Yen Kan, and Hwee Tou Ng. 2009. Recognizing implicit discourse relations in the penn discourse treebank. In *Proceedings of the 2009 Conference on Empirical Methods in Natural Language Processing*, pages 343–351, Singapore. Association for Computational Linguistics.

Ziheng Lin, Hwee Tou Ng, and Min-Yen Kan. 2014. A pdtb-styled end-to-end discourse parser. *Natural Language Engineering*, 20(02):151–184.

Thomas Meyer, Najeh Hajlaoui, and Andrei Popescu-Belis. 2015. Disambiguating discourse connectives for statistical machine translation. *IEEE Transactions on Audio, Speech, and Language Processing*, 23(7):1184–1197.

Joonsuk Park and Claire Cardie. 2012. Improving implicit discourse relation recognition through feature set optimization. In *Proceedings of the 13th Annual Meeting of the Special Interest Group on Discourse and Dialogue*, pages 108–112. Association for Computational Linguistics.

Emily Pitler, Annie Louis, and Ani Nenkova. 2009. Automatic sense prediction for implicit discourse relations in text. In *Proceedings of the 47th Annual Meeting of the Association for Computational Linguistics*, pages 683–691, Suntec, Singapore. Association for Computational Linguistics.

Emily Pitler, Mridhula Raghupathy, Hena Mehta, Ani Nenkova, Alan Lee, and Aravind K Joshi. 2008. Easily identifiable discourse relations. *Technical Reports (CIS)*, page 884.

Rashmi Prasad, Nikhil Dinesh, Alan Lee, Eleni Miltsakaki, Livio Robaldo, Aravind K. Joshi, and Bonnie L. Webber. 2008. The penn discourse treebank 2.0. In *LREC*, Marrakech, Morocco. European Language Resources Association.

Lianhui Qin, Zhisong Zhang, and Hai Zhao. 2016. Implicit discourse relation recognition with context-aware character-enhanced embeddings. In *Proceedings of COLING 2016, the 26th International Conference on Computational Linguistics*.

Lianhui Qin, Zhisong Zhang, Hai Zhao, Zhiting Hu, and Eric P. Xing. 2017. Adversarial connective-exploiting networks for implicit discourse relation classification. In *Proceedings of the 55th Annual Meeting of the Association for Computational Linguistics (Volume 1: Long Papers)*, pages 1006–1017, Vancouver, Canada. Association for Computational Linguistics.

Hannah Rohde, Anna Dickinson, Chris Clark, Annie Louis, and Bonnie Webber. 2015. Recovering discourse relations: Varying influence of discourse adverbials. In *Proceedings of the First Workshop on Linking Computational Models of Lexical, Sentential and Discourse-level Semantics*, pages 22–31.

Attapol Rutherford, Vera Demberg, and Nianwen Xue. 2017. A systematic study of neural discourse models for implicit discourse relation. In *Proceedings of the 15th Conference of the European Chapter of the Association for Computational Linguistics: Volume 1, Long Papers*, volume 1, pages 281–291.

Attapol Rutherford and Nianwen Xue. 2014. Discovering implicit discourse relations through brown cluster pair representation and coreference patterns. In *Proceedings of the 14th Conference of the European Chapter of the Association for Computational Linguistics*, pages 645–654. Association for Computational Linguistics.

Attapol Rutherford and Nianwen Xue. 2015. Improving the inference of implicit discourse relations via classifying explicit discourse connectives. In *Proceedings of the 2015 Conference of the North American Chapter of the Association for Computational Linguistics on Human Language Technology*, pages 799–808. Association for Computational Linguistics.

Wei Shi and Vera Demberg. 2017. On the need of cross validation for discourse relation classification. In *Proceedings of the 15th Conference of the European Chapter of the Association for Computational Linguistics*, pages 150–156. Association for Computational Linguistics.

Wei Shi and Vera Demberg. 2018. Learning to explicitate connectives with seq2seq network for implicit discourse relation classification. *arXiv preprint arXiv:1811.01697*.

Wei Shi, Frances Yung, Raphael Rubino, and Vera Demberg. 2017. Using explicit discourse connectives in translation for implicit discourse relation classification. In *Proceedings of the Eighth International Joint Conference on Natural Language Processing (Volume 1: Long Papers)*, volume 1, pages 484–495.

Caroline Sporleder and Alex Lascarides. 2008. Using automatically labelled examples to classify rhetorical relations: An assessment. *Natural Language Engineering*, 14(3):369–416.

Suzan Verberne, Lou Boves, Nelleke Oostdijk, and Peter-Arno Coppen. 2007. Evaluating discourse-based answer extraction for why-question answering. In *Proceedings of the 30th annual international ACM SIGIR conference on Research and development in information retrieval*, pages 735–736. ACM.

Xun Wang, Sujian Li, Jiwei Li, and Wenjie Li. 2012. Implicit discourse relation recognition by selecting typical training examples. In *Proceedings of the 24th International Conference on Computational Linguistics (COLING-2012)*, pages 2757–2772.

Nianwen Xue, Hwee Tou Ng, Sameer Pradhan, Rashmi Prasad, Christopher Bryant, and Attapol Rutherford. 2015. The conll-2015 shared task on shallow discourse parsing. In *Proceedings of the CoNLL-15 Shared Task*, pages 1–16. Association for Computational Linguistics.

Nianwen Xue, Hwee Tou Ng, Attapol Rutherford, Bonnie Webber, Chuan Wang, and Hongmin Wang. 2016. Conll 2016 shared task on multilingual shallow discourse parsing. In *Proceedings of the CoNLL-16 shared task*, pages 1–19. Association for Computational Linguistics.

Yasuhisa Yoshida, Jun Suzuki, Tsutomu Hirao, and Masaaki Nagata. 2014. Dependency-based discourse parser for single-document summarization. In *Proceedings of the 2014 Conference on Empirical Methods in Natural Language Processing (EMNLP)*, pages 1834–1839.

From News to Medical: Cross-domain Discourse Segmentation

Elisa Ferracane[1], **Titan Page**[2], **Junyi Jessy Li**[1] and **Katrin Erk**[1]

[1]Department of Linguistics, The University of Texas at Austin
[2]Department of Linguistics, University of Colorado Boulder
`elisa@ferracane.com, titan@colorado.edu`
`jessy@austin.utexas.edu, katrin.erk@mail.utexas.edu`

Abstract

The first step in discourse analysis involves dividing a text into segments. We annotate the first high-quality small-scale medical corpus in English with discourse segments and analyze how well news-trained segmenters perform on this domain. While we expectedly find a drop in performance, the nature of the segmentation errors suggests some problems can be addressed earlier in the pipeline, while others would require expanding the corpus to a trainable size to learn the nuances of the medical domain.[1]

1 Introduction

Dividing a text into units is the first step in analyzing a discourse. In the framework of Rhetorical Structure Theory (RST) (Mann and Thompson, 1988), the segments are termed elementary discourse units (EDUs), and a complete RST-style discourse analysis consists of building EDUs into a tree that spans the entire document. The tree edges are labeled with relations types, and nodes are categorized by their nuclearity (roughly, importance). RST segmentation is often regarded as a solved problem because automated segmenters achieve high performance (F1=94.3) on a task with high inter-annotator agreement (kappa=0.92) (Wang et al., 2018; Carlson et al., 2001). In fact, many RST parsers do not include a segmenter and simply evaluate on gold EDUs. However, numerous studies have shown errors in segmentation are a primary bottleneck for accurate discourse parsing (Soricut and Marcu, 2003; Fisher and Roark, 2007; Joty et al., 2015; Feng, 2015). Notably, even when using a top-performing segmenter, results degrade by 10% on the downstream tasks of span, nuclearity and relation labeling when using predicted instead of gold EDUs (Feng, 2015).

[Patients were excluded] [if they had any other major Axis I psychiatric disorder, any medical or neurological disorder] [that could influence the diagnosis or treatment of depression,] [any condition other than depression] [that was not on stable treatment for at least the past one month,] [any condition] [that could pose a health risk during a clinical trial,] [and any clinically significant abnormality or disorder] [that was newly detected during the baseline assessments.]

Table 1: An example sentence from the novel MEDICAL corpus, with EDUs annotated in square brackets.

Separately, all available discourse segmenters are trained on news, and their ability to generalize to other domains, such as medical text, has not been well-studied. In our work, we focus on the medical domain because it has garnered cross-disciplinary research interest with wide-reaching applications. For example, the Biomedical Discourse Relation Bank was created for PDTB-style discourse parsing of biomedical texts (Prasad et al., 2011), and has been used to analyze author revisions and causal relations (Zhang et al., 2016; Marsi et al., 2014).

This work studies discourse segmentation in the medical domain. In particular, we: (1) seek to identify difficulties that news-trained segmenters have on medical; (2) investigate how features of the segmenter impact the type of errors seen in medical; and (3) examine the relationship between annotator agreement and segmenter performance for different types of medical data.

To this end, we present the first small-scale medical corpus in English, annotated by trained linguists (sample in Table 1). We evaluate this corpus with three RST segmenters, finding an expected gap in the medical domain. We perform a

---

[1]Code and data available at `http://github.com/elisaF/news-med-segmentation`.

Proceedings of Discourse Relation Parsing and Treebanking (DISRPT2019), pages 22–29
Minneapolis, MN, June 6, 2019. ©2019 Association for Computational Linguistics

detailed error analysis that shows medical-specific punctuation is the largest source of errors in the medical domain, followed by different word usage in syntactic constructions which are likely caused by news-derived word embeddings. Second, by comparing segmenters which use word embeddings versus syntax trees, we find access to parsed trees may not be helpful in reducing syntactically-resolvable errors, while an improved tokenizer would provide small benefits. Third, we note patterns between humans and segmenters where both perform better on extremely short texts and worse on those with more complex discourse.

We conclude with suggestions to improve the segmenter on the medical domain and recommendations for future annotation experiments.

Our contributions in this work are two-fold: a high-quality small-scale corpus of medical documents annotated with RST-style discourse segments; a quantitative and qualitative analysis of the discourse segmentation errors in the medical domain that lays the groundwork for understanding both the strengths and limits of existing RST segmenters, and the next concrete steps towards a better segmenter for the medical domain.

2 Related Work

Corpora in non-news domains. The seminal RST resource, the RST Discourse Treebank (RST-DT) (Carlson et al., 2001), consists of news articles in English. With the wide adoption of RST, corpora have expanded to other languages and domains. Several of these corpora include science-related texts, a domain that is closer to medical, but unfortunately also use segmentation guidelines that differ sometimes considerably from RST-DT[2] (research articles in Basque, Chinese, English, Russian, Spanish (Iruskieta et al., 2013; Cao et al., 2017; Zeldes, 2017; Yang and Li, 2018; Toldova et al., 2017; Da Cunha et al., 2012); encyclopedias and science news web pages in Dutch (Redeker et al., 2012)). Specifically in the medical domain, only two corpora exist, neither of which are in English. Da Cunha et al. (2012) annotate a small corpus of Spanish medical articles, and the RST Basque Treebank (Iruskieta et al., 2013) includes a small set of medical article abstracts. Our work aims to fill this gap by creating the first cor-

---

[2]A future direction of research could revisit this domain of science if the differing segmentation schemes are adequately resolved in the forthcoming shared task of the Discourse Relation Parsing and Treebanking 2019 workshop.

Corpus	#docs	#tokens	#sents	#EDUs
RST-DT SMALL	11	4009	159	403
MEDICAL	11	3356	169	399

Table 2: Corpus statistics.

pus of RST-segmented medical articles in English. Unlike several other works, we include all parts of the article, and not just the abstract.

Segmenters in non-news domains. While corpora have expanded to other domains, most automated discourse segmenters remain focused (and trained) on news. An exception is the segmenter in Braud et al. (2017a) which was trained on different domains for the purpose of developing a segmenter for under-resourced languages. However, they make the simplifying assumption that a single corpus represents a single (and distinct) domain, and do not include the medical domain. In this work, we study the viability of using news-trained segmenters on the medical domain.

3 Corpus Creation

Medical Corpus. The MEDICAL corpus consists of 2 clinical trial reports from PubMed Central, randomly selected for their shorter lengths for ease of annotation. We expect the language and discourse to be representative of this domain, despite the shorter length. As a result of the smaller size, we hypothesize annotator agreement and segmenter performance numbers may be somewhat inflated, but we nevertheless expect the nature of the errors to be the same. We divide the reports into their corresponding sections, treating each section as a separate document, resulting in 11 labeled documents. We chose to analyze sections individually instead of an entire report because moving to larger units typically yields arbitrary and uninformative analyses (Taboada and Mann, 2006). XML formatting was stripped, and figures and tables were removed. The sections for *Acknowledgements, Competing Interests,* and *Prepublication History* were not included.

For comparison with the *News* domain, we created RST-DT-SMALL by sampling an equal number of Wall Street Journal articles from the "Test" portion of the RST-DT that were similar in length to the medical documents. The corpus statistics are summarized in Table 2.

Annotation Process. The annotation process was defined to establish a high-quality corpus that is consistent with the gold-segmented RST-DT. Two annotators participated: a Linguistics graduate student (the first author), and a Linguistics undergraduate (the second author). To train on the task and to ensure consistency with RST-DT, the annotators first segmented portions of RST-DT. During this training phase, they also discussed annotation strategies and disagreements, and then consulted the gold labels. In the first phase of annotation on the medical data, the second author segmented all documents over a period of three months using the guidelines compiled for RST-DT (Carlson and Marcu, 2001) and with minimal guidance from the first author. In the second phase of annotation, all documents were re-segmented by both annotators, and disagreements were resolved by discussion.

Agreement. Annotators achieved on average a high level of agreement for identifying EDU boundaries with kappa=0.90 (averaged over 11 texts). However, we note that document length and complexity of the discourse influence this number. On a document of 35 tokens, the annotators exhibited perfect agreement. For the *Discussion* sections that make more use of discourse, the average agreement dropped to 0.84. The lowest agreement is 0.73 on a *Methods* section, which had more complex sentences with more coordinated sentences and clauses, relative clauses and nominal postmodifiers (as discussed in Section 6.1, these syntactic constructions are also a source of error for the automated segmenters).

4 Experiment

We automatically segment the documents in RST-DT SMALL and MEDICAL using three segmenters: (1) DPLP[3] uses features from syntactic and dependency parses for a linear support vector classifier; (2) TWO-PASS (Feng and Hirst, 2014) is a CRF segmenter that derives features from syntax parses but also uses global features to perform a second pass of segmentation; (3) NEURAL (Wang et al., 2018) is a neural BiLSTM-CRF model that uses ELMo embeddings (Peters et al., 2018). We choose these segmenters because they are widely-used and publicly available (most RST parsers do not include a segmenter). DPLP has been cited in several works showing discourse helps on different NLP tasks (Bhatia et al., 2015). TWO-PASS, until recently, achieved SOTA on discourse segmentation when using parsed (not gold) syntax

---

[3]https://github.com/jiyfeng/DPLP

RST SEG	DOMAIN	F1	P	R
DPLP	*News*	82.56	81.75	83.37
	Medical	75.29	78.69	72.18
TWO-PASS	*News*	95.72	<u>97.19</u>	94.29
	Medical	84.69	86.23	83.21
NEURAL	*News*	<u>97.32</u>	95.68	<u>99.01</u>
	Medical	**91.68**	**94.86**	**88.70**

Table 3: F1, precision (P) and recall (R) of RST discourse segmenters on two domains (best numbers for *News* are underlined, for *Medical* are bolded).

trees. NEURAL now holds SOTA in RST discourse segmentation. We evaluate the segmenter's ability to detect all EDU boundaries present in the gold data (not just intra-sentential) using the metrics of precision (P), recall (R) and F1.

The DPLP and TWO-PASS segmenters, both of which employ the Stanford Core NLP pipeline (Manning et al., 2014), were updated to use the same version of this software (2018-10-05).

5 Results

Table 3 lists our results on *News* and *Medical* for correctly identifying EDU boundaries using the three discourse segmenters. As expected, the *News* domain outperforms the *Medical* domain, regardless of which segmenter is used. In the case of the DPLP segmenter, the gap between the two domains is about 7.4 F1 points. Note that the performance of DPLP on *News* lags considerably behind the state of the art (-14.76 F1 points). When switching to the TWO-PASS segmenter, the performance on *News* increases dramatically (+13 F1 points). However, the performance on *Medical* increases by only 3.75 F1 points. Thus, large gains in *News* translate into only a small gain in *Medical*. The NEURAL segmenter achieves the best performance on *News* and is also able to more successfully close the gap on *Medical*, with only a 5.64 F1 difference, largely attributable to lower recall.

6 Error Analysis

We perform an error analysis to understand the segmentation differences between domains and between segmenters.

6.1 Error Types

We first group errors of the best-performing NEURAL segmenter into *error types*. Here we discuss

ERROR TYPE	PREDICTED	GOLD
amb. lexical cue	[our performance][since the buy - out makes it imperative]	[our performance since the buy - out makes it imperative]
infinitival "to"	[the auto giants will move quickly][to buy up stakes]	[the auto giants will move quickly to buy up stakes]
correct	[you attempt to seize assets][related to the crime]	[you attempt to seize assets related to the crime]
tokenization	[as identified in clinical trials.{8-11}It][is noteworthy]	[as identified in clinical trials .][{ 8-11 }][It is noteworthy]
end emb. EDU	[Studies][confined to medical professionals have shown]	[Studies][confined to medical professionals][have shown]
punctuation	[the safety of placeboxetine][(PB) hydrochloride capsules]	[the safety of placeboxetine][(PB)][hydrochloride capsules]

Table 4: Examples of the most frequent segmentation error types with the erroneous EDU boundaries highlighted in red for *News* (top) and *Medical* (bottom) with predicted and gold EDU boundaries in square brackets (square brackets for citations are changed to curly brackets to avoid confusion). For *News*, the boundaries are inserted incorrectly (false positives) and for *Medical* they are omitted incorrectly (false negatives).

the most frequent types in each domain and give examples of each in Table 4 with the predicted and gold EDU boundaries.

ambiguous lexical cue Certain words (often discourse connectives) are strongly indicative of the beginning of an EDU, but are nonetheless ambiguous because of nuanced segmentation rules. In the Table 4 example, the discourse connective "since" typically signals the start of an EDU (e.g., in the RST discourse relations of *temporal* and *circumstance*), but is not a boundary in this case because there is no verbal element. Other problematic words include "that", signalling relative clauses (often, but not always treated as embedded EDUs), and "and" which may indicate a coordinated sentence or clause (treated as a separate EDU) but also a coordinated verb phrase (not a separate EDU). Note this phenomenon is different from distinguishing between discourse vs. non-discourse usage of a word, or sense disambiguation of a discourse connective as studied in Pitler and Nenkova (2009).

infinitival "to" The syntactic construction of `to+verb` can act either as a verbal complement (treated as the same EDU) or a clausal complement (separate EDU). In the Table 4 example, the infinitival "to buy" is a complement of the verb "move" and should remain in the same EDU, but the segmenter incorrectly segmented it.

tokenization This error type covers cases where the tokenizer fails to detect token boundaries, specifically punctuation. These tokenization errors lead to downstream segmentation errors since punctuation marks, often markers of EDU boundaries, are entirely missed when mangled together with their neighboring tokens, as in 'trials.[8-

11]It' in Table 4.

punctuation This error occurs when parentheses and square brackets are successfully tokenized, but the segmenter fails to recognize them as EDU boundaries. This error is expected for square brackets, as they do not occur in RST-DT, but frequently appear in the *Medical* corpus for citations. It is not clear why the segmenter has difficulty with parentheses as in the Table 4 example "(PB)", since they do occur in *News* and further almost invariably mark an EDU boundary.

end of embedded EDU An embedded EDU breaks up a larger EDU and is typically a relative clause or nominal postmodifier with a verbal element.[4] While the segmenter is good at identifying the beginning of an embedded EDU, it often fails to detect the end. An embedded EDU such as the one listed in Table 4 can be clearly identified from a syntactic parse: the verbal element 'have shown' attaches to the subject 'Studies' and not the nominal postmodifier as predicted by the segmenter.

correct This category describes cases where we hypothesize the annotator made a mistake and the segmenter is correct. In the Table 4 example, the nominal postmodifier with non-finite clause "related to the crime" is an embedded EDU missed by annotators.

6.2 Errors between domains

In Figure 1, we compare the distribution of the most frequent error types in *News* (left) and the most frequent in *Medical* (right).

In *News* Figure 1a, the errors are mostly false positives where the segmenter incorrectly inserts

---

[4]For a more complete definition, see the tagging manual.

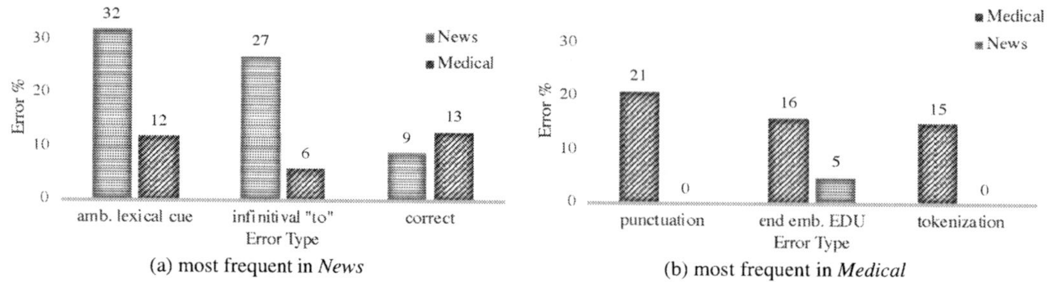

(a) most frequent in News
(b) most frequent in Medical

Figure 1: Most frequent segmentation error types by domain, using the best discourse segmenter.

boundaries before *ambiguous lexical cues*, and before *infinitival "to"* clauses (that are verbal complements). Interestingly, Braud et al. (2017a) found the tricky distinction of clausal vs. verbal infinitival complements to also be a large source of segmentation errors. These two error types also occur in *Medical*, though not as frequently, in part because the `to+verb` construction itself occurs less in the medical corpus. The third category of *correct* consists mostly of cases where the segmenter correctly identified an embedded EDU missed by annotators, illustrating both the difficulty of annotation even for experts and the usefulness of an automated segmenter for both in-domain and out-of-domain data since this error type is attested in both domains.

In *Medical* Figure 1b, we first note a stark contrast in distribution between the domains. The error types most frequent in *Medical* are hardly present in *News*; that is, errors in the *Medical* domain are often exclusive to this domain. The errors are mostly false negatives where the segmenter fails to detect boundaries around medical-specific use of *punctuation* marks, including square brackets for citations and parentheticals containing mathematical notations, which are entirely absent in *News*. The segmenter often misses the *end of embedded EDUs*, and more frequently than in *News*. The difference in this syntactically-identifiable error points to a gap in the embedding space for words signalling relative clauses and nominal postmodifiers. Given that ELMo embeddings have been shown to capture some syntax (Tenney et al., 2018), we recommend using PubMed-trained ELMo embeddings.[5] One may further hypothesize that adding syntactic parses to the segmenter would help, which we explore in

---

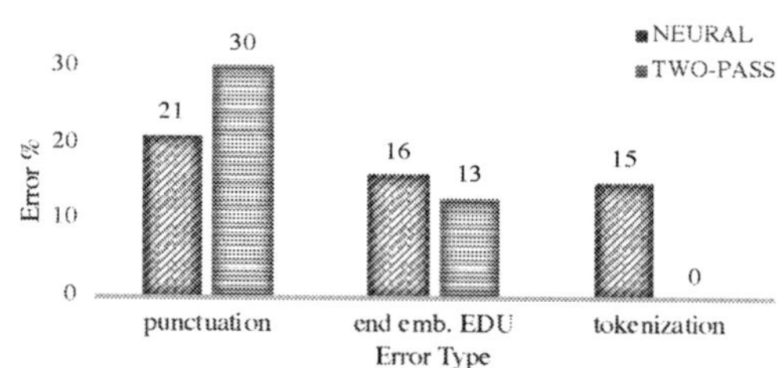

Figure 2: Distribution of the most frequent error types on *Medical* when using the NEURAL and TWO-PASS segmenter.

Section 6.3. The third error of *tokenization* occurs mainly around square brackets (citations), and this specific token never occurs in *News*.

6.3 Errors between segmenters

The rules of discourse segmentation rely heavily on syntax. Most discourse segmenters include syntax parse trees with the notable exception of the NEURAL segmenter. While this is the best-performing segmenter, we question whether it could be improved further if it had access to syntax trees. We probe this question by comparing the NEURAL segmentation errors with those found in TWO-PASS, which does use syntax trees.

Figure 2 illustrates the proportion of error types using the two segmenters. Although TWO-PASS makes use of syntax trees, the frequency of the syntactically-identifiable *end of embedded EDU* error type is only slightly lower. Because we do not have gold trees, it is also possible the news-trained parser performs poorly on medical and leads to downstream errors. We visually inspect the parse trees for these error cases and find the syntactic clause signaling the embedded EDU is correctly parsed in half the cases. Thus, bad parse trees contribute only partially to this error, and we suspect better trees may not provide much bene-

---

[5]This option is viable once the MEDICAL corpus is expanded to a large enough size for training.

SECTION	KAPPA	F1	#TOKENS
Summary	1.00	100	35
Introduction	0.96	86.58	258
Results	0.93	91.74	354
Abstract	0.89	95.08	266
Methods	0.86	92.99	417
Discussion	0.84	89.03	365

Table 5: Average inter-annotator agreement per section, ordered from highest to lowest, the corresponding average F1 of the NEURAL segmenter, and number of tokens (there are 2 documents per section, except 1 for Summary).

fit. This finding is consistent with the little help dependency trees provided for cross-lingual discourse segmentation in Braud et al. (2017b).

We further note the tokenizer for TWO-PASS makes no errors on the medical data, but conversely has a higher proportion of *punctuation* errors. This pattern suggests improving the tokenizer of the NEURAL segmenter may simply shift errors from one type to another. To test this hypothesis, we use pre-tokenized text and find roughly half the errors do shift from one type to the other, but the other half is correctly labeled. That is, performance actually improves, but only slightly (F1=+0.36, P=+0.50, R=+0.24).

6.4 Errors between annotators and segmenters

Here we compare the level of annotator agreement with the performance of the NEURAL segmenter. In Table 5, we see that both humans and the model do well on extremely short texts (*Summary*). However, high agreement does not always translate to good performance. The *Introduction* section is straightforward for the annotators to segment, but this is also where most citations occur, causing the segmenter to perform more poorly. Earlier, we had noted the *Discussion* section was the hardest for annotators to label because of the more complex discourse. These more ambiguous syntactic constructions also pose a challenge for the segmenter, with lower performance than most other sections.

7 Next Steps

Based on our findings, we propose a set of next steps for RST discourse analysis in the medical domain. A much faster annotation process can be adopted by using the NEURAL segmenter as a first pass. Annotators should skip extremely short documents and instead focus on the more challenging *Discussion* section. During training, we recommend using medical-specific word embeddings and preprocessing pipeline.[6] Addressing even one of these issues may yield a multiplied effect on segmentation improvements as the *Medical* domain is by nature highly repetitive and formulaic.

However, a future avenue of research would be to first understand what impact these segmentation errors have on downstream tasks. For example, using RST trees generated by the lowest-performing DPLP parser nevertheless provides small gains to text categorization tasks such as sentiment analysis (Ji and Smith, 2017). On the other hand, understanding the verb form, which proved to be difficult in the *Medical* domain, has been shown to be useful in distinguishing text on experimental results from text describing more abstract concepts (such as background and introductory information), which may be a more relevant task than sentiment analysis (de Waard and Maat, 2012).

8 Conclusion

As a first step in understanding discourse differences between domains, we analyze the performance of three discourse segmenters on *News* and *Medical*. For this purpose, we create a first, small-scale corpus of segmented medical documents in English. All segmenters suffer a drop in performance on *Medical*, but this drop is smaller on the best *News* segmenter. An error analysis reveals difficulty in both domains for cases requiring a fine-grained syntactic analysis, as dictated by the RST-DT annotation guidelines. This finding suggests a need for either a clearer distinction in the guidelines, or more training examples for a model to learn to distinguish them. In the *Medical* domain, we find that differences in syntactic construction and formatting, including use of punctuation, account for most of the segmentation errors. We hypothesize these errors can be partly traced back to tokenizers and word embeddings also trained on *News*. We finally compare annotator agreement with segmenter performance and find both suffer in sections with more complex discourse. Based on our findings, we have proposed (Section 7) a set of next steps to expand the corpus and improve the segmenter.

---

[6]`https://allennlp.org/elmo,https://allenai.github.io/scispacy`

Acknowledgments

We thank the anonymous reviewers for their helpful feedback. The first author was supported by the National Science Foundation Graduate Research Fellowship Program under Grant No. 2017247409. Any opinions, findings, and conclusions or recommendations expressed in this material are those of the authors and do not necessarily reflect the views of the National Science Foundation.

References

Parminder Bhatia, Yangfeng Ji, and Jacob Eisenstein. 2015. Better document-level sentiment analysis from rst discourse parsing. In *Proceedings of the 2015 Conference on Empirical Methods in Natural Language Processing*, pages 2212–2218. Association for Computational Linguistics.

Chloé Braud, Ophélie Lacroix, and Anders Søgaard. 2017a. Cross-lingual and cross-domain discourse segmentation of entire documents. In *Proceedings of the 55th Annual Meeting of the Association for Computational Linguistics (Volume 2: Short Papers)*, pages 237–243. Association for Computational Linguistics.

Chloé Braud, Ophélie Lacroix, and Anders Søgaard. 2017b. Does syntax help discourse segmentation? not so much. In *Proceedings of the 2017 Conference on Empirical Methods in Natural Language Processing*, pages 2432–2442. Association for Computational Linguistics.

Shuyuan Cao, Nianwen Xue, Iria da Cunha, Mikel Iruskieta, and Chuan Wang. 2017. Discourse segmentation for building a rst chinese treebank. In *Proceedings of the 6th Workshop on Recent Advances in RST and Related Formalisms*, pages 73–81. Association for Computational Linguistics.

Lynn Carlson and Daniel Marcu. 2001. Discourse tagging reference manual. *ISI Technical Report ISI-TR-545*, 54:56.

Lynn Carlson, Daniel Marcu, and Mary Ellen Okurovsky. 2001. Building a discourse-tagged corpus in the framework of rhetorical structure theory. In *Proceedings of the Second SIGdial Workshop on Discourse and Dialogue*, pages 1–10. Association for Computational Linguistics.

Iria Da Cunha, Eric San Juan, Juan Manuel Torres-Moreno, Marina Lloberese, and Irene Castellóne. 2012. Diseg 1.0: The first system for spanish discourse segmentation. *Expert Systems with Applications*, 39(2):1671–1678.

Vanessa Wei Feng and Graeme Hirst. 2014. Two-pass Discourse Segmentation with Pairing and Global Features. *arXiv preprint arXiv:1407.8215*.

Wei Vanessa Feng. 2015. *RST-style discourse parsing and its applications in discourse analysis*. Ph.D. thesis, University of Toronto (Canada).

Seeger Fisher and Brian Roark. 2007. The utility of parse-derived features for automatic discourse segmentation. In *Proceedings of the 45th Annual Meeting of the Association of Computational Linguistics*, pages 488–495. Association for Computational Linguistics.

Mikel Iruskieta, Mara Jesus Aranzabe, A Diaz de Ilarraza, Itziar Gonzalez, Mikel Lersundi, and O Lopez de Lacalle. 2013. The RST Basque TreeBank: an online search interface to check rhetorical relations. In *Anais do IV Workshop A RST e os Estudos do Texto*, pages 40–49. Sociedade Brasileira de Computação.

Yangfeng Ji and Noah A. Smith. 2017. Neural Discourse Structure for Text Categorization. In *Proceedings of the 55th Annual Meeting of the Association for Computational Linguistics (Volume 1: Long Papers)*, pages 996–1005. Association for Computational Linguistics.

Shafiq Joty, Giuseppe Carenini, and Raymond T. Ng. 2015. CODRA: A Novel Discriminative Framework for Rhetorical Analysis. *Computational Linguistics*, 41(3):385–435.

William C Mann and Sandra A Thompson. 1988. Rhetorical structure theory: Toward a functional theory of text organization. *Text-Interdisciplinary Journal for the Study of Discourse*, 8(3):243–281.

Christopher D. Manning, Mihai Surdeanu, John Bauer, Jenny Finkel, Steven J. Bethard, and David McClosky. 2014. The Stanford CoreNLP natural language processing toolkit. In *Association for Computational Linguistics (ACL) System Demonstrations*, pages 55–60.

Erwin Marsi, Pinar Øzturk, Elias Aamot, Gleb Valerjevich Sizov, and Murat Van Ardelan. 2014. Towards text mining in climate science: Extraction of quantitative variables and their relations.

Matthew Peters, Mark Neumann, Mohit Iyyer, Matt Gardner, Christopher Clark, Kenton Lee, and Luke Zettlemoyer. 2018. Deep contextualized word representations. In *Proceedings of the 2018 Conference of the North American Chapter of the Association for Computational Linguistics: Human Language Technologies, (Volume 1: Long Papers)*, pages 2227–2237. Association for Computational Linguistics.

Emily Pitler and Ani Nenkova. 2009. Using syntax to disambiguate explicit discourse connectives in text. In *Proceedings of Joint conference of the 47th Annual Meeting of the Association for Computational Linguistics and the 4th International Joint Conference on Natural Language Processing of the Asian Federation of Natural Language Processing*, pages 13–16. Association for Computational Linguistics.

Rashmi Prasad, Susan McRoy, Nadya Frid, Aravind Joshi, and Hong Yu. 2011. The biomedical discourse relation bank. *BMC bioinformatics*, 12(1):188.

Gisela Redeker, Ildikó Berzlánovich, Nynke van der Vliet, Gosse Bouma, and Markus Egg. 2012. Multilayer discourse annotation of a dutch text corpus. In *Proceedings of the Eighth International Conference on Language Resources and Evaluation*. European Language Resources Association.

Radu Soricut and Daniel Marcu. 2003. Sentence level discourse parsing using syntactic and lexical information. In *Proceedings of the 2003 Human Language Technology Conference of the North American Chapter of the Association for Computational Linguistics*, pages 228–235. Association for Computational Linguistics.

Maite Taboada and William C Mann. 2006. Rhetorical structure theory: Looking back and moving ahead. *Discourse studies*, 8(3):423–459.

Ian Tenney, Patrick Xia, Berlin Chen, Alex Wang, Adam Poliak, R Thomas McCoy, Najoung Kim, Benjamin Van Durme, Sam Bowman, Dipanjan Das, et al. 2018. What do you learn from context? probing for sentence structure in contextualized word representations.

Svetlana Toldova, Dina Pisarevskaya, Margarita Ananyeva, Maria Kobozeva, Alexander Nasedkin, Sofia Nikiforova, Irina Pavlova, and Alexey Shelepov. 2017. Rhetorical relations markers in russian rst treebank. In *Proceedings of the 6th Workshop on Recent Advances in RST and Related Formalisms*, pages 29–33. Association for Computational Linguistics.

Anita de Waard and Henk Pander Maat. 2012. Verb form indicates discourse segment type in biological research papers: Experimental evidence. *Journal of English for Academic Purposes*, 11(4):357–366.

Yizhong Wang, Sujian Li, and Jingfeng Yang. 2018. Toward fast and accurate neural discourse segmentation. In *Proceedings of the 2018 Conference on Empirical Methods in Natural Language Processing*, pages 962–967. Association for Computational Linguistics.

An Yang and Sujian Li. 2018. Scidtb: Discourse dependency treebank for scientific abstracts. In *Proceedings of the 56th Annual Meeting of the Association for Computational Linguistics (Volume 2: Short Papers)*, pages 444–449. Association for Computational Linguistics.

Amir Zeldes. 2017. The GUM corpus: creating multilayer resources in the classroom. *Language Resources and Evaluation*, 51(3):581–612.

Fan Zhang, Diane Litman, and Katherine Forbes-Riley. 2016. Inferring discourse relations from pdtb-style discourse labels for argumentative revision classification. In *Proceedings of the 26th International Conference on Computational Linguistics: Technical Papers*, pages 2615–2624. The COLING 2016 Organizing Committee.

Nuclearity in RST and signals of coherence relations

Debopam Das

Department of English and American Studies
Humboldt University of Berlin, Germany
dasdebop@hu-berlin.de

Abstract

We investigate the relationship between the notion of nuclearity as proposed in Rhetorical Structure Theory (RST) and the signalling of coherence relations. RST relations are categorized as either mononuclear (comprising a nucleus and a satellite span) or multinuclear (comprising two or more nuclei spans). We examine how mononuclear relations (e.g., Antithesis, Condition) and multinuclear relations (e.g., Contrast, List) are indicated by relational signals, more particularly by discourse markers (e.g., *because, however, if, therefore*). We conduct a corpus study, examining the distribution of either type of relations in the RST Discourse Treebank (Carlson et al., 2002) and the distribution of discourse markers for those relations in the RST Signalling Corpus (Das et al., 2015). Our results show that discourse markers are used more often to signal multinuclear relations than mononuclear relations. The findings also suggest a complex relationship between the relation types and syntactic categories of discourse markers (subordinating and coordinating conjunctions).

1 Introduction

Nuclearity in Rhetorical Structure Theory (RST) is explained in terms of relative importance of text spans (Mann and Thompson, 1988). The span perceived (by the reader) to be more important or central to the writer's purpose is called the nucleus, and the span perceived to be less important or peripheral to the writer's purpose is called the satellite. RST relations having spans with equal and unequal importance are known as multinuclear and mononuclear relations, respectively. Examples of multinuclear relations include Contrast, List or Sequence, and examples of mononuclear relations include Condition, Elaboration, Evidence or Summary. The notion of nuclearity in RST represents a symmetric-asymmetric divide, which also parallels with the distinction between non-hierarchical and hierarchical relations: Multinuclear relations are symmetrical or non-hierarchical relations, and mononuclear relations are asymmetric or hierarchical relations.

Coherence relations, whether multinuclear or mononuclear, are often signalled by discourse markers (henceforth DMs)[1]. For example, a Contrast relation (multinuclear) can be indicated by the DM *but*, and an Evidence relation (mononuclear) can be conveyed through the DM *because*. Research on the signalling phenomenon in discourse has, however, more recently shown that coherence relations can well be indicated by other textual signals such as certain lexical expressions or syntactic features, both in addition to or in the absence of DMs (Das and Taboada, 2018). For instance, in the Penn Discourse Treebank (PDTB 3.0) (Webber et al., 2018, p. 10) the Condition relation between the text segments (within square brackets) in Example 1 is conveyed through the use of auxiliary inversion (underlined)[2]:

(1) [. . . but would have climbed 0.6%,] [<u>had it not been</u> for the storm] (file no: wsj-0573)

In this paper, we investigate the relationship between the notion of nuclearity in RST and the signalling of coherence relations. We examine whether nuclearity has a role to play in relation marking, and whether multinuclear and mononu-

---

[1] In this paper, we define discourse markers as having the meaning of a two-place relation, and not representing elements like hedges, fillers or interjections, as in conversations. While the term 'discourse connectives' is deemed to be more appropriate, we prefer to use the term discourse markers in the spirit of the RST Signalling Corpus (Das et al., 2015), which we base our analyses on.

[2] In the PDTB 3.0, this is represented by a finer version of AltLex, called AltLexC, which records the position of the relevant lexico-grammatical signal within a sentence.

Proceedings of Discourse Relation Parsing and Treebanking (DISRPT2019), pages 30–37
Minneapolis, MN, June 6, 2019. ©2019 Association for Computational Linguistics

clear relations differ in terms of signalling. However, since a complete analysis of all kinds of relational signals is beyond the scope of the present paper, we constrain our analysis only to DMs, and do not consider any other types of signalling[3]. We address the following research questions:

1. How are mononuclear and multinuclear relations signalled in text?
2. Does one category employ more DMs than the other?
3. What types of DMs (subordinating and coordinating conjunctions) are used to indicate these two categories of relations?

DMs, although primarily representing a functional category, are generally considered to belong to four different syntactic classes: coordinating conjunction (like *and* and *but*, as when they connect two coordinated clauses), subordinating conjunction (like *if* and *since*, as when they connect a subordinate adjunct clause to a main clause), prepositional phrases (like *in addition* and *as a result*, as when they connect two main clauses or sentences), and adverbial phrases (like *however* and *nevertheless*, as used much like the above-mentioned prepositional phrases). The question that we aim to address here is to what degree these canonical signal types correspond to the categories of nuclearity in RST. More simply, we examine, for example, to what extent coordinated conjunctions are used to indicate multinuclear relations, and to what extent subordinated conjunctions are used to signal mononuclear relations. For this purpose, we examine the signalling of mononuclear and multinuclear relations in the RST Signalling Corpus (Das et al., 2015), a corpus annotated for relational signals, which is built upon the RST Discourse Treebank (Carlson et al., 2002), a corpus annotated for coherence relations.

The paper is organized as follows: In Section 2, we provide the distribution of mononuclear and multinuclear relations in the RST Discourse Treebank. Section 3 provides a brief introduction to the RST Signalling Corpus, with a special focus on DMs. In Section 4, we present the results, reporting on the distributions of mononuclear and multinuclear relations with respect to DMs. Section 5 reflects on the implications of the results,

Project	# rel	# mono	# multi	# both
M&T[4]	23	21	2	0
PCC[5]	31	26	5	0
GUM[6]	20	16	3	1
Span TB[7]	28	22	6	0
DiZer[8]	32	26	6	0
Website[9]	25	21	4	0
RST-DT[10]	78	53	8	17

Table 1: Distribution of mononuclear and multinuclear RST relations in RST-based studies

and outlines a few potential future developments of this work. Finally, Section 6 summarizes the paper, and provides the conclusion.

2 Nuclearity and RST-DT

In RST-based research, just like the way relational inventories differ from studies to studies, so does the number of mononuclear and multinuclear relations within an inventory, as shown in Table 1.

In this study, we examine the relations from the RST Discourse Treebank (henceforth the RST-DT) (Carlson et al., 2002). The corpus, as the distribution (in Table 1) shows, uses a large set of 78 relations, including 53 mononuclear and 8 multinuclear relations. Most importantly, unlike other RST-based projects (in Table 1) that only distinguish between mononuclear and multinuclear relations (exception: the GUM corpus), the RST-DT includes an additional category for relations that can appear as both mononuclear or multinuclear[11]. The taxonomy of the RST-DT relations in terms of nuclearity is provided in Table 2.

The RST-DT contains a total of 20,123 relations, which were expanded to 21,400 relations for the signalling annotation in the RST Signalling Corpus (Das and Taboada, 2017), as a result of complying with a strict binary branching requirement and thus breaking a multinuclear relation

---

[3]We believe that the signalling of relations beyond discourse markers constitutes an important topic, and is worthy of investigation in its own right. We discuss the prospects of conducting a similar analysis of other signals for nuclearity in Section 5.

[4]Mann and Thompson (1988)

[5]Potsdam Commentary Corpus (Stede, 2016)

[6]The GUM corpus (Zeldes, 2017)

[7]RST Spanish Treebank (da Cunha et al., 2011)

[8]DIscourse analyZER for Brazilian Portuguese (Maziero et al., 2011)

[9]RST website (http://www.sfu.ca/rst/)

[10]RST Discourse Treebank (Carlson et al., 2002)

[11]The assignation of nuclearity status on a particular span can sometimes be a matter of considerable difficulty, and the inclusion of the both mono and multi versions of relations in the RST-DT, as Stede (2008) suggests, provided the RST-DT annotators greater freedom in choosing what spans should be labeled nuclear.

Type	Relation
mono	Antithesis, Attribution, Background, Cause, Circumstance, Comment, Concession, Condition, Contingency, Definition, Elaboration-additional, Elaboration-set-member, Elaboration-part-whole, Elaboration-process-step, Elaboration-object-attribute, Elaboration-general-specific, Enablement, Evidence, Example, Explanation-argumentative, Hypothetical, Manner, Means, Otherwise, Preference, Purpose, Restatement, Result, Rhetorical-question, Summary, Temporal-after, Temporal-before
multi	Contrast, Cause-Result, Comment-topic, Disjunction, Inverted-sequence, List, Otherwise, Proportion, Same-unit, Sequence, Textual-organization, Topic-comment
both	Analogy, Comparison, Conclusion, Consequence, Evaluation, Interpretation, Problem-solution, Question-answer, Reason, Statement-response, Temporal-same-time, Topic-drift, Topic-shift

Table 2: Relation types in RST-DT

having more than two nuclei into more than one (multinuclear) relation. These 21,400 relations are divided into 16,526 mononuclear and 4,874 multinuclear relations.

3 RST Signalling Corpus

The RST Signalling Corpus (henceforth the RST-SC) (Das et al., 2015) provides signalling annotation for the coherence relations that are present in the RST-DT. The RST-SC implements a wide perspective of signalling, and provides annotation for a large variety of textual signals, such as reference, lexical, semantic, syntactic, graphical and genre-related features, in addition to DMs. These signals are organized hierarchically in a taxonomy of three levels: *signal class, signal type,* and *specific signal.* The top level, *signal class,* has three tags representing three major classes of signals: *single, combined* and *unsure.* For each class, a second level is identified; for example, the class *single* is divided into nine signal types (e.g., *reference, syntactic, graphical*). Finally, the third level in the hierarchy refers to specific signals; for example, *reference* type has four specific signals: *personal, demonstrative, comparative,* and *propositional reference.* The hierarchical organization of the taxonomy is provided in Figure 1[12].

The distribution of relations by signals in the RST-SC (in Table 3, from Das and Taboada

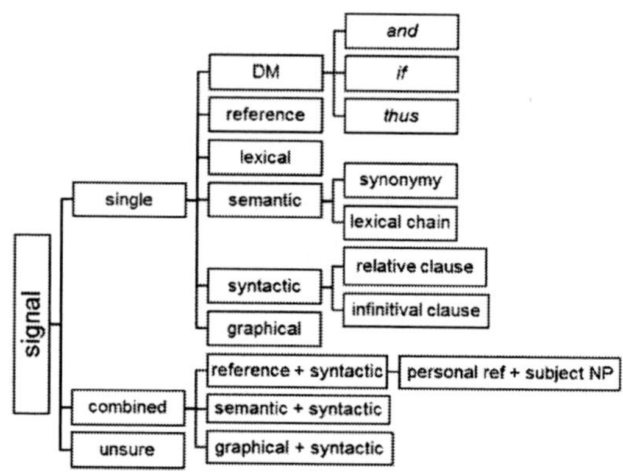

Figure 1: Hierarchical taxonomy of signals in RST-SC

(2018)) shows that an overwhelming majority of the relations in the RST-DT are signalled, and also that the majority of signalled relations are indicated by other signals rather than DMs. Only 3,896 (2,280 + 1,616) relations out of 21,400 relations (18.21% of all relations) are indicated by DMs[13]. These DMs are distributed across 201 different types, which can be further divided into coordinating conjunctions, subordinating conjunctions, prepositional and adverbial phrases.

In order to examine the relationship between nuclearity and DMs, we extract from the RST-SC (i) instances of all DMs, and (2) instances of different relations that are indicated by those DMs. A complete analysis of the relationship between the relations (78 types) and DMs (201 types) in the RST-SC, however, could not be covered in the present paper. That is why, we focus only on the most frequently occurring DMs and most frequently occurring relations in the corpus. In order to extract those tokens, we use UAM CorpusTool (O'Donnell, 2008), which was also used to annotate the RST-SC. The tool provides an efficient tag-specific search option for finding required annotated segments, and it also provides various types of statistical analyses of the corpus.

---

[12]Note that subcategories in the figure are only illustrative, not exhaustive. For the detailed taxonomy and definitions of signals, see Das (2014).

[13]One possible reason for the RST-SC for having a lower proportion of DMs than other comparable corpora is that the RST-SC employs a much stricter definition for DMs. For example, the PDTB 3.0 corpus (Webber et al., 2018), containing 45.93% relations with explicit connectives, uses more flexible parameters in the connective definition, and includes very frequently occurring words such as *also, by, from, in* or *like* as connectives. In contrast, the RST-SC considers these expressions not as DMs, but as lexical signals (more specifically, indicative words).

Relation type	Signalling type	#	%
Signalled relations	Relations exclusively signalled by DMs	2,280	10.65
	Relations exclusively signalled by other signals	15,951	74.54
	Relations signalled by both DMs and other signals	1,616	7.55
	TOTAL	19,847	92.74
Unsignalled relations	Relations not signalled by DMs or other signals	1,553	7.26
	TOTAL	21,400	100.00

Table 3: Distribution of signalled and unsignalled relations in RST-SC

4 Results

We first examine how mononuclear and multinuclear relations are distributed in the RST-SC with respect to signalling. The distribution in Table 4 shows that both mononuclear or multinuclear relations most often contain signals (over 90% of the relations). This also shows, however, that when it comes to the signalling by DMs, multinuclear relations are more often indicated by DMs than mononuclear relations: About 30% of the multinuclear relations contain a DM while only about 15% of the mononuclear relations occur with them.

Next, we find in the RST-SC the relations that are most frequently signalled by DMs (with respect to their overall frequencies in the corpus), and examine what DMs are commonly used to signal those relations. We provide the distribution of DMs for mononuclear relations in Table 5 and the distribution for multinuclear relations in Table 6. The number within parentheses after a relation name in column 1 (labeled Relation, in both tables) refers to the number of instances the relation occurs with a DM in the corpus. The number in column 3 (labeled #, in both tables) refers to the number of instances a DM (in the corresponding row) is used for marking the relation. (Note: CC = coordinating conjunction; SC = subordinating conjunction; PP = preposition (-al phrase); ADV = adverb (-ial) phrase)

Table 5 shows that a mononuclear relation is indicated by different DMs[14], which belong to different syntactic classes (e.g., CC, SC or ADV). For example, Result relations are commonly signalled by the DMs *because* (SC), *and* (CC) and *as a result* (ADV). Similar distribution of DMs for multinuclear relations is shown in Table 6. For ex-

ample, Temporal-same-time relations[15] are commonly marked by the DMs *while* (SC), *as* (SC) and *and* (CC).

Finally, we extract the most frequently used DMs in the RST-SC, and examine the relations that are signalled by them. In Table 7, we provide the distribution of the common relations for those DMs. The number in column 2 (labeled # DM) refers to the number of instances of a DM in the RST-SC, and the number in column 5 (labeled # Rel) refers to the number of instances for a relation indicated by that DM in the corpus. The distribution shows that the DMs *and* and *but* (both CC) are the two most frequent DMs (with over 600 tokens), followed by other DMs like *as* (SC), *if* (SC), *when* (SC), *because* (SC) and *however* (ADV). As we have seen in Table 5 and 6 that relations are indicated by a wide variety of DMs, Table 7 shows the opposite is also true: Each of the DMs in Table 7 indicates more than one relation in the corpus[16]. Furthermore, the relations indicated by these DMs are distributed for mononuclear and multinuclear categories. For example, the DM *while* is commonly used to indicate, on the one hand, Antithesis and Concession relations, which are mononuclear relations, and on the other hand, Contrast and List relations, which are multinuclear relations.

5 Discussion

As our results show (in Table 4), although over 90% of the RST relations in the RST-SC, regardless of their types (mononuclear or multinuclear), contain some sort of signals, only about

---

[14]The relations presented in Table 5 (and also Table 6) are indicated by an even wider variety of DMs in the RST-SC (see Das (2014)). The distribution here only records the most frequently used DMs (common DMs) for those relations.

[15]Temporal-same-time relations can be both mononuclear and multinuclear (see Table 2). Table 6 provides the distribution of DMs for Temporal-same-time when it is used as a multinuclear relation.

[16]In Table 7, the DM *if* is shown to indicate only Condition relations. In the RST-SC, however, *if* is also found to signal other relations, such as Circumstance, Contingency or Hypothetical (although with relatively lower frequencies).

Type	Total #	# signalled	% signalled	# with DM	% with DM
mono	16526	15424	93.33	2415	14.61
multi	4874	4423	90.75	1481	30.39

Table 4: Distribution of mononuclear and multinuclear relations by signalling

Relation	DM	#	Type
Concession (264)	but	100	CC
	although	28	SC
	despite	24	PP
	though	24	SC
	while	17	SC
Condition (221)	if	162	SC
	unless	12	SC
Temporal-before (38)	before	31	SC
Antithesis (330)	but	182	CC
	although	28	SC
	however	26	ADV
	though	11	ADV
Temporal-after (69)	after	48	SC
Temporal-same-time (63)	when	29	SC
	as	18	SC
	while	13	SC
Result (87)	because	25	SC
	and	23	CC
	as a result	19	ADV
Reason (112)	because	65	SC

Table 5: Common DMs for mononuclear relations

Relation	DM	#	Type
Disjunction (26)	or	19	CC
Temporal-same-time (52)	while	14	SC
	as	13	SC
	and	9	CC
Contrast (305)	but	186	CC
	however	22	ADV
	while	20	SC
	and	17	CC
Cause-result (42)	and	15	CC
	because	11	SC
Sequence (119)	and	69	CC
	then	20	ADV
List (818)	and	698	CC
	but	19	CC
	while	16	SC

Table 6: Common DMs for multinuclear relations

15% mononuclear and about 30% multinuclear relations contain a DM. This, however, implies that most often both mononuclear and multinuclear relations are conveyed by other textual signals. This is, we believe, an important issue to consider, and we will touch upon this point after we discuss our findings about DMs.

The crucial difference between mononuclear and multinuclear relations for signalling lies in the proportions of each type of relations containing a DM (15% vs. 30%). We observe that relations that differ according to nuclearity also differ with respect to two additional factors. First, all RST taxonomies (as shown in Table 1) contain significantly higher number of mononuclear relations than multinuclear relations (e.g., the GUM corpus (Zeldes, 2017) has 16 mononuclear (80%), but only 4 multinuclear (20%) relations). Furthermore, with respect to the number of tokens in a corpus, the mononuclear relations also outnumber multinuclear relations. For example, out of 21,400 relations in the RST-DT (Carlson et al., 2002), there are 16,526 mononuclear (77.22%) and only 4,874 multinuclear (22.78%) relations. The relatively lower number of multinuclear relations, both in RST taxonomies and corpora, may imply that mononuclear relations are more basic type of relations than multinuclear relations. If that is borne out, then it might also be case that when relations are multinuclear, they would require more DMs as their signals than mononuclear relations.

The distribution of DMs for mononuclear and multinuclear relations (in Table 5 and 6) shows a complex co-occurrence pattern of nuclearity type and the syntactic membership of DMs. On the one hand, we observe (in Table 5) that mononuclear relations are often conveyed by subordinating conjunctions (SCs). This is evidenced by relations such as Condition, Reason and Temporal-same-time (when used as a mononuclear relation) that (exclusively) employ SCs (among DMs) as their signals. Similarly (in Table 6), a strong association between multinuclear relations and coordinating conjunctions (CCs) is observed for Disjunction which is indicated by the CC *or*.

DM	# DM	Type	Relation	# Rel	Type
and	1043	CC	List	698	multinuclear
			Elaboration-additional	76	mononuclear
			Sequence	66	multinuclear
			Consequence	42	mononuclear
			Circumstance	20	mononuclear
but	615	CC	Contrast	186	multinuclear
			Antithesis	182	mononuclear
			Concession	100	mononuclear
			Elaboration-additional	48	mononuclear
			List	19	multinuclear
if	180	SC	Condition	162	mononuclear
when	168	SC	Circumstance	109	mononuclear
			Temporal-same-time	22	mononuclear
as	166	SC	Circumstance	64	mononuclear
			Temporal-same-time	18	mononuclear
			Comparison	15	mononuclear
because	162	SC	Reason	64	mononuclear
			Explanation-argumentative	35	mononuclear
			Consequence	21	mononuclear
			Result	14	mononuclear
			Cause-result	11	multinuclear
while	131	SC	Antithesis	24	mononuclear
			Contrast	20	multinuclear
			List	16	multinuclear
			Concession	17	mononuclear
			Temporal-same-time	14	multinuclear
after	101	SC	Temporal-after	48	mononuclear
			Circumstance	37	mononuclear
however	92	ADV	Antithesis	26	mononuclear
			Contrast	22	multinuclear
			Elaboration-additional	14	mononuclear
			Concession	11	mononuclear
because of	81	SC	Consequence	21	mononuclear
			Reason	19	mononuclear
			Result	18	mononuclear
although	62	SC	Antithesis	28	mononuclear
			Concession	28	mononuclear
before	60	SC	Temporal-before	31	mononuclear
			Circumstance	14	mononuclear
without	51	PP	Circumstance	21	mononuclear
			Manner	19	mononuclear

Table 7: Common relations for DMs

On the other hand, we observe (in Table 5 and 6) that the opposite pattern also holds, that is, mononuclear relations are often signalled by CCs and multinuclear relations frequently contain SCs. For example, a large proportion of Concession or Antithesis (both mononuclear relations) employ the CC *but* as their signal. Similarly, Temporal-same-time (as a multinuclear relation) are mostly indicated by the SCs *while* and *as*.

The complex nature of the co-occurrence of nuclearity types and DM types is further illustrated by Table 7 that presents the distribution of common relations for most frequent DMs in the RST-SC. For example, the SC *while* is used to indicate both mononuclear relations (Antithesis or Concession) and multinuclear relations (Contrast or List).

In sum, DMs are found to signal multinuclear relations more often than mononuclear relations. However, with respect to the DM types, mononuclear and multinuclear relations are indicated by both SCs ad CCs, without having any strong commitment to either type of DMs[17]. The latter finding is in line with Blühdorn (2008), who finds that hierarchy and non-hierarchy at the syntactic level (represented by subordination and coordination, respectively) does not systematically correspond to hierarchical and non-hierarchical coherence relations (in effect, mononuclear and multinuclear relations, respectively) at the discourse level.

Theoretically, the nuclearity status of a span (nucleus or satellite) in a relation is assigned by evaluating it against the other span in terms of to what degree the span is important to the intention of the writer. In practice, however, determining the relative importance of spans may not be a straightforward task. Stede (2008) identifies different factors that influence RST annotators to decide on the nuclearity status of the text segments. These factors include intention of the writer (represented in the nucleus and supported by the satellite), recurrence of an idea across different parts of a text (as a sign of emphasizing importance for a span), digression from the main topic (as a sign of less importance for a span), connectives (in German) and punctuation (e.g., parentheses) that can mark the nucleus-satellite distinction, syntactic structure (main clause vs. subordinate clause),

or the RST relation definitions themselves that prescribe the nuclearity status for a span (e.g., reporting clause as the satellite for Attribution relations). If these sources really contribute to identify the nucleus (or distinguish between the nucleus and satellite), an important venture could be to examine whether or how signalling interacts with these factors. It seems that some of the factors are closely associated with the signalling phenomenon. For example, as our results show, certain DMs (or connectives) such as *if* or *although*, which are SCs, are always used to convey mononuclear relations.

The association of potential sources of nuclearity and relation marking can possibly be made more substantial if we adopt a wider perspective of signalling, incorporating other means of signalling beyond DMs. As mentioned in Section 3, the RST-SC exploits many different types of signals, and we argue here that some of these signals may well be correlated with some of the factors affecting nuclearity. We provide a few examples to illustrate this. Syntactic signals such as auxiliary inversion (as shown in Example 1) or certain type of subordinate clauses (e.g., participial or infinitival) may exhibit a strong correlation with the factor *syntactic structure*, as suggested by Stede (2008). Also, parallel syntactic constructions (e.g., *Chris is tall; Pat is short.*) can indicate or predict the presence of a multinuclear relation. Similarly, a graphical signal such as an itemized list (called *items in sequence* in the RST-SC) can be used to signal a multinuclear (List) relation, while the content within parentheses (as also suggested by Stede (2008)) can refer to a satellite span. Furthermore, a reference feature (encoding a co-reference chain) or semantic feature (representing a lexical chain) can indicate the presence of a mononuclear relation (e.g., Elaboration or Restatement). We leave an exploration of the interaction of other relational signals and nuclearity as one of our future endeavors from this study.

Furthermore, a rather specific query about the relationship between nuclearity and signalling relates to the location of the signals, that is, where the signals occur – in nucleus, in satellite, or in both spans. We would like to examine, more particularly, which signal occurs in which span, and how frequently they occur in one (as opposed to in the other) span.

We envisage another related line of develop-

---

[17]DMs can also belong to two other syntactic classes, PPs or ADVs. However, since we find only a few DMs of these types (four ADVs (*however, though, as a result* and *then*) and two PPs (*despite* and *without*)), we do not include them in the present analysis.

ment concerning what is suggested by Marcu (2000) as the 'strong nuclearity hypothesis'. According to this hypothesis, it is postulated that when a relation holds between two (composite) text spans, it should also hold between the nuclei of those two spans. We would like to examine whether it is possible to motivate the 'strong nuclearity hypothesis' by evidence from the signalling of RST relations. The relevant question to address here would be if we disregard all the satellites in an RST analysis, whether we would still have relevant signals left in the remaining nuclei that can indicate the relations between spans.

6 Conclusion

In this paper, we have investigated how the notion of nuclearity correlates with the signalling of coherence relations by discourse markers, which are generally considered to be the most explicit and reliable signals of coherence relations. Based on a corpus analysis of RST relations and relational signals, we have examined how mononuclear and multinuclear relations are signalled by discourse markers. Our results have shown that multinuclear relations are indicated more frequently by discourse markers than mononuclear relations. However, we did not find conclusive evidence as to whether these two relation types are more or less conveyed through coordinating or subordinating conjunctions, the two primary categories of discourse markers. In order to address the complex relationship between nuclearity and signalling more adequately, we have argued for the need to incorporate in the analysis other types of relational signals (such as syntactic, graphical or reference features), which might demonstrate a more substantial correlation between the notion of nuclearity in RST and the signalling of coherence relations.

References

Hardarik Blühdorn. 2008. Subordination and coordination in syntax, semantics, and discourse: Evidence from the study of connectives. In Cathrine Fabricius-Hansen and Wiebke Ramm, editors, 'Subordination' versus 'Coordination' in Sentence and Text: A cross-linguistic perspective, pages 59–85. John Benjamins, Amsterdam.

Lynn Carlson, Daniel Marcu, and Mary Ellen Okurowski. 2002. RST Discourse Treebank, LDC2002T07. Philadelphia. Linguistic Data Consortium.

Iria da Cunha, Juan-Manuel Torres-Moreno, and Gerardo Sierra. 2011. On the Development of the RST Spanish Treebank. In Proceedings of the 5th Linguistic Annotation Workshop, LAW V '11, pages 1–10, Stroudsburg, PA, USA. Association for Computational Linguistics.

Debopam Das. 2014. Signalling of Coherence Relations in Discourse. Phd dissertation, Simon Fraser University, Canada.

Debopam Das and Maite Taboada. 2017. RST Signalling Corpus: A corpus of signals of coherence relations. Language Resources Evaluation, 52(1):149–184.

Debopam Das and Maite Taboada. 2018. Signalling of Coherence Relations in Discourse, Beyond Discourse Markers. Discourse Processes, 55(8):743–770.

Debopam Das, Maite Taboada, and Paul McFetridge. 2015. RST Signalling Corpus, LDC2015T10. Philadelphia. Linguistic Data Consortium.

William C. Mann and Sandra A. Thompson. 1988. Rhetorical Structure Theory: Toward a functional theory of text organization. Text, 8(3):243–281.

Daniel Marcu. 2000. The Theory and Practice of Discourse Parsing and Summarization. MIT Press, Cambridge, MA.

Erick Galani Maziero, Thiago Alexandre Salgueiro Pardo, Iria da Cunha, Juan-Manuel Torres-Moreno, and Eric SanJuan. 2011. DiZer 2.0 An Adaptable On-line Discourse Parser. In Proceedings of the III RST Meeting (8th Brazilian Symposium in Information and Human Language Technology, pages 1–17, Cuiabá/MT, Brazil.

Michael O'Donnell. 2008. The UAM Corpustool: Software for corpus annotation and exploration. In Proceedings of the XXVI Congreso de AESLA, pages 3–5, Almeria, Spain.

Manfred Stede. 2008. RST revisited: Disentangling nuclearity. In Cathrine Fabricius-Hansen and Wiebke Ramm, editors, 'Subordination' versus 'Coordination' in Sentence and Text: A cross-linguistic perspective, pages 33–58. John Benjamins, Amsterdam.

Manfred Stede. 2016. Rhetorische Struktur. In Manfred Stede, editor, Handbuch Textannotation: Potsdamer Kommentarkorpus 2.0. Universitätsverlag, Potsdam.

Bonnie Webber, Rashmi Prasad, Alan Lee, and Aravind Joshi. 2018. The Penn Discourse Treebank 3.0 Annotation Manual. Report, The University of Pennsylvania.

Amir Zeldes. 2017. The GUM corpus: creating multilayer resources in the classroom. Language Resources and Evaluation, 51:581–612.

The Rhetorical Structure of Attribution

Andrew Potter
Computer Science & Information Systems Department
University of North Alabama
Florence, Alabama, USA
`apotter1@una.edu`

Abstract

The relational status of ATTRIBUTION in Rhetorical Structure Theory has been a matter of ongoing debate. Although several researchers have weighed in on the topic, and although numerous studies have relied upon attributional structures for their analyses, nothing approaching consensus has emerged. This paper identifies three basic issues that must be resolved to determine the relational status of attributions. These are identified as the Discourse Units Issue, the Nuclearity Issue, and the Relation Identification Issue. These three issues are analyzed from the perspective of classical RST. A finding of this analysis is that the nuclearity and the relational identification of attribution structures are shown to depend on the writer's intended effect, such that attributional relations cannot be considered as a single relation, but rather as attributional instances of other RST relations.

1 Introduction

In the classical formulation of Rhetorical Structure Theory, Mann and Thompson (1987) considered, but decided against, QUOTE as one of the baselined relations. But this rejection of an attribution relation was by no means the final word on the subject, with debate continuing into the most recent formulation of the theory (Stede, Taboada, & Das, 2017). Even so, some basic ideas can be generally agreed upon. It would be generally agreed that if there were an attribution relation, it would likely consist of two parts, consisting of an attribution predicate and its respective attributed material (although terminology for these parts varies from one researcher to the next). It is also generally agreed that if there were, or is to be, an attribution relation, one of these parts would be an RST satellite and the other the nucleus. There is not, however, general agreement as to which one is which (e.g., Carlson & Marcu, 2001; Redeker & Egg, 2006).

Among those accepting that there is an attribution relation, as well as among some of those who reject it, the parts comprising the relation are often identified in terms of syntactical or grammatical features (e.g., Carlson & Marcu, 2001; Redeker & Egg, 2006; Wolf & Gibson, 2005). For example, the part of the putative relation that would provide the attributed material is sometimes delimited, for reasons not entirely forthcoming, to clausal complements, and thereby ruling out other possibilities, such as infinitival complements, except when including them would serve the analyst's purposes.

Alternatively among those who reject the relational status of attribution, the reasoning may be more closely aligned with the fundamentals of classical RST, based on the view that the constituents of attributions, whatever they might be from a syntactical or grammatical view, fail to meet the basic standards for discourse units (e.g., Mann & Thompson, 1987; Stede et al., 2017; Tofiloski, Brooke, & Taboada, 2009). However, given that the standards for what constitutes a discourse unit are somewhat unstable in their own right, this too leaves one on uncertain ground (Degand & Simon, 2009).

So there are three core issues here, and these will be the subject of this paper. The first of these issues may be called the *Discourse Units Issue*, and concerns whether the constituents of attributions can be plausibly construed as discourse units, elementary or otherwise. The second issue is the *Nuclearity Issue*. That is, if attributions are relations, which part is the satellite and which the nucleus? The third issue is the *Relation Identification Issue*. If we accept the finding that attributions are relational, with one part consisting

Proceedings of Discourse Relation Parsing and Treebanking (DISRPT2019), pages 38–49
Minneapolis, MN, June 6, 2019. ©2019 Association for Computational Linguistics

of a nucleus and the other a satellite, then how do we characterize whatever relations may be found between these parts? What are the constraints, and what are the intended effects? Is there only one ATTRIBUTION relation, or are there other possibilities? Addressing these issues is the objective of this study.

The analytical approach used here is based on classical RST analysis. A key determinant in addressing the issues requires analysis of the writer's *intended effect*, as understood by the analyst. Identifying the writer's intended effect is an essential means for determining relational structure. Because RST is a functional account of text organization, intended effect overrides grammatical analysis, and it is the tie-breaker for resolving otherwise simultaneous analyses. As described by Mann and Thompson (1987), RST provides an account for how intended effects are realized through relational propositions, and thus serves as a general theory of writers' goals, and this is fundamental to understanding the organization of a text.

And yet the primacy of intended effect is scarcely mentioned in discussions of attribution. It is not explicit among the reasons Mann and Thompson (1987) identified for rejecting it. Neither Carlson and Marcu (2001) nor Redeker and Egg (2006) mention it. Wolf and Gibson (2005) do not mention it. Nor do Sanders, Spooren, and Noordman (1992) nor Das, Taboada, and Stede (2017). In an earlier rejection of relational status for attributions, Stede (2008) calls attention to the lack of nuclear constraints and inattention to the intentions of the writer, an assessment shared by da Cunha and Iruskieta (2010), but for the most part intended effect, so fundamental to RST, has been ignored.

In this study, I propose to explore attributional relations from the perspective of intended effect. The claim to be developed is that attributions can be segmented into reporting and reported parts, but that the relation between these two parts will not necessarily be ATTRIBUTION *per se*, but will occur as one among several possible relations, including JUSTIFY, ELABORATION, EVIDENCE, EVALUATION, INTERPRETATION, and CAUSE.

To support this claim, I will revisit a selection of existing RST analyses containing attributions from Carlson and Marcu (2001), Redeker and Egg (2006), Taboada and Hay (2008), and Das and Taboada (2013). In addition, I have provided several original analyses. These analyses will be used to support a discussion of each of the core issues outlined above, i.e., the Discourse Units Issue, the Nuclearity Issue, and the Relation Identification Issue. This investigation is followed by discussion of the consequences of these findings along with some suggestions for further research.

2 Background

Quite a few researchers have voiced opposition to relational status for attribution. As noted in above, a frequent objection is that it fails to meet the inter-clausal criterion for coherence relations (e.g., Das et al., 2017; Mann & Thompson, 1987; Sanders et al., 1992; Stede, 2008). Despite these objections, numerous research projects have adopted ATTRIBUTION as a relation. The primary proponents are Carlson and Marcu (2001), whose *Discourse Tagging Reference Manual* and their *RST Discourse Treebank* (Carlson, Marcu, & Okurowski, 2002) have been influential among RST analysts. Redeker and Egg (2006) have also recognized the ATTRIBUTION relation, although their definition differs significantly from those of Carlson and Marcu (2001). Dahlgren, McDowell, and Stabler (1989) used ATTRIBUTION in their knowledge representation system for tracking knowledge provenance. Radev (2000) used ATTRIBUTION in his adaptation of RST for a theory of cross-document information fusion. Wolf and Gibson (2005), for their annotation of news articles, used ATTRIBUTION to distinguish between multiple and possibly conflicting reports about identical news events. Heerschop et al. (2011) used ATTRIBUTION for performing sentiment analysis. In their study of sentiment-based ranking of blog posts, Chenlo, Hogenboom, and Losada (2013) used the ATTRIBUTION relation and found that it, along with ELABORATION, occurred frequently in the postings studied. Similar results were obtained by Zhang and Liu (2016) in their study of RST relations across multiple levels of discourse unit granularity. Galitsky, Ilvovsky, and Kuznetsov (2018) used ATTRIBUTION in their text classification framework for detecting logical argumentation. The ATTRIBUTION relation has been widely included among the relations detected by RST discourse parsing systems (e.g., Heilman & Sagae, 2015; Hernault, Prendinger, duVerle, & Ishizuka, 2010; Ketui, Theeramunkong, & Onsuwan, 2012; Pardo, Nunes, & Rino, 2004; Soricut & Marcu, 2003). Abdalla, Rudzicz, and

Hirst (2018) found both ATTRIBUTION and ELABORATION to be significant indicators of Alzheimer's disease in speech. This widespread acceptance of the relation indicates an extensive reliance on it. For this reason, if for no other, it is important that concerns about its status should be investigated and perhaps even resolved.

3 The Discourse Units Issue

The reason given by Mann and Thompson (1987) for rejecting attribution as a relation is that it does not constitute a distinct entity but has only a support role, such that no relational proposition arises. Therefore it would suffice to show that relational propositions, i.e., RST relations, do under these circumstances arise, hence requiring segmentation of attribution predicates from their attributed material. Showing how these relations arise is an objective of the analyses presented below, in Section 4.

Stede et al. (2017) reject attribution for syntactical reasons. They argue that the attributed material, i.e., the reported unit is not a discourse unit because it is a clausal complement of the attribution verb. If RST were a theory of grammar, this might seem adequate. But since RST is a functional theory of text organization, this argument seems questionable. And if relational propositions are discoverable between attributions and the attributed material, then the constituents of that relation must be discourse units or text spans, and syntactical concerns are insufficient grounds for rejection. Showing how these relations arise is an objective of the analyses presented below.

4 The Nuclearity Issue

In their definition of ATTRIBUTION, Carlson and Marcu (2001) mark the attribution predicate as the satellite and the attributed material, or reported message, as the nucleus. Thus in the passage,

> 1) *Senator Chris Coons, the Delaware Democrat, told me*
> 2) *that his longtime colleague [Senator Lindsey Graham] is "hysterically funny" and "personally engaging."*

the first unit would be the satellite and the second would be the nucleus. Redeker and Egg (2006) argue that relegating the attribution predicate to satellite status can lead to misrepresentative or impossible RST analyses, particularly when the

attribution predicate is a cognitive predication that is more salient than the attribution material. They therefore mark the attribution predicate as the nucleus and the clausal complement as the satellite. And yet this too will lead to analyses that are misrepresentative or impossible. Under this regimen, in the above example, the attribution predicate, *Senator Chris Coons, the Delaware Democrat, told me* would be marked as the nucleus, but it is the assessment of Lindsey Graham that is the more salient in this passage.

This conflict is the result of a false dilemma. While attributions are clearly asymmetric, meaning that one constituent will be the nucleus and the other the satellite, there is no single pattern of asymmetry. Sometimes the attribution predicate is the more salient, and sometimes the attributed material is more salient. However, the inference to be made is not that ATTRIBUTION is not a discourse relation, nor is it that nuclearity must be decided on a case by case basis. The inference to be made is that, although attribution is relational, the relation is not necessarily ATTRIBUTION per se. Indeed, ATTRIBUTION is but one among several relations that are used in attributional constructs.

5 The Relation Identification Issue

Identification of attributions in discourse appears to be fairly straightforward, based on the presence of attribution verbs or cognitive predicates. However, this is not to say that recognition of attribution phenomena, even as relational structures, provides any assurance that an attribution is ATTRIBUTION rather than some other relation. Identification of intended effect is essential in determining the specific relation. Without identification of intended effect, it cannot be presumed that there is any relation whatsoever. In the case of attribution, the situation is complicated by the necessity for distinguishing between the writer's intended effect and the source's intended effect. Is the writer merely reporting the attribution phenomena, or is the writer leveraging the attribution source or the attribution material to achieve some change in positive regard? Attributions may be to the first person, second person, or third person. Attributions occur within the context of a discourse, and context must be considered when ascertaining the writer's intended effect. As detailed in the following, attributions are used to achieve a range of effects, with each of these having a corresponding relational function.

5.1 Attribution as JUSTIFY

Attribution is often used to justify a claim. In Carlson and Marcu's example of ATTRIBUTION, *Analysts estimated that sales at U.S. stores declined in the quarter, too,* it is significant that the analysts who have provided the estimation are presumably financial analysts, not psychoanalysts, software analysts, politicians, or human resource managers. The intended effect of JUSTIFY is to increase the reader's readiness to accept the writer's right to present the situation in the nucleus. Misconstruing the type of analyst would undermine the claim that sales in U.S. stores declined.

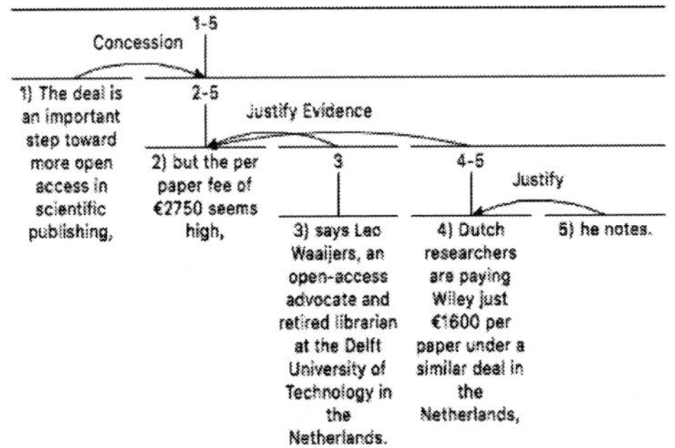

Figure 1: Attribution as JUSTIFY

In the example shown in Figure 1, a writer for *Science Magazine* uses JUSTIFY to present an argument in which the attributed material is interwoven with other elements of the argument. The topic is an open access agreement between Project Deal (a consortium of libraries, universities, and research institutes in Germany) and the Wiley publishing company. Credibility for the claim that the price per paper fee is too high is provided by the qualifications of the attribution source. Further on in the same article, the writer presents a counter-argument and again uses JUSTIFY, this time supporting the position with an attribution to the physicist Gerard Meijer, one of the negotiators for Project Deal. The function of these attributions is not just to give credit to the sources, but to provide authority for claims for which the writer lacks sufficient expertise. That is, the writer is relying on borrowed authority. To assert the two opposing perspectives without attribution would be to risk diminished credibility.

The use of attribution as a form of borrowed authority is standard practice not only in journalism but in other disciplines as well, such as rhetorical studies (Connors, 1999), scientific and technical writing (Cronin & Shaw, 2002), professional health communication (Schryer, Bell, Mian, Spafford, & Lingard, 2011), information science (Halevi & Moed, 2013), anthropology (Goodman, Tomlinson, & Richland, 2014), student writing assignments (Swales, 2014), religious texts (O'Keefe, 2015), and, of course, discourse analysis (Swales, 1986; White, 2004). As observed by Connors (1998), although the use of citation tends to be highly formalized, it is essentially rhetorical in nature.

Attribution as JUSTIFY can also occur in expressions of cognitive acts. For example, when the US politician Kirsten Gillibrand declared that *one of the reasons why I'm running for president is because I truly believe I can bring this country together*, among the intended effects is that the audience should also believe that she can achieve that lofty goal. Designating the relation as JUSTIFY is consistent with the writer's intended effect. To designate the relation as ATTRIBUTION would obscure the identification of intended effect.

5.2 Attribution as EVALUATION and INTERPRETATION

With the EVALUATION relation, the reader recognizes that the satellite assesses the nucleus and recognizes the value it assigns. In the following example, the writer uses a cognitive predicate. The intended effect is that the reader will recognize the pleasure the writer takes in having a new client:

S: We are pleased
N: that you have chosen Young Physical Therapy, Inc. Specialty Center for your physical therapy needs.

Like EVALUATION, INTERPRETATION involves an assessment of the situation presented in the nucleus, but without concern for the writer's positive regard. In the example shown in Figure 2, there are two attributions, one the cause of the other. The first is an example of attribution used for ELABORATION, which will be discussed in Section 5.4. In the second attribution relation, the writer assesses the reaction of a surgical team upon learning of the long term survival of their patient. Although the surgeons' positive regard was likely enhanced by the surprise, there is no indication that the reported event is concerned with writer's positive regard.

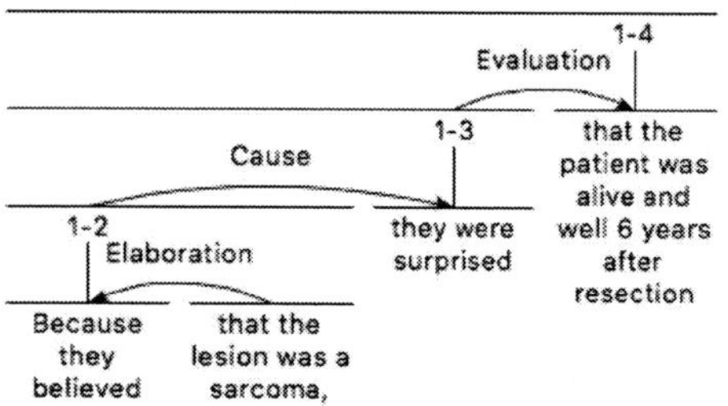

Figure 2: Attribution as ELABORATION and EVALUATION

5.3 Attribution as CAUSE

Sometimes a situation presented in the attributed material is the CAUSE of a cognitive state. These constructs are similar to EVALUATION, except the rhetorical salience is on the attribution predicate. In the example shown in Figure 3, the low ranking assigned to a football team caused outrage among college football experts. Although their outraged response is an evaluation of the ranking, it is their outrage that is the topic of the discourse.

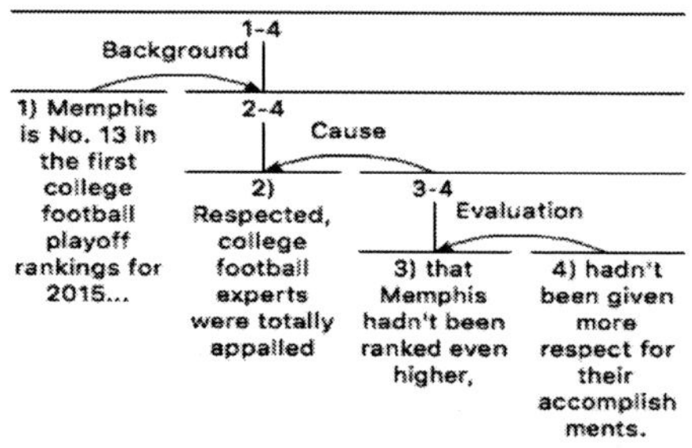

Figure 3: Attribution as CAUSE

5.4 Attribution as ELABORATION

Sometimes the attributed material simply provides more information about the activity identified in the attribution predicate. In the attribution, *Bush indicated there might be "room for flexibility" in a bill*, the significance of context in establishing intended effect becomes apparent. The attribution source is President George H. W. Bush, and the bill he was referring to would have allowed federal funding of abortions for poor women who are victims of rape and incest. The context includes the observation that *he reiterated his opposition to such funding, but expressed hope of a compromise.* Because the source of the attribution is a US president, who through his political stature and his veto power wields some authority as to whether there is "room for flexibility" in any pending legislation, the attribution might seem to be JUSTIFY. But Bush is not the writer here, and the writer is merely reporting what Bush said during a press conference. There is no indication that the writer's intent was to increase the reader's readiness to accept his or her right to present. Indeed, the press release immediately passes on to other matters. The RST relation in use here is ELABORATION.

Attributions as elaborations also include cognitive states, such as thinking and believing. As shown above in segments 1-2 of Figure 2, the satellite identifies a particular belief attributed to the subject of the nucleus. Presumably this belief or thought is one among many that could be attributed to the surgeons. As a subject matter relation, ELABORATION specifies that the reader will recognize that the satellite provides additional detail for the nucleus. It is not necessary that the reader agree with the additional detail, it is only necessary that the reader agree that, true or false, it is one of the subject's beliefs.

5.5 Attribution as EVIDENCE

In an EVIDENCE relation, the satellite is intended to increase the reader's belief in the nucleus. It is not unusual for an EVIDENCE relation to also meet the criteria for an ELABORATION relation. The difference is one of intended effect. The following example is from Redeker and Egg (2006), who recycled it from Wolf and Gibson (2005), who cite it as example of a text containing cross dependencies, and as such cannot be represented using an RST tree structure:

"Sure I'll be polite," promised one BMW driver who gave his name only as Rudolph, "as long as the trucks and the timid stay out of the left lane."

Redeker and Egg note that, if analyzed in the style of Marcu, the ATTRIBUTION satellite (*promised one BMW driver…*) would interrupt the reported text, so that what should be the nucleus of the ATTRIBUTION is split into separate segments, only one of which can be accessed by the satellite. To address this difficulty, Redeker and Egg reverse the nuclearity of the ATTRIBUTION relation and avoid the split segments by moving the embedded segments outside of the enclosing text. This practice can be given greater clarity by, in addition to moving the text, relocating them immediately following, and inserting a placeholder at the removal point:

1) "Sure I'll be polite" [3-4],
2) "as long as the trucks and the timid stay out of the left lane."
3) promised one BMW driver
4) who gave his name only as Rudolph.

However, assigning nuclearity to the attribution predicate is at odds with the rhetorical function of the text. The point of the text is the promise itself. The speaker's politeness is contingent upon slower drivers staying out of the way. That Rudolph drives a BMW and refuses to disclose his full name makes the reported warning more believable, so as shown in Figure 4, the EVIDENCE relation is used, with nuclearity assigned to the reported speech. Lest there be any doubt that 'BMW' contributes to the believability of the promise, consider substituting 'Ford Pinto' for it instead. The strength of this evidence is sufficient to assure that the CONDITION relation between segments 1-2 is one of equivalence, not just implication: failure to stay out of the left lane will assuredly result in something other than politeness. The text is an argument, for which the claim is that Rudolph will be polite only to drivers who stay out of his way, and the ground is that not only does he promise as much, but he is also the driver of a fast car and he refuses to be identified.

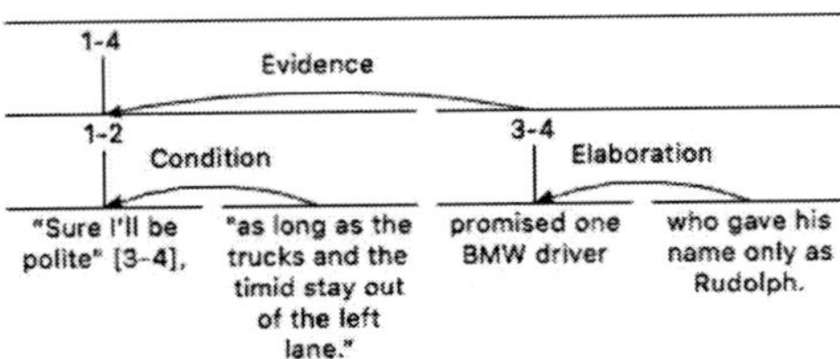

Figure 4: Attribution as EVIDENCE

5.6 Attribution as ATTRIBUTION

As an example of a text problematic for the relational status of ATTRIBUTION, Stede et al. (2017) offer the following:

Katsumoto says to Nathan on the dawn of battle, "You think a man can change his destiny?" to which Cruise replies, "I
believe a man does what he can, until his destiny is revealed."

The text comes from a review of the movie *The Last Samurai*, and can be found in the *Simon Fraser University Review Corpus*. Tom Cruise plays the part of Nathan Algren.

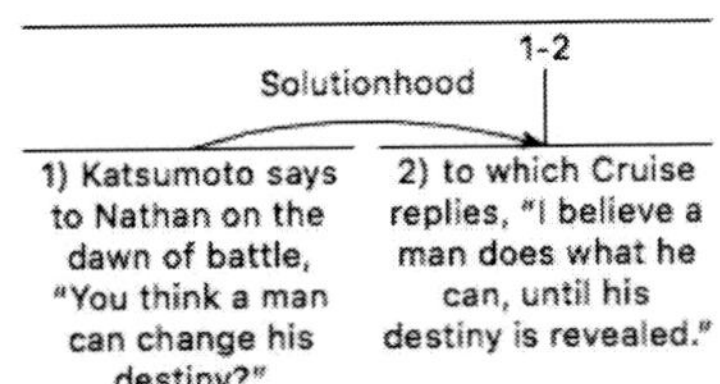

Figure 5. Non-Attributive Analysis

Following the view that attributions should not be treated as distinct discourse entities, Taboada and Hay (2008) analyze this text as shown in Figure 5. Stede et al. (2017) support this view, observing that the reporting verbs are in a relationship to each other, but that also, there is a relation between the content clauses and the reporting verbs. Moreover, it is difficult to say what these relations are, other than that they are attributive. The passage seems to be structurally ambiguous, and the relationships between the attributed material and the attribution predicates seem to be nothing more than attributive. If annotated as attributive, the text would be segmented into four units:

1) Katsumoto says to Nathan on the dawn of battle,
2) "You think a man can change his destiny?"
3) to which Cruise replies,
4) "I believe a man does what he can, until his destiny is revealed."

The structural ambiguity arises with segment 3, *to which Cruise replies*, because it refers both backward (*to which*) and forward (*Cruise replies*). But the SOLUTIONHOOD relation overrides the ambiguity because the question posed by Katsumoto is satisfied not by segment 3, but by the text span 3-4. This sense of the text is captured by the Taboada and Hay (2008) annotation shown above.

As for the possibility of the reporting verbs being nothing more than attributive, if that were so, it might provide support for an ATTRIBUTION relation as defined by Carlson and Marcu, as being reported speech, without regard for intended effect.

But the intended effect here goes beyond reporting who-said-what. As shown in Figure 6, each of the satellites support the exchange between Katsumoto and Nathan (Cruise) by engaging the reader in the drama (*on the dawn of battle*), making the reader more interested in reading the nuclei. This is akin to the definition of the PREPARATION relation, as defined by Mann and Thompson (1987). However, this relation should not be marked as PREPARATION. It does not conform with the way PREPARATION is usually used, and although, as with PREPARATION, the satellite precedes the nucleus in the text, conformance to that schema is not a reliable expectation. Therefore I suggest that the relation is ATTRIBUTION, but that its definition is not merely attributive.

In this sense the ATTRIBUTION relation could be categorized as a textual relation. Textual relations, as defined by Stede et al. (2017), are relations used

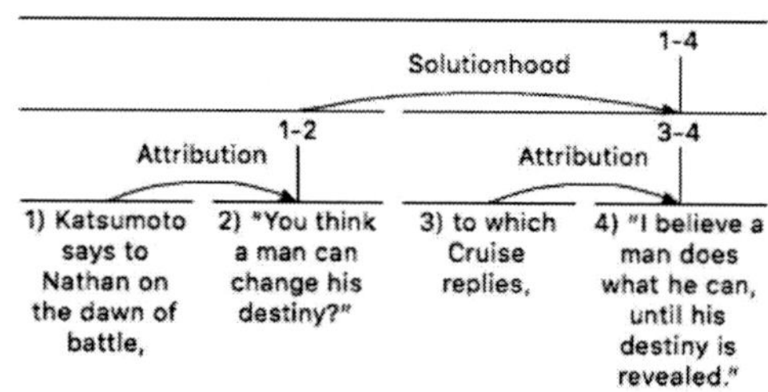

Figure 6: Attribution as ATTRIBUTION

to organize the text and make its understanding easier by providing orienting information. In Stede's classification, textual relations include PREPARATION, RESTATEMENT, and SUMMARY. With that stipulation, we can accept that sometimes an attribution is just an ATTRIBUTION.

5.7 Cognitive States as (Faux) CONCESSION

Expressions of cognitive states are sometimes used to moderate a claim with an indication of uncertainty. This involves an apparent delimitation of the claim as merely a matter of opinion. But the intended effect is not to concede uncertainty upon the claim, but to appear to concede uncertainty in order to moderate the claim's delivery, with the intended effect of assuring acceptance. In the following example from TripAdvisor, the writer tenders some advice to a prospective traveler to the Yucatán Peninsula:

Have you been to Cancun before - if not I
think you might want to reconsider using it

as a base. It is heavy traffic, and positively
the worst resort I ever went [to] in my life -
overdeveloped and literally raping you for
every dollar to be had.

This text uses *I think* to soften the advice, ostensibly allowing that *I could be wrong, but*, but the stridency of the evidence used in support of this advice leaves little doubt as to the intended effect. This equivocal use of an expression of cognitive state allows the writer to have it both ways. Similarly, in the movie *Field of Dreams*, when the ghost of baseball legend Shoeless Joe Jackson says to Ray Kinsella,

I think you'd better stay here, Ray

in denying Ray the chance to join the baseball team in the clubhouse, Jackson is not merely expressing an opinion, he is not merely floating an idea for Ray's consideration. He is directing Ray to stay put. That this is a correct interpretation is supported not only by Ray's angry response, but also by the necessity of physically restraining him from going forward: The cognitive predicate has the effect of downtoning the directive while the intent of the directive remains intact.

This use of expressions of cognitive state is particularly valuable for writers of sufficient stature to be recognized as experts in their field. The writer may blend this faux CONCESSION with JUSTIFY. Assured of their authority, the writer can moderate a claim through the rhetorical leavening arising from the disingenuous indication of uncertainty and its resulting informality, while at the same time putting the weight of their authority behind the claim. Thus, in his 1925 presidential address to the Mathematical Association, when mathematician G.H. Hardy wrote that

I think that it is time that teachers of
geometry became a little more ambitious

he could easily afford to assume a posture of less than full certainty, knowing that his words would be accorded a respect consistent with his stature. Similarly, in Michael Asimow's letter to the California Common Cause organization, as Vice-Chair and UCLA Law Professor, he could employ the same technique to avoid officiousness when urging the membership to vote against a CCC endorsement of a nuclear freeze initiative:

... I think we will be stronger and more
effective if we stick to those issues of
governmental structure and process,

broadly defined, that have formed the core of our agenda for years.

And

... I don't think endorsing a specific nuclear freeze proposal is appropriate for CCC.

Analyses of the letter from which these examples are drawn have appeared in numerous publications. It was analyzed as part of a study in relational propositions by Mann and Thompson (1983), and an RST analyses of the text is in several papers by Mann (1984), Mann and Thompson (1985), and Thompson and Mann (1987). It was analyzed from an argumentative perspective by Fries (1987). Seligman (1994) used it to substantiate development of arguments arranged as lattices. It was revisited by Matthiessen (2002a), Matthiessen (2002b), and Halliday and Matthiessen (2004) with lexicogrammatical realizations superimposed on the RST analysis. In none of these studies has this engagingly ambiguous use of language attracted attention. And yet this use of attributions as faux CONCESSION is significant to realization of an intended effect, in this case, buy-in from the membership. And this suggests that not only are attributions relational, but they are central in determining the writer's intended effect.

6   Conclusion

Writers construct attributions with diverse intentions, and this diversity is reflected in the range of RST relations discernible within these constructions. Showing that there are such relations has been an objective of this study. The means for doing so has involved determining whether the constituents of attribution constructions can be plausibly treated as discourse units (the *Discourse Units Issue*), and given that, whether these units can be said to hold satellite-nucleus relations (the *Nuclearity Issue*), and if so, what these relations are (the *Relation Identification Issue*). While this ordering of the research questions may seem like a reasonable way to present them, it is perhaps not the best order in which to answer them. This is because there is an interdependency among the three issues. The units, consisting of the attribution predicates and attributed material, are discourse units by virtue of their participation in discourse relations. That there are attributional discourse relations is established by the ability to identify applicable relations. The relations identified in this study do not necessarily comprise an exhaustive list. Others may be discovered through further analysis. But such relations as have been discovered are sufficient to satisfy the objectives of the study.

Moreover, I believe the analysis presented here resolves the discrepancy in nuclearity between the approaches presented by Carlson and Marcu (2001) and Redeker and Egg (2006). For most attributions, the nucleus is in the attributed material (ATTRIBUTION, EVIDENCE, EVALUATION, INTERPRETATION, and CONCESSION), but for the ELABORATION and CAUSE relations the nucleus is the attribution predicate. Further, to the extent that the analysis presented here is plausible, some of the criteria employed by Carlson and Marcu for excluding certain constructs as relations may need to be revisited. In particular, their exclusion of infinitival complements from attribution relations seems rhetorically arbitrary. Similarly, the exclusion of attribution predicates that do not identify a source seems unnecessarily restrictive. And passive constructions like *It is hoped that other Japanese would then follow the leader* need not be excluded. Although the apparent anonymity of the expressed hope suggests there could be difficulties in determining whether the writer is among those who hold the attributed material in positive regard, it is clear that someone does. So the relation would be either EVALUATION or INTERPRETATION – that there may be difficulty in choosing between these two is not sufficient to rule that it is neither. And in general for such constructions it would be reasonable to expect that context would be helpful in reaching a determination. In this particular case, the context identifies the parties doing the hoping as unnamed Mexican officials.

The confirmation that attributions are RST relations may seem to be a setup for a long slide down a slippery slope into intraclausal relations. Perhaps, but this descent is already well underway (e.g., de Souza, Scott, & Volpe Nunes, 1989; Garson, 1981; Grabski & Stede, 2006; Hobbs, 2010; Hovy, 1990; Krifka-Dobes & Novak, 1993; Nicholas, 1994; Roch, 2013; Rosner & Stede, 1992; Schauer & Hahn, 2000; van der Vliet, 2010; van der Vliet, Berzlánovich, Bouma, Egg, & Redeker, 2011; Vander Linden, Cumming, & Martin, 1992). Some of this work has been aimed at addressing requirements specific to a particular application. Other work has been undertaken with the objective of refining or extending general theory.

That RST analyses based on intended effect would yield different results from methods relying on syntactical and algorithmic criteria is unsurprising. Analysis using intended effect involves the use of judgments that, while not arbitrary, if allowed to pass unexplicated, may seem ad hoc. And as Carlson and Marcu (2001) observe, applying such methods to a large corpus is impractical. Even so, for the study of text organization, analyses using intended effect continues to be useful for text and analysis theory development. From such studies emerge new desiderata for development of scalable methods, and thus they are essential to continued progress.

References

Abdalla, M., Rudzicz, F., & Hirst, G. (2018). Rhetorical structure and Alzheimer's disease. *Aphasiology, 32*(1), 41-60. doi:10.1080/02687038.2017.1355439

Carlson, L., & Marcu, D. (2001). *Discourse tagging reference manual* (TR-2001-545). Marina del Rey, CA: USC Information Sciences Institute.

Carlson, L., Marcu, D., & Okurowski, M. E. (2002). *RST Discourse Treebank* (LDC2002T07). Philadelphia: Linguistic Data Consortium.

Chenlo, J. M., Hogenboom, A., & Losada, D. E. (2013). Sentiment-based ranking of blog posts using Rhetorical Structure Theory. In E. Métais, F. Meziane, M. Saraee, V. Sugumaran, & S. Vadera (Eds.), *Natural Language Processing and Information Systems* (pp. 13-24). Berlin, Heidelberg: Springer Berlin Heidelberg.

Connors, R. J. (1998). The rhetoric of citation systems—Part I: The development of annotation structures from the renaissance to 1900. *Rhetoric Review, 17*(1), 6-48. doi:10.1080/07350199809359230

Connors, R. J. (1999). The rhetoric of citation systems—Part II: Competing epistemic values in citation. *Rhetoric Review, 17*(2), 219-245.

Cronin, B., & Shaw, D. (2002). Identity-creators and image-makers: Using citation analysis and thick description to put authors in their place. *Scientometrics, 54*(1).

da Cunha, I., & Iruskieta, M. (2010). Comparing rhetorical structures in different languages: The influence of translation strategies. *Discourse Studies, 12*(5), 563.

Dahlgren, K., McDowell, J., & Stabler, E. P. (1989). Knowledge representation for commonsense reasoning with text. *Computational Linguistics, 15*(3), 149-170.

Das, D., & Taboada, M. (2013). *Signalling subject matter and presentational coherence relations in discourse: A corpus study*. Paper presented at the 2013 LACUS Conference, Brooklyn.

Das, D., Taboada, M., & Stede, M. (2017). The good, the bad, and the disagreement: Complex ground truth in rhetorical structure analysis. *Proceedings of the 6th Workshop on Recent Advances in RST and Related Formalisms* (pp. 11-19).

de Souza, C. S., Scott, D. R., & Volpe Nunes, M. d. G. (1989). Enhancing text quality in a question-answering system. In J. P. Martins & E. M. Morgado (Eds.), *EPIA'89: 4th Portuguese Conference on Artificial Intelligence* (pp. 222-233). Berlin: Springer.

Degand, L., & Simon, A. C. (2009). On identifying basic discourse units in speech: theoretical and empirical issues. *Discours, 4*.

Fries, P. H. (1987). Toward a componential approach to text. In M. A. K. Halliday, J. Gibbons, & H. Nicholas (Eds.), *Learning, Keeping and Using Language: Selected papers from the Eighth World Congress of Applied Linguistics* (Vol. 2, pp. 363-380). Sydney, Australia: Benjamins.

Galitsky, B., Ilvovsky, D., & Kuznetsov, S. O. (2018). Detecting logical argumentation in text via communicative discourse tree. *Journal of Experimental & Theoretical Artificial Intelligence, 30*(5), 637-663. doi:10.1080/0952813X.2018.1467492

Garson, J. W. (1981). Prepositional logic. *Logique et Analyse, 24*(93), 3-33.

Goodman, J. E., Tomlinson, M., & Richland, J. B. (2014). Citational practices: Knowledge, personhood, and subjectivity. *Annual Review of Anthropology, 43*, 449-463.

Grabski, M., & Stede, M. (2006). Bei: Intraclausal coherence relations illustrated with a German preposition. *Discourse Processes, 41*(2), 195-219. doi:10.1207/s15326950dp4102_5

Halevi, G., & Moed, H. F. (2013). The thematic and conceptual flow of disciplinary research: A citation context analysis of the journal of informetrics. *Journal of the American Society* for *Information Science and Technology, 64*(9), 1903-1913.

Halliday, M. A. K., & Matthiessen, C. M. I. M. (2004). *An introduction to functional grammar.* New York: Oxford University Press.

Heerschop, B., Goossen, F., Hogenboom, A., Frasincar, F., Kaymak, U., & Jong, F. d. (2011). Polarity analysis of texts using discourse structure. *Proceedings of the 20th ACM international conference on Information and knowledge management* (pp. 1061-1070). Glasgow, Scotland, UK: ACM.

Heilman, M., & Sagae, K. (2015). Fast Rhetorical Structure Theory discourse parsing. *CoRR.*

Hernault, H., Prendinger, H., duVerle, D. A., & Ishizuka, M. (2010). HILDA: A Discourse parser using Support Vector Machine classification. *Dialogue and Discourse, 1*(3), 1-33.

Hobbs, J. R. (2010). Clause-internal coherence. In P. Kühnlein, A. Benz, & C. L. Sidner (Eds.), *Constraints in Discourse 2* (pp. 15-34). Amsterdam: John Benjamins.

Hovy, E. H. (1990). Parsimonious and profligate approaches to the question of discourse structure relations. *Proceedings of the Fifth International Workshop on Natural Language Generation.* Pittsburgh, PA: Association for Computational Linguistics.

Ketui, N., Theeramunkong, T., & Onsuwan, C. (2012). A rule-based method for Thai elementary discourse unit segmentation (TED-Seg) *Seventh International Conference on Knowledge, Information and Creativity Support Systems (KICSS)* (pp. 195-202). Melbourne, VIC: IEEE.

Krifka-Dobes, Z., & Novak, H.-J. (1993). From constituent planning to text planning. In H. Horacek & M. Zock (Eds.), *New concepts in Natural Language Generation: Planning, realization and systems* (pp. 87-113).

Mann, W. C. (1984). Discourse structures for text generation *Proceedings of the 22nd Conference on Association for Computational Linguistics* (pp. 367-375). New York: ACM Press.

Mann, W. C., & Thompson, S. A. (1983). *Relational propositions in discourse.* Marina del Rey, CA: Information Sciences Institute.

Mann, W. C., & Thompson, S. A. (1985). *Assertions from discourse structure* (Technical Report No. ISI/RS-85-155). Marina del Rey, California: Information Sciences Institute.

Mann, W. C., & Thompson, S. A. (1987). *Rhetorical structure theory: A theory of text organization* (Technical Report ISI/RS-87-190). Marina del Rey, CA: University of Southern California, Information Sciences Institute (ISI).

Matthiessen, C. M. I. M. (2002a). Combining clauses into clause complexes: A multi-faceted view. In J. L. Bybee & M. Noonan (Eds.), *Complex sentences in grammar and discourse: Essays in honor of Sandra A. Thompson* (pp. 235-320). Amsterdam: John Benjamins.

Matthiessen, C. M. I. M. (2002b). Lexicogrammar in discourse development: Logogenetic patterns of wording. In G. Huang & Z. Wang (Eds.), *Discourse and Language Functions* (pp. 2-25). Shanghai:: Foreign Language Teaching and Research Press.

Nicholas, N. (1994). *Problems in the application of rhetorical structure theory to text generation.* (masters thesis), University of Melbourne, Melbourne, Australia.

O'Keefe, M. M. (2015). Borrowed authority: The American Catholic bishops' argument by citation *Written Communication, 32*(2), 150-173.

Pardo, T. A. S., Nunes, M. d. G. V., & Rino, L. H. M. (2004). DiZer: An automatic discourse analyzer for Brazilian Portuguese. *Advances in Artificial Intelligence – SBIA 2004 17th Brazilian Symposium on Artificial Intelligence, Sao Luis, Maranhao, Brazil, September 29-Ocotber 1, 2004. Proceedings.* Berlin: Springer.

Radev, D. R. (2000). A common theory of information fusion from multiple text sources step one: cross-document structure *Proceedings of the 1st SIGdial workshop on Discourse and dialogue - Volume 10* (pp. 74-83). Hong Kong: Association for Computational Linguistics.

Redeker, G., & Egg, M. (2006). Says who? On the treatment of speech attributions in discourse structure. In C. Sidner, J. Harpur, A. Benz, & P. Kuhnlein (Eds.), *Constraints in discourse* (pp. 140-146). Maynooth: National University of Ireland.

Roch, C. (2013). Influence of modality markers on the conditional interpretation of the German preposition ohne *Proceedings of the IWCS 2013 Workshop on Annotation of `Modal Meanings in Natural Language*

(WAMM) Potsdam: Association for Computational Linguistics.

Rosner, D., & Stede, M. (1992). Customizing RST for the automatic production of technical manuals *Proceedings of the Sixth International Workshop on Natural Language Geneneration* (pp. 199–214). London: Springer-Verlag.

Sanders, T. J. M., Spooren, W. P. M., & Noordman, L. G. M. (1992). Toward a taxonomy of coherence relations. *Discourse Processes, 15*, 1-35.

Schauer, H., & Hahn, U. (2000). Phrases as carriers of coherence relations *Proceedings of the Annual Meeting of the Cognitive Science Society.*

Schryer, C. F., Bell, S., Mian, M., Spafford, M. M., & Lingard, L. (2011). Professional citation practices in child maltreatment forensic letters. *Written Communication, 28*(2), 147-171

Seligman, M. (1994). *Discovery and format of input structures for tactical generation.* Paper presented at the Proceedings of the Seventh International Workshop on Natural Language Generation, Kennebunkport, Maine.

Soricut, R., & Marcu, D. (2003). *Sentence level discourse parsing using syntactic and lexical information.* Paper presented at the Human Language Technology and North American Association for Computational Linguistics Conference (HLT/NAACL), Edmonton, Canada.

Stede, M. (2008). Disambiguating rhetorical structure. *Research on Language and Computation, 6*(3), 311-332.

Stede, M., Taboada, M., & Das, D. (2017). *Annotation guidelines for rhetorical structure.* Potsdam and Burnaby: University of Potsdam and Simon Fraser University.

Swales, J. M. (1986). Citation analysis and discourse analysis. *Applied Linguistics, 7*(1), 39-56.

Swales, J. M. (2014). Variation in citational practice in a corpus of student biology papers: From parenthetical plonking to intertextual storytelling. *Written Communication, 31*(1), 118-141.

Taboada, M., & Hay, M. (2008). *Simon Fraser University Review Corpus: RST annotations.* https://www.sfu.ca/~mtaboada/SFU_Review_Corpus.html

Thompson, S. A., & Mann, W. C. (1987). Antithesis: A study in clause combining and discourse structure. In R. Steele & T. Threadgold (Eds.), *Language Topics: Essays in Honour of Michael Halliday, Volume II* (pp. 359-381). Amsterdam: John Benjamins.

Tofiloski, M., Brooke, J., & Taboada, M. (2009). A syntactic and lexical-based discourse segmenter. *Proceedings of the ACL-IJCNLP 2009 Conference Short Papers* (pp. 77-80). Suntec, Singapore: Association for Computational Linguistics.

van der Vliet, N. (2010). Syntax-based discourse segmentation of Dutch text. In M. Slavkovik (Ed.), *Proceedings of the 15th Student Session, ESSLLI* (pp. 203–210). Copenhagen, Denmark: The Association for Logic, Language and Information.

van der Vliet, N., Berzlánovich, I., Bouma, G., Egg, M., & Redeker, G. (2011). Building a discourse-annotated Dutch text corpus. In S. Dipper & H. Zinsmeister (Eds.), *Beyond semantics: Corpus-based investigations of pragmatic and discourse phenomena: Proceedings of the DGfS Workshop* (pp. 157-171). Göttingen: Bochumer Linguistische Arbeitsberichte 3.

Vander Linden, K., Cumming, S., & Martin, J. (1992, 1992//). *Using system networks to build rhetorical structures.* Paper presented at the Aspects of Automated Natural Language Generation: 6th International Workshop on Natural Language Generation Trente, Italy, April 5–7 1992 Proceedings., Berlin.

White, H. D. (2004). Citation analysis and discourse analysis revisited *Applied Linguistics, 25*(1), 89–116.

Wolf, F., & Gibson, E. (2005). Representing discourse coherence: A corpus-based analysis. *Computational Linguistics, 31*(2), 249-287.

Zhang, H., & Liu, H. (2016). Rhetorical relations revisited across distinct levels of discourse unit granularity. *Discourse Studies, 18*(4), 454-472.

Appendix. Sources for Original RST Analyses

The nuclearity issue: Senator Chris Coons…

Leibovich, M. (2019, February 25). How Lindsey Graham went from Trump skeptic to Trump sidekick. *The New York Times Magazine.* http://tinyurl.com/yxhxo3ba

Attribution as JUSTIFY: The deal is…

Kupferschmidt, K. (2019, February 21). Deal reveals what scientists in Germany are paying for open access. *Science.* http://tinyurl.com/y673es8v

Attribution as JUSTIFY: *One of the reasons why…*
Ryan, J., Mundt, T., & Raphelson, S. (2019, March 7). Democrat Kirsten Gillibrand: 'I truly believe I can bring this country together'. *Here & Now.* http://tinyurl.com/y2znf38c
Attribution as EVALUATION: *Because they…*
McLeod, R. A., & Dahlin, D. C. (1979). Hamartoma (Mesenchymoma) of the Chest Wall in Infancy. *Radiology, 131*(3).
Attribution as EVALUATION: *We are pleased…*
Young. (2017, January 24). Young Physical Therapy Patient Form. Retrieved from http://tinyurl.com/y4njblq9
Attribution as CAUSE: *Respected college football…*
Calkins, G. (2015, November 3). Tigers have become part of the national conversation. *The Commercial Appeal.*
http://tinyurl.com/y24287ga
Faux CONCESSION *I think that it is time…*
Hardy, G. H. (1925). What is geometry? *The Mathematical Gazette, 12*(175), 309-316.
Faux CONCESSION: *I think you'd better stay here…*
Robinson, P. A., Gordon, L., & Gordon, C. (Writers). (1989). Field of Dreams. United States: Universal Pictures.

Annotating Shallow Discourse Relations in Twitter Conversations

Tatjana Scheffler[1], Berfin Aktaş[1], Debopam Das[2], and Manfred Stede[1]

[1]Department of Linguistics / SFB1287, University of Potsdam, Germany
[2]Department of English and American Studies, Humboldt University of Berlin, Germany
tatjana.scheffler@uni-potsdam.de

Abstract

We introduce our pilot study applying PDTB-style annotation to Twitter conversations. Lexically grounded coherence annotation for Twitter threads will enable detailed investigations of the discourse structure of conversations on social media. Here, we present our corpus of 185 threads and annotation, including an inter-annotator agreement study. We discuss our observations as to how Twitter discourses differ from written news text wrt. discourse connectives and relations. We confirm our hypothesis that discourse relations in written social media conversations are expressed differently than in (news) text. We find that in Twitter, connective arguments frequently are not full syntactic clauses, and that a few general connectives expressing EXPANSION and CONTINGENCY make up the majority of the explicit relations in our data.

1 Introduction

The PDTB corpus (Prasad et al., 2008) is a well-known resource of discourse-level annotations, and the general idea of lexically signalled discourse structure annotation has over the years been applied to a variety of languages. A shallow approach to discourse structure in the PDTB style can also be adapted to different genres. In this paper, we consider English conversations on Twitter, and describe the first phase of our annotation, viz. that of explicit connectives whose arguments are within a single tweet. We explain the collection of the data and our annotation procedure, and the results of an inter-annotator-agreement study. We present our analysis of the specific features of this genre of conversation wrt. discourse structure, as well as corpus statistics, which we compare to the distributions in the original PDTB corpus.

We show that explicit discourse relations are frequent in English Twitter conversations, and that the distribution of connectives and relations differs markedly from the distribution in PDTB text. In particular, the Twitter threads contain many more CONTINGENCY relations (in particular, conditional and causal relations). In addition, the connective's arguments in the Twitter data are often elliptical phrases standing in for propositional content.

The upcoming second phase of the project will target connectives whose Arg1 is located in a previous tweet, as well as AltLex realizations and implicit relations. We regard this effort as complementary to approaches that applied Rhetorical Structure Theory (Mann and Thompson, 1988) and Segmented Discourse Representation Theory (Asher and Lascarides, 2003) to dialogue; the important difference being that other than RST and SDRT, PDTB does not make strong commitments as to an overarching structure of the discourse. Overall, we see this as an advantage for studying relatively uncharted territory: The structural peculiarities of social media conversations have not yet been explored in depth, and a PDTB-style annotation is one way of laying empirical groundwork for that endeavour.

2 Twitter and Discourse Relations

Recent studies indicate significant differences in the use of discourse connectives and discourse relations between written and spoken data (Rehbein et al., 2016; Crible and Cuenca, 2017). Though the PDTB approach has been applied to different text types, conversational data has not been systematically analysed yet. There is recent work on annotating spoken TED talks in several languages (Zeyrek et al., 2018), but these planned monologues do not exhibit spontaneous interaction. To our knowledge, only (Tonelli et al., 2010; Riccardi et al., 2016) have constructed PDTB annotations

Proceedings of Discourse Relation Parsing and Treebanking (DISRPT2019), pages 50–55
Minneapolis, MN, June 6, 2019. ©2019 Association for Computational Linguistics

for spoken conversations, and they work on Italian dialogs. Riccardi et al. (2016) focus on the detection of discourse connectives from lexical and acoustic features in help desk dialogs. In contrast, we investigate open topic spontaneous conversations in computer mediated communication, to abstract away from the speech mode, but retain the conversational properties.

Twitter[1] is a social media platform that publishes short "microposts" by registered users. In addition to textual content, these posts may contain embedded images or videos. Twitter users can interact by directly replying to each other's messages. Such replies are quite frequent and the resulting conversations often contain discourse connectives (Scheffler, 2014). There is some evidence that the types of relations and connectives found in Twitter conversations differs markedly from edited news text and reflects some features of spoken conversations (Scheffler, 2014; Scheffler and Stede, 2016). Here, we introduce an annotated corpus of explicit connectives in English tweets, which allows us to test genre differences between the discourse structure of newspaper texts (PDTB) and conversational writing (our Twitter corpus).

3 Collecting and Annotating the Corpus

We collected English language tweets from the Twitter stream on several (non-adjacent) days in December, 2017 and January 2018 without filtering for hashtags or topics in any way. In order to obtain conversations that are linked to each other via the *reply-to* relation, and which altogether then form a tree structure, we recursively retrieved parent tweets of those gathered via the initial search. A single *thread* in our terminology is a path from the root to a leaf node of that tree. For the purposes of the present experiment, we then selected only one of the longest threads (paths) from each tree and discarded everything else in this dataset. See (Aktaş et al., 2018) for details on the data collection. The resulting corpus consists of 1756 tweets arranged in 185 threads, and the average length of a tweet is 153 characters.[2]

So far, we only annotated explicit connectives whose two arguments are contained within the same tweet (whether a source or reply tweet).[3]

We primarily used the list of 100 explicit connectives from the PDTB corpus (Prasad et al., 2008) to identify connectives. Additionally, we found a few new connectives in our corpus, such as *by the way, plus, so long as*, and *when-then*. In practice, we annotate an explicit connective, identify its two arguments in the same tweet in which the connective occurs, and finally, label the connective sense according to the PDTB-3 relational taxonomy (Webber et al., 2018)[4]. In the event we find an ambiguous connective or interpret more than one relational reading, we assign multiple senses to the connective. The annotation was conducted using the PDTB annotator tool.

Inter-Annotator Agreement. After one author of this paper labeled the dataset in the way just described, we conducted an Inter-Annotator Agreement (IAA) study on 50 threads selected randomly. This sub-corpus consists of 683 tweets whose average length is 188 characters, and was re-annotated by a research assistant. We calculated the percent agreement for connective detection (i.e. the percentage of connectives marked by both of the annotators), Arg1 and Arg2 span selection, and all levels of sense assignment. Arg1, Arg2 and sense agreements are calculated for the relations annotated by both of the annotators. Table 1 shows the percent agreement for *exact match* and *partial match* of the selected text spans. We consider one character difference in the begin & end indices of text spans as an instance of *exact match* to eliminate disagreements because of the involvement of punctuation at the end or beginning of the texts in marked spans. In *partial match* statistics, in addition to exact matches, the argument spans having any overlapping tokens are also considered matching. We manually inspected all cases of *partial match* and observed that in all cases, one annotator's argument span is fully included in the other annotator's span.

The agreement is generally good, except for exact argument spans for Arg1. The main reason for this is the difficulty in Twitter to determine utterance and clause breaks. There was major disagreement with respect to social media specific items like hashtags and emoji (should they be included in the argument span or not?; see also Section 4).

---

[1] www.twitter.com

[2] URL strings are excluded, but user names are included in tweet length statistics throughout the paper.

[3] The only exception to this rule is when one message by a single author is split over subsequent adjacent tweets. When

the continuation is explicitly marked (e.g., with a '+' symbol at the end of an incomplete tweet), all connectives are annotated (even though the arguments may span across tweets).

[4] We do not annotate other information such as attribution features or supplementary spans for connectives.

Social media text is genuinely more difficult to annotate than news text in this regard, and we will adapt the annotation guidelines accordingly to develop clear instructions for these cases.

Table 2 shows IAA statistics for sense levels[5].

Type	% Exact	%Partial
Connective Detection	70%	-
Arg1 Span	62%	90%
Arg2 Span	89%	92%

Table 1: IAA for text spans.

Sense Level	%
Level-1	88%
Level-2	82%
Level-3	76%

Table 2: IAA for sense annotations.

4 Analysis: Twitter versus WSJ

Qualitative Analysis. As said earlier, Twitter posts, although they are written, are part of interactive conversations. While annotating these posts, we also encountered a number of phenomena that are typically found in spoken registers, and not in written texts. For example, we identified higher numbers of a small set of connectives, such as *and, but* and *when*, that frequently occur in conversations. We rarely annotated (if any) connectives like *since, therefore* or *nevertheless*, which are typically found in formal writing (e.g., newspaper, scientific genre). The most frequent connectives in our corpus and in newspaper text are shown in Tables 3 and 4, respectively.

Twitter texts, like conversations, most often represent spontaneous use of language, and thus contain instances of fragmented or incomplete utterances. In our annotation, we often encounter constructions that comprise only nouns or noun phrases, but nevertheless, are often seen to stand for a complete proposition. These phrases can function as the arguments of a connective. (e.g., "NO PROB *BUT* WHERE THE HELL DID U", or "*If* he could work on that, good prospect"). We

Connective	% in Twitter
and[6]	30.0%
but	16.2%
if	7.3%
when	6.5%
so	6.0%
because	4.5%
or	2.9%
as	2.2%
also	2.0%
before[7]	1.3%

Table 3: Top ten connectives in the Twitter corpus.

Connective	% in PDTB
and	26.4%
but	15.4%
also	7.2%
if	4.8%
when	4.4%
as	3.5%
because	3.5%
while	3.3%
after	2.4%
however	2.0%

Table 4: Top ten connectives in the PDTB.

accordingly use more flexible argument selection criteria in order to accommodate such (elliptical) structures, in addition to clauses and other constructions (nominalizations, VP-conjuncts, etc.) that typically constitute arguments in the PDTB. Furthermore, similar to the genre of instant messaging, the Twitter texts contain a wide range of acronyms for sentences/clauses that act like fixed expressions. Examples include: "idc" = I don't care; "idk" = I don't know; "idrk" = I don't really know. In our annotation, we pay special attention to these acronyms as to whether they constitute (part of) the argument of a connective or not. For example, *idc* in "idc *if* u do or not" is annotated as an argument (of *if*), while *idk* is not part of the argument in "i get your point... *but* idk the k-exol who he was talking to was comforted...".

Our Twitter data also exhibits different spellings for the same connective, for example, 'wen' = *when*; 'cos', 'cus', 'cuz' = *because*; 'btw' = *by the way*; '&', '&', 'an' = *and*. We considered these alternative forms as orthographical variants of the same connective.

Finally, we find that the parity between Twit-

---

[5]Level-1 specifies four sense classes, TEMPORAL, CONTINGENCY, COMPARISON, and EXPANSION. Level-2 provides 17 sense types, whereas Level-3 encodes only the *directionality* of the sense in the PDTB-3 schema (e.g., REASON vs. RESULT as subtypes of the Level-2 sense type CAUSE).

[6]The instances of "&" are also counted in this category.

[7]The instances of "b4" are also counted in this category.

ter texts and spoken conversations also operates at the level of annotating senses for the connectives. For examples, the additive connective *and* is frequently used in conversations (or spoken texts in general) to link upcoming utterances with the present one, even though there is no strong semantic relation between them (comparable to the Joint relation in RST). We observe similar uses of *and* in our Twitter corpus, too (e.g., "Happy new year *and* cant wait for you to come back to the UK next year").

Quantitative Analysis. We performed a quantitative analysis of our annotations. In general, we observe that explicit discourse relations are a frequent occurrence in our Twitter data. Out of 1756 tweets, over 40% contain at least one tweet-internal explicit discourse relation. Table 3 shows the relative frequency distribution of the top 10 connectives in our annotations. The calculated percentages are case insensitive (e.g., "and" and "And" are considered as different instances of the same connective). Some basic statistics of our annotation:

- # of relations: 1237

- # of tweets with a single connective: 406

- # of tweets with multiple connectives: 329

- average Arg1 length (chars): 43

- average Arg2 length (chars): 41

- average length of tweets with a single connective (chars):181

- average length of text **not** part of a discourse relation (Arg1 or Arg2) in tweets with a single connective (chars): 103

As for sense distributions, Table 5 shows the relative frequency distribution of Level-1 sense tags (i.e. *Class* level tags) in our corpus. We also calculated the relative frequencies for each *Class* level tag in the PDTB 2.0 according to frequencies of *Explicit* connectives presented in Table 4 in (Prasad et al., 2008). The second column in Table 5 shows the calculated relative frequencies in the PDTB corpus.[8] It can be seen from the distribution that there are a lot more CONTINGENCY

---

[8]The class frequencies for PDTB column presented here come from the PDTB 2.0 sense hierarchy and we are using the relations in PDTB 3.0. Since there is no change defined in (Webber et al., 2018) regarding the Class level sense tags, we consider the columns in Table 5 as comparable.

relations in our Twitter data than in the PDTB, while there are fewer COMPARISON and TEMPORAL relations. Considering that not all explicit relations have been annotated in our Twitter corpus yet (only relations contained entirely within one tweet), no final conclusions can be drawn yet, but it appears that narrative (temporal) and comparative or contrastive relations are more typical of newspaper writing than spontaneous social media conversations. This is also reflected in the lists of frequent connectives (Tables 3, 4), which show that connectives expressing CONTINGENCY relations like *if*, *when*, and *so* occur relatively more frequently on Twitter.

Class	% in Twitter	% in PDTB
EXPANSION	33.4%	33.5%
CONTINGENCY	28.0%	18.7%
COMPARISON	24.3%	28.8%
TEMPORAL	14.3%	19.0%

Table 5: Distribution of class level sense tags.

We also allowed the annotator to select more than one sense if both were deemed relevant (see Rohde et al., 2018, for a discussion of multiple concurrent relations in text); this option was chosen in 9 cases, listed in Table 6.

Connective	#	Senses
when	3	SYNCH. + CONDITION
and	2	REASON + CONJUNCT.
(and, an)		RESULT + CONJUNCT.
anytime	1	SYNCH. + CONDITION
however	1	CONTR. + CONCESSION
or	1	DETAIL + CONCESSION
while	1	SYNCH. + CONTRAST

Table 6: Connectives with 2 simultaneous senses.

5 Conclusions and Future Work

We presented initial results of our PDTB style annotation of English Twitter conversations. Social media conversations are an interesting domain for such annotation, because despite the written mode, they show many properties typical of spoken interactions. They therefore allow an investigation of the discourse structure of written multi-party interactions. Since this type of annotation is still rare for spoken data, we hope to add to what is known about discourse structure in conversations.

We reported about our annotation of intra-tweet discourse relations in 185 Twitter threads. We conducted an inter-annotator agreement study, which revealed that in particular the selection of argument spans poses new problems in the Twitter domain. We are currently adapting and further specifying our annotation guidelines to cover the phenomena found in our social media data, such as elliptical constituents, hashtags and emoji, abbreviations, missing punctuation, etc. Based on the amended guidelines, we will validate the existing annotations and edit them for consistency.

The current study only reports on intra-tweet relations, where the connective and both arguments are contributed by the same speaker. However, inter-tweet relations are also found in our data. In these cases, a subsequent reply contains a connective and Arg2, but relates to an Arg1 in a previous tweet (typically by a different speaker). We are planning to add annotations for these types of relations, as well as non-explicit discourse relations, in future work.

Finally, we showed results from a basic analysis that demonstrates how explicit discourse relations in Twitter conversations differ from the relations in the PDTB newspaper text. Due to genre differences, Twitter conversations contain more CONTINGENCY and fewer TEMPORAL and COMPARISON relations. The distribution of connectives in Twitter also differs from newspaper text. This corresponds to known differences between connectives used in spoken and written language. Finally the syntactic type and size of arguments we find in the Twitter data differs markedly from the PDTB arguments.

In current work, we are extending the annotations to include inter-tweet and non-explicit relations. We are planning to use the corpus in developing a shallow discourse parser for English social media text.

Acknowledgements

The authors would like to thank Olha Zolotarenko for assisting with the annotation. This research was funded by the Deutsche Forschungsgemeinschaft (DFG, German Research Foundation) under project nr. 317633480 – SFB 1287, project A03.

References

Berfin Aktaş, Tatjana Scheffler, and Manfred Stede. 2018. Anaphora resolution for Twitter conversations: An exploratory study. In *Proceedings of the First Workshop on Computational Models of Reference, Anaphora and Coreference*, pages 1–10.

Nicholas Asher and Alex Lascarides. 2003. *Logics of Conversation*. Cambridge University Press, Cambridge.

Ludivine Crible and Maria Josep Cuenca. 2017. Discourse markers in speech: characteristics and challenges for corpus annotation. *Dialogue and Discourse*, 8(2):149–166.

William Mann and Sandra Thompson. 1988. Rhetorical structure theory: Towards a functional theory of text organization. *TEXT*, 8:243–281.

R. Prasad, N. Dinesh, A. Lee, E. Miltsakaki, L. Robaldo, A. Joshi, and B. Webber. 2008. The Penn Discourse Treebank 2.0. In *Proc. of the 6th International Conference on Language Resources and Evaluation (LREC)*, Marrakech, Morocco.

Ines Rehbein, Merel Scholman, and Vera Demberg. 2016. Annotating discourse relations in spoken language: A comparison of the PDTB and CCR frameworks. In *Proceedings of the Tenth International Conference on Language Resources and Evaluation (LREC)*.

Giuseppe Riccardi, Evgeny A Stepanov, and Shammur Absar Chowdhury. 2016. Discourse connective detection in spoken conversations. In *International Conference on Acoustics, Speech and Signal Processing (ICASSP)*, pages 6095–6099. IEEE.

Hannah Rohde, Alexander Johnson, Nathan Schneider, and Bonnie Webber. 2018. Discourse coherence: Concurrent explicit and implicit relations. In *Proceedings of the 56th Annual Meeting of the Association for Computational Linguistics*, volume 1, pages 2257–2267.

Tatjana Scheffler. 2014. A German Twitter snapshot. In *Proc. of the 9th International Conference on Language Resources and Evaluation (LREC)*, pages 2284–2289, Reykjavik, Iceland.

Tatjana Scheffler and Manfred Stede. 2016. Realizing argumentative coherence relations in German: A contrastive study of newspaper editorials and Twitter posts. In *Proceedings of the COMMA Workshop "Foundations of the Language of Argumentation"*, Potsdam, Germany.

Sara Tonelli, Giuseppe Riccardi, Rashmi Prasad, and Aravind K Joshi. 2010. Annotation of discourse relations for conversational spoken dialogs. In *Proc. of the 7th International Conference on Language Resources and Evaluation (LREC)*.

Bonnie Webber, Rashmi Prasad, Alan Lee, and Aravind Joshi. 2018. The Penn Discourse Treebank 3.0 Annotation Manual. Report, The University of Pennsylvania.

Deniz Zeyrek, Amália Mendes, and Murathan Kurfalı.
2018. Multilingual extension of PDTB-style annotation: The case of TED multilingual discourse
bank. In *Proc. of the 11th International Conference
on Language Resources and Evaluation (LREC)*.

A Discourse Signal Annotation System for RST Trees[*]

Luke Gessler, Yang Liu, and Amir Zeldes
Department of Linguistics
Georgetown University
{lg876,yl879,amir.zeldes}@georgetown.edu

Abstract

This paper presents a new system for open-ended discourse relation signal annotation in the framework of Rhetorical Structure Theory (RST), implemented on top of an online tool for RST annotation. We discuss existing projects annotating textual signals of discourse relations, which have so far not allowed simultaneously structuring and annotating words signaling hierarchical discourse trees, and demonstrate the design and applications of our interface by extending existing RST annotations in the freely available GUM corpus.

1 Introduction

Discourse signals help language users recognize semantic and pragmatic relationships that hold between clauses and sentences in discourse, also known as coherence or rhetorical relations. Discourse markers such as coordinations (e.g. 'but'), subordinating conjunctions (e.g. 'although'), and adverbials (e.g. 'instead') are usually considered the most explicit signals and are relatively well studied, but work on other types of discourse signals has been more limited. These include semantic, syntactic, and morphological features; for example, repeated mention, parallel syntactic constructions, and inflection for tense and aspect can also signal discourse relations.

Building corpora annotated for discourse signals is important for empirical studies of how writers and speakers signal relations in naturally occurring text, and how readers or hearers are able to recognize them. However, for one of the most popular frameworks for analyzing discourse relations, Rhetorical Structure Theory (RST, Mann

and Thompson 1988), there are currently no tools which allow full-featured annotation of both RST trees and signals. RST is a functional theory of text organization that interprets discourse as a hierarchical tree of clauses or similar discourse units, meaning that annotation interfaces must accommodate the complexity of tree structures. The main contribution of this paper is in enabling a completely new type of annotation within the framework of RST, simultaneously targeting the ways in which humans construct discourse trees and identify relations in a single system. Although we base our work on an existing RST interface, the expansions presented here bridge a substantial gap in RST annotation, which has to date been unable to link complete trees to concrete discourse signal positions in a single annotation tool and format, linking specific tokens and other signaling devices to positions in the tree.

Our system, shown in Figure 1, features state of the art support for viewing and editing signals, and benefits from an underlying interface offering full RST editing capabilities, called rstWeb (Zeldes, 2016). No installation is needed for end users in a project since the tool is web-based, and annotators can easily collaborate. Docker images and a local version are available for easy deployment and we make all code available open source via GitHub.[1]

2 Previous Work

Numerous studies have examined discourse signals (e.g. Knott and Sanders 1998), but the largest corpora with signal annotations have been produced in the framework of the Penn Discourse Treebank (PDTB, Prasad et al. 2008, and similarly for Chinese, Zhou and Xue 2012, and other languages) and the RST Signalling Corpus (RST-SC, Taboada and Das 2013), both built on top of

---

[*]We would like to thank Richard Eckhart de Castilho, Debopam Das, Nathan Schneider and Maite Taboada, as well as three anonymous reviewers for valuable comments on earlier versions of this paper and the system it describes.

[1]https://github.com/amir-zeldes/rstweb

Proceedings of Discourse Relation Parsing and Treebanking (DISRPT2019), pages 56–61
Minneapolis, MN, June 6, 2019. ©2019 Association for Computational Linguistics

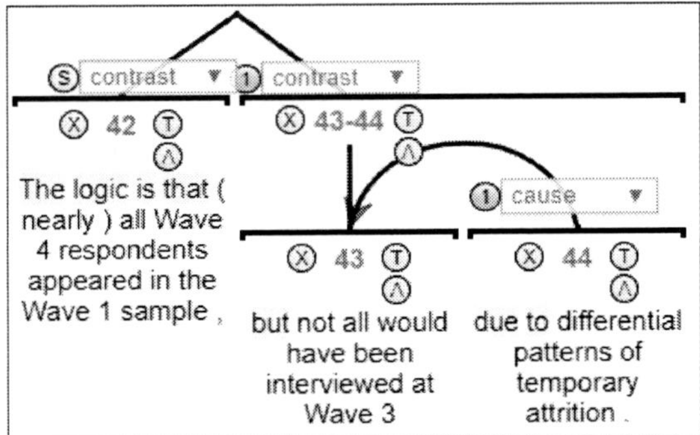

Figure 1: Signaling in a discourse tree fragment.

The $2.5 billion Byron 1 plant near Rockford, Ill., was completed in 1985. In a disputed 1985 ruling, the Commerce Commission said Commonwealth Edison could raise its electricity rates by $49 million to pay for the plant. But state courts upheld a challenge by consumer groups to the commission's rate increase and found the rates illegal. The Illinois Supreme Court ordered the commission to audit Commonwealth Edison's construction expenses and refund any unreasonable expenses.

Figure 2: PDTB connective and argument spans.

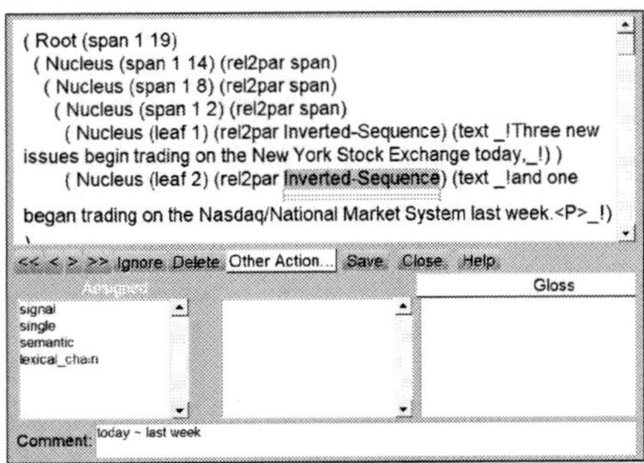

Figure 3: Signal annotation from RST-SC in the UAM tool.

the text of the Wall Street Journal corpus (Marcus et al., 1993). We examine the tools used to produce these, as well as other approaches, below.

2.1 Discourse Signals in PDTB

PDTB employs a lexically grounded approach to discourse relations and their signals by annotating 1) *Explicit* and *Implicit* connectives and their associated argument spans, which are not constrained to be single clauses or sentences; 2) *supplementary information* that is considered relevant but not required for the interpretation; 3) textual expressions that establish coherence other than connectives called *Alternative Lexicalizations* (*AltLex*); 4) relation senses for *Explicit* and *Implicit* connectives and *AltLex* relations; 5) attribution within discourse relations including categories such as *source, type, scopal polarity,* and *determinacy* (Prasad et al., 2008). Unlike RST, which identifies hierarchic structures in text, PDTB-style annotations do not form a hierarchy and need not cover the entire text.

According to Prasad et al. (2014), annotation workflow in PDTB-style resources has varied in the development of comparable corpora in other languages (e.g. Zhou and Xue 2012) and genres (e.g. Prasad et al. 2011), which could potentially affect annotator effort and inter-annotator agreement (e.g. Sharma et al. 2013). For instance, when annotating the example in Figure 2 where an Ex-

plicit connective *But* is present, one could easily identify the argument spans by highlighting them in different colors (i.e. Arg1 in yellow and Arg2 in blue in Figure 2) as well as the sense tag associated with it, in this case, *Comparison.Concession*. Thus, depending on what elements can be found in text to reliably identify relations (i.e. either an argument or a connective), the annotation workflow may differ. Moreover, potential span overlaps with other relations are not problematic, since each relation is annotated independently, and signals for multiple relations are not visualized simultaneously. Annotators can thus annotate relations and signals concurrently. However, this tool is not suitable for the type of annotation addressed by our tool, since no hierarchy of discourse units can be represented in the way required for RST trees.

2.2 Signals in RST-SC

Since RST originally did not foresee annotating relation signals, RST-SC takes existing trees in the RST Discourse Treebank (RST-DT, Carlson et al. 2003) as a ground truth, and adds explicit annotations for how each relation can be identified. Because trees are hierarchical, annotations apply not to spans of text, but to relations attached to nodes in the tree. Multiple signals corresponding to different words are possible for the same relation, and some signals do not correspond to words in the text (e.g. genre conventions, graphical layout and more). Since we also annotate signals in RST trees, this corpus is the most comparable to what we aim to produce with the tool described here.

Because of the lack of an annotation tool capable of simultaneously representing RST trees and signal spans, Taboada and Das (2013) used the UAM CorpusTool (O'Donnell, 2008), illustrated in Figure 3, to annotate the underlying LISP format files of RST-DT directly. The UAM tool is not aware of the LISP bracket structure of the RST tree: annotators simply add underlines to any span in the plain text file and categorize them, taking care to add annotations only to the position of the label of the relation being signaled, a potentially error prone process. In Figure 3, an *Inverted-Sequence* relation ("Three new issues begin trading ... and one began...", with the temporal sequence inverted) has three signals, each corresponding to a green underline. To switch between annotations, users may click on an underline – the selected one in this case has the signal type 'semantic', subtype 'lexical_chain'.

Since UAM cannot connect the signal annotation to specific tokens, RST-SC provides no information about the location of the signaling tokens. In other words, unlike in PDTB, annotations are not anchored to words in the text. For instance, the 'lexical_chain' signal shown in Figure 3 corresponds to the words 'today' and 'last week', which signal the temporal relation in the text (the comment box in the figure confirms this, though such comments are not consistently available in RST-SC, and the location of the word in the comment is not notated unambiguously, if the word occurs multiple times).

To explore the actual words corresponding to RST-SC signals, Liu and Zeldes (2019) anchored annotations to word positions using a tabular grid based interface called GitDox (Zhang and Zeldes, 2017), in addition to UAM. Annotators were asked to locate relevant information in UAM and transfer the results, including signal types/subtypes, source/target of relations and associated tokens, to GitDox. Because GitDox only provides a tabular spreadsheet-like input, relation names and positions were indicated as plain text annotations of the relevant signal tokens, a process which is slow and error prone. Liu and Zeldes (2019) reached moderate agreement on anchoring the existing signal annotations (see Table 1 below), and concluded that a better tool was critical for the task.

2.3 Other Tools

In addition to the tools mentioned above, RhetDB (Pardo, 2005) has also been used to annotate signals. RhetDB does allow for the annotation of discourse signals, but its limitations include its inability to graphically represent a full RST tree and the fact that it only runs on the Windows operating

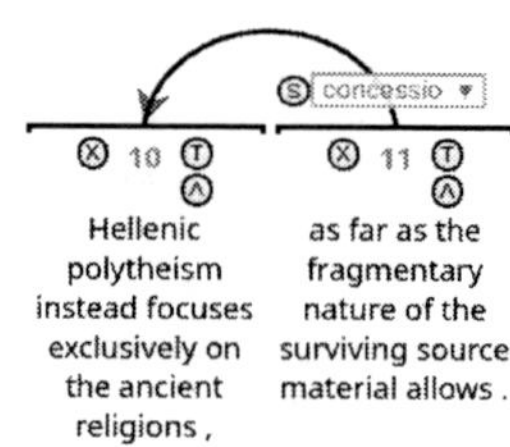

Figure 4: Two discourse units joined with a relation in the interface. The "X" clears the node's parent relation, the "T" adds a span above the node, and the "∧" creates a multinuclear relation. Relations are edited via drag-and-drop.

system locally.

The Basque RST TreeBank (Iruskieta et al., 2013) includes visualizations of discourse signals, but these signals cannot be viewed in the context of a fully graphically represented RST tree, and are instead represented as a separate annotation layer in a dedicated interface built for the corpus.

3 Implementation

3.1 rstWeb

The signal annotation system was developed on top of an existing interface, rstWeb. rstWeb (Zeldes, 2016) is a web application that allows collaborative, online annotation of RST trees. It was intended to replace an older desktop application, RSTTool (O'Donnell, 2000), which is no longer being maintained. Developed in Python and JavaScript and running in the browser, it allows administrators to set up projects for annotators, assign them multiple versions of documents for annotation experiments, and control files and schemas centrally. Annotators need only a browser and login, and all annotations and versions of files, including optional annotation step logs, are collected on a server.

rstWeb provides a solid foundation for our signal annotation system. Its feature-set for RST annotation tasks is mature and flexible, and unlike older RST interfaces, minimizes the clicks required for common tasks by avoiding multiple modes for linking/unlinking relations and creating nodes. To maintain this advantage, we chose to integrate signal annotation into the same environment used for building RST trees, rather than a separate mode (see Figure 4).

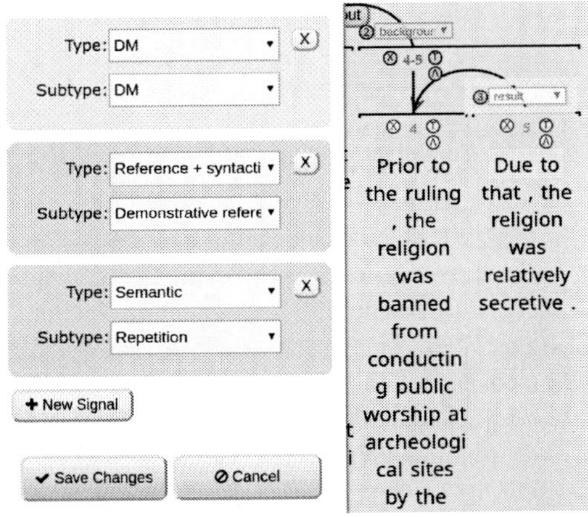

Figure 5: The signal sidebar, toggled by a button labeled "S" next to a relation. Signals have a type, subtype, and associated tokens, highlighted with a click. Here three signals indicate a RESULT relation: One, the discourse marker (DM) "due to", has been selected in the sidebar, highlighting its associated tokens. Clicking on other signals, such as Semantic, subtype Repetition below it, highlights their associated tokens.

3.2 The Signal Annotation System

Prior to this work, rstWeb had no support for signal annotation. The contribution of the present work was to build a signal annotation system on top of rstWeb to allow annotators to view and edit signal annotations and make these available for export and use in downstream tasks.

In the signal annotation system, annotators may associate signals with relations after they are created by hitting a button next to the relation which opens a sidebar (see Figure 5). Different annotation workflows are conceivable, including only annotating signals once RST trees are complete or annotating signals and building RST trees in tandem, as well as either annotating all kinds of signals by going over the entire text once, or focusing on one relation type at a time (e.g. annotating signals for all CAUSE relations first, then moving on to the next type, etc.).[2]

Once associated with a relation, a signal can be linked with any subset of tokens in the text. The significance of the signal annotation system is in enabling RST analysts to annotate discourse signals with a feature-set that is more comprehensive and ergonomic than any other existing RST interface. Signal types are fully configurable, with no restriction on the placement and number of tokens

[2]We thank an anonymous reviewer for noting these potentially different workflows.

that may be associated with a signal, and relations can be associated with multiple signals.

3.3 Data Model

A signal in our system consists of four elements:

1. A relation whose type (RESULT, CONCESSION, etc.) the signal is helping to indicate
2. A possibly empty list of tokens which comprise the signal
3. A type that categorizes the signal according to its linguistic nature
4. A more fine-grained subtype

Each relation from 1. can have multiple signals having elements 2.-4., and 2. can be an empty set, as some signals may have *no* associated tokens. For example, RST-SC assumes that factors such as genre conventions or graphical layout (e.g. a sequence of indented paragraphs or bullet points, even when no token encodes a bullet point glyph) can be used by writers to signal a meaningful structure, which readers can identify. Our interface supports such explicit, typed annotations, without reference to specific token indices.

The introduction of signals anchored to tokens creates a new complication for the representation format of RST data, the commonly used .rs3 XML format: since RST trees only connect discourse units, word level tokenization has been ignored in RST annotation tools to date. However, because our annotations associate tokens with the relations they are cues for, and users are meant to click or drag across cue words to mark them as signals, tokenization is essential to signal annotation. To address this, we have added automatic tokenization facilities for imported documents written in alphabetic languages using a Python port[3] of the TreeTagger tokenizer[4]; built-in tokenization for Asian languages and morphologically rich languages remains outstanding, but for these languages pre-tokenized data that has been processed with appropriate tools can be imported.

The signal *type* and *subtype* attributes categorize annotations based on a pre-determined annotation scheme. By default, rstWeb uses the types from RST-SC (Das and Taboada, 2018), but any annotation scheme can be defined, and multiple

[3]https://github.com/amir-zeldes/
rstWeb/blob/develop/modules/whitespace_
tokenize.py
[4]http://www.cis.uni-muenchen.de/
~schmid/tools/TreeTagger/

schemes can be maintained to accommodate multiple projects on the same installation. The `.rs3` format used by rstWeb and RSTTool was extended to include signal information. The new format, `.rs4`, is backward compatible with both tools, meaning that files containing signal information may be opened with RSTTool (though the signals cannot be displayed).

4   Evaluation

To assess the benefits of our interface for signal annotation, we re-annotated a pilot data set of three documents from RST-SC, containing 506 tokens with just over 90 signals. In Table 1 we compare our results to scores achieved for the same annotation task of anchoring RST-SC data to specific signal tokens in Liu and Zeldes (2019).

	L&Z19	**this paper**
% identical	86.0	90.9
Cohen's kappa	0.52	0.77

Table 1: Comparison with Liu and Zeldes (2019).

Next to the numerical results showing an improvement in kappa, annotators reported the new interface was much easier and faster to work with. Feedback from the original annotators of RST-SC also suggests the interface is much more suited to the signal annotation task.

5   Applications and Outlook

We are currently using the interface presented here to annotate RST signals in GUM (Zeldes, 2017), a freely available, richly annotated corpus with 126 documents and some 109,000 tokens across eight genres: academic, biography, fiction, interviews, news, travel guides, how-to guides and reddit forum discussions. Since the scheme by Das and Taboada (2017) is based solely on Wall Street Journal articles, signal types and subtypes need to be extended to cover more genres. For instance, RST-SC genre features include subtypes such as *Newspaper Layout*, *Newspaper Style Attribution* and *Newspaper Style Definition*; however, these are not enough to represent other genre-specific layouts – e.g. in academic articles (headings, formulas etc.). We are also working on search and visualization facilities to explore data annotated with discourse trees and signals. We plan to use the ANNIS platform (Krause and Zeldes, 2016), which already visualizes RST trees, and add interactive ways to explore signaling tokens in documents as well as signals for individual relations, which we view as an important extension to RST.

One of the goals of the current project is to learn which new types of signals are needed to describe signaling in different text types, and to discover differences in signals across genres. These in turn will help us to develop new models of the features used in discourse relation identification, which may be more or less general, or language and text-type specific. We are also exploring how human annotated signal spans compare with the words most attended to by neural models for automatic relation classification (see Zeldes 2018:178-188 for some first results). With the release of an easy-to-use interface for signal annotation within the RST framework, we hope that more corpora with signal-enhanced RST trees will be developed in more languages, and advance our understanding of how readers identify relations in practice.

References

Lynn Carlson, Daniel Marcu, and Mary Ellen Okurowski. 2003. Building a discourse-tagged corpus in the framework of Rhetorical Structure Theory. In *Current and New Directions in Discourse and Dialogue*, Text, Speech and Language Technology 22, pages 85–112. Kluwer, Dordrecht.

Debopam Das and Maite Taboada. 2017. Signalling of coherence relations in discourse, beyond discourse markers. *Discourse Processes*, pages 1–29.

Debopam Das and Maite Taboada. 2018. RST signalling corpus: A corpus of signals of coherence relations. *Language Resources and Evaluation*, 52(1):149–184.

Mikel Iruskieta, María Jesús Aranzabe, Arantza Diaz de Ilarraza, Itziar Gonzalez, Mikel Lersundi, and Oier Lopez de la Calle. 2013. The RST Basque TreeBank: an online search interface to check rhetorical relations. In *Proceedings of the 4th Workshop on RST and Discourse Studies*.

Alistair Knott and Ted Sanders. 1998. The classification of coherence relations and their linguistic markers: An exploration of two languages. *Journal of Pragmatics*, 30(2):135–175.

Thomas Krause and Amir Zeldes. 2016. ANNIS3: A new architecture for generic corpus query and visualization. *Digital Scholarship in the Humanities*, 31(1):118–139.

Yang Liu and Amir Zeldes. 2019. Discourse relations and signaling information: Anchoring discourse signals in RST-DT. *Proceedings of the Society for Computation in Linguistics*, 2(1):314–317.

William C. Mann and Sandra A. Thompson. 1988. Rhetorical Structure Theory: Toward a functional theory of text organization. *Text*, 8(3):243–281.

Mitchell P. Marcus, Beatrice Santorini, and Mary Ann Marcinkiewicz. 1993. Building a large annotated corpus of English: The Penn Treebank. *Computational Linguistics*, 19(2):313–330.

Michael O'Donnell. 2000. RSTTool 2.4 – a markup tool for Rhetorical Structure Theory. In *Proceedings of the International Natural Language Generation Conference (INLG 2000)*, pages 253–256, Mitzpe Ramon, Israel.

Michael O'Donnell. 2008. The UAM CorpusTool: Software for corpus annotation and exploration. In *Proceedings of the XXVI congreso de AESLA*, pages 3–5, Almeria, Spain.

Thiago Alexandre Salgueiro Pardo. 2005. *Métodos para análise discursiva automática*. Ph.D. thesis, Instituto de Ciêcias Matemáticas e de Computação, Universidade de São Paulo.

Rashmi Prasad, Nikhil Dinesh, Alan Lee, Eleni Miltsakaki, Livio Robaldo, Aravind Joshi, and Bonnie Webber. 2008. The Penn Discourse Treebank 2.0. In *Proceedings of the 6th International Conference on Language Resources and Evaluation (LREC 2008)*, pages 2961–2968, Marrakesh, Morocco.

Rashmi Prasad, Susan McRoy, Nadya Frid, Aravind Joshi, and Hong Yu. 2011. The Biomedical Discourse Relation Bank. *BMC bioinformatics*, 12(1):188.

Rashmi Prasad, Bonnie Webber, and Aravind Joshi. 2014. Reflections on the Penn Discourse Treebank, comparable corpora, and complementary annotation. *Computational Linguistics*, 40(4):921–950.

Himanshu Sharma, Praveen Dakwale, Dipti M Sharma, Rashmi Prasad, and Aravind Joshi. 2013. Assessment of different workflow strategies for annotating discourse relations: A case study with HDRB. In *International Conference on Intelligent Text Processing and Computational Linguistics*, pages 523–532. Springer.

Maite Taboada and Debopam Das. 2013. Annotation upon annotation: Adding signalling information to a corpus of discourse relations. *Dialogue and Discourse*, 4(2):249–281.

Amir Zeldes. 2016. rstWeb - a browser-based annotation interface for rhetorical structure theory and discourse relations. In *Proceedings of NAACL-HLT 2016 System Demonstrations*, pages 1–5, San Diego, CA.

Amir Zeldes. 2017. The GUM corpus: Creating multilayer resources in the classroom. *Language Resources and Evaluation*, 51(3):581–612.

Amir Zeldes. 2018. *Multilayer Corpus Studies*. Routledge Advances in Corpus Linguistics 22. Routledge, London.

Shuo Zhang and Amir Zeldes. 2017. GitDOX: A linked version controlled online XML editor for manuscript transcription. In *Proceedings of FLAIRS 2017, Special Track on Natural Language Processing of Ancient and other Low-resource Languages*, pages 619–623.

Yuping Zhou and Nianwen Xue. 2012. PDTB-style discourse annotation of Chinese text. In *Proceedings of ACL 2012*, pages 69–77, Jeju Island, Republic of Korea.

EusDisParser: improving an under-resourced discourse parser with cross-lingual data

Mikel Iruskieta
IXA group
University of the Basque Country (UPV/EHU)
`mikel.iruskieta@ehu.eus`

Chloé Braud
LORIA - CNRS
Nancy, France
`chloe.braud@loria.fr`

Abstract

Development of discourse parsers to annotate the relational discourse structure of a text is crucial for many downstream tasks. However, most of the existing work focuses on English, assuming a quite large dataset. Discourse data have been annotated for Basque, but training a system on these data is challenging since the corpus is very small. In this paper, we create the first parser based on RST for Basque, and we investigate the use of data in another language to improve the performance of a Basque discourse parser. More precisely, we build a monolingual system using the small set of data available and investigate the use of multilingual word embeddings to train a system for Basque using data annotated for another language. We found that our approach to building a system limited to the small set of data available for Basque allowed us to get an improvement over previous approaches making use of many data annotated in other languages. At best, we get 34.78 in F1 for the full discourse structure. More data annotation is necessary in order to improve the results obtained with these techniques. We also describe which relations match with the gold standard, in order to understand these results.

1   Introduction

Several theoretical frameworks exist for discourse analysis, and automatic discourse analyzers (ADA) have been developed within each framework, but mostly for English texts: i) under Rhetorical Structure Theory (RST) (Mann and Thompson, 1988): see for example (Liu and Lapata, 2017; Yu et al., 2018) ii) under Segmented Discourse Representation Theory (SDRT) (Asher and Lascarides, 2003), as the one developed by (Afantenos et al., 2015) iii) or Penn Discourse Treebank (PDTB) style (Prasad et al., 2008) as the

one described in (Lin et al., 2014).[1]

Within RST, discourse parsing is done in two steps: (i) Linear discourse segmentation: The text is divided into EDUs (Elementary Discourse Unit) ; (ii) Rhetorical annotation: All the EDUs are linked following tree structure (RS-tree). Iruskieta et al. (2014) proposed to carry out an intermediate phase, between segmentation and rhetorical labelling, the annotation of the central unit (CU annotation).

Although several ADAs exist, researchers have still face important issues:

— ADAs are not easy to test unless an online version exists.

— Most of them were developed for English or languages with a considerable amount of resources.

— The evaluation methods do not demonstrate robustness and reliability of the systems.

Moreover, when working on low resourced languages such as Basque, with few resources available, one has to deal with additional difficulties:

— Information obtained from automatic tools (e.g. PoS tags) are often less accurate, or are even sometimes not available.

— The terminology and discourse markers (or signals) are not standardised since students have developed the domain or topic.[2]

— Even in academic texts, language standards are not known nor established, and there are more writing errors.

— Finding reliable and third parties annotated corpora is challenging.

Due to these difficulties, the way to get an ADA for some languages was done step by step, follow-

---

[1] `http://wing.comp.nus.edu.sg/~linzihen/parser`.

[2] Note that the problem is not to collect ideal pieces of texts, but to work with real texts, problematic or not.

Proceedings of Discourse Relation Parsing and Treebanking (DISRPT2019), pages 62–71
Minneapolis, MN, June 6, 2019. ©2019 Association for Computational Linguistics

ing a partial labelling strategy, such as:[3] focusing on segmentation, as done for French (Afantenos et al., 2010), for Spanish (da Cunha et al., 2012) and for Basque (Iruskieta and Beñat, 2015), or on the detection of centrals units, as done for Basque (Bengoetxea et al., 2017) and for Spanish (Bengoetxea and Iruskieta, 2017). Moreover, a system has been developed for identifying nuclearity and intra-sentential relations for Spanish (da Cunha et al., 2012), and a rule-based discourse parser exist for Brazilian Portuguese (Pardo and Nunes, 2008; Maziero et al., 2011). The first versions of these tools were developed mostly following simple techniques (i.e. a rule-based approach) and, later, that results were improved using more complicated techniques, more amount of data or machine learning techniques.

Recently, from a different perspective, using a cross-lingual discourse parsing approach, Braud et al. (2017) carried out a discourse parser which includes several languages: English, Basque, Spanish, Portuguese, Dutch and German.

For Basque, Braud et al. (2017) report at best 29.5% in F1 for the full discourse structure using training data from other languages. However, we want to underline that Braud et al. (2017) do not use specific materials (e.g. word embeddings) for Basque, and they do not report results for a system trained on Basque data only. When experimenting on a low-resourced language (i.e., less that 100 document in total), such as Basque, they only report results with a union of all the training data for the other languages, possibly using some held-out documents to tune the hyper-parameters of their model.

In this paper, we investigate the use of data in another language to improve the performance of a discourse parser for Basque, an under-resourced language. Moreover, we create and evaluate the first parser for Basque, and investigate the following questions:

— Can we learn from other languages and improve the performance of a parser?
— What differences emerge between the human and machine annotation?
— Is the parser confident about same rhetorical relations as humans?

As we mentioned, a limit of this work is that more annotation data is necessary, in order to improve the results of the Basque parser.

The remainder of this paper is organized as follows: Section 2, Section 3, Section 4 and Section 5 present the system of the Basque discourse parser, the approach and the settings of the system. Section 6 lays out the evaluation of the results. Finally, section 7 sets out the conclusions, the limitations and the future work.

2 System

We use the discourse parser described in Braud et al. (2017), that has proved to give state-of-the-art results on English, and was used for the first cross-lingual experiments for discourse parsing.

This parser can take pre-trained embeddings as input, for words and for any other features mapped to real-valued vectors. The parser is based on a transition-based constituent parser (Coavoux and Crabbé, 2016) that uses a lexicalized shift-reduce transition system, here used in the static oracle setting. The optimization is done using averaged stochastic gradient descent algorithm (Polyak and Juditsky, 1992). At inference time, we used beam-search to find the best-scoring tree. [4]

3 Approach

We report results for monolingual systems, using only the data available for Basque, and cross-lingual systems using both data for Basque and for other available languages. Contrary to Braud et al. (2017), we have access to word embeddings for Basque, and thus report results using pre-trained word embeddings (see Section 5).

Monolingual systems: Since the number of documents avalaible is limited in the monolingual setting, we optimize the hyper-parameters of our systems based on cross-validation on the development set, keeping the test set separated.[5] Then, we report results with systems trained on the full development set and evaluated on the test set.

Cross-lingual systems: We evaluate two strategies: first, we build systems trained on the data available for a source language (i.e. English, Spanish and Portuguese) and evaluated on the Basque test set. In this setting, called 'Src Only',

---

[3] All of them can be tested online.

[4] The code is available at https://gitlab.inria.fr/andiamo/eusdisparser.

[5] We use the same split of the data as in Braud et al. (2017), in order to compare results and improvements. In this study, authors split the available documents into a development set and a test set.

we use the Basque development set to choose the best values for the hyper-parameters.

The second strategy is to set the values of the hyper-parameters via cross-validation (i.e. we keep the best values obtained in the monolingual setting), then we can train a model using the training data of a source language and the data available in the Basque development set. In this setting, called 'Src+Tgt', we evaluate the possible gains when including some data of the target language within our training set. Comparing this two strategies allows us to investigate the difference between corpora for discourse annotated for different languages. In both cases, we report final results on the Basque test set.

In the cross-lingual setting, we can use more data at training time than when only using monolingual data, but we need a method to represent our input into the same space (here, multilingual word embeddings, see Section 5). Also, note that the datasets annotated within RST do not follow exactly the same annotation guidelines, thus possibly degrading the results (e.g. the relations ATTRIBUTION, TOPIC-COMMENT, COMPARISON, to cite some, annotated for English are not annotated in the Basque corpus).

We also report results on the datasets used for training (i.e. English, Spanish and Portuguese) as a way to check the performance of our system when more data than for Basque are available, and when training and evaluation data come from the same dataset.

4 Data

The Basque RST DT (Iruskieta et al., 2013) contains 88 abstracts from three specialized domains –medicine, terminology and science– and opinionative texts, annotated with 31 relations. The inter-annotator agreement is 81.67% for the identification of the CDU (Iruskieta et al., 2015), and 61.47% for the identification of the relations. We split the data as done in Braud et al. (2017), keeping 38 documents as test set, the remaining are used as development set.

In our cross-lingual experiments, we also use the English RST DT (Carlson et al., 2001) that contains 385 documents in English from the Wall Street Journal annotated with 56 relations, the Spanish RST DT (da Cunha et al., 2011), containing 267 texts annotated with 29 relations, and, for Portuguese, we used, as done in Braud et al.

(2017), the merging of the four existing corpora: CST-News (Cardoso et al., 2011), Summit (Collovini et al., 2007), Rhetalho (Pardo and Seno, 2005) and CorpusTCC (Pardo and Nunes, 2003, 2004). For Portuguese, we have in total 329 documents.

The English dataset contains only news articles, while the others are more diversified, with texts written by specialists on different topics (e.g. astrophysics, economy, law, linguistics) for the Spanish corpus, and news, but also scientific articles for the Portuguese one.

Corpus	#Doc	#Words	#Rel	#Lab	#EDU
English	385	206,300	56	110	21,789
Portuguese	329	135,820	32	58	12,573
Spanish	266	69,787	29	43	4,019
Basque	85	27,982	31	50	2,396

Table 1: Number of documents (#Doc), words (#Words), relations (#Rel, originally), labels (#Lab, relation and nuclearity) and EDUs (#EDU).

Word embeddings: We used pre-trained word embeddings as input of our systems in order to deal with data sparsity.

For mono-lingual setting, we evaluate two pre-trained embeddings for Basque.

The first word embeddings for Basque were calculated by the Ixa Group on the Elhuyar web Corpus[6] (Leturia, 2012), Elhuyar Web Corpus size is around 124 million word forms and it was automatically built by scraping the web, using Gensim's (Řehůřek and Sojka, 2010) word2vec skipgram (Mikolov et al., 2013), with 350 dimensions, negative sampling and using a window of size 5.

We also evaluated the FasText word embeddings made available for 157 languages (including Basque). They were trained on Common Crawl and Wikipedia (Grave et al., 2018), using CBOW with position-weights, in dimension 300, with character n-grams of length 5, a window of size 5, and 10 negatives. [7]

These embeddings are monolingual, we only use them in the monolingual setting on Basque. For cross-lingual experiments, we need multilingual word embeddings, that is a representation where the words of different languages are embedded within the same vectorial space.

---

[6] https://labur.eus/3Ad5l.
[7] Source: https://fasttext.cc/docs/en/crawl-vectors.html

In order to obtain the bilingual word embeddings needed for our experiments, we mapped Basque and English, Spanish, Portuguese pairwise, using the FastText pre-trained word embeddings. These mappings were performed using VecMap with a semi-supervised configuration, where cognates, identical words in both languages, were used as seed dictionary (Artetxe et al., 2018).

5 Settings

Hyper-parameters: We optimize the following hyper-parameters, using 10-fold cross-validation with 5 runs in the monolingual setting, or directly on the development set in the cross-lingual setting or on languages other than Basque: number of iterations $1 < i < 10$, learning rate $lr \in \{0.01, 0.02\}$, the learning rate decay constant $dc \in \{1e-5, 1e-6, 1e-7, 0\}$, the size of the beam $\in \{1, 2, 4, 8, 16, 32\}$ and the size of the hidden layers $H \in \{64, 128, 256\}$. We fixed the number N of hidden layers to 2 as in Braud et al. (2017).

Features: We use the same representation of the data as in Braud et al. (2017), that is: the first three words and the last word along with their POS and the words in the *head set* (Sagae, 2009),[8] features that represent the position of the EDU in the document and its length in tokens, a feature indicating whether the head of the sentence is in the current EDU or outside, and 4 indicators of the presence of a date, a number, an amount of money and a percentage.

As in previous studies, we used features representing the two EDUs on the top of the stack and the EDU on the queue. If the stack contains CDUs, we use the nuclearity principle to choose the head EDU, converting multi-nuclear relations into nucleus-satellite ones as done since Sagae (2009).

When representing words, only the first 50 dimensions of the pre-trained word embeddings are kept, thus leading to an input vector of 350 dimensions for the lexical part. Other features have the following size: 16 for POS, 6 for position, 4 for length, and 2 for other features.

The data have been parsed using UDPipe.[9]

---

[8]We thus have a maximum of 7 words represented per EDU, and build a vector representing the EDU by concatenating the vectors for each word.

[9]http://ufal.mff.cuni.cz/udpipe.

6 Evaluation

6.1 Quantitative evaluation

We report both macro- and micro-average scores, since both have been reported in previous studies, as noted in Morey et al. (2017) following the quantitative evaluation mehtod of Marcu (2000).

6.1.1 Monolingual systems for Basque

After optimization via cross-validation, the model is trained on the entire development set (we use the average over 5 runs to decide on the best hyper-parameters) and evaluated on the test set. The models are built either with randomly initialized word embeddings ("Random"), or using the embeddings built by Artetxe et al. (2018) ("BasqueTeam") or the ones built using FastText ("FastText").

Using the FastText embeddings allows to improve over the state-of-the-art by 2% for the identification of the structure ("Span"), almost 5% for the nuclearity ("Nuc") and 5.28% for the full structure with relations ("Rel"). Results are lower when using the embeddings built on the Elhuyar corpus, probably partly because the corpus is smaller than the one used with FastText. Moreover, it has been shown that FastText often allows improvements over 'classical' word based techniques to train word embeddings, such as word2vec, since it takes into account subwords information, thus encoding morphology. Finally, note that even without pre-trained embeddings, our system is a bit better than the previous one, demonstrating that, even if the dataset is small, it allows to build a better system than when using a large dataset only containing data for other languages.

The best parameters on each of the 5 runs do not vary a lot: when using embeddings 'BasqueTeam', we have decay $d = 1e-05$, dimension of the hidden layer $h = 256$, best number of iterations $i = 10$, and learning rate $lr = 0.01$. Only the number of beam changes, from 1 to 16. We chose 4 in our final experiments, an average value that also corresponds to the one used in the best run. When using 'FastText', we have learning rate $lr = 0.02$ and decay $d = 1e-07$, and with randomly initialized embeddings, we have $lr = 0.02$ and $d = 1e-06$, the others being the same.

System	Macro-average			Micro-average		
	Span	Nuc	Rel	Span	Nuc	Rel
Braud et al. (2017)	76.7	50.5	29.5	-	-	-
Random	73.72	50.37	31.51	71.33	48.9	29.88
BasqueTeam	73.5	45.16	26.38	71.78	43.55	25.14
FastText	**78.98**	**55.02**	**34.78**	76.46	53.03	33.02

Table 2: Mono-lingual systems, micro- and macro-averaged F1 scores on the test set. Results reported from Braud et al. (2017) were obtained in a cross-lingual setting without the use of pre-trained embeddings.

6.1.2 Cross-lingual systems for Basque (for pairs of languages)

In the cross-lingual setting, we experiment with: i) training a model on a source language (i.e. English, Spanish or Portuguese), the hyper-parameters being optimized on the development set for Basque, or ii) training a model on an union of the training set of a source language and the development set for Basque, keeping the hyper-parameters selected in the monolingual setting. In both cases, the reported results are computed on the Basque test set.

Lg	Macro-average			Micro-average		
	Span	Nuc	Rel	Span	Nuc	Rel
Es	89.42	70.06	51.01	85.38	65.02	45.75
Braud et al. (2017)	89.3	72.7	**54.4**	-	-	-
Pt	81.54	63.71	**49.75**	79.66	62.84	47.78
(Braud et al., 2017)	81.3	62.9	48.8	-	-	-
En	84.38	70.27	**57.26**	80.85	65.47	52.06
(Braud et al., 2017)	83.5	68.5	55.9	-	-	-

Table 3: Results for the mono-lingual systems built for the source languages used in the cross-lingual setting. The systems use the bi-lingual word embeddings built by Artetxe et al. (2018).

As a recall, we use the multilingual word embeddings built by Artetxe et al. (2018). We report the monolingual results obtained for the source languages in Table 3, and the results for Basque in the cross-lingual setting in Table 4.

First, we note that our results for monolingual systems are a bit better for Portuguese and English than the ones presented in Braud et al. (2017) when using pre-trained word embeddings. This shows that the building of the embeddings using FastText and crawled data leads to a more useful word representation for the task than the ones built on EuroParl (Levy et al., 2017), a dataset more genre specific.

Looking at the results on Basque (Table 4), we

Lg.		Src Only			Src+Tgt		
	Avg	Span	Nuc	Rel	Span	Nuc	Rel
Es	Macro	73.35	46.94	21.41	77.53	53.79	**33.88**
	Micro	71.72	45.7	20.73	75.52	51.54	31.86
Pt	Macro	75.42	45.44	**22.14**	78.57	53.68	**33.22**
	Micro	73.59	44.71	21.78	76.96	52.54	32.47
En	Macro	75.67	44.73	21.73	78.99	52.69	**32.28**
	Micro	73.32	44.43	21.44	77.56	50.72	31.15

Table 4: Cross-lingual systems evaluated on Basque using the word embeddings built by Artetxe et al. (2018), results on the Basque test set. 'Src only': trained only on source language training data (the hyper-parameters are optimized using the Basque development set). 'Src+Tgt': trained on source language training data + Basque development set (the hyper-parameters are the ones used in the monolingual setting).

note, however, that the results obtained within the first cross-lingual setting ('Src Only') are lower than the ones we get in the monolingual setting, with at best 22.14% of macro-F1 (micro 21.78) for the full structure. These results are also lower than the ones presented in Braud et al. (2017) where multiple corpora were merged to build a large training set, with at best 29.5% for the full structure. This tends to show that, for the cross-lingual strategy to succeed, one needs a lot of training data. Note however that results were also mixed for cross-lingual learning of discourse structure in previous papers, using all the available data generally not leading to better results than using a small set of data coming only from the target language. As Iruskieta et al. (2015) and Hoek and Zufferey (2015) showed, some texts, when conveyed in different languages, may have different rhetorical structures. Moreover, for Basque, we have to face an important issue: while cross-lingual strategy might have proven useful for English when using data for languages such as German or Spanish (Braud et al., 2017), Basque is an isolated language, not pertaining to the same language family as the other languages used.

Finally, when including the data from the Basque development set to the training set ('Src+Tgt'), we obtain performance that are close to the one obtained in the monolingual-setting while the hyper-parameters were not directly tuned, with at best 33.88 in macro-F1 (against 34.78 in the monolingual setting). The scores obtained are largely higher than the ones obtained with the first cross-lingual strategy, i.e. when no Basque data is included at training time, and also better than the ones presented in Braud et al. (2017), i.e. no Basque data either but multiple languages in the training set. This shows that a cross-lingual approach might succeeds at improving discourse parsers scores, but we need to take into account the bias between either the languages or the corpora –since including some target data seems essential–, and we might want to access better cross-lingual representations.

We hypothesized that using pairs of close languages could give better performance than mixing all the corpora altogether. These results are encouraging for pursuing the investigation of cross-lingual approaches, even if it is clear from these results that the kind of complex structures and pragmatico-semantic relations involved within discourse analysis are not easily transferable accross languages. The difficulty of annotation for discourse makes it an attractive path of research.

6.2 Qualitative Evaluation and confusion matrix

Discourse annotation (Hovy, 2010) and its evaluation is a challenging task (Das et al., 2017; Iruskieta et al., 2015; Mitocariu et al., 2013; van der Vliet, 2010; da Cunha and Iruskieta, 2010; Maziero et al., 2009; Marcu, 2000). To understand what this parser is doing, we followed the evaluation method proposed by Iruskieta et al. (2015), and compare our best systems in order to understand what kind of RS-trees the system is producing. Note that scores per relation or confusion matrices are rarely given in studies on discourse parsing, while it would allow for a better and deeper comparison of the systems developed.

6.2.1 Basque mono-lingual system

We have compared the RS-trees obtained from our best system (FastText) with RS-trees of the Basque gold standard corpus (Iruskieta et al., 2013). We have followed this evaluation method because the evaluation proposed by Marcu (2000) has deficiencies in the description and some compared factors are conflated. This carries out that the alignment of rhetorical relations is not properly done and the aligned labels are not always RST relations, so we cannot adequately describe the confusion matrix of the parser. This confusion matrix shows where (in which rhetorical relation) is the agreement and the disagreement (see Table 6).

Central unit agreement: Furthermore, we have detected that sometimes parsers that have been trained within a genre do not label the central unit (CU) or the most important EDU of the RS-tree properly if it is parsing another genre. We think as Iruskieta et al. (2014) that structures with the same CU shows more agreement in rhetorical relations and they are more reliable. Therefore, we think that CU annotation is another evaluation factor to take into account.

CU	Agreement Total	Partial	Disagree	Texts	F_1
GMB	2	1	9	12	0.208
TERM	0	0	10	10	0.000
ZTF	1	0	6	7	0.143
SENT	3	0	6	9	0.333
Total	6	1	31	38	0.171

Table 5: Central Unit reliability

The results obtained in Table 5 regarding the CU agreement are much lower than those obtained by CU detectors in Bengoetxea et al. (2017). The reliability of this CU detector goes from 0.54 to 0.57 regarding the train or test data-set. We think that this disagreement is due to the fact that the parser follows left to right or bottom-up annotation style; whereas Bengoetxea et al. (2017) propose a top-down annotation style to detect the CU after segmenting the text.[10]

Confusion matrix: The quantitative evaluation gives the agreement rate between the gold standard (or human annotation) and the parser, but it does not describe in which rhetorical relation is this agreement and if the confusion matrix is similar to those obtained by two human annotators.

Here we will compare human's confusion matrix against the machine's confusion matrix (see Table 6) in order to identify on which relations they agree.

When we compare the parser's and human's annotations, we can identify interesting differences. As Table 7 shows, the agreement is mostly in the general and most used ELABORATION relation (101 of 164).[11] There was a match in other relations, but the frequency is very low: EVALUATION (9 of 164) and BACKGROUND (6 of 164).

---

[10] A demo of the CU detector for scientific Basque texts can be tested at http://ixa2.si.ehu.es/rst/tresnak/rstpartialparser/.

[11] Note that we do not mention the agreement in the SAME-UNIT label, because it is not a rhetorical relation.

Human \Auto	En	Jo	C	Ev	El	Ca	Co	Su	Me	Nu	Sa	Ba	Total
Enablement En	**2**			4									6
Unless												1	1
Anthitesis		1				1				1		2	5
Solution-hood		1		1	2							1	5
Condition C	1				1	1				6		2	11
Joint Jo		**1**								3			4
Restatement		3		2	7	1	1		1	1			16
Disjunction					2					4		1	7
Evaluation Ev		1		**9**	11	5	1			9	1	3	40
Evidence				1	8	1				5			15
Elaboration El	2	9		12	**101**	9	1		1	68	4	9	216
Un-conditional							1			1			2
Purpose	8	3		2	18	9			2	10	7	7	66
Interpretation		1		1	5	1				12	3	1	24
Justify	1	1		1	2	2				6	1	1	15
Cause Ca		7		2	7	**2**	2			17	1	6	44
Conjunction		21		1	3	2	1			7	1		36
Contrast Co		5		2	5					10	3	1	26
Conccesion		1	1	1	7	3	2	1		7	2	3	28
Summary Su				1	2								3
List		20		6	12	1	2		1	50	6	16	114
Means Me	6	8		2	12	8	1		**3**	26	1	7	74
Motivation				2	1					7			10
Null Nu	9	75		13	89	16	8		4		22	96	332
Result	2	8		4	8	5				12	2	1	42
Preparation		2			1					13		66	82
Same-unit Sa	1	7		1	1	1				7	**40**	5	63
Sequence		10			3					5	2	4	24
Background Ba	1	2		4	6		1			28	2	**6**	50
Circumstance	3	5				11	2			17	9	19	66
Total	36	192	1	72	314	79	22	2	12	332	107	258	1427

Table 6: Confusion matrix of the Basque monolingual parser: gold standard in files and parser output in columns. Agreement in bold

However, when we compare humans' annotations (Iruskieta et al., 2013) the agreement is significant (Fleiss Kappa) in other relations such as PURPOSE, PREPARATION, CIRCUMSTANCE, CONCESSION, CONDITION, LIST, DISJUNCTION, RESTATEMENT and MEANS. In contrast, ELABORATION has shown weak inter-annotator agreement along with BACKGROUND, SEQUENCE, CAUSE, RESULT, CONTRAST and CONJUNCTION.

To have a better look at the parser, we can also look at its confusion matrix, in order to describe the most confused relations.

RST relation	Match	
ELABORATION	101	0.616
SAME-UNIT	40	0.244
EVALUATION	9	0.055
BACKGROUND	6	0.036
MEANS	3	0.018
CAUSE	2	0.012
ENABLEMENT	2	0.012
JOINT	1	0.006
Total agreement	164	

Table 7: Description of gold and automatic label matching

There is a important difference when we compare the disagreements between human-machine and human-human. We see in Table 8 that machine tries to get the best results using a small number of relations and all of them are general

Relation	Errors	Empl. Tags
ELABORATION	213	314
BACKGROUND	252	258
JOINT	191	192
CAUSE	77	79
SAME-UNIT	67	107
EVALUATION	63	72
ENABLEMENT	29	31

Table 8: Parser annotation confusion matrix

Relation	Match	RR Tags	
ELABORATION	107	337	0.317
SAME-UNIT	41	69	0.594
ATTRIBUTION	43	60	0.717
EXPLANATION	6	43	0.139
CONTRAST	3	15	0.2
CONDITION	1	3	0.333

Table 9: Description of gold and automatic label matching for Portuguese.

relations (in the semantic scale of RRs (Kortmann, 1991)), such as: ELABORATION, BACKGROUND and JOINT. On the contrary, the agreement between humans lies in much more relations and more informative ones, because they try to be exhaustive, and they rather disagree on general, widely used and less informative relations, such as ELABORATION, LIST, BACKGROUND, RESULT and MEANS. Disagreement in ELABORATION is slightly bigger or more confused between humans (162 of 267: 0.343 F_1 agreement) than between human-machine (101 of 314: 0.321) but the big differences are in some uncommon relations, such as JOINT that was annotated only on 3 occasions in Basque treebank, but the system used widely without success (1 of 192: 0.005). Similarly, LIST was confused widely (0 of 114: 0.00).

6.2.2 Portuguese mono-lingual system

Concerning the Portuguese mono-lingual system, we followed the same evaluation method (Iruskieta et al., 2015) and investigated in which rhetorical relation our system matches with the gold standard anotation.

In Table 9 we show the relations, and frequencies, for which we have an agreement between the Portuguese gold standard corpus and our monolingual Portuguese parser.

First of all, we see that agreement is mainly in ELABORATION and ATTRIBUTION,[12] the most

---

[12]Note that in the original RST relation set (and also in

Relation	Match		RR Tags
ELABORATION	131	688	0.190
SAME-UNIT	21	36	0.583
CONTRAST	1	3	0.333
JOINT	1	129	0.008

Table 10: Description of gold and automatic label matching for Basque, using cross-lingual information from Portuguese

used relations. Besides, the system tags other relations such as EXPLANATION and CONTRAST.

If we compare these results with the results obtained from the Basque corpus, we can see some interesting things. For example, we can notice that, in the Basque corpus, there are some opinionative texts and the system could learn it using EVALUATION, and in the Portuguese corpus, there is much ATTRIBUTION relation, because some of the analysed texts were collected from newspapers and this relation is common in this genre and this tag was used in the annotation campaign.

Finally, in Table 10 we show in which relation is the agreement for the cross-lingual system trained on Portuguese and evaluated on Basque.

As we can see in Table 10 the system has used only one relation adequately and this relation is the most used and general one. i.e. the ELABORATION relation.

7 Results and Future work

This paper presents the first discourse parser for Basque. Regarding the reliability of the parser, we get promising results while relying on a very small dataset. We also show that results can be improved with more data, as performance for languages with larger datasets are higher. In this work, we conduct a multilingual experiment to augment training data and get better results for Basque. Even if our cross-lingual system did not improve over the monolingual one, we believe that this path of research should be pursued, in parallel to annotating more data.

Moreover we evaluated quantitatively, but also qualitatively our system, in order to get a better understanding of how this first Basque RST parser works, and how far it is from human behaviour. We hope that this will help us to design a better discourse parser for Basque.

We underlined that the parser does not label properly the CU and uses a set of fixed rhetorical relations to get the best results, whereas humans try to get a better description and the confusion matrix pinpoint to more informative relations. In future work, we plan to improve on central unit detection, to evaluate a top-down approach, and to move from predicting very general and uninformative relations to a system able to identify the more interesting relations despite class imbalance.

This first RST parser for Basque represents a step forward to the use of discourse information in summarisation (Atutxa et al., 2017), sentiment analysis (Alkorta et al., 2017) and in many other advanced tasks.

Moreover, authors are currently striving to annotate more Basque data, to improve the system. One hope is to get performance reliable enough to provide an interesting pre-annotation that could make the whole annotation process easier and faster.

Acknowledgments

This research was supported by the University of the Basque Country project UPV/EHU IXA Group (GIU16/16) and *Procesamiento automático de textos basado en arquitecturas avanzadas* (PES18/28) project. This work was supported partly by the french PIA project "Lorraine Universit dExcellence", reference ANR-15-IDEX-04-LUE.

References

Stergos Afantenos, Pascal Denis, Philippe Muller, and Laurence Danlos. 2010. Learning recursive segments for discourse parsing. *arXiv preprint arXiv:1003.5372*.

Stergos Afantenos, Eric Kow, Nicholas Asher, and Jérémy Perret. 2015. Discourse parsing for multi-party chat dialogues. Association for Computational Linguistics (ACL).

Jon Alkorta, Koldo Gojenola, Mikel Iruskieta, and Maite Taboada. 2017. Using lexical level information in discourse structures for Basque sentiment analysis. In *Proceedings of the 6th Workshop on Recent Advances in RST and Related Formalisms*, pages 39–47.

Mikel Artetxe, Gorka Labaka, and Eneko Agirre. 2018. A robust self-learning method for fully unsupervised cross-lingual mappings of word embeddings. In

---

other annotation campaigns) ATTRIBUTION is not considered a rhetorical relation.

Proceedings of the 56th Annual Meeting of the Association for Computational Linguistics (Volume 1: Long Papers).

Nicholas Asher and Alex Lascarides. 2003. *Logics of conversation.* Cambridge University Press.

Unai Atutxa, Mikel Iruskieta, Olatz Ansa, and Alejandro Molina. 2017. COMPRESS-EUS: I(ra)kasleen laburpenak lortzeko tresna. In *EUDIA: Euskararen bariazioa eta bariazioaren irakaskuntza-III*, pages 87–98.

Kepa Bengoetxea, Aitziber Atutxa, and Mikel Iruskieta. 2017. Un detector de la unidad central de un texto basado en técnicas de aprendizaje automático en textos científicos para el euskera. *Procesamiento del Lenguaje Natural*, 58:37–44.

Kepa Bengoetxea and Mikel Iruskieta. 2017. A Supervised Central Unit Detector for Spanish. *Procesamiento del Lenguaje Natural*, 60:29–36.

Chloé Braud, Maximin Coavoux, and Anders Søgaard. 2017. Cross-lingual RST Discourse Parsing. In *Proceedings of the European Chapter of the Association for Computational Linguistics*.

Paula C.F. Cardoso, Erick G. Maziero, Mara Luca Castro Jorge, Eloize R.M. Seno, Ariani Di Felippo, Lucia Helena Machado Rino, Maria das Gracas Volpe Nunes, and Thiago A. S. Pardo. 2011. CSTNews - a discourse-annotated corpus for single and multi-document summarization of news texts in Brazilian Portuguese. In *Proceedings of the 3rd RST Brazilian Meeting*, pages 88–105.

Lynn Carlson, Daniel Marcu, and Mary Ellen Okurowski. 2001. Building a discourse-tagged corpus in the framework of Rhetorical Structure Theory. In *Proceedings of the Second SIGdial Workshop on Discourse and Dialogue*.

Maximin Coavoux and Benoit Crabbé. 2016. Neural greedy constituent parsing with dynamic oracles. In *Proceedings of the Annual Meeting of the Association for Computational Linguistics*.

Sandra Collovini, Thiago I Carbonel, Juliana Thiesen Fuchs, Jorge César Coelho, Lúcia Rino, and Renata Vieira. 2007. Summ-it: Um corpus anotado com informaçoes discursivas visandoa sumarizaçao automática. *Proceedings of TIL*.

Iria da Cunha, Juan Manuel Torres Moreno, and Gerardo Sierra. 2011. On the development of the RST Spanish Treebank. In *Linguistic Annotation Workshop*.

Iria da Cunha, Eric SanJuan, Juan-Manuel Torres-Moreno, M. Teresa Cabré, and Gerardo Sierra. 2012. A symbolic approach for automatic detection of nuclearity and rhetorical relations among intra-sentence discourse segments in Spanish. In *International Conference on Intelligent Text Processing and Computational Linguistics*, pages 462–474. Springer.

Iria da Cunha and Mikel Iruskieta. 2010. Comparing rhetorical structures in different languages: The influence of translation strategies. *Discourse Studies*, 12(5):563–598.

Iria da Cunha, Eric San Juan, Juan-Manuel Torres-Moreno, Marina Lloberese, and Irene Castelln. 2012. DiSeg 1.0: The first system for Spanish discourse segmentation. *Expert Systems with Applications*, 39(2):1671–1678.

Debopam Das, Manfred Stede, and Maite Taboada. 2017. The good, the bad, and the disagreement: Complex ground truth in rhetorical structure analysis. In *Proceedings of the 6th Workshop on Recent Advances in RST and Related Formalisms*, pages 11–19.

Edouard Grave, Piotr Bojanowski, Prakhar Gupta, Armand Joulin, and Tomas Mikolov. 2018. Learning word vectors for 157 languages. In *Proceedings of the International Conference on Language Resources and Evaluation (LREC 2018)*.

Jet Hoek and Sandrine Zufferey. 2015. Factors influencing the implicitation of discourse relations across languages. In *Proceedings of the 11th Joint ACL-ISO Workshop on Interoperable Semantic Annotation (ISA-11)*.

Eduard Hovy. 2010. Annotation. a tutorial. In *48th Annual Meeting of the Association for Computational Linguistics*.

Mikel Iruskieta, María J. Aranzabe, Arantza Diaz de Ilarraza, Itziar Gonzalez-Dios, Mikel Lersundi, and Oier Lopez de la Calle. 2013. The RST Basque Treebank: an online search interface to check rhetorical relations. In *Proceedings of the Workshop RST and Discourse Studies*.

Mikel Iruskieta and Zapirain Beñat. 2015. EusEduSeg: a Dependency-Based EDU Segmentation for Basque. In *Procesamiento del Lenguaje Natural, 55 41-48. Consultado en http://rua.ua.es/dspace/handle/10045/49274 ISBN (edicion digital): 978-84-608-1989-9*.

Mikel Iruskieta, Iria da Cunha, and Taboada Maite. 2015. A qualitative comparison method for rhetorical structures: Identifying different discourse structures in multilingual corpora. *Language Resources and Evaluation vol. 49: 263-309*.

Mikel Iruskieta, Arantza Díaz de Ilarraza, and Mikel Lersundi. 2014. The annotation of the central unit in rhetorical structure trees: A key step in annotating rhetorical relations. In *Proceedings of COLING 2014, the 25th International Conference on Computational Linguistics: Technical Papers*, pages 466–475.

Bernd Kortmann. 1991. *Free adjuncts and absolutes in English: Problems of control and interpretation.* Psychology Press, New York.

Igor Leturia. 2012. Evaluating different methods for automatically collecting large general corpora for Basque from the web. In *24th International Conference on Computational Linguistics (COLING 2012)*, pages 1553–1570, Mumbai, India.

Omer Levy, Anders Søgaard, and Yoav Goldberg. 2017. A strong baseline for learning cross-lingual word embeddings from sentence alignments. In *Proceedings of EACL*.

Ziheng Lin, Hwee Tou Ng, and Min-Yen Kan. 2014. A PDTB-styled end-to-end discourse parser. *Natural Language Engineering*, 20(02):151–184.

Yang Liu and Mirella Lapata. 2017. Learning contextually informed representations for linear-time discourse parsing. In *Proceedings of the 2017 Conference on Empirical Methods in Natural Language Processing*.

Willian C. Mann and Sandra A. Thompson. 1988. Rhetorical Structure Theory: Toward a functional theory of text organization. *Text-Interdisciplinary Journal for the Study of Discourse*, 8(3):243–281.

Daniel Marcu. 2000. The rhetorical parsing of unrestricted texts: A surface-based approach. *Computational Linguistics*, 26(3):395–448.

Erick G. Maziero, Thiago A. S. Pardo, Iria da Cunha, Juan-Manuel Torres-Moreno, and Eric SanJuan. 2011. DiZer 2.0-an adaptable on-line discourse parser. In *Proceedings of 3rd RST Brazilian Meeting*.

Erick Galani Maziero, Thiago Alexandre Salgueiro Pardo, and Núcleo Interinstitucional de Lingüística Computacional. 2009. Automatização de um método de avaliação de estruturas retóricas. In *Proceedings of the RST Brazilian Meeting*, pages 1–9.

Tomas Mikolov, Ilya Sutskever, Kai Chen, Greg S Corrado, and Jeff Dean. 2013. Distributed representations of words and phrases and their compositionality. In C. J. C. Burges, L. Bottou, M. Welling, Z. Ghahramani, and K. Q. Weinberger, editors, *Advances in Neural Information Processing Systems 26*, pages 3111–3119. Curran Associates, Inc.

Elena Mitocariu, Daniel Alexandru Anechitei, and Dan Cristea. 2013. Comparing discourse tree structures. In *International Conference on Intelligent Text Processing and Computational Linguistics*, pages 513–522. Springer.

Mathieu Morey, Philippe Muller, and Nicholas Asher. 2017. How much progress have we made on RST discourse parsing? A replication study of recent results on the RST-DT. In *Proceedings of Empirical Methods on Natural Language Processing (EMNLP)*.

Thiago A. S. Pardo and Maria das Graças Volpe Nunes. 2003. A construção de um corpus de textos científicos em Português do Brasil e sua marcação retórica. Technical report, Technical Report.

Thiago A. S. Pardo and Maria das Graças Volpe Nunes. 2004. Relações retóricas e seus marcadores superficiais: Análise de um corpus de textos científicos em Português do Brasil. *Relatório Técnico NILC*.

Thiago A. S. Pardo and Maria das Graças Volpe Nunes. 2008. On the development and evaluation of a Brazilian Portuguese discourse parser. *Revista de Informática Teórica e Aplicada*, 15(2):43–64.

Thiago A. S. Pardo and Eloize R. M. Seno. 2005. Rhetalho: Um corpus de referência anotado retoricamente. In *Proceedings of Encontro de Corpora*.

Boris T. Polyak and Anatoli B. Juditsky. 1992. Acceleration of stochastic approximation by averaging. *SIAM J. Control Optim.*, 30(4):838–855.

Rashmi Prasad, Nikhil Dinesh, Alan Lee, Eleni Miltsakaki, Livio Robaldo, Aravind Joshi, and Bonnie Webber. 2008. The penn discourse treebank 2.0. In *Proceedings of LREC*.

Radim Řehůřek and Petr Sojka. 2010. Software Framework for Topic Modelling with Large Corpora. In *Proceedings of the LREC 2010 Workshop on New Challenges for NLP Frameworks*, pages 45–50, Valletta, Malta. ELRA.

Kenji Sagae. 2009. Analysis of discourse structure with syntactic dependencies and data-driven shift-reduce parsing. In *Proceedings of IWPT 2009*.

Nynke van der Vliet. 2010. Inter annotator agreement in discourse analysis. http://www.let.rug.nl/ nerbonne/teach/rema-stats-meth-seminar/.

Nan Yu, Meishan Zhang, and Guohong Fu. 2018. Transition-based neural rst parsing with implicit syntax features. In *Proceedings of the 27th International Conference on Computational Linguistics*.

Beyond The Wall Street Journal:
Anchoring and Comparing Discourse Signals across Genres

Yang Liu

Department of Linguistics
Georgetown University
yl879@georgetown.edu

Abstract

Recent research on discourse relations has found that they are cued not only by discourse markers (DMs) but also by other textual signals and that signaling information is indicative of genres. While several corpora exist with discourse relation signaling information such as the Penn Discourse Treebank (PDTB, Prasad et al. 2008) and the Rhetorical Structure Theory Signalling Corpus (RST-SC, Das and Taboada 2018), they both annotate the Wall Street Journal (WSJ) section of the Penn Treebank (PTB, Marcus et al. 1993), which is limited to the news domain. Thus, this paper adapts the signal identification and anchoring scheme (Liu and Zeldes, 2019) to three more genres, examines the distribution of signaling devices across relations and genres, and provides a taxonomy of indicative signals found in this dataset.

1 Introduction

Sentences do not exist in isolation, and the meaning of a text or a conversation is not merely the sum of all the sentences involved: an informative text contains sentences whose meanings are relevant to each other rather than a random sequence of utterances. Moreover, some of the information in texts is not included in any one sentence but in their arrangement. Therefore, a high-level analysis of discourse and document structures is required in order to facilitate effective communication, which could benefit both linguistic research and NLP applications. For instance, an automatic discourse parser that successfully captures how sentences are connected in texts could serve tasks such as information extraction and text summarization.

A discourse is delineated in terms of relevance between textual elements. One of the ways to categorize such relevance is through *coherence*, which

refers to semantic or pragmatic linkages that hold between larger textual units such as CAUSE, CONTRAST, and ELABORATION etc. Moreover, there are certain linguistic devices that systematically signal certain discourse relations: some are generic signals across the board while others are indicative of particular relations in certain contexts. Consider the following example from the Georgetown University Multilayer (GUM) corpus (Zeldes, 2017),[1] in which the two textual units connected by the DM *but* form a CONTRAST relation, meaning that the contents of the two textual units are comparable yet not identical.

(1) Related cross-cultural studies have resulted in insufficient statistical power, ***but*** interesting trends (e.g., Nedwick, 2014). [academic_implicature]

However, the coordinating conjunction *but* is also a frequent signal of another two relations that can express adversativity: CONCESSION and ANTITHESIS. CONCESSION means that the writer acknowledges the claim presented in one textual unit but still claims the proposition presented in the other discourse unit while ANTITHESIS dismisses the former claim in order to establish or reinforce the latter. In spite of the differences in their pragmatic functions, these three relations can all be frequently signaled by the coordinating conjunction *but*: symmetrical CONTRAST as in (1), CONCESSION as in (2), and ANTITHESIS as in (3). It is clear that *but* is a generic signal here as it does not indicate strong associations with the relations it signals.

(2) This was a very difficult decision, ***but*** one

---

[1]The square brackets at the end of each example contain the document ID from which this example is extracted. Each ID consists of its genre type and one keyword assigned by the annotator at the beginning of the annotation task.

Proceedings of Discourse Relation Parsing and Treebanking (DISRPT2019), pages 72–81
Minneapolis, MN, June 6, 2019. ©2019 Association for Computational Linguistics

that was made with the American public in mind. [news_nasa]

(3)   NATO had never rescinded it, ***but*** they had and started some remilitarization. [interview_chomsky]

As suggested by Taboada and Lavid (2003), some discourse signals are indicative of certain genres: they presented how to characterize appointment-scheduling dialogues using their rhetorical and thematic patterns as linguistic evidence and suggested that the rhetorical and the thematic analysis of their data can be interpreted functionally as indicative of this type of task-oriented conversation. Furthermore, the study of the classification of discourse signals can serve as valuable evidence to investigate their role in discourse as well as the relations they signal.

One limitation of the RST Signalling Corpus is that no information about the location of signaling devices was provided. As a result, Liu and Zeldes (2019) presented an annotation effort to anchor discourse signals for both elementary and complex units on a small set of documents in RST-SC (see Section 2.2 for details). The present study addresses methodological limitations in the annotation process as well as annotating more data in more genres in order to investigate the distribution of signals across relations and genres and to provide both quantitative and qualitative analyses on signal tokens.

2   Background

Rhetorical Structure Theory (RST, Mann and Thompson 1988) is a well-known theoretical framework that extensively investigates discourse relations and is adopted by Das and Taboada (2017) and the present study. RST is a functional theory of text organization that identifies hierarchical structure in text. The original goals of RST were discourse analysis and proposing a model for text generation; however, due to its popularity, it has been applied to several other areas such as theoretical linguistics, psycholinguistics, and computational linguistics (Taboada and Mann, 2006).

RST identifies hierarchical structure and nuclearity in text, which categorizes relations into two structural types: NUCLEUS-SATELLITE and MULTINUCLEAR. The NUCLEUS-SATELLITE structure reflects a hypotactic relation whereas the MULTINUCLEAR structure is a paratactic relation

(Taboada and Das, 2013). The inventory of relations used in the RST framework varies widely, and therefore the number of relations in an RST taxonomy is not fixed. The original set of relations defined by Mann and Thompson (1988) included 23 relations. Moreover, RST identifies textual units as Elementary Discourse Units (EDUs), which are non-overlapping, contiguous spans of text that relate to other EDUs (Zeldes, 2017). EDUs can also form hierarchical groups known as complex discourse units.

2.1   Relation Signaling

When it comes to relation signaling, the first question to ask is what a signal is. In general, signals are the means by which humans identify the realization of discourse relations. The most typical signal type is DMs (e.g. 'although') as they provide explicit and direct linking information between clauses and sentences. As mentioned in Section 1, the lexicalized discourse relation annotations in PDTB have led to the discovery of a wide range of expressions called ALTERNATIVE LEXICALIZATIONS (*AltLex*) (Prasad et al., 2010). RST-SC provides a hierarchical taxonomy of discourse signals beyond DMs (see Figure 1 for an illustration, reproduced from Das and Taboada (2017, p.752).

Intuitively, DMs are the most obvious linguistic means of signaling discourse relations, and therefore extensive research has been done on DMs. Nevertheless, focusing merely on DMs is inadequate as they can only account for a small number of relations in discourse. To be specific, Das and Taboada (2017) reported that among all the 19,847 signaled relations (92.74%) in RST-SC (i.e. 385 documents and all 21,400 annotated relations), relations exclusively signaled by DMs only account for 10.65% whereas 74.54% of the relations are exclusively signaled by other signals, corresponding to the types they proposed.

2.2   The Signal Anchoring Mechanism

As mentioned in Section 1, RST-SC does not provide information about the location of discourse signals. Thus, Liu and Zeldes (2019) presented an annotation effort to anchor signal tokens in the text, with six categories being annotated. Their results showed that with 11 documents and 4,732 tokens, 923 instances of signal types/subtypes were anchored in the text, which accounted for over 92% of discourse signals, with the signal type *se-*

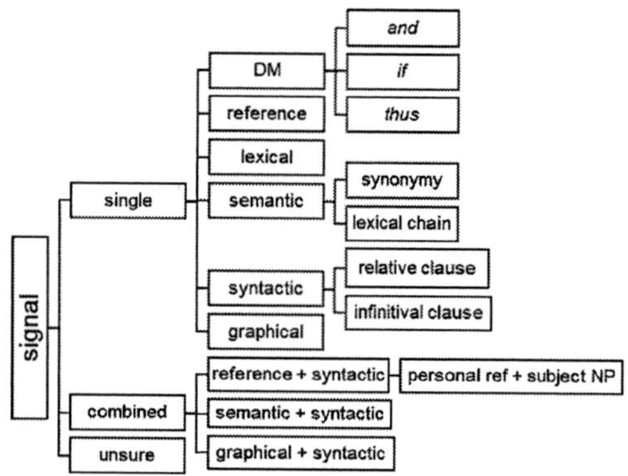

Figure 1: Taxonomy of Signals in RST-SC (Fragment).

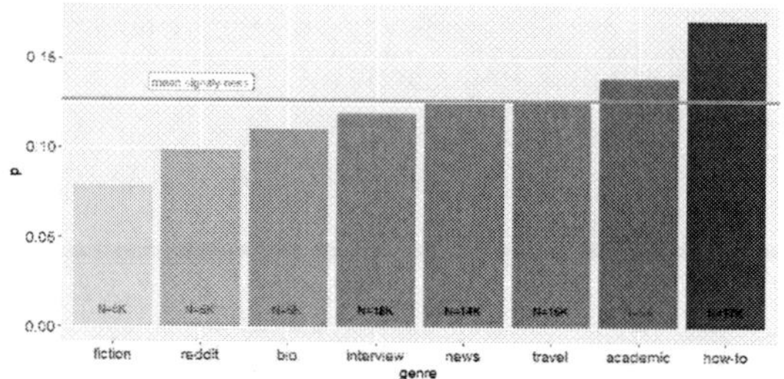

Figure 2: A Visualization of How Strongly Each Genre Signals in the GUM Corpus.

mantic representing the most cases (41.7% of signaling anchors) whereas discourse relations anchored by DMs were only about 8.5% of anchor tokens in this study, unveiling the value of signal identification and anchoring.

2.3 Neural Modeling for Signal Detection

Zeldes (2018a) trained a Recurrent Neural Network (RNN) model for the task of relation classification, and then latent associations in the network were inspected to detect signals. It is relatively easy to capture DMs such as 'then' or a relative pronoun 'which' signaling an ELABORATION. The challenge is to figure out what features the network needs to know about beyond just word forms such as meaningful repetitions and variable syntactic constructions. With the human annotated data from the current project, it is hoped that more insights into these aspects can help us engineer meaningful features in order to build a more informative computational model.

3 Methodology

Corpus. The main goal of this project is to anchor and compare discourse signals across genres, which makes the Georgetown University Multilayer (GUM) corpus the optimal candidate, in that it consists of eight genres including interviews, news stories, travel guides, how-to guides, academic papers, biographies, fiction, and forum discussions. Each document is annotated with different annotation layers including but not limited to dependency (`dep`), coreference (`ref`), and rhetorical structures (`rst`). For the purpose of this study, the `rst` layer is used as it includes annotation on discourse relations, and signaling infor-

mation will be anchored to it in order to produce a new layer of annotation. However, it is worth noting that other annotation layers are great resources to delve into discourse signals on other levels.

Moreover, due to time limitations and the fact that this is the first attempt to apply the taxonomy of signals and the annotation scheme to other genres outside RST-DT's newswire texts, four out of eight genres in the GUM corpus were selected: *academic, how-to guides, interviews,* and *news,* which include a collection of 12 documents annotated for discourse relations. The rationale for choosing these genres is that according to Zeldes (2018a)'s neural approach to discourse signal prediction on the GUM corpus, how-to guides and academic articles in the GUM corpus signal most strongly, with interviews and news articles slightly below the average and fiction and reddit texts the least signaled, as shown in Figure 2 (reproduced from Zeldes (2018b, p.19)). It is believed that the selection of these four genres is a good starting point of the topic under discussion.

Annotation Tool. One of the reasons that caused low inter-annotator agreement (IAA) in Liu and Zeldes (2019) is the inefficient and error prone annotation tools they used: no designated tools were available for the signal anchoring task at the time. We therefore developed a better tool tailored to the purpose of the annotation task. It is built over an interface offering full RST editing capabilities called rstWeb (Zeldes, 2016) and provides mechanisms for viewing and editing signals (Gessler et al., 2019).

Annotation Reliability. In order to evaluate the reliability of the scheme, a revised inter-annotator agreement study was conducted using the same metric and with the new interface on three documents from RST-SC, containing 506 tokens with just over 90 signals. Specifically, agreement is measured based on token spans. That is, for each token, whether the two annotators agree it is signaled or not. The results demonstrate an improvement in Kappa, 0.77 as opposed to the previous Kappa 0.52 in Liu and Zeldes (2019).

Taxonomy of Discourse Signals. The most crucial task in signaling annotation is the selection of signal types. The taxonomy of discourse signals used in this project is adapted from that of Das and Taboada (2017), with additional types and subtypes to better suit other genres. Two new types and four new subtypes of the existing types are proposed: the two new types are *Visual* and *Textual* in which the subtype of the former is *Image* and the subtypes of the latter are *Title, Date,* and *Attribution*. The three new subtypes are *Modality* under the type *Morphological* and *Academic article layout, Interview layout* and *Instructional text layout* under the type *Genre*.

Signal Anchoring Example. Semantic features have several subtypes, with *lexical chain* being the most common one. Lexical chains are annotated for words with the same lemma or words or phrases that are semantically related. Another characteristic of lexical chains is that words or phrases annotated as lexical chains are open to different syntactic categories. For instance, the following example shows that the relation RESTATE-MENT is signaled by a *lexical chain* item corresponding to the phrase *a lot of* in the nucleus span and *quantity* in the satellite span respectively.

(4) [They compensate for this by creating the impression that they have ***a lot of*** friends –]N [they have a '***quantity***, not quality' mentality.]S [whow_arrogant]

4 Results & Analysis

This pilot study annotated 12 documents with 11,145 tokens across four different genres selected from the GUM corpus. *Academic articles, how-to guides,* and *news* are written texts while *interview* is spoken language. Generally speaking, all 20 relations used in the GUM corpus are signaled and anchored. However, this does not mean that all occurrences of these relations are signaled and anchored. There are several signaled but unanchored relations, as shown in Table 1. In particular, the 5 unsignaled instances of the relation JOINT result from the design of the annotation scheme (see Section 5.1 for details). Additionally, the unanchored signal types and subtypes are usually asso-

ciated with high-level discourse relations and usually correspond to genre features such as *interview layout* in interviews where the conversation is constructed as a question-answer scheme and thus rarely anchored to tokens.

With regard to the distribution of the signal types found in these 12 documents, the 16 distinct signal types amounted to 1263 signal instances, as shown in Table 2. There are only 204 instances of DMs out of all 1263 annotated signal instances (16.15%) as opposed to 1059 instances (83.85%) of other signal types. In RST-SC, DM accounts for 13.34% of the annotated signal instances as opposed to 81.36%[2] of other signal types (Das and Taboada, 2017). The last column in Table 2 shows how the distribution of each signal type found in this dataset compares to RST-SC. The reason why the last column does not sum to 100% is that not all the signal types found in RST-SC are present in this study such as the combined signal type *Graphical + syntactic*. And since *Textual* and *Visual* are first proposed in this study, no results can be found in RST-SC, and the category *Unsure* used in RST-SC is excluded from this project.

4.1 Distribution of Signals across Relations

Table 3 provides the distribution of discourse signals regarding the relations they signal. The first column lists all the relations used in the GUM corpus. The second column shows the number of signal instances associated with each relation. The third and fourth columns list the most signaled and anchored type and subtype respectively.

The results show a very strong dichotomy of relations signaled by DMs and semantic-related signals: while DMs are the most frequent signals for five of the relations – CONDITION, CONCESSION, ANTITHESIS, CAUSE, and CIRCUMSTANCE, the rest of the relations are all most frequently signaled by the type *Semantic* or *Lexical*, which, broadly speaking, are all associated with open-class words as opposed to functional words or phrases. Furthermore, the type *Lexical* and its subtype *indicative word* seem to be indicative of JUSTIFY and EVALUATION. This makes sense due to the nature of the relations, which requires writers' or speakers' opinions or inclinations for the subject under discussion, which are usually expressed through positive or negative adjectives (e.g. *serious, outstanding, disappointed*) and other

---

[2]This result excludes the class *Unsure* used in RST-SC.

unanchored relations	frequency	percentage (%)
PREPARATION	28	22.2
SOLUTIONHOOD	11	32.35
JOINT	5	1.92
BACKGROUND	3	2.68
CAUSE	1	4
EVIDENCE	1	4.2
MOTIVATION	1	4.76

Table 1: Distribution of Unanchored Relations.

signal_type	frequency	percentage (%)	RST-SC (%)
Semantic	563	44.58	24.8
DM	204	16.15	13.34
Lexical	156	12.35	3.89
Reference	71	5.62	2.00
Semantic + syntactic	51	4.04	7.36
Graphical	46	3.64	3.46
Syntactic	44	3.48	29.77
Genre	30	2.38	3.22
Morphological	26	2.06	1.07
Syntactic + semantic	25	1.98	1.40
Textual	24	1.90	N/A
Numerical	8	0.63	0.09
Visual	7	0.55	N/A
Reference + syntactic	3	0.24	1.86
Lexical + syntactic	3	0.24	0.41
Syntactic + positional	2	0.16	0.23
Total	1263	100.00	92.9

Table 2: Distribution of Signal Types and its Comparison to RST-SC.

signaled relations	signal instances	signal type	signal subtype
JOINT	260	Semantic (147)	lexical chain (96)
ELABORATION	243	Semantic (140)	lexical chain (96)
PREPARATION	129	Semantic (54)	lexical chain (30)
BACKGROUND	112	Semantic (62)	lexical chain (42)
CONTRAST	68	Semantic (39)	lexical chain (31)
RESTATEMENT	60	Semantic (34)	lexical chain (28)
CONCESSION	49	DM (23)	DM (23)
JUSTIFY	49	Lexical (25)	indicative word (23)
EVALUATION	42	Lexical (31)	indicative word (31)
SOLUTIONHOOD	34	Semantic (12)	lexical chain (5)
CONDITION	31	DM (25)	DM (25)
ANTITHESIS	31	DM (12)	DM (12)
SEQUENCE	26	Semantic (7)	lexical chain (6)
CAUSE	25	DM (12)	DM (12)
EVIDENCE	24	Semantic (8)	lexical chain (7)
RESULT	21	Semantic (8)	lexical chain (7)
MOTIVATION	21	Semantic (8)	lexical chain (7)
PURPOSE	21	Syntactic (9)	infinitival clause (7)
CIRCUMSTANCE	20	DM (11)	DM (11)

Table 3: Distribution of Most Common Signals across Relations.

estingly, world knowledge such as the order of the presidents of the United States (e.g. that Bush served as the president of the United States before Obama) is also a indicative signal for SEQUENCE.

Another way of seeing these signals is to examine their associated tokens in texts, regardless of the signal types and subtypes. Table 4 lists some representative, generic/ambiguous (in bold-face), and coincidental (in italics) tokens that correspond to the relations they signal. Each item is delimited by a comma; the & symbol between tokens in one item means that this signal consists of a word pair in respective spans. The number in the parentheses is the count of that item attested in this project; if no number is indicated, then that token span only occurs once. The selection of these single-occurrence items is random in order to better reflect the relevance in contexts. For instance, lexical items like *Professor Eastman* in JOINT, *NASA* in ELABORATION, *Bob McDonnell* in BACKGROUND, and *NATO* in RESTATEMENT appear to be coincidental because they are the topics or subjects being discussed in the articles. These results are parallel to the findings in Zeldes (2018a, p.180), which employed a frequency-based approach to show the most distinctive lexemes for some relations in GUM.

4.2 Distribution of Signals across Genres

Table 6 shows the distribution of the signaled relations in different genres. Specifically, the number preceding the vertical line is the number of signals indicating the relation and the percentage fol-

syntactic categories such as nouns/noun phrases (e.g. *legacy, excitement, an unending war*) and verb phrases (e.g. *make sure, stand for*). Likewise, words like *Tips, Steps,* and *Warnings* are indicative items to address communicative needs, which is specific to a genre, in this case, the how-to guides. It is also worth pointing out that EVALUATION is the only discourse relation that is not signaled by any DMs in this dataset.

Even though some relations are frequently signaled by DMs such as CONDITION and ANTITHESIS, most of the signals are highly lexicalized and indicative of the relations they indicate. For instance, signal tokens associated with the relation RESTATEMENT tend to be the repetition or paraphrase of the token(s). Likewise, most of the tokens associated with EVALUATION are strong positive or negative expressions. As for SEQUENCE, in addition to the indicative tokens such as *First & Second* and temporal expressions such as *later*, an indicative word pair such as *stop & update* can also suggest sequential relationship. More inter-

relations	examples of anchored tokens
JOINT	; (16), **and** (15), also (10), *Professor Eastman* (3), he (3), they (2)
ELABORATION	Image (6), based on (3), – (3), *NASA* (3), *IE6* (3), More specifically (2), Additionally (2), also (2), they (2), it (2), *Professor Chomsky* (2)
PREPARATION	: (6), How to (2), Know (2), Steps (2), Getting (2)
BACKGROUND	Therefore, Indeed, build on, previous, *Bob McDonnell*, Looking back
CONTRAST	**but** (9)/**But** (4), **or** (2), Plastic-type twist ties & paper-type twist ties, in 2009 & today, deteriorate & hold up, however, bad & nice, yet
RESTATEMENT	They & they (2), *NATO* (2), In other words, realistic & real, **and**, rehashed & retell, it means that, *Microsoft & Microsoft*
CONCESSION	**but** (10), However (3), The problem is (2), though (2), at least, While, It is (also) possible that, however, best & okay, Albeit, despite, if, still
JUSTIFY	because (2), an affront & disappointed deeply, excitement, share, *the straps*, The logic is that, any reason, **so**, **since**, confirm, inspire
EVALUATION	very serious, nationally representative, a frightening idea, a true win, an important addition, issue, This study & It, misguided, pain
SOLUTIONHOOD	Well (2), arrogant, :, **So**, why, **and**, *Darfur*, How, I think, Determine
CONDITION	If (12)/if(10), even if, unless, depends on, –, once, when, until
ANTITHESIS	**but** (5)/**But**, instead of (2), In fact, counteract, won't, rather than, **Or**, not, *the Arabs*, however, better & worst
SEQUENCE	**and** (3), First & Second, examined & assessed, later, Bush & Obama, initial, *digital humanities*, A year later, stop & update
CAUSE	because (3), suggests, due to, compensate for, **as**, **since/Since**, *arrogant people*, in turn, given, brain damage, as such
EVIDENCE	( ) (2), see (2), According to, because, **as**, –, **and**, *Arabs & Turkey*, Because of, *discrimination*, biases, The report states that, Thus
RESULT	**so** (3), **and** (2), meaning (2), so that, capturing, thus, putting, *the $\chi2$ statistic*, make
MOTIVATION	will (2), easier, *the pockets*, All it takes is, **so**, last longer
PURPOSE	to (6)/To, in order to (3)/In order to (2), **so** (2), enable, The aim
CIRCUMSTANCE	when (4)/When (2), On March 13, Whether, **As/as**, With, in his MIT office, the bigger & the harsher

Table 4: Examples of Anchored Tokens across Relations.

	examples of anchored tokens in different genres
academic	*discrimination* (16), **;** (11), and (8), **:** (5), **to** (5), but (5), also (5), though (3), **hypothesized** (3), **based on** (3), **First & Second** (3), however (3), because (2), More specifically (2), in/In order to (2), as (2), ( ) (2), **see** (2), when (2), **posited**, **expected**, capturing, **Albeit**
how-to guides	but (10), If (9)/if(7), **;** (5), and (4), also (4), *arrogant people* (9), **How** (7), **:** (3), so (3), – (3), But (3), **Know** (3), **Steps** (2), Move, Challenge, **Warnings**, In other words, Empty, Fasten, **Tips**, Wash
news	*IE6* (9), *NASA* (5), and (4), but (4)/But (2), **Image** (4), **market** (4) However (2), **the major source**, the Udvar-Hazy Center, in 2009
interviews	*Sarvis* (14), **What** (12), **Why** (11), and (8), *Noam Chomsky* (8), but (5), **Wikinews** (4), because (3), **interview** (2), – (2), **Well** (2), So (2), Which

Table 5: Examples of Anchored Tokens across Genres.

relations	academic	how-to guides	news	interview
JOINT	65 | 23.13%	76 | 18.67%	65 | 25.39%	54 | 16.77%
ELABORATION	61 | 21.71%	79 | 19.41%	53 | 20.70%	50 | 15.53%
PREPARATION	25 | 8.9%	55 | 13.51	15 | 5.86%	34 | 10.56%
BACKGROUND	33 | 11.74%	24 | 5.9%	28 | 10.94%	27 | 8.39%
CONTRAST	17 | 6.05%	21 | 5.16%	19 | 7.42%	11 | 3.42%
RESTATEMENT	N/A	20 | 4.91%	11 | 4.3%	29 | 9.01%
CONCESSION	17 | 6.05%	13 | 3.19%	10 | 3.91%	9 | 2.8%
JUSTIFY	1 | 0.36%	11 | 2.7%	15 | 5.86%	22 | 6.83%
EVALUATION	10 | 3.56%	12 | 2.95%	7 | 2.73%	13 | 4.04%
SOLUTIONHOOD	2 | 0.71%	8 | 1.97%	N/A	24 | 7.45%
CONDITION	N/A	25 | 6.14%	3 | 1.17%	3 | 0.93%
ANTITHESIS	3 | 1.07%	10 | 2.46%	1 | 0.39%	17 | 5.28%
SEQUENCE	12 | 4.27%	4 | 0.98	5 | 1.95%	5 | 1.55%
CAUSE	6 | 2.14%	12 | 2.95	6 | 2.34%	1 | 0.31%
EVIDENCE	10 | 3.56%	N/A	5 | 1.95%	9 | 2.8%
RESULT	3 | 1.07%	6 | 1.47%	6 | 2.34%	6 | 1.86%
MOTIVATION	N/A	21 | 5.16%	N/A	N/A
PURPOSE	14 | 4.98%	5 | 1.23%	N/A	2 | 0.62%
CIRCUMSTANCE	2 | 0.36%	5 | 1.23%	7 | 2.73%	6 | 1.86%
Total	281 | 100%	**407** | 100%	256 | 100%	322 | 100%

Table 6: Distribution of Signaled Relations across Genres.

lowing the vertical line is the corresponding proportional frequency. The label N/A suggests that no such relation is present in the sample from that genre.

As can be seen from Table 6, how-to guides involve the most signals (i.e. 407 instances), followed by interviews, academic articles, and news. It is surprising to see that news articles selected from the GUM corpus are not as frequently signaled as they are in RST-SC, which could be attributed to two reasons. Firstly, the source data is different. The news articles from GUM are from Wikinews while the documents from RST-SC are Wall Street Journal articles. Secondly, RST-DT has finer-grained relations (i.e. 78 relations as opposed to the 20 relations used in GUM) and segmentation guidelines, thereby having more chances for signaled relations. Moreover, it is clear that JOINT and ELABORATION are the most frequently signaled relations in all four genres across the board, followed by PREPARATION in how-to guides and interviews or BACKGROUND in academic articles and news, which is expected as these four relations all show high-level representations of discourse that involve more texts with more potential signals.

Table 5 lists some signal tokens that are indicative of genre (in boldface) as well as generic and coincidental ones (in italics). The selection of these items follows the same criteria used in Section 4.1. Even though DMs *and* and *but* are present in all four genres, no associations can be established between these DMs and the genres they appear in. Moreover, as can be seen from Table 5, graphical features such as semicolons, colons, dashes, and parentheses play an important role in relation signaling. Although these punctuation marks do not seem to be indicative of any genres, academic articles tend to use them more as opposed to other genres. Although some words or phrases are highly frequent, such as *discrimination* in academic articles, *arrogant people* in how-to guides, *IE6* in news, and *Sarvis* in interviews, they just seem to be coincidental as they happen to be the subjects or topics being discussed in the articles.

Academic writing is typically formal, making the annotation more straightforward. The results from this dataset suggest that academic articles contain signals with diverse categories. As shown in Table 5, in addition to the typical DMs and some graphical features mentioned above, there are several lexical items that are very strong signals indicating the genre. For instance, the verb *hypothesized* and its synonym *posited* are indicative in that researchers and scholars tend to use them in their research papers to present their hypotheses. The phrase *based on* is frequently used to elaborate on the subject matter. Furthermore, Table 5 also demonstrates that academic articles tend to use ordinal numbers such as *First* and *Second* to structure the text. Last but not least, the word *Albeit* indicating the relation CONCESSION seems to be an indicative signal of academic writing due to the register it is associated with.

How-to Guides are the most signaled genre in this dataset. This is due to the fact that instructional texts are highly organized, and the cue phrases are usually obvious to identify. As shown in Table 5, there are several indicative signal tokens such as the *wh*-word *How*, an essential element in instructional texts. Words like *Steps*, *Tips*, and *Warnings* are strongly associated with the genre due to its communicative needs. Another distinct feature of how-to guides is the use of imperative clauses, which correspond to verbs whose first letter is capitalized (e.g. *Know, Empty, Fasten, Wash*), as instructional texts are about giving instructions on accomplishing certain tasks and imperative clauses are good at conveying such information in a straightforward way.

News articles, like academic writing, are typically organized and structured. As briefly mentioned at the beginning of this section, news articles selected in this project are not as highly signaled as the news articles in RST-SC. In addition to the use of different source data, another reason is that RST-DT employs a finer-grained relation inventory and segmentation guidelines; as a result, certain information is lost. For instance, the relation ATTRIBUTION is signaled 3,061 times out of 3070 occurrences (99.71%) in RST-SC, corresponding to the type *syntactic* and its subtype *reported speech*, which does not occur in this dataset. However, we do have some indicative signal tokens such as *market* and *the major source*.

Interviews are the most difficult genre to annotate in this project for two main reasons. Firstly, it is (partly) spoken language; as a result, they are not as organized as news or academic articles and harder to follow. Secondly, the layout of an interview is fundamentally different from the previous three written genres. For instance, the relation SOLUTIONHOOD seems specific to interviews, and most of the signal instances remain unanchored (i.e. 11 instances), which is likely due to the fact that the question mark is ignored in the current annotation scheme. As can be seen from Table 5, there are many *wh*-words such as *What* and *Why*. These can be used towards identifying interviews in that they formulate the question-answer scheme. Moreover, interviewers and interviewees are also important constituents of an interview, which explains the high frequencies of the two interviewees *Sarvis* and *Noam Chomsky* and the interviewer *Wikinews*. Another unique feature shown by the signals in this dataset is the use of spoken expressions such as *Well* and *So* when talking, which rarely appear in written texts.

5 Discussion

5.1 Annotation Scheme

For syntactic signals, one of the questions worth exploring is which of these are actually attributable to sequences of tokens, and which are not. For example, sequences of auxiliaries or constructions like imperative clauses might be identifiable, but more implicit and variable syntactic constructions are not such as ellipsis.

In addition, one of the objectives of the current project is to provide human annotated data in order to see how the results produced by machine learning techniques compare to humans' judgments. In particular, we are interested in whether or not contemporary neural models have a chance to identify the constructions that humans use to recognize discourse relations in text based on individual

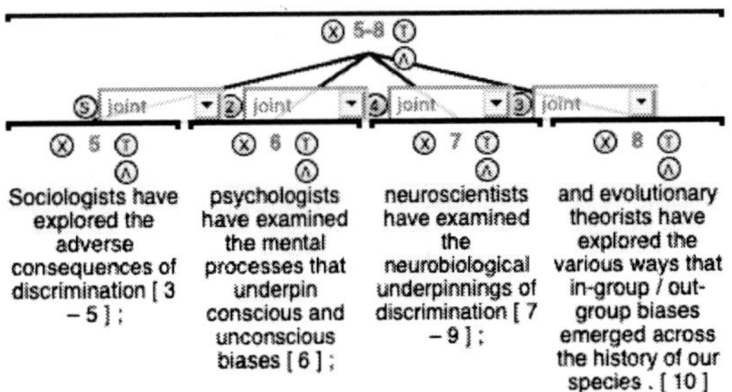

Figure 3: A Visualization of a Multinuclear Relation.

sequences of word embeddings, a language modeling technique that converts words into vectors of real numbers that are used as the input representation to a neural network model based on the idea that words that appear in similar environments should be represented as close in vector space.

Another dilemma that generally came up during the discussion about signal anchoring was whether or not to mark the first constituent of a multinuclear relation. In Figure 3, four juxtaposed segments are linked together by the JOINT relation, with associated signal tokens being highlighted. The first instance of JOINT is left unsignaled/unmarked while the other instances of JOINT are signaled. The rationale is that when presented with a parallelism, the reader only notices it from the second instance. As a result, signals are first looked for between the first two spans, and then between the second and the third. If there is no signal between the second and the third spans, then try to find signals in the first and the third spans. Because this is a multinuclear relation, transitivity does exist between spans. Moreover, the current approach is also supported by the fact that a multinuclear relation is often found in the structure like X, Y *and* Z, in which the discourse marker *and* is between the last two spans, and thus this *and* is only annotated for the relation between the last two spans but not between the first two spans. However, the problem with this approach is that the original source for the parallelism cannot be located.

5.2 Distribution of Discourse Signals

So far we have examined the distributions of signals across relations (Section 4.1) and genres (Section 4.2) respectively. Generally speaking, DMs are not only ambiguous but also inadequate as discourse signals; most signal tokens are open-class lexical items. More specifically, both perspectives have revealed the fact that some signals are highly indicative while others are generic or ambiguous. Thus, in order to obtain more valid discourse signals and parse discourse relations effectively, we need to develop models that take signals' surrounding contexts into account to disambiguate these signals.

Based on the results found in this dataset regarding the indicative signals, they can be broadly categorized into three groups: *register-related*, *communicative-need related*, and *semantics-related*. The first two are used to address genre specifications whereas the last one is used to address relation classification. Words like *Albeit* are more likely to appear in academic papers than other genres due to the register they are associated with; words like *Steps*, *Tips*, and *Warnings* are more likely to appear in instructional texts due to the communication effect they intend to achieve. Semantics-related signals play a crucial role in classifying relations as the semantic associations between tokens are less ambiguous cues, thereby supplementing the inadequacy of DMs.

5.3 Validity of Discourse Signals

It is also worth pointing out that some tokens are frequent signals in several relations, which makes their use very ambiguous. For instance, the coordinating conjunction *and* appears in JOINT, RESTATEMENT, SEQUENCE, and RESULT in this dataset. Similarly, the subordinating conjunctions *since* and *because* serve as signals of JUSTIFY, CAUSE, and EVIDENCE in these 12 documents. These ambiguities would pose difficulties to the validity of discourse signals. As pointed out by Zeldes (2018a), a word like *and* is extremely ambiguous overall, since it appears very frequently in general, and is attested in all discourse functions. However, it is noted that some 'and's are more useful as signals than others: adnominal 'and' (example (5)) is usually less interesting than intersentential 'and' (example (6)) and sentence initial 'and' (example (7)).

(5)   The owners, [William *and* Margie Hammack], are luckier than any others.[3] – ELABORATION-ADDITIONAL

---

[3]This example is chosen from the RST-DT corpus (Carlson et al., 2003) for illustration due to the apposition. Note that the relation inventory also differs.

(6)   [Germany alone had virtually destroyed Russia, twice,]$_{n1}$ [*and* Germany backed by a hostile military alliance, centered in the most phenomenal military power in history, that's a real threat.]$_{n2}$ – JOINT [interview_chomsky]

(7)   [It arrests us.]$_N$ [*And* then you say you won't commit a mistake, so you'll commit new mistakes. It doesn't matter.]$_S$ – ANTITHESIS [interview_peres]

Hence, it would be beneficial to develop computational models that score and rank signal words not just based on how proportionally often they occur with a relation, but also on how (un)ambiguous they are in contexts. In other words, if there are clues in the environment that can tell us to safely exclude some occurrences of a word, then those instances shouldn't be taken into consideration in measuring its 'signalyness'.

6   Conclusion

The current study anchors discourse signals across several genres by adapting the hierarchical taxonomy of signals used in RST-SC. In this study, 12 documents with 11,145 tokens across four different genres selected from the GUM corpus are annotated for discourse signals. The taxonomy of signals used in this project is based on the one in RST-SC with additional types and subtypes proposed to better represent different genres. The results have shown that different relations and genres have their indicative signals in addition to generic ones, and the indicative signals can be characterized into three categories: register-related, communicative-need related, and semantics-related.

The current study is limited to the `rst` annotation layer in GUM; it is worth investigating the linguistic representation of these signals through other layers of annotation in GUM such as coreference and bridging, which could be very useful resources constructing theoretical models of discourse. In addition, the current project provides a qualitative analysis on the validity of discourse signals by looking at the annotated signal tokens across relations and genres respectively, which provides insights into the disambiguation of generic signals and paves the way for designing a more informative mechanism to quantitatively measure the validity of discourse signals.

References

Lynn Carlson, Daniel Marcu, and Mary Ellen Okurowski. 2003. Building a Discourse-Tagged Corpus in the Framework of Rhetorical Structure Theory. In *Current and New Directions in Discourse and Dialogue*, Text, Speech and Language Technology 22, pages 85–112. Kluwer, Dordrecht.

Debopam Das and Maite Taboada. 2017. Signalling of Coherence Relations in Discourse, Beyond Discourse Markers. *Discourse Processes*, pages 1–29.

Debopam Das and Maite Taboada. 2018. RST Signalling Corpus: A Corpus of Signals of Coherence Relations. *Language Resources and Evaluation*, 52(1):149–184.

Luke Gessler, Yang Liu, and Amir Zeldes. 2019. A Discourse Signal Annotation System for RST Trees. In *Proceedings of 7th Workshop on Discourse Relation Parsing and Treebanking (DISRPT) at NAACL-HLT*, Minneapolis, MN. (To Appear).

Yang Liu and Amir Zeldes. 2019. Discourse relations and signaling information: Anchoring discourse signals in RST-DT. *Proceedings of the Society for Computation in Linguistics*, 2(1):314–317.

William C Mann and Sandra A Thompson. 1988. Rhetorical Structure Theory: Toward a Functional Theory of Text Organization. *Text-Interdisciplinary Journal for the Study of Discourse*, 8(3):243–281.

Mitchell P. Marcus, Beatrice Santorini, and Mary Ann Marcinkiewicz. 1993. Building a Large Annotated Corpus of English: The Penn Treebank. *Special Issue on Using Large Corpora, Computational Linguistics*, 19(2):313–330.

Rashmi Prasad, Nikhil Dinesh, Alan Lee, Eleni Miltsakaki, Livio Robaldo, Aravind Joshi, and Bonnie Webber. 2008. The Penn Discourse Treebank 2.0. In *Proceedings of the 6th International Conference on Language Resources and Evaluation (LREC 2008)*, pages 2961–2968, Marrakesh, Morocco.

Rashmi Prasad, Aravind Joshi, and Bonnie Webber. 2010. Realization of Discourse Relations by Other Means: Alternative Lexicalizations. In *Proceedings of the 23rd International Conference on Computational Linguistics: Posters*, pages 1023–1031. Association for Computational Linguistics.

Maite Taboada and Debopam Das. 2013. Annotation upon Annotation: Adding Signalling Information to a Corpus of Discourse Relations. *D&D*, 4(2):249–281.

Maite Taboada and Julia Lavid. 2003. Rhetorical and Thematic Patterns in Scheduling Dialogues: A Generic Characterization. *Functions of Language*, 10(2):147–178.

Maite Taboada and William C Mann. 2006. Applications of Rhetorical Structure Theory. *Discourse Studies*, 8(4):567–588.

Amir Zeldes. 2016. rstWeb - A Browser-based Annotation Interface for Rhetorical Structure Theory and Discourse Relations. In *Proceedings of NAACL-HLT 2016 System Demonstrations*, pages 1–5, San Diego, CA.

Amir Zeldes. 2017. The GUM Corpus: Creating Multilayer Resources in the Classroom. *Language Resources and Evaluation*, 51(3):581–612.

Amir Zeldes. 2018a. *Multilayer Corpus Studies*. Routledge Advances in Corpus Linguistics 22. Routledge, London.

Amir Zeldes. 2018b. A Neural Approach to Discourse Relation Signaling. *Georgetown University Round Table (GURT) 2018: Approaches to Discourse*.

Towards the Data-driven System for Rhetorical Parsing of Russian Texts

Elena Chistova
FRC CSC RAS / Russia, 119333
RUDN University / Russia, 117198
`chistova@isa.ru`

Maria Kobozeva, Dina Pisarevskaya
FRC CSC RAS / Russia, 119333
`kobozeva@isa.ru,`
`dinabpr@gmail.com`

Artem Shelmanov
Skoltech / Russia, 121205
FRC CSC RAS / Russia, 119333
`a.shelmanov@skoltech.ru`

Ivan Smirnov
FRC CSC RAS / Russia, 119333
`ivs@isa.ru`

Svetlana Toldova
NRU Higher School of
Economics / Russia, 101000
`toldova@yandex.ru`

Abstract

Results of the first experimental evaluation of machine learning models trained on Ru-RSTreebank – first Russian corpus annotated within RST framework – are presented. Various lexical, quantitative, morphological, and semantic features were used. In rhetorical relation classification, ensemble of CatBoost model with selected features and a linear SVM model provides the best score (macro $F_1 = 54.67 \pm 0.38$). We discover that most of the important features for rhetorical relation classification are related to discourse connectives derived from the connectives lexicon for Russian and from other sources.

1 Introduction

One of the widely used discourse models of text is the Rhetorical Structure Theory (RST) (Mann and Thompson, 1988). It represents a text as a constituency tree containing discourse (rhetorical) relations between text segments – discourse units (DUs). These units can play different roles inside a relation: nuclei contain more important information, while satellites give supplementary information. The leaves of the tree are so called elementary discourse units (EDUs), they usually are represented as clauses. Discourse units of different levels are combined by the same set of relations.

The goal of our work is the development of a data-driven system for rhetorical parsing of Russian texts. For training, we use recently released Ru-RSTreebank corpus (Pisarevskaya et al., 2017). In this paper, we describe the pipeline of the parser, present the developed featureset for relation classification task, and present the results of the first experimental evaluation of machine learning models trained on Ru-RSTreebank. Special attention is paid to the importance of discourse connectives.

Discourse connectives are clues signalling that there is a definite relation between two DUs, such as "in consequence of" for "Effect" or "because of" for "Cause". Some of them are functional words (primary connectives), the rest of them, secondary connectives, are less grammaticalized (Rysova and Rysova, 2014; Danlos et al., 2018), but also should be presented in exhaustive lexicons of connectives. We find that these cue phrases are informative features for rhetorical relation classification.

2 Related Work

First discourse parsers were trained mostly on syntactic features. The authors of (Soricut and Marcu, 2003) experiment with lexicalized syntactic trees for sentence segmentation. In (Subba and Di Eugenio, 2007), authors leverage discourse cue phrases and punctuation in addition to syntactic structure of sentences and POS tags. The same features along with information about n-grams are used to define rhetorical relations in the HILDA parser (Hernault et al., 2010). It is also suggested to use syntax and discourse production rules (Lin et al., 2009; Feng and Hirst, 2012), POS tags of the head node and the attachment node, as well as the dominance relationship between EDUs, and the distance of each unit to their nearest common ancestor (Feng and Hirst, 2014).

In addition to syntactic features, one can use lexical features, semantic similarities of verbs and nouns (Feng and Hirst, 2012) in different EDUs, tokens and POS tags at the beginning and the end of each EDU and whether both of them are in the same sentence (Li et al., 2014), bag of words along with the appearing of any possible word pair from both EDUs (Zhang et al., 2015). In (Joty and Ng., 2015), among other features, authors use discourse cues, lexical chains, and syntactic fea-

Proceedings of Discourse Relation Parsing and Treebanking (DISRPT2019), pages 82–87
Minneapolis, MN, June 6, 2019. ©2019 Association for Computational Linguistics

tures. In (Guo et al., 2018), neural tensor network with interactive attention was applied to capture the most important word pairs from two discourse arguments. These pairs were used as features in addition to word embeddings.

As discourse connectives are important for discourse parsing, recently, lexicons of connectives have been created for several languages. There are lexicons for French (Roze et al., 2012), Czech (Synková et al., 2017), German (Scheffler and Stede, 2016), English (Das and Stede, 2018). For example, DiMLex, a lexicon for German, consists of 275 connectives (Scheffler and Stede, 2016), DiMLex-Eng, the lexicon for English, contains 149 connectives (Das and Stede, 2018). There are also PDTB-based lexicons for French (Laali and Kosseim, 2017) and Portuguese (Mendes and Dombek, 2018).

Recently, deep learning models that use low-level features were adopted for discourse parsing. (Jia et al., 2018) propose a transition-based discourse parser for English that uses memory networks to take discourse cohesion into account. (Chuan-An et al., 2018) propose a framework based on recursive neural network that jointly models several subtasks including EDU segmentation, tree structure construction, as well as center and sense labeling. (Xu et al., 2018) present a text matching network that encodes the discourse units and the paragraphs by combining Bi-LSTM and CNN to capture both global dependency information and local n-gram information.

In this work, we run several experiments that let investigate the importance of various features for the first data-driven discourse parser for Russian.

3 Corpus Details

Ru-RSTreebank[1] is the first discourse corpus for Russian (Pisarevskaya et al., 2017) annotated within the RST framework. The updated version, used in this research, as well as the guidelines for annotators, are currently freely available on demand. The corpus consists of 179 texts: 79 texts of such genres as news, news analytics, popular science, and 100 research articles about linguistics and computer science (203,287 tokens in total). The corpus was manually annotated with an open-source tool called rstWeb[2]. The customized set of rhetorical relations was adapted for the Russian

language. Last value for Krippendorff's unitized alpha, that is used to measuring inter-annotator agreement, is 81%.

Following types of annotations are provided in the corpus: segmentation of EDUs, discourse units nuclearity, types of discourse relations, rhetorical tree construction. Clauses were mostly used as EDUs, with some adaptations for Russian. Verbal adverb phrases are emphasized as EDUs only if they have causal or clarifying meaning. Separate EDUs can occur without verb if they contain prepositional phrases that have cause, effect, contrast, or concession meaning. The release of this corpus unlocked the possibility to use machine learning techniques for discourse parsing.

We created a lexicon of discourse connectives, based on this corpus. The procedure is similar to that described in (Toldova et al., 2017). The connectives from the lexicon were further used as features for discourse parsing of Russian texts.

4 Parsing Approach

4.1 Parsing Pipeline

We divide the task of automated discourse parsing into five subtasks: sentence segmentation, relation prediction, discourse tree construction, classification of connected DU pairs into nuclear-satellite, and labeling relations between DUs.

Sentence segmentation task can be performed with external rule-based tools such as AOT.ru[3] and lies outside the scope of this work. Relation prediction is a simple binary classification task. Positive objects for this task are provided by gold parses of the corpus. Negative objects are generated by considering adjunct unconnected DUs in the gold parses. For construction of the connected discourse tree, we adopt an algorithm presented in (Hernault et al., 2010). The algorithm greedily merges DUs according to probabilities obtained from binary classification on the previous step.

Determining nuclear-satellite relations between DUs according to RST is a three-label classification task: "Satellite-Nucleus" (SN), "Nucleus-Satellite" (NS), "Nucleus-Nucleus" (NN). The final step, in which we predict a label of DU relations, is a multi-label classification task (we select 11 most important relations) that uses results of nuclear-satellite classification.

---

[1] http://rstreebank.ru/
[2] https://corpling.uis.georgetown.edu/rstweb/info/
[3] http://aot.ru/

4.2 Classification and Feature Selection Methods

We compare the effectiveness of various widely used supervised learning algorithms: logistic regression, support vector machine with linear kernel, and gradient boosting on decision trees (GBT) implemented in LightGBM[4] and CatBoost[5] packages. Since the feature space is too large and sparse for GBT methods, we perform feature selection in order to keep only the most informative features. For this purpose, we use a wrapper method implemented via logistic regression with L1 regularizer. The regularizer makes the model to aggressively zero feature coefficients during training, which leads to a smaller effective feature space. We also experiment with soft-voting ensembles that combine linear classifiers with GBT models.

4.3 Features

We use combinations of various lexical, quantitative, morphological, and semantic features. Lexical features contain a number of occurrences of cue phrases from a manually composed list of discourse connectives. The list contains nearly 450 items collected from three sources: expressions derived from the connectives lexicon for Russian mentioned above, conjunctions used in complex sentences in Russian described in RusGram[6], and the list of functional multi-word expressions suggested in the Russian National Corpus[7]. Each connective yields a feature according to one-hot encoding. Lexical features also include TF-IDF vectors of bags of words, cosine similarity between these vectors, BLEU, and Jaccard similarity metrics. Quantitative features include number of words, average word length, number of uppercased letters, as well as a number of words that start with uppercase. Morphological features encompass vector of counts of morphological characteristics in each DU, several similarity measures between these vectors and part of speech tags for the first and the last word pairs of each DU. Semantic features include averaged word embeddings of each DU. The word embedding model used in this work is described in (Toldova et al., 2018). The peculiarity of this model is that stop

---

[4]https://lightgbm.readthedocs.io/en/latest/
[5]https://tech.yandex.ru/catboost/
[6]http://rusgram.ru
[7]http://ruscorpora.ru/obgrams.html

Classifier	Macro F_1, %	
	mean	std
Linear SVM	63.13	0.39
Logistic Regression	63.65	1.08
CatBoost	67.79	0.57

Table 1: Performance of nuclear-satellite classification models.

words and punctuation marks were not removed during pretraining, whereby discourse connectives were not lost. For rhetorical relation classification, in addition, we use probabilities obtained in the nuclear-satellite classification step according to a stacking technique.

5 Experiments

5.1 Evaluation Procedure and Results

For experiments, we excluded "Elaboration" and "Joint" relations, since although they are the most common relations, they are also not very informative. We decided to focus on more specialized relation types. We also excluded "Same-unit", since it was used in the annotation only for utility purposes to mark discontinuous EDUs. Except aforementioned ones, we took the first 11 most representative classes, for which the dataset contains at least 320 examples. We selected 8 mono-nuclear relations ("Cause", "Preparation", "Condition", "Purpose", "Attribution", "Evidence", "Evaluation", "Background") and 3 multi-nuclear relations ("Contrast", "Sequence", "Comparison"). The dataset for experimental evaluation contains 6,790 examples. We note that the distribution of the classes is skewed. Before feature extraction, we performed the following preprocessing: tokenization, lemmatization, part-of-speech tagging, and morphological analysis using MyStem tool (Segalovich, 2003). The hyperparameters of our models are tuned using randomized search and overfitting detection tools built in gradient boosting packages. The evaluation scores are obtained using 5-fold cross-validation procedure with macro-averaging.

The results for distinguishing "Satellite-Nucleus", "Nucleus-Satellite", and "Nucleus-Nucleus" types of relations are presented in Table 1. The experiment shows that the CatBoost model outperforms linear SVM and logistic regression classifiers.

Table 2 summarizes the results of the exper-

Classifier	Macro F_1, %	
	mean	std
Logistic Regression	50.81	1.06
LGBM	51.39	2.18
Linear SVM	51.63	1.95
L_1 Feature selection + LGBM	51.64	2.22
CatBoost	53.32	0.96
L_1 Feature selection + CatBoost	53.45	2.19
voting((L_1 Feature selection + LGBM), Linear SVM)	54.67	1.80
voting((L_1 Feature selection + CatBoost), Linear SVM)	54.67	0.38

Table 2: Performance of rhetorical relation classification models.

iments with models for rhetorical relation classification. The results show that GBT models strongly outperform other methods. Also, we observe that training on the features selected by L1-regularized logistic regression reduces the variance of GBT models. Ensembles of GBT models with selected features and a linear SVM model own the best score. We should note that the qualitative performances of ensembles with LightGBM and CatBoost are almost the same, however, the computational performance of the latter is significantly better. Therefore, we used CatBoost model for the assessment of the feature importance.

5.2 Feature Importance and Error Analysis

From the whole set of features (3,624 features), CatBoost model for rhetorical type relation classification selected 2,054 informative lexical, morphological, and semantic features (word embeddings).

Important lexical features (1,941) are: occurrences of 318 cue phrases at the beginning and of 326 cue phrases at the end of the first DU; occurrences of 243 cue phrases at the beginning and of 353 cue phrases at the end of the second DU; number of occurrences of 345 cue phrases in the first DU; number of occurrences of 356 cue phrases in the second DU; 5 elements of TF-IDF vectors and 2 elements of averaged word embeddings for the first DU and 9 elements of TF-IDF vectors for the second DU. Important morphological features (97) are: combinations of punctuation, nouns, verbs, adverbs, conjunctions, adjectives, prepositions, pronouns, numerals, particles as the first word pairs of discourse units; combina-

tions of punctuation, verbs, adverbs, nouns, pronouns, adjectives, conjunctions, prepositions, particles, numerals as the last word pairs of discourse units. Therefore, most of the important features are related to discourse connectives.

The 20 least important features include 5 elements of word embeddings of the first DU, 3 elements of TF-IDF vectors and 2 elements of word embeddings of the second DU; average length of the first DU, number of finite verbs in both DUs, one occurrence of a keyword in the second DU; number of nouns in the second DU; Jaccard index between DUs; number of words that start with capital letter in both DUs; number of words in the first DU; occurrence of a period mark at the end of the first DU.

Error analysis of the models for rhetorical relation classification shows that mistakes often occur when there is semantic similarity between true and predicted class for such pairs as: "Comparison"-"Contrast", "Cause"-"Evidence". Another reason behind mistakes is the usage of connectives: for instance, if "Cause" is predicted instead of "Contrast", the error can be explained by occurrences of possible cause cue phrases in a nucleus or a satellite. Relations between long DUs that consist of several EDUs are influenced by the cue phrases inside EDUs, which sometimes results in errors. Especially it concerns the cases of "Evidence" (instead of "Contrast"), "Sequence" (instead of "Comparison") and "Cause" (instead of "Evidence").

6 Conclusion

We presented the first RST-based discourse parser for Russian. Rhetorical relation classifier and algorithm for building the RST-tree were implemented for discourse analysis of texts in Russian. Our experiments showed that the ensemble of CatBoost model with selected features and a linear SVM model provides the best results for relation classification. Feature selection procedure showed high importance of discourse connectives. In the future work, we are going to apply an extended version of discourse connectives lexicon for relation classification task, as well as implement more complex deep learning methods.

Acknowledgements

This paper is partially supported by Russian Foundation for Basic Research (project No. 17-29-

07033, 17-07-01477).

We would like to express our gratitude to the corpus annotators T. Davydova, A. Tugutova, M. Vasilyeva and Y. Petukhova.

References

Lin Chuan-An, Hen-Hsen Huang, Zi-Yuan Chen, and Hsin-Hsi Chen. 2018. A unified RvNN framework for end-to-end chinese discourse parsing. In *Proceedings of the 27th International Conference on Computational Linguistics: System Demonstrations*, pages 73–77.

Laurence Danlos, Katerina Rysova, Magdalena Rysova, and Manfred Stede. 2018. Primary and secondary discourse connectives: definitions and lexicons. *Dialogue & Discourse*, 9(1):50–78.

Tatjana Scheffler Peter Bourgonje Das, Debopam and Manfred Stede. 2018. Constructing a lexicon of english discourse connectives. In *Proceedings of the SIGDIAL 2018 Conference*, pages 360–365.

Vanessa Wei Feng and Graeme Hirst. 2012. Text-level discourse parsing with rich linguistic features. In *Proceedings of the 50th Annual Meeting of the Association for Computational Linguistics (Volume 1: Long Papers)*, volume 1, pages 60–68.

Vanessa Wei Feng and Graeme Hirst. 2014. A linear-time bottom-up discourse parser with constraints and post-editing. In *Proceedings of the 52nd Annual Meeting of the Association for Computational Linguistics (Volume 1: Long Papers)*, volume 1, pages 511–521.

Fengyu Guo, Ruifang He, Di Jin, Jianwu Dang, Long-biao Wang, and Xiangang Li. 2018. Implicit discourse relation recognition using neural tensor network with interactive attention and sparse learning. In *Proceedings of the 27th International Conference on Computational Linguistics*, pages 547–558.

Hugo Hernault, Helmut Prendinger, Mitsuru Ishizuka, et al. 2010. HILDA: A discourse parser using support vector machine classification. *Dialogue & Discourse*, 1(3).

Yanyan Jia, Yuan Ye, Yansong Feng, Yuxuan Lai, Rui Yan, and Dongyan Zhao. 2018. Modeling discourse cohesion for discourse parsing via memory network. In *Proceedings of the 56th Annual Meeting of the Association for Computational Linguistics (Volume 2: Short Papers)*, volume 2, pages 438–443.

Giuseppe Carenini Joty, Shafiq and Raymond T. Ng. 2015. CODRA: A novel discriminative framework for rhetorical analysis. *Computational Linguistics*, 41(3):385–435.

Majid Laali and Leila Kosseim. 2017. Automatic mapping of french discourse connectives to pdtb discourse relations. In *Proceedings of the SIGDIAL 2017 Conference*, pages 1–6.

Jiwei Li, Rumeng Li, and Eduard Hovy. 2014. Recursive deep models for discourse parsing. In *Proceedings of the 2014 Conference on Empirical Methods in Natural Language Processing*, pages 2061–2069.

Ziheng Lin, Min-Yen Kan, and Hwee Tou Ng. 2009. Recognizing implicit discourse relations in the penn discourse treebank. In *Proceedings of the 2009 Conference on Empirical Methods in Natural Language Processing*, pages 343–351.

William C Mann and Sandra A Thompson. 1988. Rhetorical structure theory: Toward a functional theory of text organization. *Text-Interdisciplinary Journal for the Study of Discourse*, 8(3):243–281.

Iria Del Ro Gayo Manfred Stede Mendes, Amlia and Felix Dombek. 2018. A lexicon of discourse markers for portuguese ldm-pt. In *Proceedings of the Eleventh International Conference on Language Resources and Evaluation*, pages 4379–4384.

Dina Pisarevskaya, Margarita Ananyeva, Maria Kobozeva, Alexander Nasedkin, Sofia Nikiforova, Irina Pavlova, and Alexey Shelepov. 2017. Towards building a discourse-annotated corpus of Russian. In *Computational Linguistics and Intellectual Technologies. Proceedings of the International Conference Dialogue 2017*, 16, pages 194–204.

Charlotte Roze, Laurence Danlos, and Philippe Muller. 2012. LexConn: a French lexicon of discourse connectives. *Revue Discours*, 10.

Magdalena Rysova and Katerina Rysova. 2014. The centre and periphery of discourse connectives. In *Proceedings of the 28th Pacific Asia Conference on Language, Information and Computing*, pages 452–459.

Tatjana Scheffler and Manfred Stede. 2016. Adding semantic relations to a large-coverage connective lexicon of German. In *Proceedings of the Tenth International Conference on Language Resources and Evaluation*.

Ilya Segalovich. 2003. A fast morphological algorithm with unknown word guessing induced by a dictionary for a web search engine. In *MLMTA*, pages 273–280.

Radu Soricut and Daniel Marcu. 2003. Sentence level discourse parsing using syntactic and lexical information. In *Proceedings of the 2003 Conference of the North American Chapter of the Association for Computational Linguistics on Human Language Technology-Volume 1*, pages 149–156.

Rajen Subba and Barbara Di Eugenio. 2007. Automatic discourse segmentation using neural networks. In *Proc. of the 11th Workshop on the Semantics and Pragmatics of Dialogue*, pages 189–190.

Pavlína Synková, Magdaléna Rysová, Lucie Poláková, and Jiří Mírovský. 2017. Extracting a lexicon of discourse connectives in czech from an annotated corpus. In *Proceedings of the 31st Pacific Asia Conference on Language, Information and Computation*, pages 232–240.

Svetlana Toldova, Dina Pisarevskaya, Margarita Ananyeva, Maria Kobozeva, Alexander Nasedkin, Sofia Nikiforova, Irina Pavlova, and Alexey Shelepov. 2017. Rhetorical relation markers in Russian RST treebank. In *Proceedings of the 6th Workshop on Recent Advances in RST and Related Formalisms*, pages 29–33.

Svetlana Toldova, Dina Pisarevskaya, and Maria Kobozeva. 2018. Automatic mining of discourse connectives for Russian. volume 930, pages 79–87.

Sheng Xu, Peifeng Li, Guodong Zhou, and Qiaoming Zhu. 2018. Employing text matching network to recognise nuclearity in chinese discourse. In *Proceedings of the 27th International Conference on Computational Linguistics*, pages 525–535.

Biao Zhang, Jinsong Su, Deyi Xiong, Yaojie Lu, Hong Duan, and Junfeng Yao. 2015. Shallow convolutional neural network for implicit discourse relation recognition. In *Proceedings of the 2015 Conference on Empirical Methods in Natural Language Processing*, pages 2230–2235.

RST-Tace
A tool for automatic comparison and evaluation of RST trees

Shujun Wan
Humboldt University of Berlin
Berlin, Germany
shujun.wan@hu-berlin.de

Tino Kutschbach
Independent Researcher
Berlin, Germany
tino.kutschbach@mailbox.org

Anke Lüdeling
Humboldt University of Berlin
Berlin, Germany
anke.luedeling@hu-berlin.de

Manfred Stede
University of Potsdam
Potsdam, Germany
stede@uni-potsdam.de

Abstract

This paper presents RST-Tace, a tool for automatic comparison and evaluation of RST trees. RST-Tace serves as an implementation of Iruskieta's comparison method, which allows trees to be compared and evaluated without the influence of decisions at lower levels in a tree in terms of four factors: constituent, attachment point, nuclearity as well as relation. RST-Tace can be used regardless of the language or the size of rhetorical trees. This tool aims to measure the agreement between two annotators. The result is reflected by F-measure and inter-annotator agreement. Both the comparison table and the result of the evaluation can be obtained automatically.

1 Introduction

Rhetorical Structure Theory (Mann and Thompson, 1988) is intended to describe discourse structure and text organization by labeling the discourse relations that hold between *elementary discourse units (EDU)* or between larger spans of text. It is widely used throughout the discourse community as a theory for discourse analysis. RST is defined as the reconstruction of the author's plan from the perspective of the reader (Stede, 2017), that is to say it implies a certain subjectivity. According to this view, different annotators might very well produce different analyses, which can nonetheless be equally legitimate (Das et al., 2017).

However, differences in the analysis based on the legitimate scope of explication ought to be distinguished from unexpected errors or ambiguities resulting from unclear annotation guidelines. In order to assess and ensure the accuracy and reliability of the annotation, it is crucial to measure the agreement between the annotators. Compared with other types of annotation, evaluating rhetorical structures and calculating the inter-annotator agreement are not trivial. There are several challenges: 1) RST tree parsing, 2) finding an appropriate method for comparison and evaluation, 3) applying this method efficiently.

So far, Marcu's (2000) method for the comparison of RST annotations by several annotators is widely-used. Building on Marcu's method, Maziero and Pardo (2009) developed *RSTeval* in order to obtain the results of comparison automatically. While being widely used, the method has also been criticized. For instance, da Cunha and Iruskieta (2010) argue that it amalgamates agreement coming from different sources, with the result that decisions at lower levels in the tree significantly affect agreement at the upper rhetorical relations in a tree (Iruskieta et al., 2015), and relations cannot be able to be compared where constituents do not coincide.

In this regard, Iruskieta et al. (2015) proposed an evaluation method which accepts that constituents do not need to coincide in their entirety to be compared. Iruskieta's method provides a qualitative description of dispersion annotation while allowing quantitative evaluation (details are introduced in section 2). Nevertheless, using this method to evaluate discourse structures manually is an extremely time- and resource-consuming task. Thus, inspired by RSTeval, we have developed RST-Tace as a tool for automatic comparison and evaluation of RST trees based on Iruskieta's method.

Proceedings of Discourse Relation Parsing and Treebanking (DISRPT2019), pages 88–96
Minneapolis, MN, June 6, 2019. ©2019 Association for Computational Linguistics

Example	CS1	CS2
[1]	1	1
[2]	23	23|24
[3]	17-18|26	17-18|26
[4]	10|15	11|15

Table 1: Examples of matching central subconstiutents (extracted from *CMN_008, RST German Learner Treebank*[8])

This research paper focuses on the theoretical foundations of RST-Tace as well as the implementation process. In addition, an example of using RST-Tace to compare and evaluate rhetorical trees (extracted from a self-built RST treebank) by two linguists will be presented in the final section.

2 Theoretical Framework

According to Iruskieta's method, the correspondence of constituents is not a necessary condition for comparison. Only the central subconstituent (CS)[1] which indicates the most important unit of the satellite span, has to be identical. With this restriction, discourse structures are compared using four independent factors:

- Constituent (C): the unit(s) where the satellite (or one of the nuclei in case of multinuclear relations) is located.

- Attachment point (A): the unit(s) where the constituent is linked.

- Nuclearity (N): the direction of the relation.

- Relation (R): the name of relations.

In order to use Iruskieta's method, each RST tree must first be converted into a table which consists of the four above factors as well as the central subconstituent. Subsequently, pairs should be matched according to the central subconstituent. The third stage is evaluation. According to Iruskieta's method, both agreement and disagreement are considered. Lastly, the result of the evaluation (F-measure) is calculated.

[1] According to Iruskieta (2015), there is an agreement that the most important unit of an RST tree is the "central unit(s)" (Stede, 2008) and the most important unit of a span is the "central subconstituent" (Egg and Redeker, 2010). Following this framework, Iruskieta et al. use the term "Central Subconstituent(s)" of a relation for the most important unit of the modifier span that is the most important unit of the satellite span.

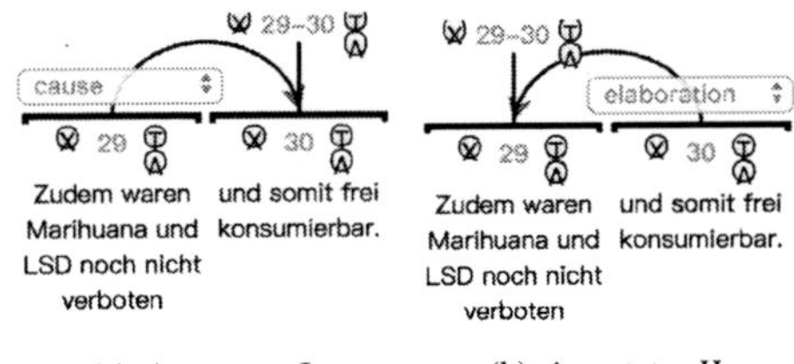

(a) Annotator I   (b) Annotator II

Figure 1: Annotations from two annotators (extracted from *DEU_006, RST German Learner Treebank*[2])

Anno	CS	R	N	C	A
I	29	cause	$\rightarrow$	29S[3]	30N[4]
II	30	elaboration	$\leftarrow$	30S	29N

Table 2: Matching table of Figure 1

Modifications

In light of the basic principles of Iruskieta's method, we highlight, in this part, some points which are crucial for the use of our tool or are slightly modified by us:

1. The use of this method for comparison and evaluation takes the harmonization of discourse segmentation as a given.

2. As a general rule, CS has to be the same so that the relations are able to be compared (see example [1] in Table 1). A case complicating the comparison occurs when multinuclear relations become involved. When there is a multinuclear relation, all of its constituents must be described as CS. Consequently, a multinuclear relation has more than one CS. Under such a circumstance, when a relation with more than one CS is able to be compared with another that has only one CS, at least one of the CSs has to be identical (see example [2] in Table 1). When two multinuclear relations are to be compared, their CSs do not have to remain the same entirely (see example [3] in Table 1). Similarly, they need to possess at least one identical CS (see example [4] in Table 1).

3. The association of CS is the prerequisite for

[2] Since we aim to show the tree structures rather than the linguistic decision, we decided not to translate the language of RST trees into English in this paper.

[3] S represents Satellite

[4] N refers to Nucleus

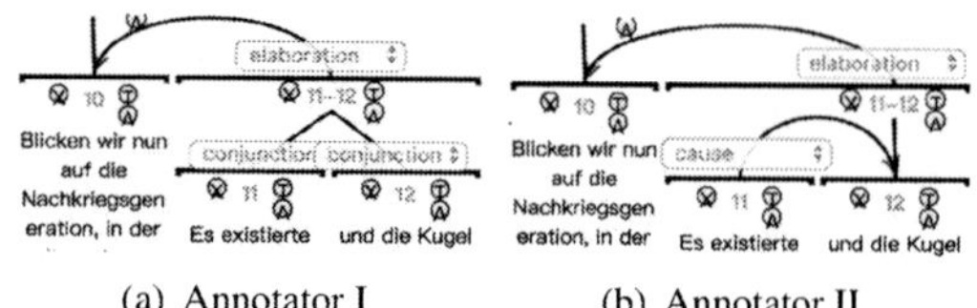

(a) Annotator I   (b) Annotator II

Figure 2: Annotations from two annotators (Extracted from *DEU_006, RST German Learner Treebank*)

Anno	CS	R	N	C	A
I	11-12	elaboration	←	11-12S	10N
II	12	elaboration	←	11-12S	10N

Table 3: Matching table of Figure 2

comparison of relations according to Iruskieta's method. However, there are two cases that still deserve to be compared, even though the CSs are not identical.

The RST tree of the example in Figure 1(a) is quite similar to the RST tree of 1(b). Apart from the names of relations which are coincidentally not the same in this example, the main reason why the two trees have different CSs, constituents and attachment points, is that they differ merely in nuclearity. However, due to the discrepancy in CS, this pair cannot be detected using Iruskieta's method. From Table 2 which is converted from the RST trees, we can observe that the CS of Figure 1(a) is 29 whereas the CS of Figure 1(b) is 30; yet, C1 equals A2 as well as C2 equaling A1.

The other case in which relations are still associated despite distinct CSs is when C1 equals C2 and A1 equals A2. The relation 10 and 11-12 of Figure 2(b) is not able to be compared with the one of Figure 2(a), because they have different CSs (see Table 3). This discrepancy stems from the micro level, i.e. the relation between EDU 10 to EDU 11.

In brief, we match relations following the decision tree below (see Figure 3).

4. Iruskieta's method is originally designed for comparing and evaluating discourse structures in different languages and/or by different annotators. Hence, in the case of disagreement, two sources of disagreement are distinguished: type A and type L for

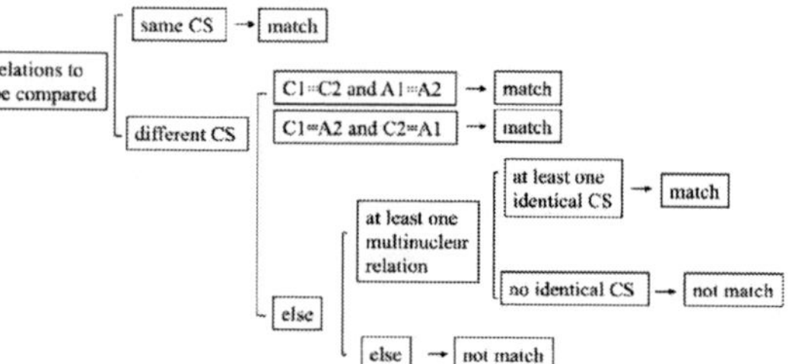

Figure 3: Decision tree for matching

annotator-based discrepancies and language-based discrepancies respectively[5]. In comparison to Iruskieta's method, we focus more on agreement instead of disagreement, because we aim to compare and evaluate annotations which are in the same language but annotated by different annotators. To check agreement in rhetorical relation, the constituent of this relation must have the same central subconstituent. If this condition is fulfilled, relation (R), constituent (C) and attachment point (A) will be further checked.

5. Concerning the results of evaluation, both F-measure and inter-annotator agreement for each factor are calculated. The agreement score for the whole RST trees is the mean value of the four factors.

3 Implementation

For evaluation, comparison, and analysis of RST trees, RST-Tace supports three main use cases:

1. Analysis of a single RST tree (i.e. extraction and listing of all annotated relations), see section 3.3.

2. Comparison of the annotated relations of a pair of RST trees, see section 3.4.

3. Statistical evaluation of a whole dataset.

These use cases depend on each other, e.g. in order to compare the annotated relations of a pair of RST trees (second use case), the annotated relations of both trees are first extracted and listed (first use case).

---

[5]For more details and examples regarding the evaluation of disagreement, refer to (Iruskieta et al., 2015), p.15-20.

3.1 Commandline Interface

In its current state, RST-Tace can be used via a commandline interface (command: *rsttace*), and each of the main use cases has its own command (*analyse / compare / evaluate*):

```
$ rsttace
Usage: rsttace [OPTIONS] COMMAND [ARGS]...

This tool analyses, compares, and evaluates RST trees.

Options:
--help  Show this message and exit.

Commands:
analyse   Parse single RST trees, analyse
          and list their annotated relations.
compare   Parse RST tree pairs and compare
          them with each other.
evaluate  Perform a statistical evaluation
          of a set of RST tree pairs.
```

The results are either written back to the commandline, or to csv-files if needed. For example, the command for comparing two rs3-files and writing the result to a CSV-file is:

```
$ rsttace compare file1.rs3 file2.rs3 \
          -o result.csv
```

As the tool is currently under active development the user interface may still be subject to change. For up-to-date information and complete documentation, please refer to the GitHub repository of *RST-Tace*.[6]

Before we discuss how each of the three tasks is performed in detail, the parsing process of rs3-files will be described.

3.2 RST Tree Parsing

After a set of texts has been annotated with tools such as *RSTTool* (O'Donnell, 1997) and *rstWeb* (Zeldes, 2016), the resulting RST trees are typically exported as **.rs3*-files. In order to work with the RST trees efficiently, these files have to be parsed and converted into an internal tree based data structure, which allows convenient data access for the desired evaluation task.

File Format

RSTTool and *rstWeb* both use the same file format for exported rs3-files with only minor differences. The file parser of *RST-Tace* is designed to handle the rs3-files of both tools.

The file format is based on XML and contains a header and a body. Figure 4 shows an example of a RST tree annotated with *RSTTool*. The header defines which relations are used in the RST tree and

[6]https://github.com/tkutschbach/
RST-Tace

```
<rst>
<header>
 <relations>
  <rel name="background" type="rst"/>
  <rel name="antithesis" type="rst"/>
   ...
  <rel name="reason" type="rst"/>
  <rel name="summary" type="rst"/>
   ...
  <rel name="sequence" type="multinuc"/>
  <rel name="joint" type="multinuc"/>
  <rel name="contrast" type="multinuc"/>
  <rel name="list" type="multinuc"/>
 </relations>
</header>
<body>
 &lt;segment id="1" parent="45" relname="span"&gt;Man muss vor ...
 &lt;segment id="2" parent="1" relname="reason"&gt;da die erst ...
 &lt;segment id="4" parent="5" relname="background"&gt;Nehmen wir.
  ...
 &lt;segment id="8" parent="7" relname="condition"&gt;wenn sie ...
 &lt;segment id="46" parent="68" relname="span"&gt;Wenn man es ...
 &lt;segment id="9" parent="69" relname="contrast"&gt;Die Kriegs..
 &lt;segment id="10" parent="11" relname="span"&gt;Blicken wir ...
 &lt;segment id="13" parent="51" relname="conjunction"&gt;Es ex...
 &lt;segment id="12" parent="51" relname="conjunction"&gt;und die.
  ...
 <group id="3" type="span" parent="49" relname="contrast"/>
 <group id="47" type="span" parent="6" relname="evidence"/>
 <group id="48" type="span" parent="49" relname="contrast"/>
  ...
 <group id="75" type="span" parent="76" relname="span"/>
 <group id="76" type="span"/>
  ...
</body>
</rst>
```

Figure 4: Example of an rs3-file, encoding an RST tree

their corresponding type, i.e. either mono- or multinuclear. The body represents the actual RST tree. An rs3-file consists of a list of XML elements (either *segments* and *groups*), each of which has the following attributes: *Node ID, parent ID, relation name*. Elements of the type *segment* correspond to the EDUs and contain the corresponding text of the EDU. *Group* elements have an additional attribute *type*, encoding whether the element is a span or corresponds to a multinuclear relation.

As shown in Figures 1(a), 1(b), and 2(a), 2(b): each leaf node of an RST tree has an EDU-ID, and higher level nodes have ranges of EDU-IDs which depend on the EDU-IDs of their child nodes.

In the XML file format, the *segment* elements correspond to the EDUs; their order inside the body corresponds the order of occurence of the EDUs in the original text. For example, the first *segment* element in the body corresponds to the first EDU (i.e. having the EDU-ID "1"), the third *segment* element in the body corresponds to the third EDU (i.e. having the EDU-ID "3"), and so on.

For the case of rs3-files from *RSTTool*, it is important to note that the IDs encoded in the *segment* elements do not necessariliy correspond to the desired EDU-IDs, as shown in Figure 4[7].

[7]In the example in Figure 4, the third *segment* has the ID

Because the proposed evaluation method of RST trees relies on correct EDU-IDs, the parser of *RST-Tace* infers the EDU-ID of each segment itself based on its position inside the list. The IDs of the *segment* and *group* elements are then used to reconstruct the tree structure. Afterwards, the ranges of EDU-IDs that higher level nodes span (i.e. represented by the *group* elements) can be inferred.

Internal Data Representation

As mentioned above, the data arrangement of rs3-files does not precisely represent an RST tree structure, which would allow convenient data access for the proposed evaluation method. As a remedy, the given data is parsed and converted into an internal tree representation, which consists of nodes and three different types of edges.

The three different types of edges are:

1. Horizontal edges, connecting two nodes on the same level: Encoding mononuclear relations.

2. Vertical edges, connecting one parent node with multiple child nodes one level below: Encoding multinuclear relations.

3. Vertical edges, connecting one parent node with one child node one level below: Encoding spans.

The tree nodes correspond to the *segment* and *group* elements in the rs3-file format. Each node is connected to a parent node via an edge and can have one horizontal edge connecting it to another node on the same level. Furthermore, it can have one vertical edge, connecting it to one or several child nodes on the next lower level. Additionally, the nodes encode their corresponding EDU ID or ID-range. If a node is a leaf node, then it also contains the text information of its corresponding EDU.

Parsing Process

The encoding step is implemented straightforwardly by first reading all XML elements and searching the element which corresponds to the root node of the RST tree (which is characterized by a missing parent ID, e.g. the element with $id = 76$ in Figure 4). Afterwards, for all elements

that refer to this root as parent, nodes and edges are generated and connected depending on the type of their relation. In the next step, all elements that refer to those nodes are processed respectively. This process is repeated until all elements have been appended as nodes to the internal data structure.

Finally, after the complete tree has been built, the EDU ID-ranges of the higher level nodes have to be inferred based on their corresponding lower level children, because only the EDU IDs of the leaf nodes can be directly extracted from the rs3-file. This inference is done by iterating over the whole tree bottom-up, i.e. from the leaf nodes towards the root node, and gradually augmenting the higher nodes level-by-level until the root node is reached.

3.3 Extraction of Annotated Relations

In order to compare and evaluate an RST tree using Iruskieta's method, its annotated relations have to be extracted and listed together with additional information (e.g. *constituent*, *nuclearity*).

Once the RST tree is available in the form of the previously described data structure, the extraction of relations becomes a simple task of iterating over the set of edges in the tree and listing their corresponding relations. Also, the additional information is directly accessible: The *nuclearity* corresponds to the direction of an edge, and the other information such as *constituent*, *attachment-point* and *central sub-constituent* can be directly acquired from EDU IDs and ID-ranges encoded in the nodes that each edge is connected to.

3.4 Comparison of RST Tree Pairs

An important task in RST research is comparing different RST annotations (of different annotators) for a single text or a set of texts. Under the condition that two annotations of a text are based on the same segmentation of EDUs, RST-Tace can compare the two different RST trees and calculate an equivalence score.

In order to compare the RST annotations of two trees using Iruskieta's method, the annotation lists of both RST trees are generated first, as described in section 3.3. Afterwards, the annotated relations of both RST trees have to be associated to each other.

As mentioned above, two different annotators might create RST trees with different structures for the same text; thus, it is not always clear which annotated relation in one tree corresponds

---

"4" instead of "3", and the on the *segment* with ID "8" follows the *segment* with ID "46", which itself is followed by the *segment* with ID "9".

Equivalence	Cost
Same CS	0
$C1 = C2$ and $A1 = A2$	1
$C1 = A2$ and $C2 = A1$	2
At least one identical CS	3
No matching	4

Table 4: Cost values used for matching annotated relations of two RST trees

to which one in the other. This ambiguity means that the association is not a trivial task.

Optimal Association

RST-Tace deals with this ambiguity by searching for an optimal association. For this, each annotated relation of the first RST tree is compared to each annotated relation of the second RST tree by the scheme introduced previously and shown in Figure 3. Because each of the possible matching outcomes stands for a different degree of equivalence, they can be prioritized by assigning cost values to each of them (low cost values for high priorities, high cost values for low priorities). The cost values used in this work are shown in Table 4.

While comparing all annotated relations of both RST trees with each other, these cost values are used to populate a cost matrix $\mathbf{C}$. With N being the number of relations annotated in the first RST tree and M being the number of relations annotated in the second tree, the matrix $\mathbf{C}$ has the form $N \times M$. An element $\mathbf{C}_{i,j}$ represents the cost of matching relation i in the first tree with relation j of the second tree.

The optimal association is then calculated by applying the Hungarian algorithm (Kuhn, 1955), also known as Kuhn-Munkres algorithm, to this cost matrix. Matches are categorized as completely identical CS, C1=C2 and A1=A2, C1=A2 and C2=A1, partially identical CS as well as no matching.

Evaluation and Results

After the annotations of both RST trees have been associated, all annotation pairs are compared according to Iruskieta's method, i.e. their nuclearities (N), relations (R), constituents (C), and attachment points (A) are compared and marked as equal or non-equal. These values are then used to calculate F-measure and inter-annotator agreement.

RST-Tace also offers the possiblity to process a whole batch of RST tree pairs and calculate the equivalence scores and inter-annotator agreement over a whole dataset.

4 An Example of Comparison and Evaluation using RST-Tace

In this section, we provide an example of using RST-Tace to compare and evaluate RST trees. Extracted from *RST German Learner Treebank*[8], two annotations [9] on the same German text by two linguists are compared and evaluated. A part of the two RST trees where the annotations are different is shown in Figure 5; the comparison table and the results of evaluation are presented in Figure 6.

5 Summary

To conclude, RST-Tace allows comparison and evaluation of RST trees by different annotators automatically. It can be used for rhetorical structures in any language as well as with any size. The modifications that are made based on Iruskieta's method provide a further perspective of RST related theories. Currently, the statistical part of the implementation, i.e. the automatic calculation of F-measure and inter-annotator agreement, is under active development. In the future, additional features could be added to RST-Tace, for instance, a user-friendly interface, or a more sophisticated statistical analysis of larger datasets and RST treebanks.

Acknowledgments

This work was financially supported by the *China Scholarship Council*. We wish to express our appreciation to Felix Golcher from IDSL, Humboldt University of Berlin, who provided his statistical expertise that greatly assisted the research, and to Shuyuan Cao from Polytechnic University of Catalonia for his theoretical support. We would like to thank Matthew Plews and Dawn Nichols for proofreading this paper. We also owe our special thanks to the anonymous reviewers for their valuable comments.

---

[8] RST German Learner Treebank consists of 40 RST trees. The texts in the treebank are argumentative essays (around 25,000 tokens in total) extracted from Kobalt-DaF Corpus (Zinsmeister et al., 2012). All the data was annotated by two professional linguists according to the guidelines of the Potsdam Commentary Corpus (Stede, 2016), which was designed for German pro-contra essays. The quantity of EDUs of each text is between 40-80.

[9] Segmentation has been harmonized before annotating.

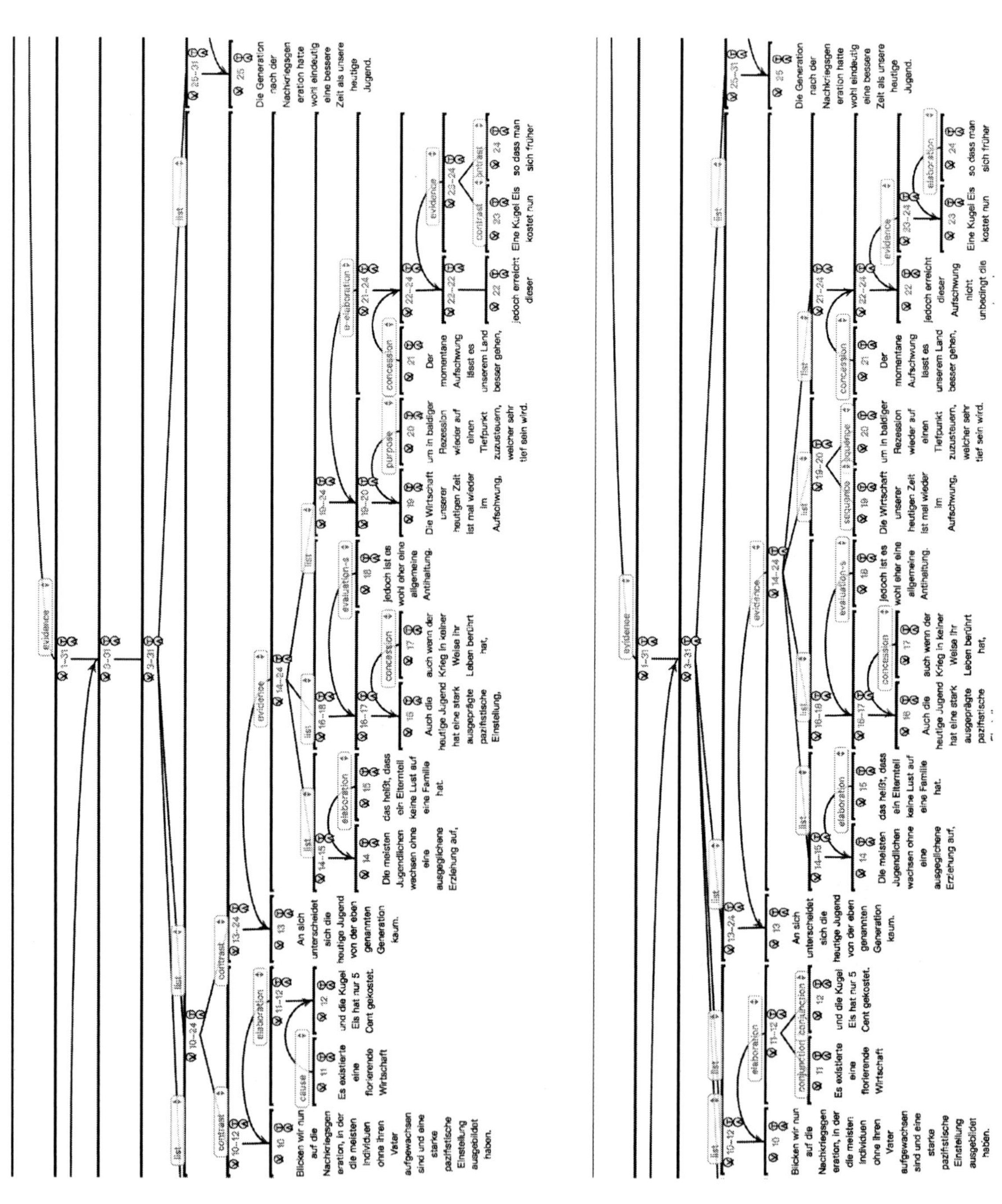

Figure 5: RST trees from two annotators. *DEU_006, RST German Learner Treebank*

ID	CS-A	Relation-A	Nuc-A	C1-A	C2-A	CN-A	A1-A	A2-A	AN-A	CS-B	Relation-B	Nuc-B	C1-B	C2-B	CN-B	A1-B	A2-B	AN-B	Matching	N	R	C	A
1	1	preparation	→	1	2	S	3	31	N	1	preparation	→	1	2	S	3	31	N	Completely identical CS	✓	✓	✓	✓
2	3-31	evidence	→	1	31	S	32	37	N	3-31	evidence	→	1	31	S	32	39	N	Completely identical CS	✓	✓	✓	✗
3	32-37|38-41	joint	↔	1	37	N	38	41	N										No matching	✗	✗	✗	✗
4										40-41	evaluation-s	←	40	41	S	1	39	N	No matching	✗	✗	✗	✗
5	2	reason	←	2	2	S	1	1	N	2	reason	←	2	2	S	1	1	N	Completely identical CS	✓	✓	✓	✓
6	3	background	→	3	3	S	4	4	N	3	background	→	3	3	S	4	4	N	Completely identical CS	✓	✓	✓	✓
7	3-7	evidence	→	3	7	S	8	8	N	3-7	evidence	→	3	7	S	8	8	N	Completely identical CS	✓	✓	✓	✓
8	8|9	contrast	↔	3	8	N	9	9	N	8|9	contrast	↔	3	8	N	9	9	N	Completely identical CS	✓	✓	✓	✓
9	4|5	contrast	↔	3	4	N	5	7	N	4|5	contrast	↔	3	4	N	5	7	N	Completely identical CS	✓	✓	✓	✓
10	3-9|10-24|25	list	↔	3	9	N	10	31	N	3-9|10|13|25	list	↔	3	9	N	10	31	N	C1=C2 and A1=A2	✓	✓	✓	✓
11	6	evidence	←	6	7	S	5	5	N	6	evidence	←	6	7	S	5	5	N	Completely identical CS	✓	✓	✓	✓
12	7	circumstance	←	7	7	S	6	6	N	7	condition	←	7	7	S	6	6	N	Completely identical CS	✓	✗	✓	✓
13	10-24|25	list	↔	10	24	N	25	31	N	10|13|25	list	↔	10	12	N	13	31	N	Partially identical CS	✓	✓	✓	✗
14	10|13	contrast	↔	10	12	N	13	24	N	13|25	list	↔	13	24	N	25	31	N	Partially identical CS	✓	✗	✗	✗
15	11	cause	→	11	11	S	12	12	N	11|12	conjunction	↔	11	11	N	12	12	N	C1=C2 and A1=A2	✗	✗	✗	✓
16	12	elaboration	←	11	12	S	10	10	N	11-12	elaboration	←	11	12	S	10	10	N	C1=C2 and A1=A2	✓	✓	✓	✓
17	14-24	evidence	←	14	24	S	13	13	N	14-24	evidence	←	14	24	S	13	13	N	Completely identical CS	✓	✓	✓	✓
18	14|16-17|19-20	list	↔	14	15	N	16	24	N	14|16-17|19-20|22-24	list	↔	14	15	N	16	24	N	C1=C2 and A1=A2	✓	✓	✓	✓
19	15	elaboration	←	15	15	S	14	14	N	15	elaboration	←	15	15	S	14	14	N	Completely identical CS	✓	✓	✓	✓
20	16-17|19-20	list	↔	16	18	N	19	24	N	16-17|19-20|22-24	list	↔	16	18	N	19	24	N	C1=C2 and A1=A2	✓	✓	✓	✓
21	17	concession	←	17	17	S	16	16	N	17	concession	←	17	17	S	16	16	N	Completely identical CS	✓	✓	✓	✓
22	18	evaluation-s	←	18	18	S	16	17	N	18	evaluation-s	←	18	18	S	16	17	N	Completely identical CS	✓	✓	✓	✓
23	20	purpose	←	20	20	S	19	19	N	19|20	sequence	↔	19	19	N	20	20	N	C1=A2 and A1=C2	✗	✗	✗	✗
24	21	concession	→	21	21	S	22	24	N	21	concession	→	21	21	S	22	24	N	Completely identical CS	✓	✓	✓	✓
25	22-24	e-elaboration	←	21	24	S	19	20	N	19-20|22-24	list	↔	19	20	N	21	24	N	C1=A2 and A1=C2	✗	✗	✗	✗
26	23-24	evidence	←	23	24	S	22	22	N	23	evidence	←	23	24	S	22	22	N	C1=C2 and A1=A2	✓	✗	✗	✗
27	23|24	contrast	↔	23	23	N	24	24	N	24	elaboration	←	24	24	S	23	23	N	C1=A2 and A1=C2	✗	✗	✗	✗
28	26-31	evidence	←	26	31	S	25	25	N	26-31	evidence	←	26	31	S	25	25	N	Completely identical CS	✓	✓	✓	✓
29	26|27|28|30|31	list	↔	26	26	N	27	31	N	26|27|28-30|31	list	↔	26	26	N	27	31	N	C1=C2 and A1=A2	✓	✓	✓	✓
30	27|28|30|31	list	↔	27	27	N	28	31	N	27|28-30|31	list	↔	27	27	N	28	31	N	C1=C2 and A1=A2	✓	✓	✓	✓
31	28|30|31	list	↔	28	28	N	29	31	N	28|29	list	↔	28	28	N	29	30	N	Partially identical CS	✓	✓	✓	✗
32	29	interpretation	→	29	29	S	30	30	N	30	elaboration	←	30	30	S	29	29	N	C1=A2 and A1=C2	✗	✗	✗	✗
33	30|31	list	↔	29	30	N	31	31	N	28-30|31	list	↔	28	30	N	31	31	N	Partially identical CS	✓	✓	✓	✗
34	32	concession	→	32	32	S	33	35	N	32	concession	→	32	32	S	33	35	N	Completely identical CS	✓	✓	✓	✓
35	33-35	antithesis	→	32	35	S	36	36	N	33-35	antithesis	→	32	35	S	36	39	N	Completely identical CS	✓	✓	✓	✗
36	36	reason	→	32	36	S	37	37	N	36	reason	→	36	36	S	37	37	N	Completely identical CS	✓	✓	✗	✓
37	34	circumstance	←	34	34	S	33	33	N	34	circumstance	←	34	34	S	33	33	N	Completely identical CS	✓	✓	✓	✓
38	35	evidence	←	35	35	S	33	34	N	35	evidence	←	35	35	S	33	34	N	Completely identical CS	✓	✓	✓	✓
39	38	circumstance	→	38	38	S	39	39	N	38	cause	→	38	38	S	39	39	N	Completely identical CS	✓	✗	✓	✓
40	39|40-41	joint	↔	38	39	N	40	41	N	39	elaboration	←	38	39	S	37	37	N	Partially identical CS	✗	✗	✗	✗
41	40|41	list	↔	40	40	N	41	41	N	40|41	list	↔	40	40	N	41	41	N	Completely identical CS	✓	✓	✓	✓

Results	Nuclearity	Relation	Constituent	Attachment point	RST trees
F-Measure:	(33 of 40) → 0.804	(30 of 41) → 0.731	(29 of 41) → 0.707	(29 of 41) → 0.707	0.737
Inter-Annotator Agreement:	0.71	0.698	0.57	0.59	0.567

Figure 6: Comparison table and the results for text *DEU_006, RST German Learner Treebank*, using RST-TACE

References

Iria da Cunha and Mikel Iruskieta. 2010. Comparing rhetorical structures in different languages: The influence of translation strategies. *Discourse Studies*, 12(5):563–598.

Debopam Das, Maite Taboada, and Manfred Stede. 2017. The Good , the Bad , and the Disagreement : Complex ground truth in rhetorical structure analysis. In *In workshop on Recent Advances in RST and Related Formalisms*, Santiago de Compostela, Spain.

Markus Egg and Gisela Redeker. 2010. How Complex is Discourse Structure ? How Complex is Discourse Structure ? (May 2014).

Mikel Iruskieta, Iria da Cunha, and Maite Taboada. 2015. A qualitative comparison method for rhetorical structures: identifying different discourse structures in multilingual corpora. *Language Resources and Evaluation*, 49(2):263–309.

H. W. Kuhn. 1955. The hungarian method for the assignment problem. *Naval Research Logistics Quarterly*, 2(1-2):83–97.

William C. Mann and Sandra A. Thompson. 1988. Rhetorical Structure Theory: Toward a functional theory of text organization. *Text*, 8(3):243–281.

Daniel Marcu. 2000. The Rhetorical Parsing of Unrestricted Texts: A Surface-based Approach. *Computational Linguistics*, 26(3):395–448.

E Maziero and Thiago AS Pardo. 2009. Metodologia de avaliação automática de estruturas retóricas. In *Proceedings of the III RST Meeting (7th Brazilian Symposium in Information and Human Language Technology), Brasil.*

Michael O'Donnell. 1997. RST-Tool: An RST analysis tool. *Proceedings of the 6th European Workshop on Natural Language Generation*, (March).

Manfred Stede. 2008. RST Revisited : Disentangling Nuclearity. In Benjamins, editor, *'Subordination' versus 'coordination' in sentence and text – from a cross-linguistic perspective.* Amsterdam.

Manfred Stede. 2016. *Handbuch Textannotation. Potsdamer Kommentarkorpus 2.0.* Universitätsverlag Potsdam, Potsdam.

Manfred Stede. 2017. Annotation Guidelines for Rhetorical Structure.

Amir Zeldes. 2016. rstWeb – A Browser-based Annotation Interface for Rhetorical Structure Theory and Discourse Relations. 2016:1–5.

Heike Zinsmeister, Marc Reznicek, Julia Ricart Brede, Christina Rosén, and Dirk Skiba. 2012. Das Wissenschaftliche Netzwerk „Kobalt-DaF". *Zeitschrift für germanistische Linguistik*, 40(3):457–458.

The DISRPT 2019 Shared Task on Elementary Discourse Unit Segmentation and Connective Detection *

Amir Zeldes
Georgetown University
az364@georgetown.edu

Debopam Das
University of Potsdam
ddas@sfu.ca

Erick Galani Maziero
Federal University of Lavras
erick.maziero@ufla.br

Juliano Desiderato Antonio
Universidade Estadual de Maringa
jdantonio@uem.br

Mikel Iruskieta
University of the Basque Country
mikel.iruskieta@ehu.eus

Abstract

In 2019, we organized the first iteration of a shared task dedicated to the underlying units used in discourse parsing across formalisms: the DISRPT Shared Task on Elementary Discourse Unit Segmentation and Connective Detection. In this paper we review the data included in the task, which cover 2.6 million manually annotated tokens from 15 datasets in 10 languages, survey and compare submitted systems and report on system performance on each task for both annotated and plain-tokenized versions of the data.

1 Introduction

The past few years have seen substantial advances in both the development of new discourse annotated corpora for diverse languages (e.g. Iruskieta et al. 2013, Zhou et al. 2014, Afantenos et al. 2012) and approaches to automatic discourse parsing relying on neural and other architectures (Braud et al. 2017, Wang and Lan 2015, Li et al. 2016, Perret et al. 2016). Across frameworks, most work producing substantial amounts of data in multiple languages has been developed within Rhetorical Structure Theory (Mann and Thompson, 1988), the Penn Discourse Treebank's framework (Prasad et al., 2014) and Segmented Discourse Representation Theory (Asher, 1993).

At the same time, there is reason to believe that performance on discourse parsing still has a substantial way to go (Morey et al., 2017), with scores on deep discourse parsing for well studied and homogeneous resources such as the English RST Discourse Treebank (Carlson et al., 2003) still well behind human annotators, and results

for other datasets, especially in less studied and lower resource languages lagging much farther behind. To make matters worse, the vast majority of deep discourse parsing papers work with gold segmented discourse units, which allow for easier comparisons of scores, but represent an unrealistically easy scenario. In their recent survey of discourse parsing results, Morey et al. (2017, 1322) point out that "all the parsers in [their] sample except [two] predict binary trees over manually segmented EDUs",[1] meaning that we have very limited information on the accuracy of discourse parsing in realistic settings. In order for discourse parsing to come closer to the reliability of syntactic parsing, a similarly reliable state of the art (SOA) for segmentation into terminal units must be reached.

The comparison with work on syntax parsing brings another point of interest into focus: the recent success of Universal Dependencies (Nivre et al., 2017) as a standard bringing together resources from different languages has been instrumental in creating generic NLP tools that are flexible and applicable to a variety of tasks. This is not only due to converging cross-linguistic annotation guidelines and the codification of a uniform format based on the CoNLL shared task datasets, but also due to the community building afforded by the organization of joint workshops which bring together researchers from a range of domains.

Within this landscape, the first multilingual and cross-framework task on discourse unit segmentation and connective detection aims to promote the development of reliable tools for working with the basic building blocks of discourse annotation. Although it is clear that there are substantial dif-

---

*Discourse Relation Parsing and Treebanking (DISRPT): 7th Workshop on Rhetorical Structure Theory and Related Formalisms (https://sites.google.com/view/disrpt2019) was held in conjunction with Annual Conference of the NAACL 2019 in Minneapolis, MN.

---

[1]EDUs or Elementary Discourse units are non-overlapping "minimal building blocks of a discourse tree" (Carlson et al., 2003). EDUs are, mostly, (sentences or) clauses, except for complement and restrictive clauses.

Proceedings of Discourse Relation Parsing and Treebanking (DISRPT2019), pages 97–104
Minneapolis, MN, June 6, 2019. ©2019 Association for Computational Linguistics

EDU segmentation

corpus	language	framework	sentences	tokens	documents	units
deu.rst.pcc	German	RST	2,193	33,222	176	3,018
eng.rst.gum	English	RST	5,274	98,615	114	7,311
eng.rst.rstdt	English	RST	8,318	205,824	385	21,789
eng.sdrt.stac	English	SDRT	10,020	47,741	41	11,531
eus.rst.ert	Basque	RST	1,660	35,313	140	2,910
fra.sdrt.annodis	French	SDRT	1,318	32,411	86	3,709
nld.rst.nldt	Dutch	RST	1,707	24,920	80	2,371
por.rst.cstn	Portuguese	RST	1,950	54,656	136	4,734
rus.rst.rrt	Russian	RST	12,513	272,664	178	19,906
spa.rst.rststb	Spanish	RST	2,136	58,591	267	3,349
spa.rst.sctb	Spanish	RST	478	16,512	50	744
zho.rst.sctb	Mandarin	RST	563	14,442	50	744

Connective detection

corpus	language	framework	sentences	tokens	documents	units
eng.pdtb.pdtb	English	PDTB	48,630	1,156,648	2,162	26,048
tur.pdtb.tdb	Turkish	PDTB	31,196	496,355	197	8,397
zho.pdtb.cdtb	Mandarin	PDTB	2,891	73,314	164	1,660

Table 1: Datasets in the DISRPT 2019 shared task.

ferences in guidelines and goals across different formalisms and datasets, we hope that the shared task will contribute to a broad discussion of discourse annotation standards and goals, and put less studied resources in focus, next to more frequently addressed corpora such as PDTB (Prasad et al., 2008) and RST-DT (Carlson et al., 2003). Additionally, the release of the DISRPT 2019 shared task dataset[2] in a uniform format, modeled on the CoNLL-U format used by Universal Dependencies, is meant as a first step in creating a multilingual testing grounds for discourse parsing systems, starting with the basic task of identifying the minimal locus at which discourse relations apply: discourse units and connectives.

2 Shared task data

The DISRPT 2019 shared task dataset comprises 15 datasets in 10 languages, 12 of which target elementary discourse unit segmentation, and 3 dedicated to explicit connective annotation. Table 1 gives an overview of the datasets. Of the 15 datasets, 14 were released approximately 1.5 months before the shared task deadline, while the final one, connective annotations from the Turkish Discourse Bank, was released as a 'surprise' dataset/language together with dev and test sets just two weeks before the announced deadline. For four of the datasets, licensing constraints prevented online publication of the underlying texts (e.g. Wall Street Journal material), meaning that the public repository contains only annotations

for those corpora, with tokens replaced by underscores. A script included in the shared task repository was provided in order to reconstruct the data, which requires users to have access to the original LDC releases of the underlying corpora.

The short names for every dataset begin with an ISO 639-3 three letter code for the language, a framework designation (RST/SDRT/PDTB) and an acronym for the corpus. The names correspond to the following included corpora:

— deu.rst.pcc - Potsdam Commentary Corpus (Stede and Neumann, 2014).

— eng.pdtb.pdtb - Penn Discourse Treebank (Prasad et al., 2014).

— eng.rst.gum - Georgetown University Multilayer corpus (Zeldes, 2017).

— eng.rst.rstdt - RST Discourse Treebank (Carlson et al., 2003).

— eng.sdrt.stac - Strategic Conversations corpus (Asher et al., 2016).

— eus.rst.ert - Basque RST Treebank (Iruskieta et al., 2013).

— fra.sdrt.annodis - ANNOtation DIScursive (Afantenos et al., 2012).

— nld.rst.nldt - Dutch Discourse Treebank (Redeker et al., 2012).

— por.rst.cstn - Cross-document Structure Theory News Corpus (Cardoso et al., 2011).

— rus.rst.rrt - Russian RST Treebank (Toldova et al., 2017).

---

[2]https://github.com/disrpt/sharedtask2019.

```
# sent_id = GUM_interview_stardust-23
# text = Yes [see below].
1    Yes    yes    INTJ   UH                                        _    0    root        _    BeginSeg=Yes
2    [      [      PUNCT  -LSB-                                     _    3    punct       _    BeginSeg=Yes|SpaceAfter=No

3    see    see    VERB   VBP    Mood=Ind|Tense=Pres|VerbForm=Fin   _    1    parataxis   _    _
4    below  below  ADV    RB                                        _    3    advmod      _    SpaceAfter=No
5    ]      ]      PUNCT  -RSB-                                     _    3    punct       _    SpaceAfter=No
6    .      .      PUNCT  .                                         _    1    punct       _    _
--------------------------------------------------------------------------------------------------------------
411  Yes    _      _      _                                         _    _    _           _    BeginSeg=Yes
412  [      _      _      _                                         _    _    _           _    BeginSeg=Yes
413  see    _      _      _                                         _    _    _           _    _
414  below  _      _      _                                         _    _    _           _    _
415  ]      _      _      _                                         _    _    _           _    _
416  .      _      _      _                                         _    _    _           _    _
```

Figure 1: Data formats: treebanked (*.conll, top) and plain (*.tok, bottom)

— spa.rst.rststb - RST Spanish Treebank (da Cunha et al., 2011).

— spa.rst.sctb - RST Spanish-Chinese Treebank (Spanish) (Shuyuan et al., 2018).

— tur.pdtb.tdb - Turkish Discourse Bank (Zeyrek et al., 2010).

— zho.pdtb.cdtb - Chinese Discourse Treebank (Zhou et al., 2014).

— zho.rst.sctb - RST Spanish-Chinese Treebank (Chinese) (Shuyuan et al., 2018).

As Table 1 shows, these datasets range from small (under 15,000 tokens for the smallest corpus, zho.rst.sctb), to the larger RST corpora (over 200,000 tokens for RST-DT and the Russian RST Treebank), to the largest PDTB-style datasets (almost half a million tokens for Turkish, and over a million for the English PDTB). The variability in sizes, languages, frameworks, and corpus-specific annotation guidelines were expected to challenge systems, but also promote architectures which can be extended to more languages in the future, and ideally stay robust for low resource settings.

Data was released for all corpora in two formats, corresponding to two scenarios: Treebanked data (*.conll), which included an (ideally gold) dependency parse, including gold sentence splits and POS tags, and unannotated, plain tokens (*.tok). For datasets that had Universal POS tags and/or UD dependencies, including these was preferred, though we followed the CoNLL-U format's convention of allowing two POS tag fields (UPOS for universal tags, XPOS for language specific tags), a morphology field with unlimited morphological annotations, and a secondary dependency field (only used in the Dutch dataset). The tenth column (MISC in CoNLL-U) was used for gold standard labels and additional annotations (e.g. SpaceAfter to indicate whitespace in underlying data), which all followed the CoNLL-U key=value format: BeginSeg=Yes for EDU segmentation and BI tags for connectives, Seg=B-Conn and Seg=I-Conn, versus _ for unannotated tokens. The second scenario included no annotations except for tokenization and the same document boundary annotations found in the treebanked files. No sentence splits were provided in this scenario. Figure 1 illustrates both formats.

The shared task repository also contained an evaluation script to score systems on each dataset. For both evaluations, we opted to compute precision, recall and F1 score on discourse unit segmentation and connective detection, micro-averaged within each dataset, and macro-averaged results across all corpora for each system in each scenario (treebank/plain tokens). Similarly to evaluation of NER performance, scores reward only the positive classes, i.e. precision and recall of segmentation is judged purely based on identification of segmentation points, with no reward for recognizing negative cases.

For connective detection, the evaluation targets exact span retrieval, meaning that precision and recall are calculated out of the total connective spans (not tokens) available in the gold data. This means that partial credit was not given: a system identifying the span in Example (1) is given one precision error and one recall error, since it misses the gold span and invents one not present in gold data.

(1)   Gold: In/B-Conn order/I-Conn to/_
       Pred: In/B-Conn order/I-Conn to/I-Conn

Dataset	ToNy			GumDrop			DFKI RF			IXA			Mean
(treebanked)	P	R	F	P	R	F	P	R	F	P	R	F	
deu.rst.pcc	95.22	94.76	**94.99**	93.33	90.48	91.88	95.33	83.33	88.93	90.91	91.84	91.37	91.86
eng.rst.gum	95.84	90.74	93.21	96.47	90.77	**93.53**	97.96	83.71	90.27	95.52	88.61	91.94	92.38
eng.rst.rstdt	95.29	96.81	**96.04**	94.88	96.46	95.67	93.65	85.47	89.37	94.56	94.93	94.75	93.99
eng.sdrt.stac	94.34	96.22	95.27	95.26	95.39	**95.32**	97.65	91.94	94.71	92.51	90.71	91.60	94.24
eus.rst.ert	89.77	82.87	**86.18**	90.89	74.03	81.60	92.77	60.54	73.27	91.19	80.27	85.38	82.40
fra.sdrt.annodis	94.42	88.12	**91.16**	94.38	86.47	90.25	94.04	81.18	87.13	91.10	90.50	90.79	89.96
nld.rst.nldt	97.90	89.59	93.56	96.44	94.48	**95.45**	98.38	88.08	92.95	90.91	93.02	91.95	93.60
por.rst.cstn	92.78	93.06	**92.92**	91.77	89.92	90.84	93.18	77.36	84.54	93.01	92.38	92.69	90.37
rus.rst.rrt	86.65	79.49	**82.91**	83.47	75.52	79.30	82.79	67.51	74.37	73.22	74.11	73.67	77.75
spa.rst.rststb	92.03	89.52	**90.74**	89.02	81.80	85.26	93.01	76.54	83.99	85.68	87.94	86.80	86.86
spa.rst.sctb	91.43	76.19	**83.12**	89.76	67.86	77.29	95.28	60.12	73.72	93.22	65.48	76.92	79.20
zho.rst.sctb	87.07	76.19	81.27	80.95	80.95	80.95	88.81	75.60	**81.67**	90.37	73.57	81.11	81.54
mean	92.73	87.80	**90.11**	91.38	85.34	88.11	93.57	77.61	84.58	90.18	85.28	87.41	87.84

Table 2: EDU segmentation results on treebanked data.

3 Results

We report precision, recall and F1 for systems in the two tasks, each consisting of two scenarios: EDU segmentation and connective detection, with treebanked and plain tokenized data. Four systems were submitted to the shared task, all of which attempted the EDU segmentation task, and three of which also approached the connective detection task for at least some datasets. For teams that submitted multiple systems, we selected the system that achieved the best macro-averaged F-score across datasets as the representative submission.

3.1 EDU segmentation

The main results for EDU segmentation on the test sets are given in Table 2 for treebanked data, and in Table 3 for plain tokenized data. No one system performs best on all corpora, suggesting that the different approaches have different merits in different settings. Overall, ToNy (Muller et al., 2019) performs best on the most datasets, and on average has the highest F-scores (90.11, computed by averaging five runs of the system, since GPU training was not deterministic). The next best systems by average F-score are GumDrop (Yu et al. 2019, 88.11 F_1), IXA (Iruskieta et al. 2019, 87.18 F_1) and DFKI RF (Bourgonje and Schäfer 2019, 84.56 F_1).

For the treebanked scenario, the best configuration for ToNy (using contextualized Bert embeddings, Devlin et al. 2018), receives the highest F-score on 8 datasets, the next best system, GumDrop, does so on 3 datasets, and DFKI's system on one: the Chinese RST dataset, which is notably the smallest one in the shared task with around 14,000 tokens.

Results for all systems show clearly that preci-sion is usually higher than recall across the board. This suggests that some 'safe' strategies, such as assuming segment boundaries at the beginnings of sentences (which are gold standard split in most cases), yield good results, with the challenge being much more the identification of non-obvious segmentation points within sentences. Another obvious trend is the comparatively high performance on datasets that are large and gold-treebanked. The counterexample to the generalization that large corpora fare well is rus.rst.rrt, which can be explained by the lack of gold parses for this dataset, as well as some tricky conventions, such as handling segmentation differently within academic abstracts and bibliographies.

For the established RST benchmark dataset, RST-DT, two systems exceed the previous state of the art score (93.7, Bach et al. 2012), suggesting substantial progress (ToNy: 96.04; GumDrop: 95.67) compared to results previous to the shared task. For other languages, previous benchmark results using different corpora include F-scores of 80 for Spanish (Da Cunha et al., 2010), 73 for French (Afantenos et al., 2010), 83 for Basque (Iruskieta and Zapirain, 2015) and between 88 and 93 for German (Sidarenka et al., 2015).

For automatically parsed data, two systems submitted results, and results were extracted for a third system by shared task testers. The two systems that included results for this scenario in their papers were conincidentally also the top scoring systems overall, suggesting that numbers may represent the state of the art for this task. Inria's system ToNy achieves top performance on all but one dataset, and the best average F-score, possibly owing to the document-level model adopted by the system, in addition to the use of contextualized embeddings (see Section 4). Both top sys-

Dataset	ToNy			GumDrop			DFKI RF			Mean
(plain)	P	R	F	P	R	F	P	R	F	
deu.rst.pcc	94.88	94.49	**94.68**	91.99	89.80	90.88	94.20	71.77	81.47	89.35
eng.rst.gum	92.28	82.89	**87.33**	94.03	77.22	84.80	90.29	64.17	75.02	83.11
eng.rst.rstdt	93.60	93.27	**93.43**	89.56	91.43	90.49	45.96	35.85	40.28	74.87
eng.sdrt.stac	87.56	80.78	**83.99**	84.24	77.45	80.70	80.21	50.30	61.82	76.34
eus.rst.ert	87.43	80.94	**84.06**	90.06	73.36	80.86	88.21	58.01	69.99	79.21
fra.sdrt.annodis	94.31	89.15	**91.65**	94.46	85.29	89.64	93.47	67.35	78.29	87.07
nld.rst.nldt	94.81	89.97	**92.32**	94.72	88.41	91.45	95.14	68.12	79.39	88.26
por.rst.cstn	93.04	90.72	**91.86**	92.95	85.08	88.84	90.82	67.17	77.22	86.41
rus.rst.rrt	83.37	78.44	**80.83**	82.06	74.84	78.28	57.27	42.11	48.53	69.53
spa.rst.rststb	89.11	90.09	**89.60**	87.50	79.82	83.49	89.23	63.60	74.26	82.97
spa.rst.sctb	87.16	76.79	**81.65**	85.27	65.48	74.07	88.35	54.17	67.16	75.57
zho.rst.sctb	66.26	64.29	65.26	76.97	69.64	**73.13**	85.71	57.14	68.57	69.66
mean	88.65	84.31	**86.38**	88.65	79.82	83.89	83.24	58.31	68.5	80.19

Table 3: EDU segmentation results on plain tokenized data.

tems exceed the previous SOA of 89.5 on unparsed RST-DT: Georgetown's system GumDrop reaches 90.49, and ToNy achieves a remarkable 93.43, almost as high as previous results on gold parsed data. GumDrop performs better by a wide margin on the small Chinese dataset, but is overall well behind on many of the larger datasets, and about 2.5 F-score points lower on average than the best system, ToNy.

3.2 Connective detection

The main results for connective detection are given in Table 4. Three systems approached this task, though the DFKI system was not adapted substantially from the segmentation scenario, leading to low performance (Bourgonje and Schäfer, 2019), and did not report results on automatically parsed data.

ToNy again has the highest scores for the most datasets, obtaining the highest mean F-score for the plain tokenized scenario, and coming second to GumDrop only on the Turkish dataset in the gold syntax scenario. The margin for this particular result is however very wide, with GumDrop leading by almost 10 points, resulting in GumDrop obtaining the highest average F-score on gold syntax connective detection (though this score is in fact below the best plain tokenized result). This surprising result remained robust across 5 runs of the ToNy system (GumDrop was deterministically seeded and therefore reproducible in a single run).

Overall the connective detection results demonstrate that syntax is not central to the task (treebanked and plain results are close) and that accuracy is correlated with dataset size, presumably because the inventory of possible explicit connectives and their disambiguating environments is

more exhaustively attested as the dataset grows.

4 Analysis of systems

The four systems submitted to the task all use either RNNs with word embeddings (ToNy, IXA), decision tree ensembles on linguistic features (DFKI's best system) or both (GumDrop). For two of the systems approaching both shared tasks, the same architecture is used for both connective detection and EDU segmentation, whereas GumDrop uses a slightly different architecture in each case. The high performance of ToNy on both tasks is remarkable in that a generic sequence labeling approach achieves excellent results despite not using engineered features or a tailored learning approach.

Looking at the internal distribution of scores for each system, we can observe that ToNy performs well on some of the less consistent resources, in particular for the automatically parsed and segmented Russian data, which all other systems degrade on, and on corpora with automatic parses but gold or very high quality sentence splits, such as the Spanish datasets and German. For some of the corpora with gold parses in the gold scenario, GumDrop takes the lead, perhaps thanks to the use of a large number of linguistic features next to character and word embeddings (notably for GUM, which has manually produced dependencies, rather than conversion from constituents in RST-DT).

ToNy's high scores on almost all datasets in the plain tokenized scenario seem to be related not only to contextualized embeddings substituting for missing morphosyntactic information, but also to the whole-document or large chunk approach (see Muller et al. 2019), which makes reli-

Dataset	ToNy			GumDrop			DFKI RF		
(treebanked)	P	R	F	P	R	F	P	R	F
eng.pdtb.pdtb	89.39	87.84	**88.60**	87.91	88.78	88.35	84.84	74.64	79.41
tur.pdtb.tdb	76.89	64.00	69.85	76.69	81.86	**79.19**	72.29	62.63	67.11
zho.pdtb.cdtb	82.67	76.25	**79.32**	81.27	70.22	75.35	73.21	43.22	54.35
mean	82.98	76.03	79.25	81.91	80.21	**80.93**	76.78	60.16	66.96
(plain)	P	R	F	P	R	F	P	R	F
eng.pdtb.pdtb	91.32	87.84	**89.54**	84.56	82.81	83.68	–	–	–
tur.pdtb.tdb	84.06	86.74	**85.37**	76.76	81.74	79.17	–	–	–
zho.pdtb.cdtb	81.64	71.07	**75.99**	80.62	67.31	73.37	–	–	–
mean	85.67	81.88	**83.63**	80.65	77.29	78.77	–	–	–

Table 4: Connective detection results.

able sentence splitting less crucial. At the same time, the performance advantage of the system is not found for the smallest corpus, zho.rst.sctb. DFKI was able to perform substantially better than ToNy for the gold scenario, while the next best system, GumDrop, takes the lead for Chinese on plain data, perhaps thanks to a high accuracy ensemble sentence splitter included in the system. The higher scores on this corpus for both DFKI and GumDrop, which employ Gradient Boosting and/or Random Forests, may suggest that the robustness of tree ensembles against overfitting allows for better generalization to the test data in the lowest resource scenario.

For connective detection, the best DFKI system using Random Forests does not attain good scores, probably due to the need to memorize sequences of vocabulary items. For English PDTB, ToNy and GumDrop are very close, suggesting that both systems can memorize the inventory of connectives and disambiguate ambiguous cases with similar success. For the smaller datasets, with the exception of the unexpectedly low performance on gold Turkish, ToNy has a more substantial lead. It is also worth noting that in 4/6 scenarios (all but Chinese), GumDrop has higher recall than precision, while ToNy has higher precision than recall in 5/6 scenarios, perhaps pointing to imbalanced learning issues for the latter versus weaker disambiguation capacity for the former.

5 Conclusion

By organizing the first shared task on EDU segmentation and connective detection, we hope to have pushed the field further in terms of bringing together resources and researchers from related fields, and making systems available that are flexible enough to tackle different datatset guidelines, but accurate enough to form the basis for deeper discourse parsing tasks in the future.

One particular point of progress has been making an official scorer and providing data in a uniform format based on the popular CoNLL-U specification used by Universal Dependencies. We expect this will make it easier to provide discourse annotations together with manually treebanked or automatically parsed data, as well as to compare future results with scores from this shared task. We also plan to maintain the DISRPT dataset and possibly extend it for future editions of the workshop.

References

Stergos Afantenos, Nicholas Asher, Farah Benamara, Myriam Bras, Ccile Fabre, Mai Ho-dac, Anne Le Draoulec, Philippe Muller, Marie-Paule Pry-Woodley, Laurent Prvot, Josette Rebeyrolle, Ludovic Tanguy, Marianne Vergez-Couret, and Laure Vieu. 2012. An empirical resource for discovering cognitive principles of discourse organisation: The ANNODIS corpus. In *Proceedings of LREC 2012*, pages 2727–2734, Istanbul, Turkey.

Stergos Afantenos, Pascal Denis, Philippe Muller, and Laurence Danlos. 2010. Learning recursive segments for discourse parsing. *arXiv preprint arXiv:1003.5372*.

Nicholas Asher. 1993. *Reference to Abstract Objects in Discourse*. Kluwer, Dordrecht.

Nicholas Asher, Julie Hunter, Mathieu Morey, Farah Benamara, and Stergos D. Afantenos. 2016. Discourse structure and dialogue acts in multiparty dialogue: the STAC corpus. In *Proceedings of LREC 2016*, pages 2721–2727, Portorož, Slovenia.

Ngo Xuan Bach, Nguyen Le Minh, and Akira Shimazu. 2012. A reranking model for discourse segmentation using subtree features. In *Proceedings of SIGDial 2012*, pages 160–168, Seoul, South Korea.

Peter Bourgonje and Robin Schäfer. 2019. Multilingual and cross-genre discourse unit segmentation.

In *Proceedings of Discourse Relation Treebanking and Parsing (DISRPT 2019)*, Minneapolis, MN.

Chloé Braud, Maximin Coavoux, and Anders Søgaard. 2017. Cross-lingual RST Discourse Parsing. In *Proceedings of EACL 2017*, pages 292–304, Valencia, Spain.

Paula Christina Figueira Cardoso, Erick Galani Maziero, Maria Lucía del Rosario Castro Jorge, M. Eloize, R. Kibar Aji Seno, Ariani Di Felippo, Lucia Helena Machado Rino, Maria das Graças Volpe Nunes, and Thiago Alexandre Salgueiro Pardo. 2011. CSTNews - a discourse-annotated corpus for single and multi-document summarization of news texts in Brazilian Portuguese. In *Proceedings of the 3rd RST Brazilian Meeting*, pages 88–105, Cuiabá, Brazil.

Lynn Carlson, Daniel Marcu, and Mary Ellen Okurowski. 2003. Building a discourse-tagged corpus in the framework of Rhetorical Structure Theory. In *Current and New Directions in Discourse and Dialogue*, Text, Speech and Language Technology 22, pages 85–112. Kluwer, Dordrecht.

Iria da Cunha, Juan-Manuel Torres-Moreno, and Gerardo Sierra. 2011. On the development of the RST Spanish Treebank. In *Proceedings of the Fifth Linguistic Annotation Workshop (LAW V)*, pages 1–10, Portland, OR.

Iria Da Cunha, Eric SanJuan, Juan-Manuel Torres-Moreno, Marina Lloberes, and Irene Castellón. 2010. Discourse segmentation for Spanish based on shallow parsing. In *Mexican International Conference on Artificial Intelligence*, pages 13–23. Springer.

Jacob Devlin, Ming-Wei Chang, Kenton Lee, and Kristina Toutanova. 2018. BERT: Pre-training of deep bidirectional transformers for language understanding.

Mikel Iruskieta, María Jesús Aranzabe, Arantza Diaz de Ilarraza, Itziar Gonzalez-Dios, Mikel Lersundi, and Oier Lopez de Lacalle. 2013. The RST Basque TreeBank: An online search interface to check rhetorical relations. In *4th Workshop on RST and Discourse Studies*, pages 40–49, Fortaleza, Brasil.

Mikel Iruskieta, Kepa Bengoetxea, Aitziber Atutxa, and Arantza Diaz de Ilarraza. 2019. Multilingual segmentation based on neural networks and pre-trained word embeddings. In *Proceedings of Discourse Relation Treebanking and Parsing (DISRPT 2019)*, Minneapolis, MN.

Mikel Iruskieta and Benat Zapirain. 2015. Euseduseg: A dependency-based EDU segmentation for Basque. *Procesamiento del Lenguaje Natural*, 55:41–48.

Qi Li, Tianshi Li, and Baobao Chang. 2016. Discourse parsing with attention-based hierarchical neural networks. In *Proceedings of EMNLP 2016*, pages 362–371, Austin, TX.

William C. Mann and Sandra A. Thompson. 1988. Rhetorical Structure Theory: Toward a functional theory of text organization. *Text*, 8(3):243–281.

Mathieu Morey, Philippe Muller, and Nicholas Asher. 2017. How much progress have we made on RST discourse parsing? A replication study of recent results on the RST-DT. In *Proceedings of EMNLP 2017*, pages 1319–1324, Copenhagen, Denmark.

Philippe Muller, Chloé Braud, and Mathieu Morey. 2019. ToNy: Contextual embeddings for accurate multilingual discourse segmentation of full documents. In *Proceedings of Discourse Relation Treebanking and Parsing (DISRPT 2019)*, Minneapolis, MN.

Joakim Nivre, Željko Agić, Lars Ahrenberg, Maria Jesus Aranzabe, Masayuki Asahara, Aitziber Atutxa, Miguel Ballesteros, John Bauer, Kepa Bengoetxea, Riyaz Ahmad Bhat, Eckhard Bick, Cristina Bosco, Gosse Bouma, Sam Bowman, Marie Candito, Gülşen Cebiroğlu Eryiğit, Giuseppe G. A. Celano, Fabricio Chalub, Jinho Choi, Çağrı Çöltekin, Miriam Connor, Elizabeth Davidson, Marie-Catherine de Marneffe, Valeria de Paiva, Arantza Diaz de Ilarraza, Kaja Dobrovoljc, Timothy Dozat, Kira Droganova, Puneet Dwivedi, Marhaba Eli, Tomaž Erjavec, Richárd Farkas, Jennifer Foster, Cláudia Freitas, Katarína Gajdošová, Daniel Galbraith, Marcos Garcia, Filip Ginter, Iakes Goenaga, Koldo Gojenola, Memduh Gökırmak, Yoav Goldberg, Xavier Gómez Guinovart, Berta Gonzáles Saavedra, Matias Grioni, Normunds Grūzītis, Bruno Guillaume, Nizar Habash, Jan Hajič, Linh Hà Mỹ, Dag Haug, Barbora Hladká, Petter Hohle, Radu Ion, Elena Irimia, Anders Johannsen, Fredrik Jørgensen, Hüner Kaşıkara, Hiroshi Kanayama, Jenna Kanerva, Natalia Kotsyba, Simon Krek, Veronika Laippala, Lê Hông, Alessandro Lenci, Nikola Ljubešić, Olga Lyashevskaya, Teresa Lynn, Aibek Makazhanov, Christopher Manning, Cătălina Mărănduc, David Mareček, Héctor Martínez Alonso, André Martins, Jan Mašek, Yuji Matsumoto, Ryan McDonald, Anna Missilä, Verginica Mititelu, Yusuke Miyao, Simonetta Montemagni, Amir More, Shunsuke Mori, Bohdan Moskalevskyi, Kadri Muischnek, Nina Mustafina, Kaili Müürisep, Luong Nguyễn Thị, Huyền Nguyễn Thị Minh, Vitaly Nikolaev, Hanna Nurmi, Stina Ojala, Petya Osenova, Lilja Øvrelid, Elena Pascual, Marco Passarotti, Cenel-Augusto Perez, Guy Perrier, Slav Petrov, Jussi Piitulainen, Barbara Plank, Martin Popel, Lauma Pretkalniņa, Prokopis Prokopidis, Tiina Puolakainen, Sampo Pyysalo, Alexandre Rademaker, Loganathan Ramasamy, Livy Real, Laura Rituma, Rudolf Rosa, Shadi Saleh, Manuela Sanguinetti, Baiba Saulīte, Sebastian Schuster, Djamé Seddah, Wolfgang Seeker, Mojgan Seraji, Lena Shakurova, Mo Shen, Dmitry Sichinava, Natalia Silveira, Maria Simi, Radu Simionescu, Katalin Simkó, Mária Šimková, Kiril Simov, Aaron Smith, Alane Suhr, Umut Sulubacak, Zsolt Szántó, Dima Taji, Takaaki Tanaka, Reut Tsarfaty, Francis Tyers, Sumire Uematsu, Larraitz Uria, Gertjan van Noord, Viktor Varga, Veronika Vincze, Jonathan North Washington, Zdeněk Žabokrtský, Amir Zeldes, Daniel Zeman, and Hanzhi Zhu. 2017. Universal dependencies 2.0. Technical report, LINDAT/CLARIN digital library at the Institute of Formal and Applied Linguistics (ÚFAL), Faculty of Mathematics and Physics, Charles University.

Jerémy Perret, Stergos Afantenos, Nicholas Asher, and Mathieu Morey. 2016. Integer linear programming for discourse parsing. In *Proceedings of NAACL 2016*, pages 99–109, San Diego, CA.

Rashmi Prasad, Nikhil Dinesh, Alan Lee, Eleni Miltsakaki, Livio Robaldo, Aravind Joshi, and Bonnie Webber. 2008. The Penn Discourse Treebank 2.0. In *Proceedings of the 6th International Conference on Language Resources and Evaluation (LREC 2008)*, pages 2961–2968, Marrakesh, Morocco.

Rashmi Prasad, Bonnie Webber, and Aravind Joshi. 2014. Reflections on the Penn Discourse TreeBank, comparable corpora, and complementary annotation. *Computational Linguistics*, 40(4):921–950.

Gisela Redeker, Ildikó Berzlánovich, Nynke van der Vliet, Gosse Bouma, and Markus Egg. 2012. Multilayer discourse annotation of a Dutch text corpus. In *Proceedings of LREC 2012*, pages 2820–2825, Istanbul, Turkey.

Cao Shuyuan, Iria da Cunha, and Mikel Iruskieta. 2018. The RST Spanish-Chinese Treebank. In *Proceedings of the Joint Workshop of Linguistic Annotation, Multiword Expression and Constructions (LAW-MWE-CxG-2018)*, pages 156–166, Santa Fe, NM.

Uladzimir Sidarenka, Andreas Peldszus, and Manfred Stede. 2015. Discourse segmentation of German texts. *JLCL*, 30(1):71–98.

Manfred Stede and Arne Neumann. 2014. Potsdam Commentary Corpus 2.0: Annotation for discourse research. In *Proceedings of the Language Resources and Evaluation Conference (LREC '14)*, pages 925–929, Reykjavik.

Svetlana Toldova, Dina Pisarevskaya, Margarita Ananyeva, Maria Kobozeva, Alexander Nasedkin, Sofia Nikiforova, Irina Pavlova, and Alexey Shelepov. 2017. Rhetorical relation markers in Russian RST Treebank. In *Proceedings of the 6th Workshop Recent Advances in RST and Related Formalisms*, pages 29–33, Santiago de Compostela, Spain.

Jianxiang Wang and Man Lan. 2015. A refined end-to-end discourse parser. In *Proceedings of CoNLL 2015*, pages 17–24, Beijing.

Yue Yu, Yilun Zhu, Yang Liu, Yan Liu, Siyao Peng, Mackenzie Gong, and Amir Zeldes. 2019. GumDrop at the DISRPT2019 shared task: A model stacking approach to discourse unit segmentation and connective detection. In *Proceedings of Discourse Relation Treebanking and Parsing (DISRPT 2019)*, Minneapolis, MN.

Amir Zeldes. 2017. The GUM corpus: Creating multilayer resources in the classroom. *Language Resources and Evaluation*, 51(3):581–612.

Deniz Zeyrek, Işın Demirşahin, Ayışığı B. Sevdik Çallı, and Ruket Çakıcı. 2010. The first question generation shared task evaluation challenge. *Dialogue and Discourse*, 3:75–99.

Yuping Zhou, Jill Lu, Jennifer Zhang, and Nianwen Xue. 2014. Chinese Discourse Treebank 0.5 LDC2014T21.

Multi-lingual and Cross-genre Discourse Unit Segmentation

Peter Bourgonje and Robin Schäfer

Applied Computational Linguistics
University of Potsdam / Germany
`firstname.lastname@uni-potsdam.de`

Abstract

We describe a series of experiments applied
to data sets from different languages and
genres annotated for coherence relations according to different theoretical frameworks.
Specifically, we investigate the feasibility of a
unified (theory-neutral) approach toward discourse segmentation; a process which divides
a text into minimal discourse units that are involved in some coherence relation. We apply a RandomForest and an LSTM based approach for all data sets, and we improve over
a simple baseline assuming simple sentence or
clause-like segmentation. Performance however varies a lot depending on language, and
more importantly genre, with f-scores ranging
from 73.00 to 94.47.

1 Introduction

The last few decades have seen several different theories and frameworks being proposed for
the task of *discourse processing*, or *discourse
parsing*; the analysis and (automatic) extraction
of coherence relations from a text. Among the
most popular approaches are Rhetorical Structure
Theory (RST) (Mann and Thompson, 1988), the
Penn Discourse Treebank (PDTB) (Prasad et al.,
2008), Segmented Discourse Representation Theory (SDRT) (Asher et al., 2003) and the Cognitive
approach to Coherence Relations (CCR) (Sanders
et al., 1992). While each of these approaches may
serve a different purpose or have a specific focus,
to a certain extent they all rely on segmenting texts
into segments that express specific propositions
which make up the arguments or components of
some relation. The 2019 DISRPT workshop aims
to contribute to a shared understanding of coherence relations by providing training and evaluation data from several available treebanks in the
RST, SDRT and PDTB formalisms. Because each
of these formalisms have their specific character-

istics for the various stages of analyses (i.e. differences in segmentation, relation inventory, flat or
tree-like representations, etc.) the shared task[1] accompanying the workshop is meant to promote the
design of flexible methods for dealing with these
differences. The focus is on the first (and com-
parably easiest) step in the process; segmenting a
text into minimal units, as a standard for discourse
segmentation would, in addition to a better general understanding, allow treebanks or resources
annotated according to one theoretical framework
to help in (manually or automatically) annotating
data according to other frameworks. In this paper we describe a set of experiments using the collection of data sets provided in the context of the
shared task, including nine different languages and
a variety of genres.

The rest of the paper is structured as follows:
Section 2 describes related work in this direction.
Section 3 describes the three formalisms that are
present among the data sets and the data sets themselves. Section 4 describes our approach toward
the segmentation task. Sections 5 and 6 present
and discuss the results, respectively, and finally,
Section 7 sums up our approach and main findings.

2 Related Work

Since the introduction of RST in Mann and
Thompson (1988), several discourse parser for English have been proposed ((Soricut and Marcu,
2003), (Hernault et al., 2010), (Ji and Eisenstein,
2014), (Joty et al., 2015)). Additionally, the release of the PDTB (Prasad et al., 2008) helped further enabling machine-learning approaches toward
shallow discourse parsing through its relatively
large size (compared to RST and also SDRT cor-

---

[1] `https://github.com/disrpt/`
`sharedtask2019`

Proceedings of Discourse Relation Parsing and Treebanking (DISRPT2019), pages 105–114
Minneapolis, MN, June 6, 2019. ©2019 Association for Computational Linguistics

pora). More recently, the 2015 and 2016 CoNLL shared tasks, following the PDTB framework, sparked interest for the task of shallow discourse parsing, with Wang and Lan (2015) and Oepen et al. (2016) as winning systems, respectively. The tasks featured both English and Chinese discourse parsing. With the generation of several treebanks in other languages over the last decade(s) (see Table 1 in Section 3 for an overview), training and evaluation data became available for several other languages as well (where before systems had to be rule-based, as the one described in Pardo and Nunes (2008)). On the topic of multi-lingual parsing, Braud et al. (2017) describe a cross-lingual approach to RST parsing, using 6 of the 9 corpora used in our experiments, but use language-specific segmenters for the languages they work with (Basque, Dutch, English, German, Spanish and Brazilian Portuguese). Iruskieta et al. (2016) look at a particular kind of segment and detect central units in both Basque and Brazilian Portuguese, where they define central units (CUs) to be units that "(do) not function as satellite of any other unit or text span.". Earlier work on unifying discourse parsing frameworks is described in Rehbein et al. (2016), Benamara and Taboada (2015), Bunt and Prasad (2016), Chiarcos (2014) and Sanders et al. (2018) from a theoretical perspective, and in Demberg et al. (2017) from a practical perspective, but their main focus is on relation senses. Although this presupposes some sort of mapping of units, language- and data-set individual segmentation can be, and in many cases is used. The 2019 DISRPT shared task will undoubtedly generate many more contributions to the segmentation task specifically.

3 Data

The data that is featured in the shared task stems from three different formalisms and covers nine different languages. An overview of the data sets, their formalism and size is shown in Table 1. Note that the indicated number of tokens are for the training and development sets only[2].

The three different formalisms that the treebanks originated from, each have their own conventions, underlying theory and potential application scenarios. While these bridges may be too large to gap for the entire representation of co-

herence relations, when it comes to just text segmentation, interesting synergies, and perhaps even unified approaches can be explored. In what follows, we will briefly explain the most important specifics with regard to segmentation of each of the three theories featured in the shared task, to conclude with our expectations in terms of overlap when dealing with the sub-task of segmentation alone.

3.1 RST

Introduced by Mann and Thompson (1988), RST aims to represent a text as a single tree structure, in which every single token is included in some elementary discourse unit (EDU) which serves as either a satellite or a nucleus in some relation. EDUs can be sequences of tokens at text level, or can be complex sub-trees which hierarchically represent a larger body of text. In RST, segmentation is an important first step in analysing a text (and consequently generating a tree); before a hierarchy of EDUs can be considered, the EDUs themselves have to be identified, which puts the segmentation task at the center of any RST analysis.

3.2 PDTB

In contrast to RST, in the PDTB framework, which originated as a discourse annotation layer over the Penn Treebank (Miltsakaki et al., 2004), no commitment to the overall structure of the text is made, an approach typically referred to as shallow discourse parsing. Relations between two (often adjacent, but not necessarily so) pieces of text are classified according to a set of relation senses. This is first done by locating explicit connectives and their two arguments (internal, or *arg2* and external, or *arg1*). Subsequently, adjacent sentences inside the same paragraph that are not yet connected through an explicit relation are classified according to an (implicit) relation sense, or as entrel or no-rel (see Prasad et al. (2008) for more details). Segmentation plays a less central role and is somewhat less formally defined. The two arguments of a relation should refer to *propositions* and typically include a finite verb, but under certain circumstances exceptions are made (for nominalized constructions such as "the uprising of the Bolsheviks" for example).

3.3 SDRT

SDRT (Asher et al., 2003) was proposed as an extension to Discourse Representation Theory

---

[2]The test sets were added only in the final stage of the shared task.

Corpus name	Language	Annotation style	Tokens
RSTBT (Iruskieta et al., 2013)	Basque	RST	28,658
CDTB (Zhou and Xue, 2015)	Chinese	PDTB	63,239
SCTB (Cao et al., 2018)	Chinese	RST	11,067
NLDT (Redeker et al., 2012)	Dutch	RST	21,355
PDTB (Prasad et al., 2008)	English	PDTB	1,100,990
GUM (Zeldes, 2017)	English	RST	82,691
RSTDT (Carlson et al., 2002)	English	RST	184,158
STAC (Asher et al., 2016)	English	SDRT	41,666
ANNODIS (Afantenos et al., 2012)	French	SDRT	25,050
PCC (Stede and Neumann, 2014)	German	RST	29,883
RRST (Toldova et al., 2017)	Russian	RST	243,896
RSTSTB (da Cunha et al., 2011)	Spanish	RST	50,565
SCTB (Cao et al., 2018)	Spanish	RST	12,699
CSTN (Cardoso et al., 2011)	Brazilian Portuguese	RST	51,041

Table 1: Shared task data sets

(Kamp, 1981). By including propositions as variables to reason over and discourse relations to rule out certain antecedents or promote others, it accounts for relations in a text beyond the sentence level (where dynamic semantic approaches often fail). Because our contribution deals with discourse segmentation only, and the two corpora included in this paper that have SDRT annotations both use RST-style EDUs for initial segmentation, the differences between the two theories are irrelevant for the segmentation task at hand.

3.4 Segmentation & Overlap

Segmentation of text into minimal units is not the first step in processing some piece of text in all of the frameworks described above. In PDTB for example, typically explicit signals in the form of connectives are identified first, upon which their arguments are extracted. Subsequently extracting implicit relations more or less means filling in the blanks between explicit relations. In RST and in the two corpora with SDRT annotations, it plays a much more central role, and segmenting a text into EDUs is the first step in constructing a tree for some text. Annotating coherence relations is a time-consuming and difficult task, as is reflected by low inter-annotator agreement scores compared to other NLP tasks, especially when using the RST framework (because of its requirement to end up with one single tree-like representation covering the entire text). As a result, available annotated corpora are relatively small and sparse. For this reason alone, attempting to unify the first, and rel-

atively simple (compared to what follows) step of segmenting some piece of text into minimal units can be very beneficial. Apart from this practical motivation, investigating segmentation characteristics over multiple different frameworks may lead to a broader understanding of the ways meaningful propositions are realised in the languages covered in this shared task. Most of the data in the shared task (i.e. the RST and SDRT data sets from Table 1) is annotated for segment boundaries and in addition is provided with dependency trees which, for most data sets, follows the Universal Dependencies scheme, meaning that we have sentence segmentation, part-of-speech tags and position and function for every word in the dependency tree. For the PDTB data sets, instead of segments (EDUs), connectives were labeled, meaning that the information in this data set is of a very different type. Also, the dependency trees were provided for these data sets. Furthermore, note that we did not have access to the Chinese Discourse Treebank, so though labels were provided in the shared task, we do not apply our methods to this data set[3]. Since we worked on the data sets as they were provided by the organisers, for more specific information related to the data sets we refer the reader either to the corresponding publications included in Table 1, or to the shared task website referred to in Section 1.

---

[3] In the final stage of the shared task, a Turkish data set was added to which we also had no access.

4   Method

To compare results against a simple, yet for some languages and data sets already relatively effective baseline, we first implement our baseline system which either assumes a segment boundary (segment start) at the beginning of each sentence, or at the beginning of each sentence and after every comma. To give a realistic impression of the performance of the other algorithms, the score for the baseline system in Table 2 represents whichever version scored best. This was the version basically assuming every sentence to be a segment for the *RSTBT*, *PDTB*, *GUM*, *RRST*, *RSTSTB* and Spanish *SCTB* data sets. The version assuming a segment boundary after every comma as well performed better for the Chinese *SCTB*, *NLDT*, *RSTDT*, *STAC*, *ANNODIS* and *CSTN* data sets.

4.1   RandomForest

To improve over the baseline, we try two different approaches. The RandomForest method (based on Scikit-learn (Pedregosa et al., 2011)) uses a combination of information present in the CoNLL-format files of the shared task (i.e. the dependency tree) and augment this, where available, with constituency syntax features. The base set of features we use for all languages consists of the surface form of the word itself; the surface forms of the next and previous word; the distance of this word to its parent in the dependency tree; the function of the parent word; the functions of the previous and next word; the part-of-speech tags (both coarse and fine-grained) tag for the previous, current and next word and the parent; binary features for whether or not the previous, current and parent word are starting with an uppercase character; absolute position in the sentence; relative position in the sentence (absolute position divided by sentence length); whether or not there is a verb ((lowercased) coarse part-of-speech tag starts with a "v") in between the current word and the next punctuation mark[4]. We are using the Stanford CoreNLP lexicalized PCFG parser (Klein and Manning, 2003) to obtain constituency trees for the languages supported (Chinese, English, French, German, and Spanish). For data sets in these languages, we additionally use as features the category of the parent node; the categories of the left and right siblings in the tree; the

path to the root node and the compressed path to the root node, where consecutive identical nodes are deleted (i.e. [N → NP → S → S] becomes [N → NP → S]). These features are inspired by the approach of Pitler and Nenkova (2009) for connective disambiguation.

4.2   LSTM

The LSTM-based method (based on Keras (Chollet et al., 2015)) uses a smaller feature set, including the distance to the parent, (grammatical) function of the parent and the current word, the parent's pos-tag and the current word's pos-tag, a binary feature for whether or not the first character of the word is uppercased and the relative position in the sentence. For the encoding of the word itself, we use two different approaches; either we use pre-trained word embeddings (Grave et al., 2018), or we use the embeddings from the corpus itself. The approach with pre-trained embeddings performed better for the *RSTBT*, *NLDT*, *RSTDT*, *RRST*, *RSTSTB*, Spanish *SCTB* and *CSTN* corpora, whereas the approach using the embeddings from the corpus itself performed better for the Chinese *SCTB*, *GUM*, *STAC*, *ANNODIS*, *PDTB* and *PCC* corpora. In general though, the scores for the two LSTM approaches were often very close together.

The results when training on the training and development section of every corpus and evaluating on the test section (as defined by the shared task setup) are shown in Table 2. The baseline rows include results for the baseline approach and the RandomForest rows include results using the above-mentioned feature set with the RandomForest classifier. The LSTM rows show the results for the best scoring LSTM system (either the one with pre-trained embeddings or the embeddings from the corpus itself, as explained above). Note that due to a much larger variation in scores over individual runs, for the LSTM approach (regardless of which one specifically), scores are macro-averaged over 10 runs[5]. Our code is publicly available at *reference_anonymised*.

5   Results

For all data sets, we beat the baseline, be it with a small margin for some (*STAC* and the Spanish *SCTB* for example). We did not check for

---

[4] Any character in the set
{!"#$%&'()*+,-./:;¡=¿?@[\]^_'— }

[5] Except for the *RRST* and *PDTB* corpora. Due to their relatively large size, hence longer processing time, these scores were averaged over 5 runs.

			precision	recall	f1 score
Basque	*RSTBT*	baseline	**98.13**	52.95	68.78
		RandomForest	92.60	61.21	73.71
		LSTM	87.75	**68.63**	**75.95**
Chinese	*SCTB*	baseline	87.23	73.21	79.61
		RandomForest	**88.89**	76.19	**82.05**
		LSTM	77.40	**77.32**	76.74
Dutch	*NLDT*	baseline	87.79	**87.54**	87.66
		RandomForest	**98.04**	86.96	**92.17**
		LSTM	90.00	85.94	86.92
English	*PDTB*	baseline	0.13	0.24	0.02
		RandomForest	**38.80**	**35.74**	**37.21**
		LSTM	9.14	9.46	9.29
	GUM	baseline	**100**	73.98	85.05
		RandomForest	97.76	83.54	**90.10**
		LSTM	93.20	**84.69**	88.41
	RSTDT	baseline	66.16	56.10	60.72
		RandomForest	93.89	87.13	90.38
		LSTM	**94.58**	**90.27**	**92.35**
	STAC	baseline	93.47	**94.80**	94.13
		RandomForest	**98.19**	91.49	**94.47**
		LSTM	95.42	90.45	92.81
French	*ANNODIS*	baseline	**93.63**	69.12	79.53
		RandomForest	93.50	80.44	**86.48**
		LSTM	89.61	**82.31**	85.32
German	*PCC*	baseline	**100**	72.45	84.02
		RandomForest	95.74	**84.01**	**89.49**
		LSTM	92.29	82.41	86.90
Russian	*RRST*	baseline	76.04	49.00	59.60
		RandomForest	82.98	67.02	74.15
		LSTM	**84.48**	**70.05**	**76.42**
Spanish	*RSTSTB*	baseline	**97.36**	64.69	77.73
		RandomForest	93.51	75.88	**83.78**
		LSTM	86.21	**76.21**	79.97
	SCTB	baseline	**97.00**	57.74	72.39
		RandomForest	94.33	**59.52**	**73.00**
		LSTM	68.92	55.60	61.45
Brazilian Portuguese	*CSTN*	baseline	64.47	73.96	68.90
		RandomForest	92.07	78.87	84.96
		LSTM	**92.33**	**82.26**	**86.43**

Table 2: Results for the different data sets

statistical significance, so claiming overall improvement over the baseline may not be justified. While the principle behind EDUs is taken to be language-neutral, it is interesting to see that the operationalisations vary greatly among languages and data sets/domains. This is demonstrated by the fluctuation in the baseline scores; from 59.60 (f1 score) for Russian (*RRST*), to 94.13 for English (*STAC*). For all but *STAC* and *CSTN*, precision is higher than recall (and in general comparatively high), meaning that the lower scoring languages have more EDUs per sentence, or just longer sentences on average. The latter is indeed what we see for Brazilian Portuguese, Russian and Basque, with average sentence lengths of 26.87, 21.85 and 19.93 words per sentence, respectively (compared to average lengths of 14.07, 14.74 and 5.05 for the much higher scoring German, Dutch and English STAC data sets, respectively). Since sentence length is a more informative property of domain than of language[6], this may suggest that a language-wise division is not the ideal one, and perhaps the domain should instead serve as the main indicator for performance. In line with the numbers above, we see that the Brazilian Portuguese, Russian and Basque data sets include scientific writing in their corpora, while the German and Dutch data sets tend more to (popular) news commentary, encyclopedia texts (targeted at the general public instead of scientists) and fund-raising letters and commercial advertisements. The English STAC data set is a domain of its own (in-game chats), with very short average sentences. If one takes the level of experience of the author and targeted reader as indications of text complexity (and also as properties of domain), this is likely to correlate to segmentation agreement figures. Unfortunately, mapping domain and complexity onto some shared dimensional space (allowing correlations to arise) is not straightforward. In addition, the creators of corpora used in our experiments do no use a single, easily unify-able metric to calculate Inter-Annotator Agreement (IAA) for EDU segmentation. We do note however that, again, for the higher scoring corpora, IAA was relatively high; Carlson et al. (2002) note a Kappa of 0.97 for RSTDT, Asher et al. (2016) note an initial agreement of 90% for automatic segmentation in STAC, and segmentation is manually improved after this automatic procedure, and Redeker et al. (2012) note an agreement of 97% for EDU segmentation in NLDT. On the other end of the spectrum, Iruskieta et al. (2013) report an EDU agreement of 81.35% for RSTBT and Toldova et al. (2017) report Krippendorf's α figures of 0.2792, 0.3173 and 0.4965 where they consider figures around 0.8 to be acceptable for RRST.

6 Discussion

Figure 1 plots performance for the RandomForest and LSTM approaches (and the baseline for comparison) on the Y axis (f1 score) and the corpora ordered by size (increasing from left to right)

on the X axis, illustrating that there is no clear correlation between corpus size and performance. The largest two corpora by a considerable margin[7] (*RSTDT* and *RRST*) do not score better than many of the other, smaller corpora. Regarding the

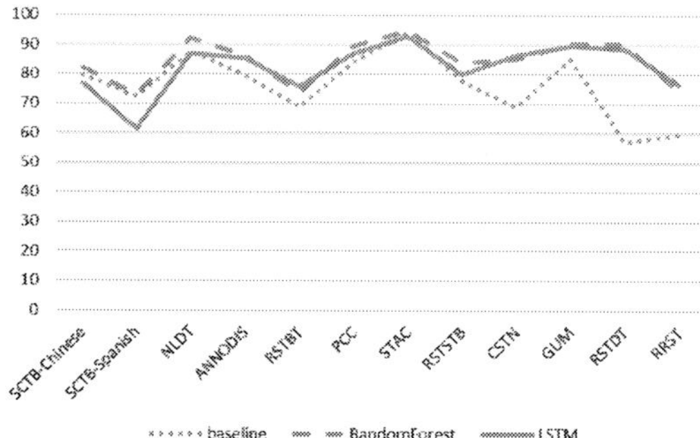

Figure 1: Results for the baseline, RandomForest and LSTM.

RandomForest and LSTM performance, the figure shows that the two come closer together and LSTM outperforms RandomForest on the larger corpora. Overall, RandomForest performs best in 9 data sets, whereas LSTM performs best in 4 cases. The difference however is typically small, and as we did not check for statistical significance, drawing conclusion based on this may not be justified in the cases where the two score close together. The cases where there is a large gap between the baseline and either of the two approaches (CSTN, RSTDT and RRST most notably) all contain (at least a portion of) text from the news domain, but two other corpora containing (a portion of) news text, i.e. PCC and ANNODIS, show much less of a gap. More investigation would be needed for these corpora to find the cause of this gain when using a classifier, compared to the baseline performance.

Figure 2 shows the information gain per feature for the RandomForest classifier for all data sets. Recall that the syntax features based on the constituency tree were not used for all data sets, hence blank for some.

The grammatical function in the dependency tree, (coarse) part-of-speech tag of the parent, position in the sentence, previous word and its part-of-speech tag play an important role for all data sets. For some data sets, the word itself plays

---

[6]For highly agglutinative languages, depending on tokenisation procedures average sentence lengths may of course be shorter, but given the set of languages here, excluding Chinese, difference in morphology plays a less prominent role.

[7]Excluding the *PDTB*, as explained in the remainder of this section.

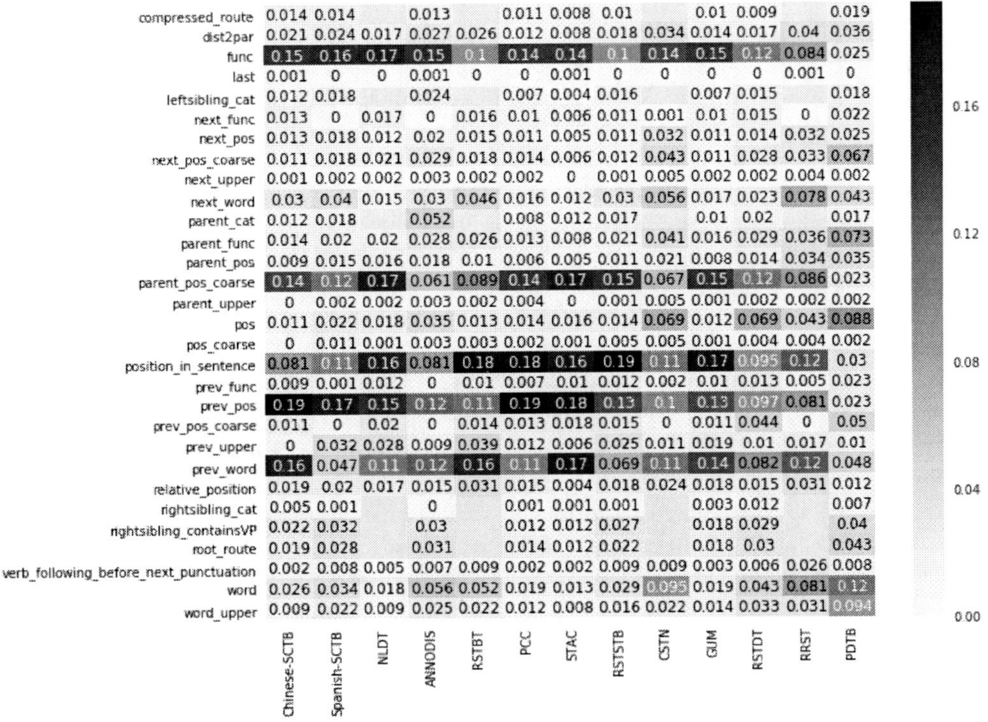

feature	Chinese-SCTB	Spanish-SCTB	NLDT	ANNODIS	RSTBT	PCC	STAC	RSTSTB	CSTN	GUM	RSTDT	RRST	PDTB
compressed_route	0.014	0.014		0.013		0.011	0.008	0.01		0.01	0.009		0.019
dist2par	0.021	0.024	0.017	0.027	0.026	0.012	0.008	0.018	0.034	0.014	0.017	0.04	0.036
func	0.15	0.16	0.17	0.15	0.1	0.14	0.14	0.1	0.14	0.15	0.12	0.084	0.025
last	0.001	0	0	0.001	0	0	0.001	0	0	0	0	0.001	0
leftsibling_cat	0.012	0.018		0.024		0.007	0.004	0.016		0.007	0.015		0.018
next_func	0.013	0	0.017	0	0.016	0.01	0.006	0.011	0.001	0.01	0.015	0	0.022
next_pos	0.013	0.018	0.012	0.02	0.015	0.011	0.005	0.011	0.032	0.011	0.014	0.032	0.025
next_pos_coarse	0.011	0.018	0.021	0.029	0.018	0.014	0.006	0.012	0.043	0.011	0.028	0.033	0.067
next_upper	0.001	0.002	0.002	0.003	0.002	0.002	0	0.001	0.005	0.002	0.002	0.004	0.002
next_word	0.03	0.04	0.015	0.03	0.046	0.016	0.012	0.03	0.056	0.017	0.023	0.078	0.043
parent_cat	0.012	0.018		0.052		0.008	0.012	0.017		0.01	0.02		0.017
parent_func	0.014	0.02	0.02	0.028	0.026	0.013	0.008	0.021	0.041	0.016	0.029	0.036	0.073
parent_pos	0.009	0.015	0.016	0.018	0.01	0.006	0.005	0.011	0.021	0.008	0.014	0.034	0.035
parent_pos_coarse	0.14	0.12	0.17	0.061	0.089	0.14	0.17	0.15	0.067	0.15	0.12	0.086	0.023
parent_upper	0	0.002	0.002	0.003	0.002	0.004	0	0.001	0.005	0.001	0.002	0.002	0.002
pos	0.011	0.022	0.018	0.035	0.013	0.014	0.016	0.014	0.069	0.012	0.069	0.043	0.088
pos_coarse	0	0.011	0.001	0.003	0.003	0.002	0.001	0.005	0.005	0.001	0.004	0.004	0.002
position_in_sentence	0.081	0.11	0.16	0.081	0.18	0.18	0.16	0.19	0.11	0.17	0.095	0.12	0.03
prev_func	0.009	0.001	0.012	0	0.01	0.007	0.01	0.012	0.002	0.01	0.013	0.005	0.023
prev_pos	0.19	0.17	0.15	0.12	0.11	0.19	0.18	0.13	0.1	0.13	0.097	0.081	0.023
prev_pos_coarse	0.011	0	0.02	0	0.014	0.013	0.018	0.015	0	0.011	0.044	0	0.05
prev_upper	0	0.032	0.028	0.009	0.039	0.012	0.006	0.025	0.011	0.019	0.01	0.017	0.01
prev_word	0.16	0.047	0.11	0.12	0.16	0.11	0.17	0.069	0.11	0.14	0.082	0.12	0.048
relative_position	0.019	0.02	0.017	0.015	0.031	0.015	0.004	0.018	0.024	0.018	0.015	0.031	0.012
rightsibling_cat	0.005	0.001		0		0.001	0.001	0.001		0.003	0.012		0.007
rightsibling_containsVP	0.022	0.032		0.03		0.012	0.012	0.027		0.018	0.029		0.04
root_route	0.019	0.028		0.031		0.014	0.012	0.022		0.018	0.03		0.043
verb_following_before_next_punctuation	0.002	0.008	0.005	0.007	0.009	0.002	0.002	0.009	0.009	0.003	0.006	0.026	0.008
word	0.026	0.034	0.018	0.056	0.052	0.019	0.013	0.029	0.095	0.019	0.043	0.081	0.12
word_upper	0.009	0.022	0.009	0.025	0.022	0.012	0.008	0.016	0.022	0.014	0.033	0.031	0.094

Figure 2: Information gain for the RandomForest classifier.

a relatively important role, while for others this is much less informative. Looking specifically at data sets from the same language (allowing to factor out language differences, and in some cases maintaining a genre difference only), the most notable differences is the informativeness of the part-of-speech tag when comparing *GUM*, *RSTDT* and *STAC* (i.e. it is informative for *RSTDT* but not for the other English data sets). The binary feature for last word in the sentence is partially encoded by relative sentence position as well and in general is very uninformative (with no information gain for most data sets). Surprising is the difference in granularity for the part-of-speech tags. We included both the fine-grained and the coarse tag, suspecting that the fine-grained one may exhibit too much variation for the classifier to pick up on. This does not seem to be the case for the part-of-speech tag of the word itself and that of the previous word. For the parent however, the coarse part-of-speech tag is generally more informative than its more fine-grained version. The data sets in Figure 2 are ordered by size (smallest to largest), but it does not seem to be the case that certain features become more or less informative once data sizes

increase.

Note that we largely leave the PDTB, by far the biggest resource of them all, out of this discussion (and consequently also out of Figure 1) due to its different nature of segmentation (at least in the context of the shared task). The task description here notes that for the PDTB-style corpora, "the task is to identify the spans of discourse connectives that explicitly identify the existence of a discourse relation." While this sounds like the task is about discourse connective identification, we note that the data set as published in the shared task includes many instances of words that would not be considered connectives by the usual definitions, such as verbs, nouns and in general includes many alternative lexicalisations. In this case, the baseline scores exceptionally low, as it makes little sense to assume a connective at the start of every sentence. Figure 2 also shows that all the syntactic features[8] add little information for the *PDTB*, and the focus on the surface form could be evidence that the classifier just tries to memorise the words

---

[8] Although the part-of-speech tag, which can be seen as some kind of syntactic information, does seem to be informative.

as the only thing to go on. However, because we did not investigate this in much detail, we intentionally and equally leave it out of the discussion regarding feature information gain. While due to its size, this data set can potentially contribute a lot to machine-learning based approaches, we argue that a higher degree of unification in the segmentation procedure should be realised before cross-fertilisation can happen. Even though standardising the segmentation task in a theory-neutral way is at the core of the shared task at hand, we found that a better definition and corresponding annotated data set would be needed before reliable classifiers can be constructed. For an idea of connective disambiguation scores on the *PDTB*, we refer to *reference_anonymised*.

We experimented with multilingual word embeddings (Conneau et al., 2017) to have a shared representation for the word and used the syntax features from the dependency layer (as this follows the Universal Dependencies scheme). This allows training on the entire collection (all data sets), and evaluating on just the development set of interest. This however did not improve results compared to using just the data set's corresponding training set.

It seems then that the language usage (i.e. factors like domain, complexity and target audience) plays a more important role in the task of discourse segmentation than the language (i.e. Spanish, Dutch or English for example) in which it is written does. This is also noted by Iruskieta et al. (2016) who look at Basque and Brazilian Portuguese specifically, but equally include and compare texts from different genres. Text from a particular genre from language can thus potentially serve as training data for text from that same genre, but in a language for which no training data for this task is available. We consider further investigation into this direction, adhering to a genre-based distinction rather than a language-based one, the most important pointer to future work and the most promising for performance improvement. First concrete steps in this direction can be the grouping of the data sets included in our experiments in combination with the multilingual word embeddings approach mentioned above.

With regard to the unification of different frameworks, as demonstrated in our experiments, the same systems that work well for EDU segmentation perform very poor for the PDTB-style segmentation defined for the purpose of this shared task. Since shallow annotations are typically easier to obtain and therefore their corresponding corpora can grow larger more easily, the mapping of segments and their properties from a (shallow) theoretical framework (i.e. PDTB) to another (i.e. RST, SDRT or CCR) is a promising direction, but also one that needs more research. Earlier work in this direction ((Demberg et al., 2017), (Sanders et al., 2018) and (Scheffler and Stede, 2016)) may help in the definition of a unifying minimal segment for future attempts at the segmentation task.

7 Conclusion & Outlook

We perform the task of discourse segmentation for various languages, genres and data sets, focusing on segmenting a text into EDUs. Experimenting with 14 data sets from 9 languages representing a variety of domains, we try a RandomForest classifier and an LSTM classifier, and use the same setup for different languages and domains. With the results of the two approaches being close together and no clear winner emerging, the main take-away is that not the language, but the genre seems the most reliable indicator of segmentation performance. We consider more research into genre differences with respect to discourse segmentation the most important suggestion for future work. In addition, while a large corpus with shallow annotations like the PDTB has a lot of potential for improving machine-learning based approaches, we argue that a more refined, unified notion of a minimal segment is needed for cross-theory segmentation to succeed.

Acknowledgments

Funded by the Deutsche Forschungsgemeinschaft (DFG, German Research Foundation) - 323949969. We would like to thank the anonymous reviewers for their helpful comments on an earlier version of this manuscript.

References

Stergos Afantenos, Nicholas Asher, Farah Benamara, Myriam Bras, Cécile Fabre, Lydia-Mai Ho-Dac, Anne Le Draoulec, Philippe Muller, Marie-Paule Péry-Woodley, Laurent Prevot, Josette Rebeyrolle, Ludovic Tanguy, Marianne Vergez-Couret, and Laure Vieu. 2012. An empirical resource for discovering cognitive principles of discourse organisation: the ANNODIS corpus. In *Proceedings of the Eight International Conference on Language Resources and Evaluation (LREC'12)*, pages –, Istanbul, Turkey. European Language Resources Association (ELRA).

N. Asher, A. Lascarides, S. Bird, B. Boguraev, D. Hindle, M. Kay, D. McDonald, and H. Uszkoreit. 2003. *Logics of Conversation*. Studies in Natural Language Processing. Cambridge University Press.

Nicholas Asher, Julie Hunter, Mathieu Morey, Farah Benamara, and Stergos D. Afantenos. 2016. Discourse structure and dialogue acts in multiparty dialogue: the STAC corpus. In *LREC*. European Language Resources Association (ELRA).

Farah Benamara and Maite Taboada. 2015. Mapping different rhetorical relation annotations: A proposal. In *Proceedings of the Fourth Joint Conference on Lexical and Computational Semantics*, pages 147–152. Association for Computational Linguistics.

Chloé Braud, Maximin Coavoux, and Anders Søgaard. 2017. Cross-lingual RST Discourse Parsing. In *Proceedings of the 15th Conference of the European Chapter of the Association for Computational Linguistics: Volume 1, Long Papers*, pages 292–304. Association for Computational Linguistics.

Harry Bunt and R. Prasad. 2016. ISO DR-Core (ISO 24617-8): Core Concepts for the Annotation of Discourse Relations. In *Proceedings 10th Joint ACL-ISO Workshop on Interoperable Semantic Annotation*, pages 45–54.

Shuyuan Cao, Iria da Cunha, and Mikel Iruskieta. 2018. The RST Spanish-Chinese Treebank.

P.C.F. Cardoso, E.G. Maziero, M.L.C. Jorge, E.M.R. Seno, A. Di Felippo, L.H.M. Rino, M.G.V. Nunes, and T.A.S. Pardo. 2011. CSTNews - A Discourse-Annotated Corpus for Single and Multi-Document Summarization of News Texts in Brazilian Portuguese. In *Proceedings of the 3rd RST Brazilian Meeting, pp. 88-105. October 26, Cuiab/MT, Brazil*.

Lynn Carlson, Daniel Marcu, and Mary Ellen Okurowski. 2002. RST Discourse Treebank, ldc2002t07.

Christian Chiarcos. 2014. Towards interoperable discourse annotation. discourse features in the ontologies of linguistic annotation. In *Proceedings of the Ninth International Conference on Language Resources and Evaluation (LREC'14)*, Reykjavik, Iceland. European Language Resources Association (ELRA).

François Chollet et al. 2015. Keras. `https://keras.io`.

Alexis Conneau, Guillaume Lample, Marc'Aurelio Ranzato, Ludovic Denoyer, and Hervé Jégou. 2017. Word translation without parallel data. *arXiv preprint arXiv:1710.04087*.

Iria da Cunha, Juan-Manuel Torres-Moreno, and Gerardo Sierra. 2011. On the Development of the RST Spanish Treebank. In *Proceedings of the 5th Linguistic Annotation Workshop*, LAW V '11, pages 1–10, Stroudsburg, PA, USA. Association for Computational Linguistics.

Vera Demberg, Fatemeh Torabi Asr, and Merel Scholman. 2017. How consistent are our discourse annotations? insights from mapping RST-DT and PDTB annotations. *CoRR*, abs/1704.08893.

Edouard Grave, Piotr Bojanowski, Prakhar Gupta, Armand Joulin, and Tomas Mikolov. 2018. Learning word vectors for 157 languages. In *Proceedings of the International Conference on Language Resources and Evaluation (LREC 2018)*.

Hugo Hernault, Helmut Prendinger, David A. duVerle, and Mitsuru Ishizuka. 2010. HILDA: A Discourse Parser Using Support Vector Machine Classification. *Dialogue and Discourse*, 1(3).

M. Iruskieta, M. Aranzabe, A. Diaz de Ilarraza, I. Gonzalez, I. Lersundi, and O. Lopez de Lacalle. 2013. The RST Basque TreeBank: an online search interface to check rhetorical relations. In *4th Workshop RST and Discourse Studies, 40-49, Sociedad Brasileira de Computacao, Fortaleza, CE, Brasil. October 20-24 (http://encontrorst2013.wix.com/encontro-rst-2013)"*.

Mikel Iruskieta, Gorka Labaka, and Juliano D. Antonio. 2016. Detecting the central units in two different genres and languages: a preliminary study of brazilian portuguese and basque texts. *Procesamiento del Lenguaje Natural*, 56:65–72.

Yangfeng Ji and Jacob Eisenstein. 2014. Representation learning for text-level discourse parsing. In *Proceedings of the 52nd Annual Meeting of the Association for Computational Linguistics (Volume 1: Long Papers)*, pages 13–24. Association for Computational Linguistics.

Shafiq Joty, Giuseppe Carenini, and Raymond T Ng. 2015. CODRA: A Novel Discriminative Framework for Rhetorical Analysis. 41:3.

Hans Kamp. 1981. A Theory of Truth and Semantic Representation. In J. A. G. Groenendijk, T. M. V. Janssen, and M. B. J. Stokhof, editors, *Formal Methods in the Study of Language*, volume 1, pages 277–322. Mathematisch Centrum, Amsterdam.

Dan Klein and Christopher D. Manning. 2003. Accurate unlexicalized parsing. In *Proceedings of the 41st Annual Meeting on Association for Computational Linguistics - Volume 1*, ACL '03, pages 423–430, Stroudsburg, PA, USA. Association for Computational Linguistics.

William Mann and Sandra Thompson. 1988. Rhetorical Structure Theory: Towards a Functional Theory of Text Organization. *Text*, 8:243–281.

Eleni Miltsakaki, Aravind K. Joshi, Rashmi Prasad, and Bonnie L. Webber. 2004. Annotating discourse connectives and their arguments. In *FCP@NAACL-HLT*.

Stephan Oepen, Jonathon Read, Tatjana Scheffler, Uladzimir Sidarenka, Manfred Stede, Erik Velldal, and Lilja Øvrelid. 2016. OPT: OsloPotsdamTeesside—Pipelining Rules, Rankers, and Classifier Ensembles for Shallow Discourse Parsing. In *Proceedings of the CONLL 2016 Shared Task*, Berlin.

T. A. S. Pardo and M. G. V. Nunes. 2008. On the Development and Evaluation of a Brazilian Portuguese Discourse Parser. *RITA*, 15:43–64.

Fabian Pedregosa, Gael Varoquaux, Alexandre Gramfort, Vincent Michel, Bertrand Thirion, Olivier Grisel, Mathieu Blondel, Peter Prettenhofer, Ron Weiss, Vincent Dubourg, Jake Vanderplas, Alexandre Passos, David Cournapeau, Matthieu Brucher, Matthieu Perrot, and Edouard Duchesnay. 2011. Scikit-learn: Machine Learning in Python. *Journal of Machine Learning Research*, 12:2825–2830.

Emily Pitler and Ani Nenkova. 2009. Using syntax to disambiguate explicit discourse connectives in text. In *Proceedings of the ACL-IJCNLP 2009 Conference Short Papers*, ACLShort '09, pages 13–16. Association for Computational Linguistics.

Rashmi Prasad, Nikhil Dinesh, Alan Lee, Eleni Miltsakaki, Livio Robaldo, Aravind Joshi, and Bonnie Webber. 2008. The Penn Discourse Treebank 2.0. In *Proceedings of LREC*.

Gisela Redeker, Ildik Berzlnovich, Nynke van der Vliet, Gosse Bouma, and Markus Egg. 2012. Multilayer discourse annotation of a dutch text corpus. In *Proceedings of the Eight International Conference on Language Resources and Evaluation (LREC'12)*, Istanbul, Turkey. European Language Resources Association (ELRA).

Ines Rehbein, Merel Scholman, and Vera Demberg. 2016. Annotating Discourse Relations in Spoken Language: A Comparison of the PDTB and CCR Frameworks. In *LREC*.

Ted J.M. Sanders, Vera Demberg, Jet Hoek, Merel C.J. Scholman, Fatemeh Torabi Asr, Sandrine Zufferey, and Jacqueline Evers-Vermeul. 2018. Unifying dimensions in coherence relations: How various annotation frameworks are related. *Corpus Linguistics and Linguistic Theory*, 0(0). Exported from https://app.dimensions.ai on 2019/02/06.

Ted J.M. Sanders, Wilbert P.M.S. Spooren, and Leo G.M. Noordman. 1992. Toward a taxonomy of coherence relations. *Discourse Processes*, 15(1):1–35.

Tatjana Scheffler and Manfred Stede. 2016. Mapping pdtb-style connective annotation to RST-style discourse annotation. In *Proceedings of KONVENS*, Bochum, Germany.

Radu Soricut and Daniel Marcu. 2003. Sentence level discourse parsing using syntactic and lexical information. In *Proceedings of the 2003 Conference of the North American Chapter of the Association for Computational Linguistics on Human Language Technology - Volume 1*, NAACL '03, pages 149–156, Stroudsburg, PA, USA. Association for Computational Linguistics.

Manfred Stede and Arne Neumann. 2014. Potsdam Commentary Corpus 2.0: Annotation for discourse research. In *Proceedings of the Ninth International Conference on Language Resources and Evaluation (LREC'14)*, Reykjavik, Iceland. European Language Resources Association (ELRA).

Svetlana Toldova, Dina Pisarevskaya, Margarita Ananyeva, Maria Kobozeva, Alexander Nasedkin, Sofia Nikiforova, Irina Pavlova, and Alexey Shelepov. 2017. Rhetorical relations markers in Russian RST Treebank. In *Proceedings of the 6th Workshop on Recent Advances in RST and Related Formalisms*, pages 29–33. Association for Computational Linguistics.

Jianxiang Wang and Man Lan. 2015. A refined end-to-end discourse parser. In *Proceedings of the Nineteenth Conference on Computational Natural Language Learning - Shared Task*, pages 17–24. Association for Computational Linguistics.

Amir Zeldes. 2017. The GUM corpus: creating multilayer resources in the classroom. *Language Resources and Evaluation*, 51(3):581–612.

Yuping Zhou and Nianwen Xue. 2015. The Chinese Discourse TreeBank: A Chinese Corpus Annotated with Discourse Relations. *Lang. Resour. Eval.*, 49(2):397–431.

ToNy: Contextual embeddings for accurate multilingual discourse segmentation of full documents

Philippe Muller
IRIT, CNRS, University of Toulouse
Toulouse, France
philippe.muller@irit.fr

Chloé Braud
LORIA
CNRS
Nancy, France
chloe.braud@loria.fr

Mathieu Morey
Datactivist
Aix-en-Provence, France
mathieu@datactivist.coop

Abstract

Segmentation is the first step in building practical discourse parsers, and is often neglected in discourse parsing studies. The goal is to identify the minimal spans of text to be linked by discourse relations, or to isolate explicit marking of discourse relations. Existing systems on English report F1 scores as high as 95%, but they generally assume gold sentence boundaries and are restricted to English newswire texts annotated within the RST framework. This article presents a generic approach and a system, ToNy, a discourse segmenter developed for the DisRPT shared task where multiple discourse representation schemes, languages and domains are represented. In our experiments, we found that a straightforward sequence prediction architecture with pretrained contextual embeddings is sufficient to reach performance levels comparable to existing systems, when separately trained on each corpus. We report performance between 81% and 96% in F1 score. We also observed that discourse segmentation models only display a moderate generalization capability, even within the same language and discourse representation scheme.

1 Introduction

Discourse segmentation corresponds to the identification of Elementary Discourse Units in a document, i.e. the minimal spans of text that will be linked by discourse relations within the discourse structure, and/or the explicit markings of a discourse relations. The task definition differs slightly across the various existing and competing formalisms: in Rhetorical Structure Theory (RST) (Mann and Thompson, 1988), all segments are adjacent while in Segmented Discourse Representation Theory (SDRT) (Asher and Lascarides, 2003), segments can be embedded in one another; In the Penn Discourse TreeBank (PDTB) (Prasad et al., 2008), the task is expressed as finding the arguments of a discourse connective, whether this connective is implicit or explicit. Combining the existing corpora is thus a challenge, while the lack of annotated data makes it an appealing solution.

Even within a given framework, the criteria for identifying EDUs differ between the annotation projects: for instance, the RST-DT corpus (Carlson et al., 2001) and the RST GUM corpus (Zeldes, 2016) have very different segmentation guidelines. While discourse analysis mainly involves semantic and pragmatic questions, discourse segmentation is closer to the syntactic level, as is reflected in the annotation guidelines, which tend to equate segments with various kinds of clauses. Most existing work considers segmentation at the sentence level (intra-sentential segmentation), implicitly assuming that the task of sentence boundary detection can be done perfectly. This assumption is rarely questioned even though the performance of sentence boundary detection systems is far from perfect and very sensitive to noisy input. Also, it is crucial for some languages to consider document-level segmentation.

Within the framework of the shared task, we investigate performance at the document-level with no gold sentence information, and compare it to the performance when assuming gold sentence boundaries. We present different sequence prediction architectures with different pre-trained embeddings, and show that the best configurations using contextual embeddings (Peters et al., 2018; Devlin et al., 2018) seem sufficient to reach comparable performances to existing systems, when separately trained on each corpus, while using more generic resources.[1] Our best system consistently improves over the state-of-the-art models at the document level without the use of any addi-

---

[1]The code is available on https://gitlab.inria.fr/andiamo/tony.

Proceedings of Discourse Relation Parsing and Treebanking (DISRPT2019), pages 115–124
Minneapolis, MN, June 6, 2019. ©2019 Association for Computational Linguistics

tional information apart from words, obtaining F1
scores between 80% and 94% when no gold sentence boundaries are given.

2 Related work

The first discourse segmenters built on the English RST-DT were rule-based: they used punctuations, POS tags, some syntactic information and the presence of specific discourse connectives to identify discourse boundaries (Le Thanh et al., 2004; Tofiloski et al., 2009). Rule based segmenters also exist for Brazilian Portuguese (Pardo and Nunes, 2008) (51.3% to 56.8%, depending on the genre), for Spanish (da Cunha et al., 2010, 2012) (80%) and for Dutch (van der Vliet, 2010) (73% with automatic parse, 82% with gold parse).

More recent approaches, on the English RST-DT, used binary classifiers at the word level (Soricut and Marcu, 2003; Fisher and Roark, 2007; Joty et al., 2015; Subba and Di Eugenio, 2007), or cast the task as a sequence labeling problem (Sporleder and Lapata, 2005; Hernault et al., 2010; Xuan Bach et al., 2012; Braud et al., 2017a,b; Wang et al., 2018).

While earlier studies investigated the usefulness of various sources of information, notably syntactic information using chunkers (Sporleder and Lapata, 2005) or full trees (Fisher and Roark, 2007; Braud et al., 2017b), recent studies mostly rely on word embeddings as input of neural network sequential architectures (Wang et al., 2018; Li et al., 2018).

Most of these studies only consider intrasentential discourse segmentation, however, thus leaving sentence segmentation as a pre-processing step. In this setting, the best current results on the English RST-DT are presented in (Wang et al., 2018) where the authors trained a BiLSTM-CRF using ELMo and self attention. They report at best 94.3% in F1.

The first results at the document level were presented in (Braud et al., 2017a), where the authors investigated cross-lingual and cross-domain training, and in (Braud et al., 2017b), a study focused on the use of syntactic information. In these studies, the best performing system for the English RST-DT obtained 89.5% in F1, showing that the task is more difficult when the sentence boundaries are not given. Scores for other datasets are also reported: 83.0% in F1 for Portuguese, 79.3% for Spanish, 86.2% for German, 82.6% for

Dutch and 68.1% for the English GUM corpus. Most of these results were obtained when combining words and morpho-syntactic information (Penn Treebank or Universal Dependencies POS tags), the authors showing that using words alone leads to scores 6 to 10 points lower. They did not use any pre-trained word embeddings. Note that the results presented in this paper are not directly comparable to these studies, since the test sets are different and there are also differences on the training data (see Section 3).

3 Data

3.1 Discourse corpora

The shared task organizers provided 15 corpora annotated with discourse boundaries, 4 of which are not freely available. There is no public procedure to get the text for the Chinese PDTB corpus hence we were unable to include it in our experiments.[2]

The generic term of "discourse annotated" corpora covers a variety of heterogeneous datasets bundled together:

Multilingual Annotated data are provided for 9 different languages. 4 datasets are in English (Carlson et al., 2001; Prasad et al., 2008; Asher et al., 2016; Zeldes, 2016), 2 are in Spanish (da Cunha et al., 2011; Cao et al., 2018) and 2 in Mandarin Chinese (Zhou et al., 2014; Cao et al., 2018). The other datasets are in German (Stede and Neumann, 2014), French (Afantenos et al., 2012), Basque (Iruskieta et al., 2013), Portuguese (Cardoso et al., 2011), Russian (Pisarevskaya et al., 2017), Turkish (Zeyrek et al., 2013) and Dutch (Redeker et al., 2012). To the best of our knowledge, this is the first time models are suggested for discourse segmentation of Russian, Turkish, and Chinese.

Multi-formalisms The 3 main frameworks for discourse are represented, namely RST, SDRT and PDTB. The latter two are only represented by two and three corpora. For PDTB, the English corpus is the largest one, but for SDRT, both the French and the English ones are very small. Moreover, the English eng.sdrt.stac corpus is the only corpus containing dialogues. Finally, note that labels are

---

[2]The organizers however trained and ran our final system on this corpus and provided us with the results reported in Table 3.

Corpus	Lg	# Doc.			Sent seg	# Sents.	# Disc. Bound.	Vocab. Size
		Train	Dev	Test		Train	Train	Train
PDTB								
eng.pdtb.pdtb	en	1,992	79	91	manual	44,563	23,850	49,156
tur.pdtb.tdb	tr	159	19	19	manual	25,080	6,841	75,891
RST								
eng.rst.rstdt	en	309	38	38	manual	6,672	17,646	17,071
eng.rst.gum	en	78	18	18	manual	3,600	5,012	10,587
deu.rst.pcc	de	142	17	17	manual	1,773	2,449	7,072
eus.rst.ert	eu	84	28	28	manual	991	1,713	7,300
nld.rst.nldt	nl	56	12	12	manual	1,202	1,679	3,942
por.rst.cstn	pt	110	14	12	manual	1,595	3,916	6,323
rus.rst.rrt	ru	140	19	19	UD-Pipe	9,859	15,804	41,231
spa.rst.stb	es	203	32	32	manual	1,577	2,474	7,715
spa.rst.sctb	es	32	9	9	manual	304	473	2,657
zho.rst.sctb	zh	32	9	9	manual	344	473	2,205
SDRT								
eng.sdrt.stac	en	29	6	6	manual	7,689	8,843	3,127
fra.sdrt.annodis	fr	64	11	11	manual	880	2,411	5,403

Table 1: Statistics on the corpora.

the same for all RST and SDRT data, with labels indicating the beginning of an EDU (BIO format, without the Inside tag), but the task is quite different for PDTB corpora where the system has to identify the beginning of a connective span and all its inside tokens (BIO format).

The results for this shared task are not directly comparable with the ones presented in (Braud et al., 2017a,b) because for the shared task, the GUM corpus has been extended – from 54 to 78 documents – while the Portuguese corpus is restricted to the 110 documents of the CSTNews corpus (Cardoso et al., 2011) – against 330 in (Braud et al., 2017a) where all the discourse corpora available for this language were merged.

3.2 Statistics

We provide a summary on the corpora used in this paper in Table 1, showing the wide differences in sizes, numbers of documents, vocabularies, and number of sentences per document, from about 10 sentences on average, to a maximum of 70 for the Russian corpus. We note that 7 corpora contain less than 100 documents, which will probably make it harder to learn from them.

Leaving out PDTB-style corpora that include a different kind of annotations, the proportion of intra-sentential boundaries varies across corpora: e.g., in eng.rst.gum, the number of sentences is close to the number of boundaries, while the eng.rst.rstdtcontains largely more intra-sentential

discourse boundaries than sentence boundaries. This is an indication of the difficulty of the task, since, at least in principle, intra-sentential boundaries are harder to detect than sentence frontiers.

4 Approach

In this paper, we investigate the usefulness of contextual pre-trained embeddings, and evaluate the effect of using sentence splitter as a pre-processing step. We compare our systems to rule-based baselines and a simple sequence labelling model using a bi-directional LSTM.

4.1 Baselines

Rule based Sentence segmentation is generally considered as given in discourse segmenters. However, performance of sentence splitters are far from perfect, especially for specific genres and low-resourced languages.

In this shared task, sentence boundaries are given in the CoNLL files, and are either gold or predicted (for rus.rst.rrt). Since sentence boundaries are always discourse boundaries for RST and SDRT style segmentation, the performance of a sentence splitter is a lower bound for our systems. Moreover, we propose systems relying on sentence segmentation as a way to reduce the size of the input, and thus help the model.

We use StanfordNLP [3] (Qi et al., 2018) with language-specific models to predict sentence seg-

---

[3] version 0.1.1

mentation. StanfordNLP performs sentence and token segmentation jointly but the corpora provided for the shared task were already tokenized. We approximately rebuilt the original text from the tokens, applied StanfordNLP's tokenizer, then mapped the predicted sentence boundaries onto the given tokens.

We report the performance of the baseline system based of the sentence segmentation produced in Table 2 (see Section 6) .

Bi-LSTM: As an additional baseline, we trained single-layer bi-directional LSTM models (Hochreiter and Schmidhuber, 1997; Graves and Schmidhuber, 2005) performing sequence labeling. These models read the input in both regular and reverse order, and are thus able, in principle, to better take into account both right and left contexts. Our implementation is based on PyTorch.

These models take as input the whole documents or a sequence of sentences, both corresponding to a sequence of words represented by real-valued vectors, here either initialized randomly or using pre-trained vectors. At the upper level, we use SoftMax to get predictions for each word based on a linear transformation, and we use a negative log likelihood loss.

4.2 Multilingual models with pretrained contextual embeddings

Our main experiment was to study the impact of contextual embeddings, i.e. vector representations for words that are computed taking into account the sentence the word appears in, on a sequence to sequence model predicting discourse segmentation labels. Two popular models have been proposed recently: ELMo (Peters et al., 2018) uses the conjunction of a left-to-right language model and a right-to-left language model, and BERT (Devlin et al., 2018) uses a single language model predicting a word given the whole sentential context. Both models show interesting results on various semantic tasks, and have been trained on corpora in multiple languages.

We applied here a simplified version of named entity recognition built on these embeddings, with a single-layer LSTM encoding a document or a sentence on top of character-based convolution filters and contextual word embeddings. ELMo reaches good results on CoNLL 2003 NER tasks with a 2-layer LSTM and a CRF on top to lever-

age dependencies between labels, but the rarity of segmentation labels and the small size of most discourse corpora encouraged us to use a smaller model. It was not possible, within the limited time frame of the shared task, to test too many different setups, but it is certainly worth exploring more expressive models, especially for connective identification where there are more label types and more dependencies between them.

We used the development set on English to test whether ELMo or BERT seemed to yield better results in this setup, and consequently chose the BERT-based model to train segmenters on each dataset, and for the two given configurations: (i) the sentence-level segmentation where gold sentences are given, and (ii) the document level where the whole document is passed to the model.

The BERT authors provide a multilingual model, where embeddings are made available simultaneously for several languages, rendering the model more generic and convenient to test. However, one disadvantage of using BERT in the discourse-level setting is that encoding sentences are limited to 512 WordPieces (subtokens of tokens showing a good regularity in the training corpus), while a lot of documents are longer than that in the task. In that configuration we thus preprocessed documents with the StanfordNLP pipeline to have a reasonable sentence splitting process, after checking that precision on the development set seemed high enough.

Since using ELMo with language-specific models involved separate and heterogeneous trained models, we decided to use only the multilingual generic one, but did a more precise comparison of performances on English datasets.

5   Settings

For the baseline models based on a bi-LSTM, we used randomly initialized or pre-trained word embeddings with a dimension of 50 or 300. For monolingual experiments, we used the FastText monolingual embeddings available for 157 languages (Grave et al., 2018), with 300 dimensions.[4] We also tested with GloVe (Pennington et al., 2014) and 50 dimensions for English datasets, since these embeddings are the ones used by our main model.[5]

---

[4] `https://fasttext.cc/docs/en/ crawl-vectors.html`
[5] `https://nlp.stanford.edu/projects/ glove/`

The other hyper-parameters are: one hidden layer with 100 dimensions, a dropout of 0.5, the Adam optimizer, a learning rate of 0.001 and 10 epochs.

For the BERT-based sequence prediction model, we used a configuration close to the NER ELMo system provided by the Allen NLP library (Gardner et al., 2017), with convolution filters at the character level combined to word-level embeddings, where BERT replaces ELMo embeddings. As explained above, we removed the CRF layer, and kept a bi-LSTM with only one layer, with 100 dimensions for the state representation. We found that small batches were better, and that the loss converged quickly, always in less than 10 epochs. We used the BERT-Adam optimizer with learning rate of 0.001. The English ELMo-based model is similar, with 50-dimensions GloVe embeddings and ELMo embeddings as provided by AllenNLP.

Two datasets required some preprocessing: we replaced URLs and special symbols in the Russian dataset, and arbitrarily split long sentences at 180 tokens on the Turkish dataset to comply with the 512 WordPiece limit on BERT embeddings[6].

6 Results

We report the F1 scores of our systems on 14 corpora (all corpora for this shared task but the Chinese PDTB) in Table 2. The left side of the table corresponds to the document-level setting where a document is provided as a plain sequence of tokens (`.tok` files). The right side of the table corresponds to the sentence-level setting where a document is provided as a sequence of sentences and a sentence is a sequence of tokens (`.conll` files). In the document-level setting, 2 systems directly process the whole document while 3 systems first segment the document into sentences. We report F1 scores on the dev and test sets, except for the two rule-based systems (rb-ssplit and rb-CoNLL).

6.1 Baselines

Our baseline systems are of two kinds: rule-based or using a simple bi-LSTM.

Rule based The rule-based systems for segmentation in the RST and SDRT frameworks obtain relatively high F1 scores given their extreme simplicity. In the sentence-level setting, the sentence

splits provided in the CoNLL files suffice to obtain a very high precision except for the Russian (rus.rst.rrt) and to a lesser extent Chinese (zho.rst.sctb) RST corpora. Both corpora contain a number of very long segments spanning more than one sentence, and the Russian RST corpus is the only corpus where sentence segmentation was not manually annotated but predicted, which means that some sentence-initial boundaries are lost. In this setting, the F1 scores of the rule-based systems are largely driven by recall, hence directly reflects the proportion of intra-sentential segment boundaries.

In the document-level setting, F1 scores degrade with the performance of the sentence segmenter on certain languages and genres. The sentence segmenter used in this study nevertheless gives largely better results than the UDPipe segmenter used in (Braud et al., 2017a) for Portuguese (62.92 vs 49.0), Spanish (72.21-71.89 vs 64.9) and German (78.51 vs 69.7), and similar results for English (RST-DT and GUM) and Dutch.

Bi-LSTM: Our additional baselines are single layer bi-LSTM models using randomly initialized word embeddings or pre-trained word embeddings (FastText or GloVe for English). In addition to the results presented in Table 2, we report English specific results in Table 5.

In general, these baseline models already give rather high performances, between 69.1% in F1 at the lowest for zho.rst.sctb (according to the results on the development set, using FastText is the best option for this corpus), and 88.11% at best for fra.sdrt.annodis. On the eng.rst.rstdt, our best system gets 87.37% in F1, lower than the 89.5% reported in (Braud et al., 2017a). This seems to indicate that FastText embeddings do not capture the syntactic information provided by POS tags in the latter study. However, we get better results on nld.rst.nldt, with at best 85.85% in F1 compared to 82.6% in (Braud et al., 2017a).

As expected, the use of pre-trained embeddings most often leads to better results than randomly initialized word vectors ('Rand.-300d' vs 'FastText-300d'). Improvements are especially high for the Spanish SCTB (+5.39 when using FastText), for the Russian corpus (+3.59), for fra.sdrt.annodis (+2.85), and around 2 points for the eng.rst.rstdt and por.rst.cstn.

The only exceptions are eng.sdrt.stac (-2.66 when using FastText), deu.rst.pcc (-2.53),

---

[6]This was also necessary for the Chinese PDTB corpus that was not available to us at submission time.

	Plain format (.tok)								Treebank format (.conll)				
	whole doc				predicted sentence (ssplit)					gold sentence (ssplit)			
	Rand.-300d		FastText-300d		rb-ssplit	FastText-300d-ssplit		BERT-M-doc		rb-CoNLL	FastText-300d-CoNLL		BERT-M-CoNLL	
	Dev	Test	Dev	Test	Test	Dev	Test	Dev	Test	Test	Dev	Test	Dev	Test
eng.pdtb.pdtb	81.55	79.87	80.16	80.02	-	80.20	80.29	92.39	**89.89**	-	79.61	76.72	91.21	**87.90**
tur.pdtb.tdb	64.55	64.25	68.18	71.61	-	68.05	72.64	81.97	**84.01**	-	00.27	00.26	75.6	**72.18**
deu.rst.pcc	85.66	86.23	85.43	83.7	78.51	69.01	67.92	93.36	**94.1**	84.02	62.92	63.39	95.75	**93.98**
eng.rst.gum	80.65	82.17	81.45	83.43	77.26	62.34	56.19	88.17	**87.27**	85.05	21.27	23.31	91.34	**96.35**
eng.rst.rstdt	84.06	85.06	86.05	87.37	52.27	84.5	84.88	93.28	**93.72**	56.73	81.02	82.59	91.2	**92.77**
eus.rst.ert	82.85	77.53	82.4	78.75	71.47	69.98	67.97	87.87	**85.79**	68.78	61.84	60.29	88.46	**85.46**
nld.rst.nldt	84.31	84.59	86.78	85.85	79.60	71.43	76.83	90.96	**90.69**	83.78	53.86	55.33	91.97	**93.55**
por.rst.cstn	80.44	82.98	81.78	85.16	62.92	74.53	80.55	89.09	**91.32**	62.89	41.83	38.6	89.34	**92.11**
rus.rst.rrt	71.72	71.42	73.95	75.01	52.22	68.67	68.82	80.77	**81.04**	59.60	46.06	45.29	82.96	**83.07**
spa.rst.stb	79.05	81.78	81.28	80.87	72.21	75.22	74.8	93.76	**88.22**	77.73	73.02	71.05	93.24	**90.73**
spa.rst.sctb	73.02	69.86	81.28	75.25	71.89	44.66	56.25	85.44	**80.81**	72.39	62.5	65.93	86.87	**82.58**
zho.rst.sctb	66.98	69.33	75.76	69.1	34.82	67.74	**70.9**	65.28	66.67	**81.33**	31.58	45.77	84	80.89
eng.sdrt.stac	82.12	80.96	79.75	78.3	46.75	79.76	77.77	84.36	**84.45**	93.32	17.94	16.43	95.1	**95.15**
fra.sdrt.annodis	83.75	85.26	86.66	88.11	46.79	84.99	86.59	90.06	**90.45**	47.36	84.27	86.44	91.28	**90.96**

Table 2: F1 scores on 14 datasets for all our systems: Baseline rule-based systems ("rb"), models based on a bi-LSTM with random initialization of the word embeddings ("Rand.") or using pre-trained word embeddings ("FastText") with 300 dimensions ("300d"), and models based on Multilingual BERT ("BERT-M"). Models are trained directly at the document level, or using gold or predicted sentence splits (resp. "CoNLL" and "ssplit" for the baseline and bi-LSTM models, "BERT-M-CoNLL" and "BERT-M-doc" for BERT-M). Best scores are in bold, underlined scores are the highest among baseline and bi-LSTM systems.

spa.rst.stb (-0.8), and for zho.rst.sctb both systems give similar results. eng.sdrt.stac has probably more out-of-vocabulary words, since it contains conversations, thus making the pre-trained vectors less useful. It is less clear why FastText does not help for German, but note that on the dev, results for both systems are very similar, we thus hypothesize that these lower results are due to some difference in the test set rather than to the quality of the pre-trained word embeddings.

In this setting, the preliminary segmentation of documents into sentences does not help much. It even really hurts performance in many cases, especially when using the sentence splitting given in the CoNLL files (e.g. 23.31% in F1 on the eng.rst.gum against 83.43% at best when the input is a whole document). The architecture of our system seems able to tackle long input sequences, and to take advantage of the whole document structure to learn regularities for the task.

6.2 Contextual embeddings

The results presented in Table 2 indicate that the sequence prediction model based on BERT contextual embeddings beats all other systems on all datasets – except the Chinese RST treebank[7] –, often by a large margin. This advantage holds in both configurations: sentential (with gold sentence segmentation, 'BERT-M-CoNLL' col-

input	corpus	P	R	F1
conll	eng.pdtb.pdtb	89.39	87.84	88.6
	tur.pdtb.tdb	76.89	64	69.85
	zho.pdtb.cdtb	82.67	76.25	79.32
	mean	82.98	76.03	79.26
tok	eng.pdtb.pdtb	91.32	87.84	89.54
	tur.pdtb.tdb	84.06	86.74	85.37
	zho.pdtb.cdtb	81.64	71.07	75.99
	mean	85.67	81.88	83.63

Table 3: Final detailed scores on connective tagging with multilingual BERT, on the syntactically processed corpora (conll) and on the tokenized-only documents (tok), after preprocessing for sentence boundaries. Scores are averaged on 5 runs, courtesy of the Shared task organizers.

---

[7] Since none of the authors is a Mandarin speaker, it is hard to analyze the source of the discrepancy for now.

umn) and document-level ('BERT-M-Doc'), even though for the latter the model is used on the output of a sentence segmenter that probably degrades its performances. This is due to BERT embeddings limitations on the lengths of the input (512 subwords), which is reasonable on sentences but too restrictive on unsegmented documents. With respect to that factor, it would be interesting to analyze results for different sentence or document lengths, although one must be prudent when comparing across corpora, as the size of the training set is probably the most crucial parameter influencing the results (see for instance the wide difference between the Spanish RST corpora).

As there were a lot of small differences in scores between our experiments and the reproduced experiments carried out by the shared task organizers, we suggested averaging on a few runs to have a more reliable estimation of the performance. These more reliable scores are reported for our best system in tables 3 and 4. They are the the average of 5 runs done by the task organizers themselves, and we also report their average estimates for precision and recall. The organizers also provided the details of the runs, from which we computed the standard errors on the measure estimates. We found that variance is greater for connective prediction (0.7 and 1.1 points on average respectively on the document or the CoNLL file, with a maximum at 1.6), while it is reasonable on segmentation prediction (0.26 and 0.24 on document and CoNLL with a maximum at 0.8).

We compared BERT and ELMo on the English datasets, and it is clear that when they operate on the same setup (either CoNLL input or preprocessed sentences for both), BERT achieves better performance, so it is safe to conclude that the WordPiece threshold is a crucial factor in document-level segmentation. It is also worth noting that using multilingual BERT yields better results in some cases (only tested on English) than the language specific BERT embeddings. This goes beyond the scope of the present article, but it would be interesting to make a more controlled comparison, if more language specific models become available (ELMo has already been trained in the relevant languages).

To have a better view of the performance level attainable by ELMo-based sequence predictors, we compared BERT- and ELMo-based systems on English using their best setups at the document-level; ie. ELMo is trained and tested on whole documents, and BERT is trained and tested on automatically split documents. The results reported in Table 5 show that ELMo obtains the best scores on discourse segmentation, however by no more than 0.4 points on the RST corpora. The BERT based models outperform ELMo on discourse marker identification, hypothetically because sentence segmentation errors are less crucial in this context since positive labels are probably further away from sentence boundaries. On the eng.sdrt.stac conversation dataset, ELMo has a clear advantage, but it could be because sentence segmentation is much harder. The version of the STAC corpus used in the shared task does not provide dialogue turn boundaries, and the StanfordNLP pipeline is not trained on this kind of input. In this context, having a bad sentence segmentation is worse than not having one at all. The "whole document" setup in this shared task is a bit artificial for STAC, since the boundaries of speakers' interventions are available in the raw data provided by the chat software.

Last, it is worth noting that the shared task provides an opportunity to assess the homogeneity of discourse segmentation guidelines within the same language, and within the *same theory*. Two datasets annotated in the RST framework are available for English and Spanish. Training on the STB and evaluating on the SCTB dataset in Spanish resulted in a 7 point decrease (from 90% to 83%). This relative stability contrasts with the large differences observed between the English RST datasets. Training on GUM and testing on RST-DT results in a drop from 96% to 66% in F1 and training on RST-DT to test on GUM from 93% to 73% (all these scores assume a gold sentence segmentation). The reason is that there are many more segments in RST-DT, so the models overpredicts segment boundaries (and vice versa). Of course, it would be better to evaluate transfer on different corpora annotated with identical or nearly identical guidelines, but the fact that no such pair of corpora exists also raises the issue of the reproducibility of annotations within the same discourse framework.

7 Conclusion

The datasets provided in the shared task allow for the investigation of discourse segmentation in

input	corpus	P	R	F1
conll	deu.rst.pcc	95.22	94.76	94.99
	eng.rst.gum	95.84	90.74	93.21
	eng.rst.rstdt	95.29	96.81	96.04
	eng.sdrt.stac	94.34	96.22	95.27
	eus.rst.ert	89.77	82.87	86.18
	fra.sdrt.annodis	94.42	88.12	91.16
	nld.rst.nldt	97.9	89.59	93.56
	por.rst.cstn	92.78	93.06	92.92
	rus.rst.rrt	86.65	79.49	82.91
	spa.rst.rststb	92.03	89.52	90.74
	spa.rst.sctb	91.43	76.19	83.12
	zho.rst.sctb	87.07	76.19	81.27
	mean	92.73	87.80	90.11
tok	deu.rst.pcc	94.88	94.49	94.68
	eng.rst.gum	92.28	82.89	87.33
	eng.rst.rstdt	93.6	93.27	93.43
	eng.sdrt.stac	87.56	80.78	83.99
	eus.rst.ert	87.43	80.94	84.06
	fra.sdrt.annodis	94.31	89.15	91.65
	nld.rst.nldt	94.81	89.97	92.32
	por.rst.cstn	93.04	90.72	91.86
	rus.rst.rrt	83.37	78.44	80.83
	spa.rst.rststb	89.11	90.09	89.6
	spa.rst.sctb	87.16	76.79	81.65
	zho.rst.sctb	66.26	64.29	65.26
	mean	88.65	84.32	86.39

Table 4: Final detailed scores on segmentation with multilingual BERT, on the syntactically processed corpora (conll) and on plain tokenized documents (tok) with predicted sentence boundaries. Scores are averaged on 5 runs, courtesy of the Shared task organizers.

	Rand.-50d	GloVe-50d	BERT-E	BERT-M	ELMo
eng.pdtb.pdtb	77.08	65.17	**90.83**	89.89	88.40
eng.rst.gum	80.58	78.28	86.29	87.27	**87.65**
eng.rst.rstdt	78.97	83.21	94.41	93.72	**94.75**
eng.sdrt.stac	77.43	71.70	84.65	84.45	**86.06**

Table 5: Specific results on English test data at the document level. 'Rand.-50d' and 'GloVe-50d' correspond to the baseline model, taking a whole document as input. BERT models are still pipelined to a sentence-splitter, but ELMo-based models take the whole document as input. BERT-E uses English embeddings and BERT-M uses multilingual embeddings.

a multilingual setting, and enable comparisons within a language or framework. We presented good baseline systems at the sentence and document levels, and showed that contextual embeddings can be usefully leveraged for the task of discourse segmentation, as on other tasks involving structural and lexical information, yielding state of the art performance.

Acknowledgments

This work was supported partly by the french PIA project "Lorraine Université d'Excellence", reference ANR-15-IDEX-04-LUE

References

Stergos Afantenos, Nicholas Asher, Farah Benamara, Myriam Bras, Ccile Fabre, Lydia-Mai Ho-Dac, Anne Le Draoulec, Philippe Muller, Marie-Paule Pery-Woodley, Laurent Prvot, Josette Rebeyrolles, Ludovic Tanguy, Marianne Vergez-Couret, and Laure Vieu. 2012. An empirical resource for discovering cognitive principles of discourse organisation: the annodis corpus. In *Proceedings of LREC*.

Nicholas Asher, Julie Hunter, Mathieu Morey, Farah Benamara, and Stergos Afantenos. 2016. Discourse structure and dialogue acts in multiparty dialogue: the stac corpus. In *Proceedings of LREC*.

Nicholas Asher and Alex Lascarides. 2003. *Logics of conversation*. Cambridge University Press.

Chloé Braud, Ophélie Lacroix, and Anders Søgaard. 2017a. Cross-lingual and cross-domain discourse segmentation of entire documents. In *Proceedings of ACL*.

Chloé Braud, Ophélie Lacroix, and Anders Søgaard. 2017b. Does syntax help discourse segmentation? not so much. In *Proceedings of EMNLP*.

Shuyuan Cao, Iria da Cunha, and Mikel Iruskieta. 2018. The RST spanish-chinese treebank. In *Proceedings of LAW-MWE-CxG*.

Paula C.F. Cardoso, Erick G. Maziero, Mara Luca Castro Jorge, Eloize R.M. Seno, Ariani Di Felippo, Lucia Helena Machado Rino, Maria das Gracas Volpe Nunes, and Thiago A. S. Pardo. 2011. CSTNews - a discourse-annotated corpus for single and multi-document summarization of news texts in Brazilian Portuguese. In *Proceedings of the 3rd RST Brazilian Meeting*, pages 88–105.

Lynn Carlson, Daniel Marcu, and Mary Ellen Okurowski. 2001. Building a discourse-tagged corpus in the framework of Rhetorical Structure Theory. In *Proceedings of the Second SIGdial Workshop on Discourse and Dialogue*.

Iria da Cunha, Eric SanJuan, Juan-Manuel Torres-Moreno, Marina Lloberas, and Irene Castellón. 2010. DiSeg: Un segmentador discursivo automático para el español. *Procesamiento del lenguaje natural*, 45:145–152.

Iria da Cunha, Eric SanJuan, Juan-Manuel Torres-Moreno, Marina Lloberes, and Irene Castellón. 2012. DiSeg 1.0: The first system for Spanish discourse segmentation. *Expert Syst. Appl.*, 39(2):1671–1678.

Iria da Cunha, Juan-Manuel Torres-Moreno, and Gerardo Sierra. 2011. On the development of the RST Spanish Treebank. In *Proceedings of the Fifth Linguistic Annotation Workshop, LAW*.

Jacob Devlin, Ming-Wei Chang, Kenton Lee, and Kristina Toutanova. 2018. BERT: pre-training of deep bidirectional transformers for language understanding. *arXiv preprint arXiv:1810.04805*.

Seeger Fisher and Brian Roark. 2007. The utility of parse-derived features for automatic discourse segmentation. In *Proceedings of ACL*.

Matt Gardner, Joel Grus, Mark Neumann, Oyvind Tafjord, Pradeep Dasigi, Nelson F. Liu, Matthew Peters, Michael Schmitz, and Luke S. Zettlemoyer. 2017. Allennlp: A deep semantic natural language processing platform. arXiv:1803.07640.

Edouard Grave, Piotr Bojanowski, Prakhar Gupta, Armand Joulin, and Tomas Mikolov. 2018. Learning word vectors for 157 languages. In *Proceedings of LREC*.

Alex Graves and Jürgen Schmidhuber. 2005. Framewise phoneme classification with bidirectional LSTM and other neural network architectures. *Neural Networks*, pages 5–6.

Hugo Hernault, Danushka Bollegala, and Mitsuru Ishizuka. 2010. A sequential model for discourse segmentation. In *Proceedings of CICLing*.

Sepp Hochreiter and Jürgen Schmidhuber. 1997. Long short-term memory. *Neural Computation*, 9(8):1735–1780.

Mikel Iruskieta, María J. Aranzabe, Arantza Diaz de Ilarraza, Itziar Gonzalez-Dios, Mikel Lersundi, and Oier Lopez de la Calle. 2013. The RST Basque Treebank: an online search interface to check rhetorical relations. In *Proceedings of the 4th Workshop RST and Discourse Studies*.

Shafiq Joty, Giuseppe Carenini, and Raymond T. Ng. 2015. Codra: A novel discriminative framework for rhetorical analysis. *Computational Linguistics*, 41:3.

Huong Le Thanh, Geetha Abeysinghe, and Christian Huyck. 2004. Generating discourse structures for written text. In *Proceedings of COLING*.

Jing Li, Aixin Sun, and Shafiq Joty. 2018. Segbot: A generic neural text segmentation model with pointer network. In *Proceedings of IJCAI*.

William C. Mann and Sandra A. Thompson. 1988. Rhetorical Structure Theory: Toward a functional theory of text organization. *Text*, 8:243–281.

Thiago A. S. Pardo and Maria das Graças Volpe Nunes. 2008. On the development and evaluation of a Brazilian Portuguese discourse parser. *Revista de Informática Teórica e Aplicada*, 15(2):43–64.

Jeffrey Pennington, Richard Socher, and Christopher D. Manning. 2014. GloVe: Global vectors for word representation. In *Proceedings of EMNLP*.

Matthew Peters, Mark Neumann, Mohit Iyyer, Matt Gardner, Christopher Clark, Kenton Lee, and Luke Zettlemoyer. 2018. Deep contextualized word representations. In *Proceedings of NAACL-HLT*.

Dina Pisarevskaya, Margarita Ananyeva, Maria Kobozeva, A Nasedkin, S Nikiforova, I Pavlova, and A Shelepov. 2017. Towards building a discourse-annotated corpus of russian. In *Proceedings of the International Conference on Computational Linguistics and Intellectual Technologies "Dialogue"*.

Rashmi Prasad, Nikhil Dinesh, Alan Lee, Eleni Miltsakaki, Livio Robaldo, Aravind Joshi, and Bonnie Webber. 2008. The Penn Discourse TreeBank 2.0. In *Proceedings of LREC*.

Peng Qi, Timothy Dozat, Yuhao Zhang, and Christopher D. Manning. 2018. Universal dependency parsing from scratch. In *Proceedings of the CoNLL 2018 Shared Task: Multilingual Parsing from Raw Text to Universal Dependencies*, Brussels, Belgium.

Gisela Redeker, Ildik Berzlnovich, Nynke van der Vliet, Gosse Bouma, and Markus Egg. 2012. Multilayer discourse annotation of a Dutch text corpus. In *Proceedings of LREC*.

Radu Soricut and Daniel Marcu. 2003. Sentence level discourse parsing using syntactic and lexical information. In *Proceedings of NAACL*.

Caroline Sporleder and Mirella Lapata. 2005. Discourse chunking and its application to sentence compression. In *Proceedings of EMNLP*.

Manfred Stede and Arne Neumann. 2014. Potsdam Commentary Corpus 2.0: Annotation for discourse research. In *Proceedings of LREC*.

Rajen Subba and Barbara Di Eugenio. 2007. Automatic discourse segmentation using neural networks. In *Workshop on the Semantics and Pragmatics of Dialogue*.

Milan Tofiloski, Julian Brooke, and Maite Taboada. 2009. A syntactic and lexical-based discourse segmenter. In *Proceedings of ACL-IJCNLP*.

Nynke van der Vliet. 2010. Syntax-based discourse segmentation of Dutch text. In *15th Student Session, ESSLLI.*

Yizhong Wang, Sujian Li, and Jingfeng Yang. 2018. Toward fast and accurate neural discourse segmentation. In *Proceedings of EMNLP.*

Ngo Xuan Bach, Nguyen Le Minh, and Akira Shimazu. 2012. A reranking model for discourse segmentation using subtree features. In *Proceedings of Sigdial.*

Amir Zeldes. 2016. The GUM corpus: Creating multilayer resources in the classroom. In *Proceedings of LREC.*

Deniz Zeyrek, Demirsahin Isın, A. Sevdik-Çallı, and Ruket Çakıcı. 2013. Turkish discourse bank: Porting a discourse annotation style to a morphologically rich language. *Dialogue and Discourse.*

Yuping Zhou, Jill Lu, Jennifer Zhang, and Nianwen Xue. 2014. Chinese discourse treebank 0.5 ldc2014t21. Web Download. Philadelphia: Linguistic Data Consortium.

Multilingual segmentation based on neural networks and pre-trained word embeddings[*]

Mikel Iruskieta and **Kepa Bengoetxea** and **Aitziber Atutxa** and **Arantza Diaz de Ilarraza**
Ixa Group. University of the Basque Country. UPV/EHU.
{mikel.iruskieta,kepa.bengoetxea,aitziber.atucha,a.diazdeilarraza}@ehu.eus

Abstract

The DISPRT 2019 workshop has organized a shared task aiming to identify cross-formalism and multilingual discourse segments. Elementary Discourse Units (EDUs) are quite similar across different theories. Segmentation is the very first stage on the way of rhetorical annotation. Still, each annotation project adopted several decisions with consequences not only on the annotation of the relational discourse structure but also at the segmentation stage. In this shared task, we have employed pre-trained word embeddings, neural networks (BiLSTM+CRF) to perform the segmentation. We report F_1 results for 6 languages: Basque (0.853), English (0.919), French (0.907), German (0.913), Portuguese (0.926) and Spanish (0.868 and 0.769). Finally, we also pursued an error analysis based on clause typology for Basque and Spanish, in order to understand the performance of the segmenter.

1 Introduction

The need to understand and automatically process texts motivates the construction of discourse parsers. Nowadays, discourse parsing is a challenging task, essential to correctly perform other NLP interesting tasks such as sentiment analysis, question answering, summarization, and others. Discourse parsing is usually divided into two main steps: i) text segmentation (discourse segmentation) which is done automatically with a discourse segmenter, and ii) relation identification linking the segments using rhetorical relations (discourse parsing).

As Iruskieta and Zapirain (2015) report, segmentation proposals are based on the following three basic concepts, or some combinations of these basic concepts:

— Linguistic "form" (or category).

— "Function" (the function of the syntactical components).

— "Meaning" (the coherence relation between propositions).

Some segmentation guidelines follow the same function-form based approach, in different languages. For instance, Tofiloski et al. (2009) for English, Iruskieta et al. (2015) for Basque and da Cunha et al. (2012) for Spanish. Following this approach, we consider an Elementary Discourse Units (EDU) to be a text span functioning as an independent unit. Under this view, only main clauses and adverbial clauses[1] with a verb (form constraint) are EDUs. Other subordinate clauses such as complements —functioning as noun phrases— and relative clauses —functioning as noun modifiers— are not considered to be EDUs.

The first step to annotate a text is to identify EDUs. The aim of discourse segmentation is to identify all the EDUs in the text. Note that granularity of an EDU is nowadays controversial even under the same theoretical approach (van der Vliet, 2010) and granularity is determined in each annotation project.

From our point of view, these are the main problems to tackle when pursuing discourse segmentation:

— Circularity: segmenting and annotating rhetorical relations at the same time. It happens if we use a relation list that includes the ATRIBUTION relation because between the segmented EDUs there is no other competing relation.

— SAME-UNIT: a clause embedded in another clause. Discourse markers and other kind of syntactic structures guide the reader, splitting

---

[*]All authors contributed equally.

[1]Functioning as modifiers of verb phrases or entire clauses, and providing the main clause with a (discourse) thematic role.

Proceedings of Discourse Relation Parsing and Treebanking (DISRPT2019), pages 125–132
Minneapolis, MN, June 6, 2019. ©2019 Association for Computational Linguistics

Language forms considered as EDUs

Clause type	Example
Independent sentence	[*Whipple (EW) gaixotasunak hesteei* **eragiten die** *bereziki.*]₁ GMB0503 [Whipple's (EW) disease usually affects to the intestine.]₁
Main, part of sentence	[pT1 tumoreko 13 kasuetan ez *zen* gongoila inbasiorik *hauteman;*]₁ [aldiz, pT1 101 tumoretatik 19 kasutan (18.6%) inbasioa *hauteman zen*, eta pT1c tumoreen artetik 93 kasutan (32.6%).]₂ GMB0703 [In 13 cases of tumour pT1, no invasive ganglia was detected;]₁ [on the other hand, 19 invasive pT1 tumours (18.6%) and PT1c tumours were detected in 93 cases (32.6%).]₂
Finite adjunct	[Haien sailkapena egiteko hormona hartzaileen eta c-erb-B2 onkogenearen gabeziaz baliatu gara,]₁ [*ikerketa anatomopatologikoetan erabili ohi diren zehaztapenak direlako.*]₂ GMB0702 [We have used the classification of their hormone receptors and c-erb-B2 oncogenetics]₁ [because they are the specifics used in anatomopathological studies.]₂
Non-finite adjunct	[Ohiko tratamendu motek porrot eginez gero,]₁ [gizentasun erigarriaren kirurgia da epe luzera egin daitekeen tratamendu bakarra.]₂ GMB0502 [If the usual treatment fails,]₁ [the surgical treatment of graft is the only treatment that can be done in the long term.]₂
Non-restrictive relative	[Dublin Hiriko Unibertsitateko atal bat da Fiontar,]₁ [zeinak Ekonomia, Informatika eta Enpresa-ikasketetako Lizentziatura ematen baitu, irlanderaren bidez.]₂ TERM23 [Fiontar is a section of the University of Dublin City,]₁ [which teaches a Bachelor of Economics, Computing and Business Studies, through Ireland.]₂

Table 1: Main clause structures in Basque

the clause in two spans sometimes. Consequently, only one of the spans will satisfy the EDU constraints of form and function, making more challenging discourse segmentation and discourse parsing. [2]

We present in Table 1 examples of different clause types in Basque (and translations) showing the ones that could potentially be EDUs. This table follows the notion of hierarchical downgrading (Lehmann, 1985) that goes from independent structures (EDUs) to subordinated clauses (no-EDUs). This notion will be very useful to understand which is the granularity adopted by the multilingual segmenter in two language: Basque and Spanish.

2 Related works

After Ejerhed (1996) published the first English segmenter for RST, several segmenters were built for different languages.

- For English, Le Thanh et al. (2004) developed a segmenter in the framework of the PDTB and Tofiloski et al. (2009) developed an rule based segmenter under RST.[3]
- For German, Lüngen et al. (2006) developed a segmenter.
- For French, Afantenos et al. (2010) developed an EDU segmenter based on machine learning techniques in the framework of SDRT.
- For Brazilian Portuguese, a segmenter which can be used easily online for first time,[4] which is the first step of the RST DiZer parser (Maziero et al., 2011) in RST.
- For Dutch, van der Vliet (2010) build a rule-base segmenter in RST.
- For Spanish, (da Cunha et al., 2012) developed a rule-based segmenter under RST.[5]
- For Arabic, Keskes et al. (2012) built a clause-based discourse segmenter in RST.
- For Thai language Ketui et al. (2013) developed a rule based segmenter in RST.

---

[2]Note that for example, this kind of structures is widespread. For example, SAME-UNIT structure affects to 12.67% (318 of 2,500) of the segments in the Basque RST treebank.

[3]English spoken language was also studied by Passonneau and Litman (1993).

[4]Available at `http://143.107.183.175:21480/segmenter/`.

[5]Available at: `http://dev.termwatch.es/esj/DiSeg/WebDiSeg/`.

Language	Corpus	Dataset	Docs	Sents	Toks	EDUs
Basque	eus.ert	Train	84	990	21,122	1,869
		Dev	28	350	7,533	656
		Test	28	100	3,813	549
Spanish	spa.sctb	Train	32	304	10,249	473
		Dev	9	74	2,450	103
		Test	9	100	3,813	168
	spa.rststb	Train	203	1,577	43,034	2,474
		Dev	32	256	7,531	419
		Test	32	303	8,026	456
Portuguese	por.cstn	Train	110	1,595	44,808	3,916
		Dev	14	232	6,233	552
		Test	12	123	3,615	265
French	fra.sdrt	Train	64	880	22,278	2,032
		Dev	11	227	4,987	517
		Test	11	211	5,146	680
English	eng.gum	Train	78	3,600	67,098	5,012
		Dev	18	784	15,593	1,096
		Test	18	890	15,924	1,203
German	deu.pcc	Train	142	1,773	26,831	2,449
		Dev	17	207	3,152	275
		Test	17	213	3,239	294

Table 2: Corpus for Segmentation tasks.

— For Basque, Iruskieta et al. (2013) created the Basque RST Treebank and Iruskieta and Zapirain (2015) developed also a rule-based segmenter in RST.[6]

As mentioned before, the segmentation task is the first elemental stage in discourse parsing. Some English parsers (Joty et al., 2015; Feng and Hirst, 2014; Ji and Eisenstein, 2014) and Portuguese parsers (Pardo and Nunes, 2004) –just to cite some– have their segmenter. Braud et al. (2017) proposed a multilingual (English, Basque, Spanish, Portuguese, Dutch and German) discourse parser, where each analyzed language has its own segmenter.

3 Resources and Methods

3.1 Corpora

The segmenter has been tested on 6 languages and 7 treebanks. Table 2 shows the information of the selected treebanks.[7]

3.2 Features for discourse segmentation

We employed both lexicalized (word embeddings and character embeddings) and delexicalized (UPOS, XPOS and ATTRs) features. When we refer to lexicalized features, we used external word embeddings for all languages (Basque included) and IXA team calculated word embeddings exclusively for Basque:

1. External word embeddings: 300-dimensional standard word embeddings using Facebook's FastText (Bojanowski et al., 2017);

2. IXA team calculated word embeddings: Basque word embeddings were calculated on the Elhuyar web Corpus (Leturia, 2012) using gensim's (Řehůřek and Sojka, 2010) word2vec skip-gram (Mikolov et al., 2013). They have a dimension of 350, and we employed a window size of 5. The Elhuyar Web corpus was automatically built by scraping the web, and it contains around 124 million Basque word forms.

We pursued the discourse segmentation phase in

---

[6]Available at `http://ixa2.si.ehu.es/EusEduSeg/EusEduSeg.pl`.

[7]For more information `https://github.com/disrpt/sharedtask2019#statistics`.

Token	WordForm	Lema	POS	CASE	Head	Func.	EDU
1	Ernalketa	ernalketa	NOUN	Case=Abs|Number=Sing	2	obl	BeginSeg=Yes
2	gertatzeko	gertatu	VERB	Case=Loc	3	advcl	
3	espermatozoideek	espermatozoide	NOUN	Case=Erg|Number=Plur	5	nmod	BeginSeg=Yes
4	emearen	eme	NOUN	Case=Gen|Number=Sing	5	nmod	
5	umetoki-tronpara	umetoki-tronpa	NOUN	Case=All|Number=Sing	6	obl	
6	heldu	heldu	VERB	VerbForm=4Part	8	xcomp	
7	behar	behar	NOUN	Case=Abs	8	compound	
8	dute	ukan	VERB	Aspect=Prog|Mood=Ind	0	root	
9	,	,	PUNCT	-	8	punct	

Table 3: A training example sentence of BIZ04.

two steps following the form-function approach:

1. Preprocess the data to obtain the features corresponding to each word. The preprocess results in the input for BiLSTM+CRF, more precisely: *a)* The word embedding. *b)* The POS (if the language provided it otherwise CPOS). *c)* The syntactic relation concatenated:

   - to the case mark or the subordination mark (Basque and German) and

   - to the gerund mark, if the POS of the verb had this label (Spanish).

2. Employ a BiLSTM+CRF to perform the actual segmentation.

Instead of randomly initializing the embedding layer, we employed the aforementioned pre-trained word embeddings.

We used the morphological and syntactic information provided by the Shared Task; the case and subordination mark associated to each word was obtained using UDPipe (Straka et al., 2016).

(1) *Ernalketa gertatzeko espermatozoideek emearen umetoki-tronpara heldu behar dute,* In order to occur the fertilization, sperm must reach the uterus stem of the female, [TRANSLATION]

Table 3 and the dependency tree in Figure 1 shows the information provided by the Shared Task Data of the Example (1).

LSTM (Hochreiter and Schmidhuber, 1997) neural networks are widely used for sequential labelling where the input-output correspondence depends on the previously tagged elements. This dependency gets realized, at each time step, in the corresponding LSTM cell by using as input for each hidden state, the output of the previously hidden state as shown in Fig 2. So, the segmentation process consists of obtaining an input sequence

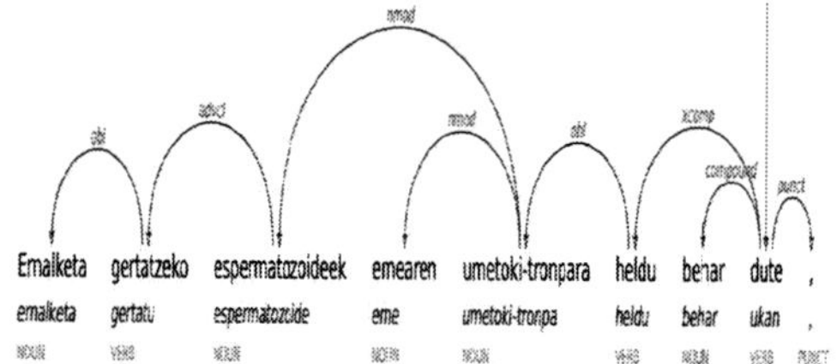

Figure 1: Dependency tree of BIZ04 with Arborator https://arborator.github.io/live.html

$(x_1, x_2, x_3, \cdots, x_n)$ and obtain the corresponding segmentation tag output $(h_1, h_2, h_3, \cdots, h_n)$ at each time step depending not only on the information of the current input word, but of the already processed input. Contrary to other algorithms (perceptron (Afantenos et al., 2010)). BiLSTMs are a special case of LSTM where two LSTM nets are employed, one treating the input sequence from left to right (forward LSTM) and the other from right to left (backward LSTM). LSTMs use a gate-based system, to automatically regulate the quantity of "previous" context to be kept and the quantity that has to be renewed. Each hidden state of an LSTM concentrates all relevant previous sequential context in one only vector. BiLSTM allows to combine information from both directions. The CRF performs the assigment of the segmentation tag taking as input the hidden states provided by each LSTM.

For this work we adopted the implementation by Lample et al. (2016), to accept not only the embeddings but additional information like POS or CPOS and syntactic relation concatenated to the case and syntactic subordination information at each time step. The equations below describe a memory cell formally in this implementation:

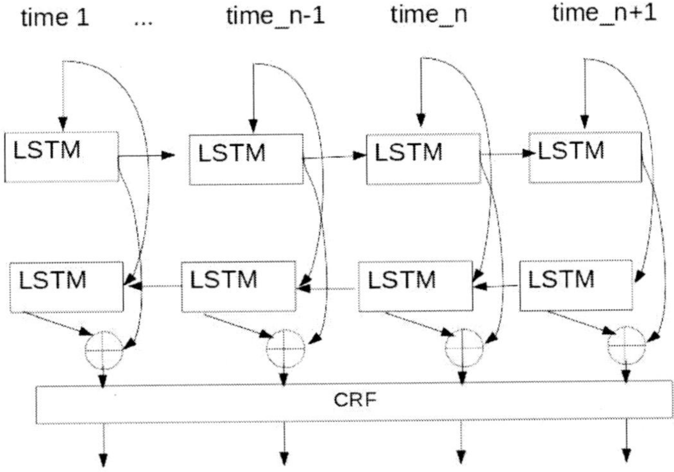

Figure 2: Graphical view of the segmenter

$$i_t = \sigma(W_{x_i}x_t + W_{h_i}h_{t-1} + W_{c_i}c_{t-1} + b_i)$$
$$\tilde{c}_t = \tanh(W_{x_c}x_t + W_{h_c}h_{t-1} + W_{c_i}c_{t-1} + b_c)$$
$$c_t = (1 - i_t) \odot c_{t-1} + i_t \odot \tilde{c}_t$$
$$o_t = \sigma(W_{x_o}x_t + W_{h_o}h_{t-1} + W_{c_o}c_t + b_o)$$
$$h_t = o_t \odot \tanh(c_t)$$

- σ and tanh the sigmoid and hyperbolic tangent respectively, which introduce in the worl non-linearity, increasing network's predictive power.
- t and $t-1$ current and previous time steps, respectively.
- c_t current state of the memory cell considering how much of the previous state cell must be forgotten $((1 - i_t) \odot c_{t-1})$ and how much information must be updated ($i_t \odot \tilde{c}_t$).
- i_t values that will get updated.
- $\tilde{c}_t$ which new candidates could be added to the state.
- o_t through the sigmoid (σ), defines which part of the information stored in the cell gets outputed.
- h_t the hidden state. Being a Bi-LSTM h_t gets calculated by concatenation right and left contexts (right to left $\overrightarrow{h_t}$ and left to right $\overleftarrow{h_t}$).

4 Results and Discussion

To evaluate the segmenter, we have used precision (P), recall (R) and F_1. We summarized our results in Table 4 showing IXAsegmenter's individual task scores for each language.

Data	P	R	F_1
deu.rst.pcc	0.909	0.918	0.913
eng.rst.gum	0.955	0.886	0.919
eus.ert+skip-gram	0.911	0.802	0.853
eus.ert	0.915	0.782	0.843
fra.sdrt	0.911	0.905	0.907
por.cstn	0.930	0.923	0.926
spa.rststb	0.856	0.879	0.868
spa.sctb	0.932	0.654	0.769

Table 4: Results of the segmenter.

As mentioned before, we have employed FastText and word2vec skip-gram pre trained word embeddings for Basque. The remaining languages were only tested using FastText. Basque results turn to be better using word2vec skip-gram embeddings (see the third row in the Table 4). In general terms, results show that the improvement is bigger in terms of precision than in terms of recall. This improvement may be because the size of the corpus is an essential factor when we are employing neural networks. Improving recall is very important at this stage because segmentation has a considerable impact on later parsing. We have obtained a recall higher than 0.9 in German, English, French and Portuguese.

4.1 Evaluation

With the aim of understanding the results of this cross-formalism and multilingual segmentation task, we analyzed all the discourse segments regarding the hierarchical downgrading:

a) Non adverbial segments (non EDUs): *i)* complements (functions as noun phrases) and *ii)* relative clauses (functions as noun modifiers).

b) Adberbial segments (EDUs): *i)* non-finite adjunct clauses, *iii)* finite adjunct clauses, *iv)* independent clause part of the sentence, *v)* one sentence and *vi)* text spans from more than one sentence.

4.2 Basque

For understanding what the segmenter did within the Basque test dataset, we carried out a comprehensive manual evaluation, annotating the output of the parser. During this evaluation, we carefully checked whether the EDUs obtained from the segmenter fulfilled EDU's constraints (see Table 1).[8]

Following this evaluation method, we found that 428 EDUs out of 500 fulfilled EDU's constraints and 72 did not. Under the notion of the hierarchical downgrading (Lehmann, 1985) from independent sentences or clauses to subordinated clauses, as we show in Table 5 in the frontier of what an EDU is: most of the exceeded errors occur because some complement clauses (28 of 72: 38.89%) were wrongly segmented and most of the missed error occurs because non-finite adjuncts (19 of 72: 26.39%) were not segmented.

The segmenter tried to learn how to segment the smallest EDUs and segmented some of them that do not follow EDU constraint. It is worth noting that here (frontier of what an EDU is) the syntactic complexity is much bigger and most of the times there is a lack of punctuation marks or punctuation marks are used for several functions. This is the reason why these kind of clauses are hard to identify by the syntactic parser; in fact, most of the times these clauses get an incorrect syntactic dependency tag. This leads us to think that improving the results of the syntactic parser should have a positive effect over the segmentation because the segmenter uses syntactic tags as input.

Other errors occur in text spans bigger than one sentence (see Table 5 multiple sentences and one sentence (7 of 72: 7.72%)). We think that the source of those errors is the PoS analysis.

Function	Units	Miss	Exc.
Non sub. (EDU)	Multiple sentences	5	1
	One sentence	2	0
	Independent clause	6	1
Subord. (EDU)	Finite adjunct	2	1
	Non-finite adjunct	19	1
EDU limit			
Subord. (No-EDU)	Adjunct without a verb	0	6
	Complement	0	28
Errors		**34**	**38**

Table 5: Error analysis of Basque test data-set.

4.3 Spanish

In the Spanish test data-set, we found that 288 EDUs out of 440 fulfilled EDUs constraints and other 152 do not. Table 6 shows differences regarding Basque output. It is worth mentioning that the system did not segment those EDUs with a discourse marker as the first word and a verb phrase afterwards (finite adjunct clauses 47 and non-finite adjunct clauses 31).

Function	Units	Miss	Exc.
Non sub. (EDU)	Sentences	0	3
	A sentence	13	5
	Independent clause	3	0
Subord.	Finite adjunct	31	0
	DM+ finite ad.	47	2
(EDU)	Non-finite adjunct	20	0
	DM+ non-finite ad.	31	0
EDU limit			
Subord. (No-EDU)	Adjunct without a verb	0	0
	Complement	6	0
Errors		**142**	**10**

Table 6: Error analysis of Spanish test data-set.

If we compare both outputs, we see that Basque segmentation (Table 5) is more fine-grained than the Spanish one (Table 6). The reason is that the errors are not allocated right above what an EDU is.

5 Conclusions and future work

We have conducted the DISRPT 2019 shared task, cross-formalism and multilingual segmentation shared task. In this segmentation task, we have provided results for 6 languages: German, Basque, Spanish, French, Portuguese and English.

Results were different if we take into account languages (and also a slightly different segment granularity): we reported above 90% in Portuguese (92.69%), English (91.94%), German (91.37%) and French (90.79%); from 80% to 90% reported for Basque and Spanish (rststb). Moreover, we report one result under 80% for Spanish (sctb) (76.92%).

Besides, we performed an error analysis of two languages (Basque and Spanish), and we underlined the different granularities in each language. We think that there is still room for improvement by applying a post-process.

Authors are currently striving to achieve the following aims:

— To design a pos-process in segmentation in order to improve results.

— To include this segmenters to the Central Unit detectors for Spanish (Bengoetxea and Iruskieta, 2017) and Portuguese (Bengoetxea et al., 2018).

Acknowledgments

This research was supported by the Spanish Ministry of Economy and Competitiveness (MINECO/FEDER, UE) project PROSA-MED (TIN2016-77820-C3-1-R), University of the Basque Country project UPV/EHU IXA Group (GIU16/16), *Procesamiento automático de textos basado en arquitecturas avanzadas* project (PES18/28) and QUALES KK-2017/00094 (Gobierno Vasco).

References

Stergos Afantenos, Pascal Denis, Philippe Muller, and Laurence Danlos. 2010. Learning recursive segments for discourse parsing. *arXiv preprint arXiv:1003.5372*.

Kepa Bengoetxea, Juliano D. Antonio, and Mikel Iruskieta. 2018. Detecting the Central Units of Brazilian Portuguese argumentative answer texts. *Procesamiento del Lenguaje Natural*, 61:23–30.

Kepa Bengoetxea and Mikel Iruskieta. 2017. A Supervised Central Unit Detector for Spanish. *Procesamiento del Lenguaje Natural*, 60:29–36.

Piotr Bojanowski, Edouard Grave, Armand Joulin, and Tomas Mikolov. 2017. Enriching word vectors with subword information. *Transactions of the Association for Computational Linguistics*, 5:135–146.

Chloé Braud, Maximin Coavoux, and Anders Søgaard. 2017. Cross-lingual RST Discourse Parsing. In *Proceedings of the European Chapter of the Association for Computational Linguistics*.

Iria da Cunha, Erick San Juan, Juan-Manuel Torres-Moreno, Marina Lloberese, and Irene Castellne. 2012. DiSeg 1.0: The first system for Spanish discourse segmentation. *Expert Systems with Applications*, 39(2):1671–1678.

Eva Ejerhed. 1996. Finite state segmentation of discourse into clauses. *Natural Language Engineering*, 2(04):355–364.

Vanessa Wei Feng and Graeme Hirst. 2014. A linear-time bottom-up discourse parser with constraints and post-editing. In *Proceedings of the 52nd Annual Meeting of the Association for Computational Linguistics (Volume 1: Long Papers)*, volume 1, pages 511–521.

Sepp Hochreiter and Jürgen Schmidhuber. 1997. Long short-term memory. *Neural computation*, 9(8):1735–1780.

Mikel Iruskieta, Maria Jesus Aranzabe, Arantza Diaz de Ilarraza, Itziar Gonzalez, Mikel Lersundi, and Oier Lopez de la Calle. 2013. The RST Basque TreeBank: an online search interface to check rhetorical relations. In *4th Workshop "RST and Discourse Studies"*, Brasil.

Mikel Iruskieta, Arantza Diaz de Ilarraza, and Mikel Lersundi. 2015. Establishing criteria for RST-based discourse segmentation and annotation for texts in Basque. *Corpus Linguistics and Linguistic Theory*, 11(2):303–334.

Mikel Iruskieta and Beñat Zapirain. 2015. EusEduSeg: a Dependency-Based EDU Segmentation for Basque. *Procesamiento del Lenguaje Natural*, 55:41–48.

Yangfeng Ji and Jacob Eisenstein. 2014. Representation learning for text-level discourse parsing. In *Proceedings of the 52nd Annual Meeting of the Association for Computational Linguistics (Volume 1: Long Papers)*, volume 1, pages 13–24.

Shafiq Joty, Giuseppe Carenini, and Raymond T Ng. 2015. Codra: A novel discriminative framework for rhetorical analysis. *Computational Linguistics*.

Iskandar Keskes, Farah Benamara, and Lamia Hadrich Belguith. 2012. Clause-based discourse segmentation of arabic texts. In *LREC*, pages 2826–2832.

Nongnuch Ketui, Thanaruk Theeramunkong, and Chutamanee Onsuwan. 2013. Thai elementary discourse unit analysis and syntactic-based segmentation. *International Information Institute (Tokyo). Information*, 16(10):7423.

Guillaume Lample, Miguel Ballesteros, Sandeep Subramanian, Kazuya Kawakami, and Chris Dyer. 2016. Neural architectures for named entity recognition. In *HLT-NAACL*, pages 260–270. ACL.

Huong Le Thanh, Geetha Abeysinghe, and Christian Huyck. 2004. Automated discourse segmentation by syntactic information and cue phrases. In *Proceedings of the IASTED International Conference on Artificial Intelligence and Applications (AIA 2004), Innsbruck, Austria*, pages 411–415.

Christian Lehmann. 1985. Towards a typology of clause linkage. In *Conference on Clause Combining*, volume 1, pages 181–248.

Igor Leturia. 2012. Evaluating different methods for automatically collecting large general corpora for basque from the web. In *24th International Conference on Computational Linguistics (COLING 2012)*, pages 1553–1570, Mumbai, India.

Harald Lüngen, Csilla Puskás, Maja Bärenfänger, Mirco Hilbert, and Henning Lobin. 2006. Discourse segmentation of german written texts. In *Advances in Natural Language Processing*, pages 245–256. Springer.

Erick Maziero, Thiago A.S. Pardo, Iria da Cunha, Juan-Manuel Torres-Moreno, and Eric SanJuan. 2011. Dizer 2.0-an adaptable on-line discourse parser. In *Proceedings of 3rd RST Brazilian Meeting*, pages 1–17.

Tomas Mikolov, Ilya Sutskever, Kai Chen, Greg S Corrado, and Jeff Dean. 2013. Distributed representations of words and phrases and their compositionality. In C. J. C. Burges, L. Bottou, M. Welling, Z. Ghahramani, and K. Q. Weinberger, editors, *Advances in Neural Information Processing Systems 26*, pages 3111–3119. Curran Associates, Inc.

Thiago A.S. Pardo and Maria G.V. Nunes. 2004. Dizer - um analisador discursivo automático para o português do brasil [ENGLISH TRANSLATION]. In *In Anais do IX Workshop de Teses e Dissertações do Instituto de Ciências Matemáticas e de Computação*, pages 1–3, So Carlos-SP, Brasil. 19 a 20 de Novembro.

Rebecca J Passonneau and Diane J Litman. 1993. Intention-based segmentation: Human reliability and correlation with linguistic cues. In *Proceedings of the 31st annual meeting on Association for Computational Linguistics*, pages 148–155. Association for Computational Linguistics.

Radim Řehůřek and Petr Sojka. 2010. Software Framework for Topic Modelling with Large Corpora. In *Proceedings of the LREC 2010 Workshop on New Challenges for NLP Frameworks*, pages 45–50, Valletta, Malta. ELRA.

Milan Straka, Jan Hajic, and Jana Straková. 2016. Udpipe: Trainable pipeline for processing conll-u files performing tokenization, morphological analysis, pos tagging and parsing. In *LREC*.

Milan Tofiloski, Julian Brooke, and Maite Taboada. 2009. A syntactic and lexical-based discourse segmenter. In *47th Annual Meeting of the Association for Computational Linguistics*, pages 77–80, Suntec, Singapore. ACL.

Nynke van der Vliet. 2010. Syntax-based discourse segmentation of Dutch text. In *15th Student Session, ESSLLI*, pages 203–210, Ljubljana, Slovenia.

GumDrop at the DISRPT2019 Shared Task: A Model Stacking Approach to Discourse Unit Segmentation and Connective Detection

Yue Yu
Computer Science
Georgetown University

Yilun Zhu
Linguistics
Georgetown University

Yang Liu
Linguistics
Georgetown University

Yan Liu
Analytics
Georgetown University

Siyao Peng
Linguistics
Georgetown University

Mackenzie Gong
CCT
Georgetown University

Amir Zeldes
Linguistics
Georgetown University

`{yy476,yz565,yl879,yl1023,sp1184,mg1745,az364}@georgetown.edu`

Abstract

In this paper we present GumDrop, Georgetown University's entry at the DISRPT 2019 Shared Task on automatic discourse unit segmentation and connective detection. Our approach relies on model stacking, creating a heterogeneous ensemble of classifiers, which feed into a metalearner for each final task. The system encompasses three trainable component stacks: one for sentence splitting, one for discourse unit segmentation and one for connective detection. The flexibility of each ensemble allows the system to generalize well to datasets of different sizes and with varying levels of homogeneity.

1 Introduction

Although discourse unit segmentation and connective detection are crucial for higher level shallow and deep discourse parsing tasks, recent years have seen more progress in work on the latter tasks than on predicting underlying segments, such as Elementary Discourse Units (EDUs). As the most recent overview on parsing in the framework of Rhetorical Structure Theory (RST, Mann and Thompson 1988) points out (Morey et al., 2017, 1322) "all the parsers in our sample except [two] predict binary trees over manually segmented EDUs". Recent discourse parsing papers (e.g. Li et al. 2016, Braud et al. 2017a) have focused on complex discourse unit span accuracy above the level of EDUs, attachment accuracy, and relation classification accuracy. This is due in part to the difficulty in comparing systems when the underlying segmentation is not identical (see Marcu et al. 1999), but also because of a relatively stable SOA accuracy of EDU segmentation as evaluated on the largest RST corpus, the English RST Discourse Treebank (RST-DT, Carlson et al. 2003), which already exceeded 90% accuracy in 2010 (Hernault et al., 2010).

However, as recent work (Braud et al., 2017b) has shown, performance on smaller or less homogeneous corpora than RST-DT, and especially in the absence of gold syntax trees (which are realistically unavailable at test time for practical applications), hovers around the mid 80s, making it problematic for full discourse parsing in practice. This is more critical for languages and domains in which relatively small datasets are available, making the application of generic neural models less promising.

The DISRPT 2019 Shared Task aims to identify spans associated with discourse relations in data from three formalisms: RST (Mann and Thompson, 1988), SDRT (Asher, 1993) and PDTB (Prasad et al., 2014). The targeted task varies actoss frameworks: Since RST and SDRT segment texts into spans covering the entire document, the corresponding task is to predict the starting point of new discourse units. In the PDTB framework, the basic locus identifying explicit discourse relations is the spans of discourse connectives which need to be identified among other words. In total, 15 corpora (10 from RST data, 3 from PDTB-style data, and 2 from SDRT) in 10 languages (Basque, Chinese, Dutch, English, French, German, Portuguese, Russian, Spanish, and Turkish) are used as the input data for the task. The heterogeneity of the frameworks, languages and even the size of the training datasets all render the shared task challenging: training datasets range from the smallest Chinese RST corpus of 8,960 tokens to the largest English PDTB dataset of 1,061,222 tokens, and all datasets have some different guidelines. In this paper, we therefore focus on creating an architecture that is not only tailored to resources like RST-DT, and takes into account the crucial importance of high accuracy sentence splitting for real-world data, generalizing well to different guidelines and datasets.

Proceedings of Discourse Relation Parsing and Treebanking (DISRPT2019), pages 133–143
Minneapolis, MN, June 6, 2019. ©2019 Association for Computational Linguistics

Our system, called GumDrop, relies on model stacking (Wolpert, 1992), which has been successfully applied to a number of complex NLP problems (e.g. Clark and Manning 2015, Friedrichs et al. 2017). The system uses a range of different rule-based and machine learning approaches whose predictions are all fed to a 'metalearner' or blender classifier, thus benefiting from both neural models where appropriate, and strong rule-based baselines coupled with simpler classifiers for smaller datasets. A further motivation for our model stacking approach is curricular: the system was developed as a graduate seminar project in the course LING-765 (Computational Discourse Modeling), and separating work into many sub-modules allowed each contributor to work on a separate sub-project, all of which are combined in the complete system as an ensemble. The system was built by six graduate students and the instructor, with each student focusing on one module (notwithstanding occasional collaborations) in two phases: work on a high-accuracy ensemble sentence splitter for the automatic parsing scenario (see Section 3.2), followed by the development of a discourse unit segmenter or connective detection module (Sections 3.3 and 3.4).

2   Previous Work

Following early work on rule-based segmenters (e.g. Marcu 2000, Thanh et al. 2004), Soricut and Marcu (2003) used a simple probabilistic model conditioning on lexicalized constituent trees, by using the highest node above each word that has a right-hand sibling, as well as its children. Like our approach, this and subsequent work below perform EDU segmentation as a token-wise binary classification task (boundary/no-boundary). In a more complex model, Sporleder and Lapata (2005) used a two-level stacked boosting classifier on syntactic chunks, POS tags, token and sentence lengths, and token positions within clauses, all of which are similar to or subsumed by some of our features below. They additionally used the list of English connectives from Knott (1996) to identify connective tokens.

Hernault et al. (2010) used an SVM model with features corresponding to token and POS trigrams at and preceding a potential segmentation point, as well as features encoding the lexical head of each token's parent phrase in a phrase structure syntax tree and the same features for the sibling node on the right. More recently, Braud et al. (2017b) used a bi-LSTM-CRF sequence labeling approach on dependency parses, with words, POS tags, dependency relations and the same features for each word's parent and grand-parent tokens, as well as the direction of attachment (left or right), achieving F-scores of .89 on segmenting RST-DT with parser-predicted syntax, and scores in the 80s, near or above previous SOA results, for a number of other corpora and languages.

By contrast, comparatively little work has approached discourse connective detection as a separate task, as it is usually employed as an intermediate step for predicting discourse relations. Pitler and Nenkova (2009) used a Max Entropy classifier using a set of syntactic features extracted from the gold standard Penn Treebank (Marcus et al., 1993) parses of PDTB (Prasad et al., 2008) articles, such as the highest node which dominates exactly and only the words in the connective, the category of the immediate parent of that phrase, and the syntactic category of the sibling immediately to the left/right of the same phrase. Patterson and Kehler (2013) presented a logistic regression model trained on eight relation types extracted from PDTB, with features in three categories: *Relation-level* features such as the connective signaling the relation, attribution status of the relation, and its relevance to financial information; *Argument-level* features, capturing the size or complexity of each of its two arguments; and *Discourse-level* features, which incorporate the dependencies between the relation in question and its neighboring relations in the text.

Polepalli Ramesh et al. (2012) used SVM and CRF for identifying discourse connectives in biomedical texts. The Biomedical Discourse Relation Bank (Prasad et al., 2011) and PDTB were used for in-domain classifiers and novel domain adaptation respectively. Features included POS tags, the dependency label of tokens' immediate parents in a parse tree, and the POS of the left neighbor; domain-specific semantic features included several biomedical gene/species taggers, in addition to NER features predicted by ABNER (A Biomedical Named Entity Recognition).

3   GumDrop

Our system is organized around three ensembles which implement model stacking.

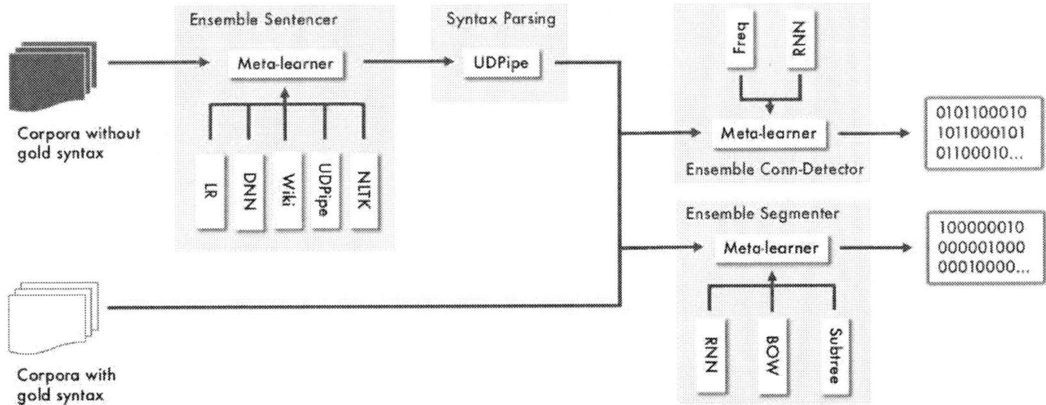

Figure 1: System architecture. The raw text from corpora without gold syntax is first split into sentences by the ensemble sentencer. Sentences are then parsed using UDPipe. Corpora with predicted or gold syntax can then be utilized for discourse unit segmentation and connective detection.

1. A trainable sentencer ensemble which feeds an off-the-shelf dependency parser

2. A discourse unit segmenter ensemble, operating on either gold or predicted sentences

3. A connective detector ensemble, also using gold or predicted sentences

Each module consists of several distinct sub-modules, as shown in Figure 1. Predicted labels and probabilities from sub-modules, along with features for every token position are fed to a blender classifier, which outputs the final prediction for each token. By learning which modules perform better on which dataset, in which scenario (gold or predicted syntax) and in what linguistic environments, the ensemble remains robust at both tasks in both settings.

Since the sub-modules and the ensembles are trained on the same training data, a crucial consideration is to avoid over-reliance on modules, which may occur if the metalearner learns about module reliability from data that the sub-modules have already seen. To counter this, we use 5-fold multitraining: each base module is trained five times, each time predicting labels for a disjoint held-out subset of the training data. These predictions are saved and fed to the ensemble as training data, thereby simulating the trained sub-modules' behavior when exposed to unseen data. At test time, live predictions are gathered from the sub-modules, whose reliability has been assessed via the prior unseen multitraining data.

3.1 Features

Table 1 gives an overview of the features we extract from the shared task data, and the modules using those features for sentence splitting and EDU segmentation/connective detection. Features derived from syntax trees are not available for sentence splitting, though automatic POS tagging using the TreeTagger (Schmid, 1994) was used as a feature for this task, due to its speed and good accuracy in the absence of sentence splits.

Most modules represent underlying words somehow, usually in a 3 or 5-gram window centered around a possible split point. An exception is the LR module, which uses only the first/last (f/l in Table 1) characters to prevent sparseness, but which also uses #char_types features, which give the count of digits, consonant, vowel and other characters per word. Modules with 'top 200/100' use only the n most frequent items in the data, and otherwise treat each word as its POS category. Neural modules (DNN, RNN) use 300 dimensional FastText (Bojanowski et al., 2017) word embeddings, and in the case of the RNN, character embeddings are also used. For Chinese in the LR module, we use the first/last byte in each word instead of actual characters.

The feature genre gives the genre, based on a substring extracted from document names, in corpora with multiple genres. The features quot/paren indicate, for each token, whether it is between quotation marks or parentheses, allowing modules to notice direct speech or uncompleted parentheses which often should not be split. The feature sent% gives the quantile position of

Feature	Sentence splitting						EDU/connective segmentation			
	LR	NLTK	UDPipe	WikiSent	DNN	Meta	Subtree	RNN	BOW	Meta
word	n	y	y	y	y	top 100	top 200	y	top 200	top 100
chars	f/l	n	y	n	n	n	n	y	n	n
upos/xpos	y	n	n	n	n	y	y	y	y	y
case	y	n	n	n	n	y	y	n	n	y
#char_types	y	n	n	n	n	n	n	n	n	n
tok_len	y	n	n	n	n	y	y	n	n	y
tok_frq	y	n	n	n	n	n	n	n	n	n
genre	n	n	n	n	n	y	y	y	n	y
quot/paren	n	n	n	n	n	n	y	n	n	y
sent%	n	n	n	n	n	y	y	n	n	y
deprel	–	–	–	–	–	–	y	y	n	y
headdist	–	–	–	–	–	–	y	bin	n	y
depbracket	–	–	–	–	–	–	y	y	n	y
children	–	–	–	–	–	–	y	n	n	n

Table 1: Features for sentence splitting and EDU segmentation modules.

the current sentence in the document as a number between 0–1. This can be important for datasets in which position in the document interacts with segmentation behavior, such as abstracts in early portions of the academic genres in the Russian corpus, which often leave sentences unsegmented.

The features `deprel`, `headdist` and `depbracket` are not available for sentence splitting, as they require dependency parses: they give the dependency relation, distance to the governing head token (negative/positive for left/right parents), and a BIEO (Begin/Inside/End/Out) encoded representation of the smallest relevant phrase boundaries covering each token for specific phrase types, headed by clausal functions such as 'advcl', 'xcomp' or 'acl' (see Figure 2). For the RNN, `headdist` is binned into 0, next-left/right, close-left/right (within 3 tokens) and far-left/right. The `children` feature set is unique to the Subtree module and is discussed below.

3.2 Sentence Splitting

DNN Sentencer A simple Deep Neural Network classifier, using 300 dimensional word embeddings in a Multilayer Perceptron for tokens in a 5–9-gram window. Optimization on dev data determines the optimal window size for each dataset. Flexible window sizes enable the DNN model to remember the surrounding tokens in both small and large datasets. Starting and ending symbols ('<s>' and '</s>') for each document guarantee the model can always predict the correct label when a new document starts.

Logistic Regression Sentencer The Logistic Regression (LR) Sentencer uses sklearn's (Pedregosa et al., 2011) LogisticRegressionCV implementation to predict sentence boundaries

given a variety of character-level information. The beginning/ending characters (*first/last letter*), auto-generated POS tags and character/frequency count representations (*number of consonants/vowels/digits/other, token length, token frequency*) are applied to a sliding 5-gram window (categorical features are converted into 1-hot features). One advantage of the LR model is its reliability for smaller datasets where character-level features prevent sparseness (including the *top 200* feature decreases performance).

Wiki-Based Sentencer The Wiki-Based Sentencer relies on the frequencies and ratios of paragraph-initial tokens extracted from Wikipedia articles obtained from Wikipedia database dumps for all languages.[1] The rationale is that even though we have no gold sentence splits for Wikipedia, if a token occurs paragraph-initial, then it must be sentence-initial. For each Wiki paragraph, we extract the first "sentence" based on text up to the first sentence final character (./?/!), and then the first word is obtained based on automatic tokenization. Though this approach is coarse, we are able to get a good approximation of frequently initial words thanks to the large data. The frequencies and ratios of tokens being sentence initial are recorded, and thresholds of frequency>10 and ratio > 0.5 are set to collect the most relevant tokens. The main purpose of this module is to capture potential sentence split points such as headings, which are not followed by periods (e.g. *Introduction* in English).

UDPipe + NLTK Additionally, we used UDPipe and NLTK's freely available models as pre-

---

[1] Traditional Chinese characters were converted into simplified Chinese to be consistent with shared task data.

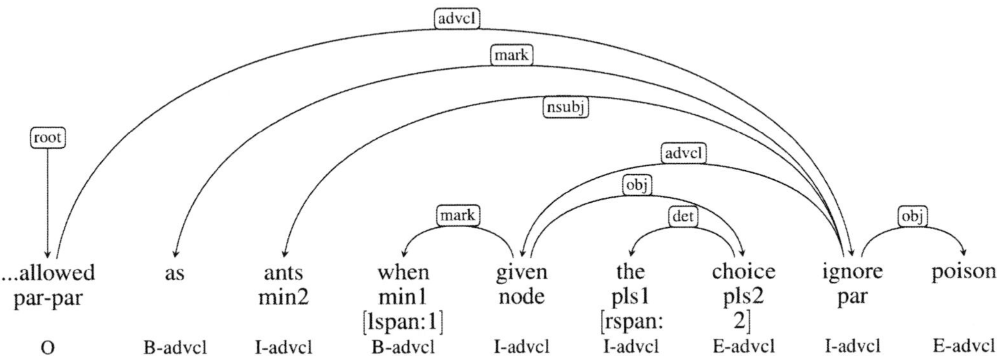

Figure 2: Dependency features from a sentence fragment for a window surrounding 'given' in SubtreeSegmenter.

dictors for the ensemble. For Simplified Chinese, we retrained UPipe using data from the Chinese Treebank, not overlapping CDTB's shared task data.

EnsembleSentencer As a metalearner receiving input from the base-modules, we used tree-based algorithms selected via optimization on dev data, either RandomForest, ExtraTrees, GradientBoosting (using sklearn's implementation), or XGBoost (Chen and Guestrin, 2016). In addition to the submodules' probability estimates, the metalearner was given access to token features in a trigram window, including word identity (for the top 100 items), POS tags, and orthographic case.

3.3 Discourse Unit Segmentation

The feature space for segmentation is much larger than for sentence splitting, due to availability of syntactic features (cf. Table 1). Additionally, as usefulness of features varies across datasets (for example, some lanaguage use only the UPOS column, or UPOS is trivially predictable from XPOS), we performed automatic variable filtering per dataset for both the Subtree and the Ensemble module below. We removed all categorical variables with a Theil's U value of implication above .98 (meaning some feature A is predictable based on some feature B), and for numerical variables, based on Pearson's r>0.95.

SubtreeSegmenter This module focuses on dependency subgraphs, looking at a trigram around the potential split point. In addition to word, orthographic case, POS, and deprel features from Table 1, the module uses a `children` feature set, extracting information for the node token, neigh-

bors, parent and grandparent, including:

- their labels and depth (rank) in the tree
- labels of closest/farthest L/R children
- left/right span length and clause BIOE
- whether L/R neighbors share their parent

The features are illustrated in Figure 2. If we consider a split at the node word 'given', we collect features for two tokens in each direction, the parent ('ignore') and grandparent ('allowed'). The left span of children of 'given' is 1 token long, and the right 2 tokens long. We additionally collect for each of these tokens whether they have the same parent as their neighbor to the right/left (e.g. 'ants' has the same parent as 'as'), as well as the nearest and farthest dependency label on descendents to each side of the node (here, *mark* for both closest and farthest left child of 'given', and *det* (closest) and *obj* (farthest) on the right. The BIOE bracket feature is a flattened 'chunk' feature indicating clauses opening and closing (B-ADVCL, etc.) These features give a good approximation of the window's syntactic context, since even if the split point is nested deeper than a relevant clausal function, discrepancies in neighbors' dependency features, and distances implied by left/right spans along with dependency functions allow the reconstruction of pertinent subtree environments for EDU segmentation. The feature count varied between 86–119 (for rus.rst.rrt and eng.sdrt.stac respectively), due to automatic feature selection.

BOWCounter Rather than predicting exact split points, the BOWCounter attempts to predict the number of segments in each sentence, using a

Ridge regressor with regularization optimized via cross-validation. The module uses the top 200 most frequent words as well as POS tags in a bag of words model and predicts a float which is fed directly to the ensemble. This allows the module to express confidence, rather than an integer prediction. We note that this module is also capable of correctly predicting 0 segmentation points in a sentence (most frequent in the Russian data).

RNNSegmenter To benefit from the predictive power of neural sequence models and word embeddings with good coverage for OOV items, we used NCRF++ (Yang and Zhang, 2018), a bi-LSTM/CNN-CRF sequence labeling framework. Features included Glove word embeddings for English (Pennington et al., 2014) and FastText embeddings (Bojanowski et al., 2017) for other languages, trainable character embeddings, as well as the features in Table 1, such as POS tags, dependency labels, binned distance to parent, genre, and BIEO dependency brackets, all encoded as dense embeddings. We optimized models for each dataset, including using CNN or LSTM encoding for character and word embeddings.

Ensemble Segmenter For the metalearner we used XGBoost, which showed high accuracy across dataset sizes. The ensemble was trained on serialized multitraining data, produced by training base-learners on 80% of the data and predicting labels for each 20% of the training data separately. At test time, the metalearner then receives live predictions from the sub-modules, whose reliability has been assessed using the multitraining data. In addition to base module predictions, the metalearner is given access to the most frequent lexemes, POS tags, dependency labels, genre, sentence length, and dependency brackets, in a trigram window.

3.4 Connective Detection

Frequency-based Connective Detector This module outputs the ratios at which sequences of lexical items have been seen as connectives in training data, establishing an intelligent 'lookup' strategy for the connective detection task. Since connectives can be either a single B-CONN or a B-CONN followed by several I-CONNs, we recover counts for each attested connective token sequence up to 5 tokens. For test data, the module reports the longest possible connective sequence containing a token and the ratio at which it is known to be a connective, as well as the training frequency of each item. Rather than select a cutoff ratio for positive prediction, we allow the ensemble to use the ratio and frequency dynamically as features.

RNN Connective Detector This module is architecturally identical to the RNN EDU segmenter, but since connective labels are non-binary and may form spans, it classifies sequences of tokens with predicted connective types (i.e. B-CONN, I-CONN or not a connective). Rather than predicted labels, the system reports probabilities with which each label is suspected to apply to tokens, based on the top 5 optimal paths as ranked by the CRF layer of NCRF++'s output.

Ensemble Connective Detector The connective ensemble is analogous to the segmenter ensemble, and relies on a Random Forest classifier fed the predicted labels and probabilities from base connective detectors, as well as the same features fed to the segmenter ensemble above.

4 Results

Sentence Splitting Although not part of the shared task, we report results for our Ensemble-Sentencer and LR module (best sub-module on average) next to a punctuation-based baseline (split on '.', '!', '?' and Chinese equivalents) and NLTK's (Bird et al., 2009) sentence tokenizer (except for Chinese, which is not supported). Since most sentence boundaries are also EDU boundaries, this task is critical, and Table 2 shows the gains brought by using the ensemble. GumDrop's performance is generally much higher than both baselines, except for the Portuguese corpus, in which both the system and the baseline make exactly 2 precision errors and one recall error, leading to an almost perfect tied score of 0.988. Somewhat surprisingly, NLTK performs worse on average than the conservative strategy of using sentence final punctuation. The LR module is usually slightly worse than the ensemble, but occasionally wins by a small margin.

Discourse Unit Segmentation Table 3 gives scores for both the predicted and gold syntax scenarios. In order to illustrate the quality of the sub-modules, we also include scores for Subtree (the best non-neural model) and the RNN (best neural model), next to the ensemble. The baseline is provided by assuming EDUs overlap exactly with sentence boundaries.

	Baseline (./!/?)			NLTK			LR			GumDrop		
corpus	P	R	F	P	R	F	P	R	F	P	R	F
deu.rst.pcc	1.00	.864	.927	1.00	.864	.927	.995	.953	.974	.986	.986	**.986**
eng.pdtb.pdtb	.921	.916	.918	.899	.863	.880	.891	.970	.929	.963	.948	**.955**
eng.rst.gum	.956	.810	.877	.943	.807	.870	.935	.885	.909	.977	.874	**.923**
eng.rst.rstdt	.901	.926	.913	.883	.900	.891	.897	.991	.942	.963	.946	**.954**
eng.sdrt.stac	.961	.290	.446	.990	.283	.440	.805	.661	.726	.850	.767	**.806**
eus.rst.ert	.964	1.00	.982	.945	.972	.958	1.00	1.00	**1.00**	1.00	.997	.998
fra.sdrt.annodis	.970	.910	.939	.965	.910	.937	.957	.943	.950	.985	.905	**.943**
nld.rst.nldt	.991	.919	.954	.983	.919	.950	.951	.931	.941	.980	.964	**.972**
por.rst.cstn	.984	.992	**.988**	.967	.967	.967	.984	.992	**.988**	.984	.984	**.988**
rus.rst.rrt	.867	.938	.901	.737	.927	.821	.948	.980	**.964**	.952	.972	.962
spa.rst.rststb	.912	.851	.881	.938	.845	.889	.996	.934	**.964**	.993	.934	.963
spa.rst.sctb	.860	.920	.889	.852	.920	.885	.889	.960	**.923**	.857	.960	.906
tur.pdtb.tdb	.962	.922	.942	.799	.099	176	.979	.979	.979	.983	.984	**.983**
zho.pdtb.cdtb	.959	.866	.910	.–	.–	.–	.954	.975	.965	.980	.975	**.978**
zho.rst.sctb	.879	.826	.852	.–	.–	.–	1.00	.811	**.895**	.991	.795	.882
mean	.939	.863	.888	.915	.790	.815	.945	.931	.937	.963	.933	**.947**
std	.046	167	128	.079	.273	.235	.055	.089	.065	.046	.070	**.050**

Table 2: GumDrop sentence splitting performance.

Overall the results compare favorably with previous work and exceed the previously reported state of the art for the benchmark RST-DT dataset, in both gold and predicted syntax (to the best of our knowledge, 93.7 and 89.5 respectively). At the same time, the ensemble offers good performance across dataset sizes and genres: scores are high on all English datasets, covering a range of genres, including gold STAC (chat data), as well as on some of the smaller datasets, such as Dutch, French and German (only 17K, 22K and 26K training tokens each). Performance is worse on the SCTB corpora and Russian, which may be due to low-quality parses in the gold scenario, and some inconsistencies, especially in the Russian data, where academic abstracts and bibliographies were sometimes segmented and sometimes not. Comparing the ensemble to the RNN or subtree modules individually shows that although they each offer rather strong performance, the ensemble outperforms them for all datasets, except German, where Subtree outperforms it by a small margin, and STAC, where the RNN is slightly better, both showing just half a point of improvement.

For automatically parsed data, the table clearly shows that *eng.rst.stac*, *eng.rst.gum* and *zho.rst.sctb* are the most problematic, in the first case since chat turns must be segmented automatically into sentences. This indicates that a trustworthy sentencer is crucial for discourse unit segmentation and thus very useful for this shared task. Here the EnsembleSentencer brings results up considerably from the punctuation based baseline. The ensemble achieves top performance for most datasets and on average, but the RNN per-forms better on French, Subtree on Portuguese, and both are tied for Spanish RSTSTB.

Connective Detection Results for connective detection are shown in Table 4. As a baseline, we consider assigning each word in the test data a connective label if and only if it is attested exclusively as a connective in the training set (case-sensitive). As the results show, the baseline has low recall but high precision, correlated with the size of the corpus (as exhaustivity of exclusive connective words increases with corpus size).

The frequency-based connective detector gives a reasonable result with a rather simple strategy, using a threshold of 0.5 as the connective detection ratio. More importantly, it is useful as input for the ensemble that outperforms the sequence labeling RNN by itself on every dataset. We suspect at least two factors are responsible for this improvement: firstly, the imbalanced nature of connective annotations (the vast majority of words are not connectives) means that the RNN achieves over 99% classification accuracy, and may have difficulty generalizing to rare but reliable connectives. Secondly, the RNN may overfit spurious features in the training data, to which the frequency detector is not susceptible. Coupled with the resistance of tree ensembles to overfitting and imbalanced problems, the ensemble is able to give a better solution to the task.

5 Error Analysis

5.1 EDU Segmenter

In both gold and predicted syntax scenarios, the RST corpora in Russian, Spanish and Chinese

Gold syntax	Baseline			Subtree			RNN			GumDrop		
corpus	P	R	F	P	R	F	P	R	F	P	R	F
deu.rst.pcc	1.0	.724	.840	.960	.891	**.924**	.892	.871	.881	.933	.905	.919
eng.rst.gum	1.0	.740	.850	.974	.888	.929	.950	.877	.912	.965	.908	**.935**
eng.rst.rstdt	1.0	.396	.567	.951	.945	.948	.932	.945	.939	.949	.965	**.957**
eng.sdrt.stac	.999	.876	.933	.968	.930	.949	.946	.971	**.958**	.953	.954	.953
eus.rst.ert	.981	.530	.688	.890	.707	.788	.889	.754	.816	.909	.740	**.816**
fra.sdrt.annodis	1.0	.310	.474	.943	.854	.897	.894	.903	.898	.944	.865	**.903**
nld.rst.nldt	1.0	.721	.838	.979	.927	.952	.933	.892	.912	.964	.945	**.954**
por.rst.cstn	.878	.435	.582	.911	.827	.867	.815	.903	.857	.918	.899	**.908**
rus.rst.rrt	.760	.490	.596	.809	.745	.775	.821	.710	.761	.835	.755	**.793**
spa.rst.rststb	.974	.647	.777	.921	.792	.851	.759	.855	.804	.890	.818	**.853**
spa.rst.sctb	.970	.577	.724	.938	.631	.754	.901	.649	.754	.898	.679	**.773**
zho.rst.sctb	.924	.726	.813	.880	.744	.806	.843	.768	.804	.810	.810	**.810**
mean	.957	.598	.724	.927	.823	.870	.881	.841	.858	.914	.853	**.881**
Pred syntax	**Baseline**			**Subtree**			**RNN**			**GumDrop**		
corpus	P	R	F	P	R	F	P	R	F	P	R	F
deu.rst.pcc	1.0	.626	.770	.924	.867	.895	.876	.867	.872	.920	.898	**.909**
eng.rst.gum	.956	.599	.737	.948	.777	.854	.910	.805	.854	.940	.772	**.848**
eng.rst.rstdt	.906	.368	.524	.916	.871	.893	.883	.911	.897	.896	.914	**.905**
eng.sdrt.stac	.956	.253	.401	.849	.767	.806	.819	.814	.817	.842	.775	**.807**
eus.rst.ert	.970	.543	.696	.917	.705	.797	.877	.747	.807	.901	.734	**.809**
fra.sdrt.annodis	.980	.285	.442	.938	.824	.877	.892	.915	**.903**	.945	.853	.896
nld.rst.nldt	.991	.663	.794	.951	.849	.897	.938	.835	.883	.947	.884	**.915**
por.rst.cstn	.879	.440	.586	.935	.867	**.900**	.788	.883	.833	.930	.851	.888
rus.rst.rrt	.664	.463	.545	.825	.717	.767	.813	.731	.770	.821	.748	**.783**
spa.rst.rststb	.912	.566	.698	.934	.772	**.845**	.820	.871	.845	.875	.798	.835
spa.rst.sctb	.888	.565	.691	.870	.637	.735	.813	.595	.687	.853	.655	**.741**
zho.rst.sctb	.798	.589	.678	.806	.643	.715	.803	.607	.692	.770	.696	**.731**
mean	.908	.497	.630	.901	.775	.832	.853	.798	.822	.887	.798	**.839**

Table 3: Subtree, RNN and full GumDrop discourse unit segmentation performance.

(rst.rus.rrt, spa.rst.sctb and zho.rst.sctb) achieve the lowest F-scores on this task. Leaving the sentencer performance aside, this error analysis for EDU segmentation will mainly focus on the gold syntax scenario of these three corpora.

Coordinating Conjunctions (CCONJ) Only particular types of coordinated structure consist of two discourse units in different corpora, e.g. VP coordination, or each coordinate predicate having its own subject, etc. For example, in eng.rst.gum, two coordinated verb phrases (*[John is athletic but hates hiking]* are annotated as one discourse unit whereas *[John is athletic] [but he hates hiking]* is divided into two units since both coordinates have their own subjects. Additionally, if one coordinate VP has a dependent adverbial clause, multiple units are annotated. However, even with dependency features included in GumDrop, precision and recall errors happen with different coordinating conjunctions. These include *and, or* in English, *y* ('and'), *o* ('or') in Spanish, and *i* ('and'), *a* ('but'), *ili* ('or') in Russian.

Subordinating Conjunctions (SCONJ) GumDrop sometimes fails when there is an ambiguity between adpositions and subordinating conjunc-

tions. Words that can function as both cause problems for segmentation since subordinate clauses are discourse units but adpositional phrases are not in most datasets. Ambiguous tokens include *to, by, after, before* in English, *en* ('in'), *de* ('of'), *con* ('with'), *por* ('by') in Spanish, as well as *zai* ('at') in Chinese.

Classifying the boundary of subordinate clauses is another problem. The *depbracket* feature can identify the beginning of a subordinate clause when the main clause precedes it. However, when they are in reverse order as in Figure 3, GumDrop fails to identify the beginning of the second discourse unit possibly due to the absence of a second B-feature at *jiaoshi*.

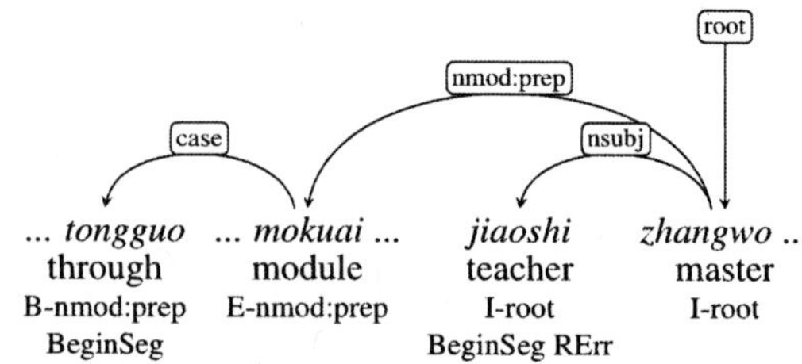

Figure 3: Example of a main clause preceded by a subordinate clause in zho.rst.sctb that causes a Recall Error (RErr) on the second instance of BeginSeg.

Gold syntax	Baseline			Freq			RNN			GumDrop		
corpus	P	R	F	P	R	F	P	R	F	P	R	F
eng.pdtb.pdtb	.964	.022	.044	.836	.578	.683	.859	.871	.865	.879	.888	**.884**
tur.pdtb.tdb	.333	.001	.002	.786	.355	.489	.759	.820	.788	.766	.816	**.790**
zho.pdtb.cdtb	.851	.259	.397	.715	.618	.663	.726	.628	.674	.813	.702	**.754**
mean	.716	.094	.148	.779	.517	.612	.781	.773	.776	.819	.802	**.809**
Pred syntax	**Baseline**			**Freq**			**RNN**			**GumDrop**		
corpus	P	R	F	P	R	F	P	R	F	P	R	F
eng.pdtb.pdtb	.964	.022	.044	.836	.578	.683	.811	.798	.805	.846	.828	**.837**
tur.pdtb.tdb	.333	.001	.002	.786	.355	.489	.761	.821	.790	.768	.817	**.792**
zho.pdtb.cdtb	.851	.259	.397	.715	.618	.663	.705	.590	.642	.806	.673	**.734**
mean	.716	.094	.148	.779	.517	.612	.759	.736	.746	.806	.773	**.788**

Table 4: Connective detection performance.

Enumerations and Listings In rus.rst.rrt, the special combination of a number, a backslash and a period, e.g. *1\\. , 2\\.* etc., is used for enumeration. However, their dependency labels vary: *root, flat, nmod* etc. Due to the instability of the labels, these tokens may result in recall errors, suggesting possibile improvements via parser postprocessing. Similar errors also occur with *1, 2* in Spanish and variants of hyphens/dashes in Russian.

5.2 Connective Detection

Co-occurring Connective Spans Unlike EDU segmentation, where only splits are marked, connectives are spans that consist of a mandatory B-Conn and possible I-Conn labels. However, in Chinese, it is possible for a a connective to consist of discontinuous spans. In (1), both *zai* 'at' and the localizer *zhong*, are connectives and are required to co-occur in the context. However, the system fails to capture the relationship between them.

(1) **zai**   cunmin   zizhi   **zhong** ...
    P : at   villager   autonomy   LC:in
    B-Conn   B-Conn
    'Under the autonomy of villagers...'

Syntactic Inversions Syntactic inversion as a connective is also problematic since no content words are involved: For instance, though the system is able to identify B-Conn in both (2) and (3), it is hard to determine whether content words, such as the verbs (*fueling* and *yinrenzhumu*), belong to the connective span or not. The model can be potentially improved by handling these using dependency features.

(2) **Further** **fueling**   the belief that ...
    B-Conn   I-Conn

(3) ... **geng**   **yinrenzhumude**   de   shi ...
    more   striking   DE   COP
    B-Conn   I-Conn
    'the more striking thing is that ...'

6 Conclusion and Future Work

A main lesson learned from the present work has been that while RNNs perform well on large and consistent datasets, such as RST-DT, they are not as robust when dealing with smaller datasets. This was especially apparent in the predicted syntax scenario, where decision tree ensembles outperformed the RNN on multiple datasets. At the same time, the model stacking approach offers the advantage of not having to choose between neural and tree-based models, by letting a metalearner learn who to believe and when.

Although we hope these results on the shared task dataset represent progress on discourse unit segmentation and connective detection, we would also like to point out that high accuracy (95% or better) is still out of reach, and especially so for languages with fewer resources and in the realistic 'no gold syntax' scenario. Additionally, the architecture used in this paper trades improvements in accuracy for a higher level of complexity, including complex training regimes due to multitraining and a variety of supporting libraries. In future work, we plan to integrate a simplified version of the system into tools that are easier to distribute. In particular, we aim to integrate automatic segmentation facilities into rstWeb (Zeldes, 2016), an open source RST editor interface, so that end users can more easily benefit from system predictions.

References

Nicholas Asher. 1993. *Reference to Abstract Objects in Discourse*. Kluwer, Dordrecht.

Steven Bird, Edward Loper, and Ewan Klein. 2009. *Natural Language Processing with Python.* O'Reilly, Sebastopol, CA.

Piotr Bojanowski, Edouard Grave, Armand Joulin, and Tomas Mikolov. 2017. Enriching word vectors with subword information. *TACL*, 5:135–146.

Chloé Braud, Maximin Coavoux, and Anders Søgaard. 2017a. Cross-lingual RST discourse parsing. In *Proceedings of EACL 2017*, pages 292–304, Valencia, Spain.

Chloé Braud, Ophélie Lacroix, and Anders Søgaard. 2017b. Does syntax help discourse segmentation? not so much. In *Proceedings of EMNLP 2017*, pages 2432–2442, Copenhagen.

Lynn Carlson, Daniel Marcu, and Mary Ellen Okurowski. 2003. Building a discourse-tagged corpus in the framework of Rhetorical Structure Theory. In *Current and New Directions in Discourse and Dialogue*, Text, Speech and Language Technology 22, pages 85–112. Kluwer, Dordrecht.

Tianqi Chen and Carlos Guestrin. 2016. XGBoost: A scalable tree boosting system. In *KDD '16 Proceedings of the 22nd ACM SIGKDD International Conference on Knowledge Discovery and Data Mining*, pages 785–794, San Francisco, CA.

Kevin Clark and Christopher D. Manning. 2015. Entity-centric coreference resolution with model stacking. In *Proceedings of the 53rd Annual Meeting of the Association for Computational Linguistics and the 7th International Joint Conference on Natural Language Processing (ACL-IJCNLP 2015)*, pages 1405–1415, Beijing.

Jasper Friedrichs, Debanjan Mahata, and Shubham Gupta. 2017. InfyNLP at SMM4H task 2: Stacked ensemble of shallow convolutional neural networks for identifying personal medication intake from Twitter. In *Proceedings of SMM4H@AMIA 2017*, Washington, DC.

Hugo Hernault, Helmut Prendinger, David A. duVerle, and Mitsuru Ishizuka. 2010. HILDA: A discourse parser using support vector machine classification. *Dialogue and Discourse*, 1(3):1–33.

Alistair Knott. 1996. *A Data-Driven Methodology for Motivating a Set of Coherence Relations.* Ph.D. thesis, University of Edinburgh, University of Edinburgh.

Qi Li, Tianshi Li, and Baobao Chang. 2016. Discourse parsing with attention-based hierarchical neural networks. In *Proceedings of EMNLP 2016*, pages 362–371, Austin, TX.

William C. Mann and Sandra A. Thompson. 1988. Rhetorical Structure Theory: Toward a functional theory of text organization. *Text*, 8(3):243–281.

Daniel Marcu. 2000. *The Theory and Practice of Discourse Parsing and Summarization.* MIT Press, Cambridge, MA.

Daniel Marcu, Estibaliz Amorrortu, and Magdalena Romera. 1999. Experiments in constructing a corpus of discourse trees. In *Proceedings of the ACL Workshop Towards Standards and Tools for Discourse Tagging*, pages 48–57, College Park, MD.

Mitchell P. Marcus, Beatrice Santorini, and Mary Ann Marcinkiewicz. 1993. Building a large annotated corpus of English: The Penn Treebank. *Special Issue on Using Large Corpora, Computational Linguistics*, 19(2):313–330.

Mathieu Morey, Philippe Muller, and Nicholas Asher. 2017. How much progress have we made on RST discourse parsing? a replication study of recent results on the RST-DT. In *Proceedings of EMNLP 2017*, pages 1319–1324, Copenhagen, Denmark.

Gary Patterson and Andrew Kehler. 2013. Predicting the presence of discourse connectives. In *Proceedings of EMNLP 2013*, pages 914–923.

Fabian Pedregosa, Gaël Varoquaux, Alexandre Gramfort, Vincent Michel, Bertrand Thirion, Olivier Grisel, Mathieu Blondel, Peter Prettenhofer, Ron Weiss, and Vincent Dubourg. 2011. Scikit-learn: Machine learning in Python. *Journal of Machine Learning Research*, 12:2825–2830.

Jeffrey Pennington, Richard Socher, and Christopher D. Manning. 2014. GloVe: Global vectors for word representation. In *Proceedings of EMNLP 2014*, pages 1532–1543, Doha, Qatar.

Emily Pitler and Ani Nenkova. 2009. Using syntax to disambiguate explicit discourse connectives in text. In *Proceedings of the ACL-IJCNLP 2009 Conference Short Papers*, pages 13–16, Suntec, Singapore.

Balaji Polepalli Ramesh, Rashmi Prasad, Tim Miller, Brian Harrington, and Hong Yu. 2012. Automatic discourse connective detection in biomedical text. *Journal of the American Medical Informatics Association*, 19(5):800–808.

Rashmi Prasad, Nikhil Dinesh, Alan Lee, Eleni Miltsakaki, Livio Robaldo, Aravind Joshi, and Bonnie Webber. 2008. The Penn Discourse Treebank 2.0. In *Proceedings of the 6th International Conference on Language Resources and Evaluation (LREC 2008)*, pages 2961–2968, Marrakesh, Morocco.

Rashmi Prasad, Susan McRoy, Nadya Frid, Aravind Joshi, and Hong Yu. 2011. The Biomedical Discourse Relation Bank. *BMC bioinformatics*, 12(1):188.

Rashmi Prasad, Bonnie Webber, and Aravind Joshi. 2014. Reflections on the Penn Discourse Treebank, comparable corpora, and complementary annotation. *Computational Linguistics*, 40(4):921–950.

Helmut Schmid. 1994. Probabilistic part-of-speech tagging using decision trees. In *Proceedings of the Conference on New Methods in Language Processing*, pages 44–49, Manchester, UK.

Radu Soricut and Daniel Marcu. 2003. Sentence level discourse parsing using syntactic and lexical information. In *Proceedings of HLT-NAACL 2003*, pages 149–156, Edmonton.

Caroline Sporleder and Mirella Lapata. 2005. Discourse chunking and its application to sentence compression. In *Proceedings of EMNLP 2005*, pages 257–264, Vancouver.

Huong Le Thanh, Geetha Abeysinghe, and Christian Huyck. 2004. Generating discourse structures for written text. In *Proceedings of COLING 2004*, pages 329–335, Geneva, Switzerland.

David H. Wolpert. 1992. Stacked generalization. *Neural Networks*, 5(2):241–259.

Jie Yang and Yue Zhang. 2018. NCRF++: An open-source neural sequence labeling toolkit. In *Proceedings of the 56th Annual Meeting of the Association for Computational Linguistics*, pages 74–79, Melbourne.

Amir Zeldes. 2016. rstWeb - a browser-based annotation interface for Rhetorical Structure Theory and discourse relations. In *Proceedings of NAACL-HLT 2016 System Demonstrations*, pages 1–5, San Diego, CA.

Towards discourse annotation and sentiment analysis of the Basque Opinion Corpus

Jon Alkorta
Ixa Group / UPV/EHU

Koldo Gojenola
Ixa Group / UPV/EHU

Mikel Iruskieta
Ixa Group / UPV/EHU

{jon.alkorta, koldo.gojenola, mikel.iruskieta}@ehu.eus

Abstract

Discourse information is crucial for a better understanding of the text structure and it is also necessary to describe which part of an opinionated text is more relevant or to decide how a text span can change the polarity (strengthen or weaken) of other span by means of coherence relations. This work presents the first results on the annotation of the Basque Opinion Corpus using Rhetorical Structure Theory (RST). Our evaluation results and analysis show us the main avenues to improve on a future annotation process. We have also extracted the subjectivity of several rhetorical relations and the results show the effect of sentiment words in relations and the influence of each relation in the semantic orientation value.

1 Introduction

Sentiment analysis is a task that extracts subjective information for texts. There are different objectives and challenges in sentiment analysis: i) document level sentiment classification, that determines whether an evaluation is positive or negative (Pang et al., 2002; Turney, 2002); ii) subjectivity classification at sentence level which determines if one sentence has subjective or objective (factual) information (Wiebe et al., 1999) and iii) aspect and entity level in which the target of one positive or negative opinion is identified (Hu and Liu, 2004).

In order to attain those objectives, some resources and tools are needed. Apart from basic resources as a sentiment lexicon, a corpus with subjective information for sentiment analysis is indispensable. Moreover, such corpora are necessary for two approaches to sentiment analysis. One approach is based on linguistic knowledge, where a corpus is needed to analyze different linguistic phenomena related to sentiment analysis. The second approach is based on statistics and, in this case, the corpus is useful to extract patterns of different linguistic phenomena.

The aim of this work is to annotate the rhetorical structure of an opinionated corpus in Basque to check out the semantic orientation of rhetorical relations. This annotation was performed following the *Rhetorical Structure Theory* (RST) (Mann and Thompson, 1988). We have used the Basque version of SO-CAL tool to analyze the semantic orientation of this corpus (Taboada et al., 2011).

This paper has been organized as follows: after presenting related work in Section 2, Section 3 describes the theoretical framework, the corpus for study and the methodology of annotation as well as the analysis of the corpus carried out. Then, Section 4 explains the results of the annotation process, the inter-annotator agreement and the results with regard to analysis in the subjectivity of the corpus. After that, Section 5 discusses the results. Finally, Section 6 concludes the paper, also proposing directions for future work.

2 Related work

The creation of a specific corpus and its annotation at different linguistic levels has been very a common task in natural language processing. As far as a corpus for sentiment analysis is concerned, information related to subjectivity and different grammar-levels has been annotated in different projects.

Refaee and Rieser (2014) annotate the Arabic Twitter Corpus for subjectivity and sentiment analysis. They collect 8,868 tweets in Arabic by random search. Two native speakers of Arabic annotated the tweets. On the one hand, they annotate the semantic orientation of each tweet. On the other hand, they also annotate different grammatical characteristics of tweets such as syntactic, morphological and semantic features as well

144

Proceedings of Discourse Relation Parsing and Treebanking (DISRPT2019), pages 144–152
Minneapolis, MN, June 6, 2019. ©2019 Association for Computational Linguistics

as stylistic and social features. They do not annotate any discourse related feature. They obtain a Kappa inter-annotator agreement of 0.84.

The majority of corpora for sentiment analysis are annotated with subjectivity information. There are fewer corpora annotated with discourse information for the same task. Chardon et al. (2013) present a corpus for sentiment analysis annotated with discourse information. They annotate the corpus using Segmented Discourse Representation Theory (SDRT), creating two corpora: i) movie reviews from *AlloCinéf.fr* and ii) news reaction from *Lemonde.fr*. They collect 211 texts, annotated at EDU and document level. At the EDU level, subjectivity is annotated while at the document level, subjectivity and discourse relations are annotated. Results in subjectivity show that, at EDU level, Cohen's Kappa varies between 0.69 and 0.44 depending on the corpus and, at the document level, Kappa is between 0.73 and 0.58, respectively. They do not give results regarding the annotation of discourse relations.

Asher et al. (2009) create a corpus with discourse and subjectivity annotation. They categorize opinions in four groups (REPORTING, JUDGMENT, ADVISE and SENTIMENT), using SDRT as the annotation framework for discourse. Exactly, they use five types of rhetorical relations (CONTRAST/CORRECTION, EXPLANATION, RESULT and CONTINUATION). They collect three corpora (movie reviews, letters and news reports) in English and French. 150 texts are in French and 186 texts in English. According to Kappa measure, in opinion categorization, the inter-annotator agreement is 95% while in discourse segmentation it is 82%.

Mittal et al. (2013) follow a similar methodology. By the annotation of negation and discourse relations in a corpus, they measure the improvement made in sentiment classification. They collect 662 reviews in Hindi from review websites (380 with a positive opinion and 282 with a negative one). Regarding discourse, they annotate violating expectation conjunctions that oppose or refute the current discourse segment. According to their results, after implementing negation and discourse information to HindiSentiWordNet (HSWN), the accuracy of the tool increases from 50.45 to 80.21. They do not mention the inter-annotating agreement of violating expectation conjunctions.

To sum up, this section gives us a general overview about discourse-based annotated corpora for sentiment analysis. Corpora have been made for specific aims, annotating only some characteristics or features related to discourse and discourse relations. This situation differs from our work, because our work describes the annotation process of the relational discourse structure and how the function in the rhetorical relation affect to the analysis in the semantic orientation.

3 Theoretical framework and methodology

3.1 Theoretical framework: Rhetorical Structure Theory

We have annotated the opinion text corpus using the principles of *Rhetorical Structure Theory* (RST) (Mann and Thompson, 1988; Taboada and Mann, 2006), as it is the most used framework in the annotation of discourse structure and coherence relations in Basque where there are some tools (Iruskieta et al., 2013, 2015b) to study rhetorical relations. According to this framework, a text is coherent when it can be represented in one discourse-tree (RS-tree). In a discourse-tree, there are elementary discourse units (EDU) that are interrelated. The relations are called *coherence relations* and the sum of these coherence relations forms a discourse-tree. Moreover, the text spans present in a discourse relation may enter into new relations, so relations can form compound and recursive structures.

Elementary discourse units are text spans that usually contain a verb, except in some specific situations. The union of two or more EDUs creates a coherence relation. There are initially 25 types of coherence relations in RST. In some cases, one EDU is more important than other one and, in this case, the most important EDU in the relation is called *nucleus*-unit (basic information) while the less important or the auxiliary EDU is called *satellite*-unit (additional information). Coherence relations of this type are called *hypotactic relations*. In contrast, in other relations, EDUs have the same importance and, consequently, all of them are nucleus. The relations with EDUs of same rank are called *paratactic relations*. The task that selects the nucleus in a relation is called *nuclearity*.

Hypotactic relations are also divided into two groups according to their effect on the reader. Some relations are *subject matter* and they are related to the content of text spans. For example, CAUSE, CONDITION or SUMMARY are subject matter relations. On the other hand, the aim of other relations is to create some effect on the reader. They are more rhetorical in their way of functioning. EVIDENCE, ANTITHESIS or MOTIVATION belong to this group.

Figure 1 presents a partial discourse-tree of an opinion text (tagged with the code LIB29). The text is segmented and each text span is a discourse unit (EDU). The discourse units are linked by different types of rhetorical relations. For instance, the EDUs numbered with 15 and 16 are linked by an ELABORATION relation and the EDUs ranging from 15 to 20 are linked by LIST (multinuclear relation). On the other hand, the EDU numbered 2 is the central unit of this text because other relations in the text are linked to it and this text span is not attached to another one (with the exception of multinuclear relations).

According to Taboada and Stede (2009), there are three steps in RST-based text annotation:

1- Segmentation of the text in text spans. Spans are usually clauses.

2- Examination of clear relations between the units. If there is a clear relation, then mark it. If not, the unit belongs to a higher-level relation. In other words, the text span is part of a larger unit.

3- Continue linking the relations until all the EDUs belong to one relation.

Following Iruskieta et al. (2014) we think that it is recommendable, after segmenting the corpus, to identify first the central unit, and then mark the relations between different text spans.

3.2 The Basque Opinion Corpus

The corpus used for this study is the *Basque Opinion Corpus* (Alkorta et al., 2016). This corpus has been created with 240 opinion texts collected from different websites. Some of them are newspapers (for instance, Berria and Argia) while others are specialized websites (for example, Zinea for movies and Kritiken Hemeroteka for literature).

The corpus is multidomain and, in total, there are opinion texts of six different domains: sports, politics, music, movies, literature books and weather. The corpus is doubly balanced. That

is, each domain has the same quantity of opinion texts (40 per domain) and each semantic orientation (positive or negative subjectivity) has the same quantity of opinion texts per each domain (20 positive and 20 negative texts per domain). We extract preliminary corpus information using the morphosyntactical analysis tool Analhitza (Otegi et al., 2017): 52,092 tokens and 3,711 sentences.

We made preliminary checks to decide whether the corpus is useful for sentiment analysis. The opinion texts are subjective, so the frequency information of the first person should be high. The results show that the first person appearance is of 1.21% in a Basque objective corpus (Basque Wikipedia) whereas its appearance is of 8.37% in the Basque Opinion Corpus. As far as the presence of adjectives is concerned, both corpora show similar results. From all the types of grammatical categories, 8.50% of the words correspond to adjectives in Basque Wikipedia and 9.82% in the corpus for study. Other interesting features for sentiment analysis, such as negation, *irrealis blocking* and discourse markers, have also been found in the corpus.

3.3 Methodological steps

We have followed several steps to annotate the Basque Opinion Corpus using the RST framework:

	A1	A2	Total
Movie	21 + 9	9	30
Weather	10 + 5	5	15
Literature	5	20 + 5	25
Total	50	39	70

Table 1: Number of texts annotated by two annotators. The number after the sum sign indicates the quantity of texts with double annotation.

1- Limiting the annotating work. Annotating 240 texts needs a lot of work and time. For that reason, we have thought to annotate some part of the corpus initially and, if the results of the annotation are acceptable, continue with the work. Taking into account the previously described data, both annotators have worked with 70 texts (29.16%) of three different domains. 21 texts from the movie domain have been annotated by one annotator and other 9 texts have been annotated by the two annotators. 10 texts from weather have been annotated once and other 5 texts of the same domain by two annotators. Finally, 25 texts

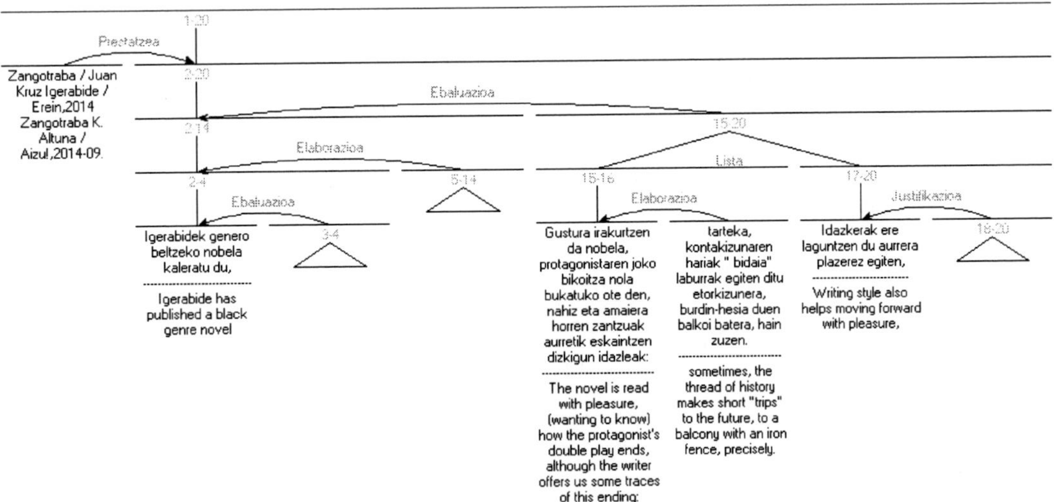

Figure 1: Part of a discourse-tree of the LIB29 review annotated with the RST framework.

of literature reviews have been annotated by one annotator and other 5 texts from the same domain by two. In total, 19 texts from 70 (27.14%) have been annotated by two annotators.

2- Annotation procedure and process. We decided to follow the annotation guidelines proposed by Das and Taboada (2018). Each person annotated four or five texts per day during two or three weeks. The time to annotate documents varied according to the domain. The texts corresponding to the weather domain are shorter and, consequently, easier to annotate while texts about movies as well as those of the literature domain are more difficult because their writing style is more implicit (less indicators and relation signals) and complex (longer at least). Approximately, each weather text was annotated in 20 minutes while movie and literature texts were annotated in one hour.

3- Measurement of inter-annotator agreement. In order to check the quality of the annotation process, inter-annotator agreement was measured. This was calculated manually following the qualitative evaluation method (Iruskieta et al., 2015a) using F-measure. In this measurement, in contrast with the automatic tool, the central subconstituent factor was not taken into account.

4- Semantic orientation extraction. Using the Basque version of the SO-CAL tool (Taboada et al., 2011), we have extracted the subjective information of rhetorical relations in the three domains of the corpus in order to check how the type

of rhetorical relation affects their sentiment valence. SO-CAL needs a sentiment lexicon where words have a sentiment valence between -5 and $+5$. The Basque version of the sentiment lexicon contains 1,237 entries.

We have extracted the sentiment valence of 75 instances if CONCESSION and EVALUATION relations. From the 75 CONCESSION relations, 16 come from the weather domain, 34 from literature and 25 from movies. In the case of EVALUATION, 19 come from weather, 31 from literature and 25 from weather.

5- Results. On the one hand, we have calculated the percentage of rhetorical relations with the same label annotated by two persons. On the other hand, we have measured accumulated values of sentiment valences in nuclei and satellites in texts of different domains.

4 Results

4.1 Inter-annotator agreement

Table 2 shows the inter-annotator agreement of rhetorical relations (RR) between both annotators. This agreement was calculated following the qualitative method (Iruskieta et al., 2015a). According to these results, the highest agreement has been reached in the domain of weather where 17 of 39 relations (43.59%) have been annotated with the same relation label. After that, inter-annotator agreement in literature is 41.67% (70 from 168). Finally, the domain of movies obtained the lowest results, since the agreement is 37.73% (83 of

220). Taking all domains into account, 39.81% of the rhetorical relations have been annotated in the same way (170 relations of 427). The disagreements are due to different reasons: i) both annotators have to train more to reach a higher agreement and to obtain better results. ii) opinionative texts are more open than news or scientific abstracts. Therefore, there is more place for different interpretations.

Domain	Agreement (%)	Agreement (RR)
Weather	43.59	17 of 39
Literature	41.67	70 of 168
Movies	37.73	83 of 220
Total	**39.81**	**170 of 427**

Table 2: Inter-annotator agreement in different domains of the corpus measured by hand.

4.2 Subjectivity extraction from rhetorical relations

The annotation of the corpus using Rhetorical Structure Theory allows us to check the usefulness of the corpus. We have extracted the subjectivity from different types of rhetorical relations using the Basque version of the SO-CAL tool and we have been able to check the distribution of words with sentiment valence in each type of rhetorical relation and domain.

We have analyzed how words with sentiment valence appear in nuclei as well as satellites of CONCESSION and EVALUATION[1] in three domains. The results[2] are presented in Table 3. In the case of CONCESSION, the presence of words with sentiment valence in nuclei (47.21%) and satellites (52.79%) is similar in the three domains, although satellites show a higher proportion. In contrast, in the case of EVALUATION, words with sentiment valence are more concentrated on satellites (55.00%) in comparison with nuclei (45.00%). The only exception is weather, where nucleus prevail over satellites as far as the concentration of words with sentiment valence is concerned[3].

This information contrast between discourse

[1] We decide to choose these rhetorical relations, because we think they are more related to opinions and emotions.

[2] In order to measure the presence of words with subjectivity, we have calculated the sum of all the sentiment valences without taking into account their sign.

[3] In the weather domain, one of rhetorical relations has a very long nucleus compared to satellite. This situation may have influenced the results. In other cases, the length of nucleus and satellites has been similar.

and sentiment analysis provides us the option to understand what happens there. For example, in **CONCESSION**, the nucleus presents a situation affirmed by the author and the satellite shows a situation which is apparently inconsistent but also affirmed by the author (Mann and Taboada, 2005). In other words, the probability of an opinion appearance is similar in both. The sentiment valence of the nucleus prevails over the satellite but the application of Basque SO-CAL does not give the correct result because the tool does not apply any discourse processing and, consequently, in this CONCESSION relation, nuclei as well as satellite are given the same weight.

(1) [S[Puntu ahulak izan arren,]$_{-1.5}$ N[film erakargarri eta berezia da Victoria.]$_{+6}$]$_{+4.5}$ (ZIN19)
 [S[Although it has weak points,]$_{-1.5}$ N[Victoria is an entertaining and special movie.]$_{+6}$]$_{+4.5}$

(2) [N[Joxek emaztea eta lagunak dauzka,]$_{-1.5}$ S[gaizki tratatzen baditu ere.]$_{-4.5}$]$_{-2.5}$ (SENTAIZ02)
 [N[Joxe has a wife and friends,]$_{+2}$ S[although he treats them badly]$_{-4.5}$]$_{-2.5}$

(3) [S[Eta Redmaynen lana oso ona bada ere,]$_{+1}$ N[Vikanderrena bikaina da.]$_{+5}$]$_{+6}$ (ZIN15)
 [S[Although Redmayn's work is very good]$_{+1}$, N[Vikander's is excellent.]$_{+5}$]$_{+6}$

In Example (1), the semantic orientation of the nucleus is positive while the semantic orientation of the satellite is negative. The sum is positive and, in this case, SO-CAL correctly assigns the semantic orientation of the overall rhetorical relation. In contrast, in Example (2), according to SO-CAL, the sentiment orientation of the relation is negative but it should be positive, because the semantic orientation of the nucleus is positive. This example clarifies how discourse information is needed in lexicon-based sentiment classifiers such as SO-CAL. Finally, in Example (3), the nucleus as well as the satellite and the rhetorical relation have positive semantic orientation and SO-CAL assigns correctly the semantic orientation.

Another type of rhetorical relation is **EVALUATION**, where the satellite makes an evaluative comment about the situation presented in the nucleus (Mann and Taboada, 2005). That means that the words with subjective information are more likely to appear in the satellite.

Sum of sentiment valences	CONCESSION		EVALUATION	
	Nucleus	Satellite	Nucleus	Satellite
Weather	39.41	39.75	49.86	33.35
Literature	61.02	68.73	53.13	80.30
Movies	13.98	19.45	26.01	45.58
Total	114.41 (47.21 %)	127.93 (52.79 %)	128.99 (45.00%)	159.23 (55.00%)

Table 3: Accumulated values of sentiment valences in nuclei and satellites for each domain.

(4) [N[Arrate Mardarasek bere lehen liburua argitaratu du berriki, Pendrive,]$_0$ S[eta apustu ausarta egin du bertan.]$_{+3}$]$_{+3}$ (SENTBER04)
[N[Arrate Mardaras has published her first book recently, Pendrive,]$_0$ S[and she has made a daring bet there.]$_{+3}$]$_{+3}$

(5) [N[Bada, erraz ikusten den filma da "The danish girl".]$_{+1}$ S[Atsegina da, hunkigarria, entretenigarria]$_{+6}$]$_{+7}$ (ZIN15).
[N[So, "The danish girl" is a film easy to watch.]$_{+1}$ S[It is nice, touching, entertaining.]$_{+6}$]$_{+7}$

(6) [N[Talde lana izatetik pertsonaia bakarraren epika izatera pasako da erdialdetik aurrera]$_{+0.5}$ S[eta horretan asko galduko du filmak.]$_{-3.9}$]$_{-3.4}$ (ZIN39)
[N[It is going to pass from being team work to epic of one person]$_{+0.5}$ S[and in that, the film will lose a lot.]$_{-3.9}$]$_{-3.4}$

Here, we can see some specific characteristics of each rhetorical relation. Unlike CONCESSION, there is a concentration of words with sentiment valence in the satellite while words with sentiment valence have little presence in the nucleus. In fact, the sentiment valence of nuclei is never higher than $+1$ whereas satellites have a higher sentiment valence than ±3 in all the cases. In these three Examples (4, 5 and 6), the Basque version of the SO-CAL tool guesses correctly the semantic orientation of rhetorical relations. For example, in Example (6), the semantic orientation of nucleus is positive and of satellite is negative. The sum of the two EDUs is negative and SO-CAL correctly assigns a -3.4 sentiment valence. This does not happen in all cases because the tool has not implemented any type of discourse information processing. Anyway, the tool provides information about semantic orientation that is necessary to study the relation between sentiment analysis and rhetorical relations.

5 Discussion

5.1 Inter-annotator agreement

Regarding inter-annotator agreement (Table 2), the agreement goes from 37.73% to 43.59%. However, some domains do not show regularity regarding agreement. For example, in the case of reviews (domain of literature), inter-annotator agreement is situated between 38% and 48%, except in two texts where the agreement is lower (26% and 30%). In the same line, in the weather domain, some texts show higher agreement than the average in the domain.

If we evaluate this doubly annotated corpus by automatic means in a more strict scenario (if and only if the central subconstituent is the same) following Iruskieta et al. (2015a), we can observe and evaluate other aspects of rhetorical structure, such as:

- **Constituent (C)** describes all the EDUs that compose each discourse unit or span.

- **Attachment point** is the node in the RS-tree to which the relation is attached.

- **N-S** or nuclearity specifies if the compared relations share the same direction (NS, NS or NN).

- **Relation** determines if both annotators have assigned[4] the same type of rhetorical relation to the attachment point of two or more EDUs in order to get the same effect.

Another aspect to take into consideration is that the manual and automatic evaluation does not show the same results with regard to inter-annotator agreement of the type of relation. According to a manual evaluation, inter-annotator

---

[4]If the central subconstituent is not described with the same span label and compared position (NS or SN), there is no possibility of comparing relations.

	Constituent		Attachment		N-S		Relation	
Domain	**Match**	**F1**	**Match**	**F1**	**Match**	**F1**	**Match**	**F1**
Weather	20 of 37	0.54	9 of 37	0.24	22 of 37	0.59	15 of 37	0.41
Literature	84 of 155	0.54	67 of 155	0.43	105 of 155	0.68	48 of 155	0.31
Movies	112 of 221	0.56	88 of 221	0.40	147 of 221	0.67	68 of 221	0.31
Total	**216 of 413**	**0.52**	**164 of 413**	**0.40**	**274 of 413**	**0.66**	**131 of 413**	**0.32**

Table 4: Inter-annotator agreement results given by the automatic tool.

agreement is 39.81% while the automatic evaluation shows an agreement of 31.72%. As we have noted before, this difference comes due to the fact that the automatic comparison is made in a strict scenario and some relations are not compared, because the description of the central subconstituent of such relations is slightly different.

The inter-annotator agreement results given by the automatic tool offer complementary information related to the annotation of the corpus. As Table 4 shows, the inter-annotator agreement is low in the case of type of relation but the results are better in other aspects of rhetorical relations such as constituent and nuclearity. The agreement in attachment point achieves 0.40 that is low still but constituent as well as nuclearity have achieved the inter-annotator agreement of 0.52 and 0.66, respectively.

On the other hand, another interesting aspect is that there is no difference between domains as far as the agreement of different aspects related to writing style is concerned. It is surprising because the type and the way to express opinions are very different for each domain. In the weather domain, texts are short and clear and the language is direct. In contrast, in literature and movies, texts are longer, more diffuse and they use figurative expression many times. Even so, the weather domain obtains lowest results in three aspects mentioned in Table 4 but the type of relation obtains a better result compared to other domains.

The interpretation of inter-annotator agreement suggests that in the evaluation of some rhetorical relations the agreement is lower while other aspects related to rhetorical relations like constituent and nuclearity obtain a better agreement. We have also discovered that specially ELABORATION, EVALUATION and some multinuclear relations show higher disagreement.

5.1.1 Relevant RR disagreement: confusion matrix

In order to know the differences of these disagreements, we have also measured the type of rhetorical relations with the highest disagreement. With that aim, we have calculated a confusion matrix, and then we have identified the most controversial rhetorical relations. Results are shown in Table 5.

A1	A2		
RRs		**#**	**Total**
ELABORATION	MOTIVATION	9	
ELABORATION	INTERPRETATION	6	19
RESULT	ELABORATION	4	
INTERPRETATION	JUSTIFICATION	4	4
CONCESSION	CONTRAST	6	
EVALUATION	CONTRAST	4	14
LIST	CONJUNCTION	4	

Table 5: Disagreement in rhetorical relations.

According to Table 5, ELABORATION has been used by one annotator whereas the other has employed a more informative relation. In two cases, the first annotator (A1) has annotated an EVALUATION relation while the other annotator (A2) has annotated MOTIVATION and INTERPRETATION. In other case, A2 has annotated ELABORATION whereas A1 has tagged RESULT. In total, there are 19 instances in which ELABORATION has been annotated by one of the annotators. Moreover, there are 4 instances of disagreement between INTERPRETATION and JUSTIFICATION. Finally, there are also disagreements in multinuclear relations. While A2 has annotated CONTRAST in 10 relations, A1 has employed CONCESSION and EVALUATION. There are also 4 instances of disagreement between LIST and CONJUNCTION.

Our interpretation of this results is that one annotator (A1) tends to annotate more general rhetorical relations (e. g. ELABORATION) while other annotator (A2) annotates more precise relations. When it comes to multinuclear relations, it seems that A1 annotator has a tendency to not annotate multinuclear relations.

5.2 Checking the usefulness of the corpus for sentiment analysis

The second aim of this work has been to check the usefulness of the corpus for sentiment analysis. Firstly, the results have shown that in some cases the Basque version of SO-CAL does not assign a suitable semantic orientation to all the rhetorical relations, even when the semantic orientation of EDUs of the relation is correct. This means that the information of rhetorical relations would be needed in order to make a lexicon-based sentiment classification. In other words, this suggests that it would be recommendable to assign weights to EDUs of rhetorical relations to model their effect on sentiment analysis. Each type of rhetorical relation has different characteristics and, consequently, the way to assign weights to EDUs in each relation must be different.

For that reason, we have made a preliminary study with the purpose of checking how different types of rhetorical relations present a semantic orientation and what is the distribution of words with sentiment valence in rhetorical relations. The study of CONCESSION has shown that *i)* the probability of sentiment words appearing in nuclei as well as satellites is similar, and that *ii)* nucleus always prevails over the satellite and, consequently, the semantic orientation of nucleus must be the semantic orientation of all the rhetorical relation. However, the semantic orientation of the satellite must be also taken into consideration in the semantic orientation of all the rhetorical relation. Although comparing with nucleus, satellite has to be less important.

The opposite situation happens in EVALUATION. Here, we can see that words with sentiment valence concentrate more on the satellite while there are fewer words with sentiment valence in the nucleus. That means that the weight must be assigned to the satellite because that part of the relation is more important from the point of view of sentiment analysis.

This interpretation of the results suggests that the Basque Opinion Corpus annotated using RST can be useful for different tasks of sentiment analysis, in fact, the preliminary analysis made with rhetorical relations shows some characteristics and differences that are related to rhetorical relations.

6 Conclusion and Future Work

In this work, we have annotated a part of the Basque Opinion Corpus using Rhetorical Structure Theory. Then, we have measured interannotator agreement. The manual evaluation of the results shows that the inter-annotator agreement of the type of rhetorical relations is 39.81%. On the other hand, using an automatic tool we have obtained more fine-grained results regarding aspects of relations and attachment, as well as nuclearity, with an inter-annotator agreement higher than 0.5. We have also identified that ELABORATION, EVALUATION and some multinuclear relations show the highest disagreement.

On the other hand, we have also checked the usefulness of this annotated corpus for sentiment analysis and the first results show that it is useful to extract subjectivity information of different rhetorical relations. In CONCESSION relations, the semantic orientation of the nucleus always prevails but the valence of the satellite must also be taken into consideration. In EVALUATION relations, words with sentiment valence concentrate on satellite.

In future, firstly, we plan to build extended annotation guidelines to annotate the corpus with more reliability. This would be the previous step before annotating the entire corpus. On the other hand, we would like to continue analyzing how the subjective information is distributed in relations.

Acknowledgments

This research is partially supported by a Basque Government scholarship (PRE_2018_2_0033), the Spanish Ministry of Economy and Competitiveness (MINECO/FEDER, UE) project PROSA-MED (TIN2016-77820-C3-1-R), University of the Basque Country project UPV/EHU IXA Group (GIU16/16) and project Procesamiento automático de textos basado en arquitecturas avanzadas (PES18/28).

References

Jon Alkorta, Koldo Gojenola, and Mikel Iruskieta. 2016. Creating and evaluating a polarity-balanced corpus for Basque sentiment analysis. In *IWoDA16 Fourth International Workshop on Discourse Analysis*, pages 58–62.

Nicholas Asher, Farah Benamara, and Yvette Yannick Mathieu. 2009. Appraisal of opinion expressions in discourse. *Lingvisticæ Investigationes*, 32(2):279–292.

Baptiste Chardon, Farah Benamara, Yannick Mathieu, Vladimir Popescu, and Nicholas Asher. 2013. Measuring the effect of discourse structure on sentiment analysis. In *International Conference on Intelligent Text Processing and Computational Linguistics*, pages 25–37. Springer.

Debopam Das and Maite Taboada. 2018. RST Signalling Corpus: A Corpus of Signals of Coherence Relations. *Lang. Resour. Eval.*, 52(1):149–184.

Minqing Hu and Bing Liu. 2004. Mining and summarizing customer reviews. In *Proceedings of the tenth ACM SIGKDD international conference on Knowledge discovery and data mining*, pages 168–177. ACM.

Mikel Iruskieta, María Jesus Aranzabe, Arantza Diaz de Ilarraza, Itziar Gonzalez, Mikel Lersundi, and Oier Lopez de Lacalle. 2013. The RST Basque TreeBank: an online search interface to check rhetorical relations. In *4th workshop RST and discourse studies*, pages 40–49.

Mikel Iruskieta, Iria Da Cunha, and Maite Taboada. 2015a. A qualitative comparison method for rhetorical structures: identifying different discourse structures in multilingual corpora. *Language resources and evaluation*, 49(2):263–309.

Mikel Iruskieta, Arantza Díaz de Ilarraza, and Mikel Lersundi. 2014. The annotation of the central unit in rhetorical structure trees: A key step in annotating rhetorical relations. In *Proceedings of COLING 2014, the 25th International Conference on Computational Linguistics: Technical Papers*, pages 466–475.

Mikel Iruskieta, Arantza Diaz de Ilarraza, and Mikel Lersundi. 2015b. Establishing criteria for RST-based discourse segmentation and annotation for texts in Basque. *Corpus Linguistics and Linguistic Theory*, 11(2):303–334.

William C Mann and Maite Taboada. 2005. RST web site.

William C Mann and Sandra A Thompson. 1988. Rhetorical Structure Theory: Toward a functional theory of text organization. *Text-Interdisciplinary Journal for the Study of Discourse*, 8(3):243–281.

Namita Mittal, Basant Agarwal, Garvit Chouhan, Nitin Bania, and Prateek Pareek. 2013. Sentiment Analysis of Hindi Reviews based on Negation and Discourse Relation. In *Proceedings of the 11th Workshop on Asian Language Resources*, pages 45–50.

Arantxa Otegi, Oier Imaz, Arantza Diaz de Ilarraza, Mikel Iruskieta, and Larraitz Uria. 2017. ANALHITZA: a tool to extract linguistic information from large corpora in Humanities research. *Procesamiento del Lenguaje Natural*, (58):77–84.

Bo Pang, Lillian Lee, and Shivakumar Vaithyanathan. 2002. Thumbs up?: sentiment classification using machine learning techniques. In *Proceedings of the ACL-02 conference on Empirical methods in natural language processing-Volume 10*, pages 79–86. Association for Computational Linguistics.

Eshrag Refaee and Verena Rieser. 2014. An Arabic Twitter Corpus for Subjectivity and Sentiment Analysis. In *LREC*, pages 2268–2273.

Maite Taboada, Julian Brooke, Milan Tofiloski, Kimberly Voll, and Manfred Stede. 2011. Lexicon-based methods for sentiment analysis. *Computational Linguistics*, 37(2):267–307.

Maite Taboada and William C. Mann. 2006. Rhetorical Structure Theory: looking back and moving ahead. *Discourse studies*, 8(3):423–459.

Maite Taboada and Manfred Stede. 2009. Introduction to RST (Rhetorical Structure Theory). *ESSLLI2016*.

Peter D Turney. 2002. Thumbs up or thumbs down?: semantic orientation applied to unsupervised classification of reviews. In *Proceedings of the 40th annual meeting on association for computational linguistics*, pages 417–424. Association for Computational Linguistics.

Janyce M Wiebe, Rebecca F Bruce, and Thomas P O'Hara. 1999. Development and use of a gold-standard data set for subjectivity classifications. In *Proceedings of the 37th annual meeting of the Association for Computational Linguistics*, pages 246–253.

Using Rhetorical Structure Theory to Assess Discourse Coherence for Non-native Spontaneous Speech

Xinhao Wang[1], **Binod Gyawali**[2], **James V. Bruno**[2], **Hillary R. Molloy**[1],
Keelan Evanini[2], **Klaus Zechner**[2]

Educational Testing Service

[1]90 New Montgomery St #1500, San Francisco, CA 94105, USA

[2]660 Rosedale Road, Princeton, NJ 08541, USA

{xwang002, bgyawali, jbruno, hmolloy}@ets.org

{kevanini, kzechner}@ets.org

Abstract

This study aims to model the discourse structure of spontaneous spoken responses within the context of an assessment of English speaking proficiency for non-native speakers. Rhetorical Structure Theory (RST) has been commonly used in the analysis of discourse organization of written texts; however, limited research has been conducted to date on RST annotation and parsing of spoken language, in particular, non-native spontaneous speech. Due to the fact that the measurement of discourse coherence is typically a key metric in human scoring rubrics for assessments of spoken language, we conducted research to obtain RST annotations on non-native spoken responses from a standardized assessment of academic English proficiency. Subsequently, automatic parsers were trained on these annotations to process non-native spontaneous speech. Finally, a set of features were extracted from automatically generated RST trees to evaluate the discourse structure of non-native spontaneous speech, which were then employed to further improve the validity of an automated speech scoring system.

1 Introduction

The spread of English as the main global language for education and commerce is continuing, and there is a strong interest in developing assessment systems that can automatically score spontaneous speech from non-native speakers with the goals of reducing the burden on human raters, improving reliability, and generating feedback that can be used by language learners (Zechner et al., 2009; Higgins et al., 2011). Various features related to different aspects of speaking proficiency have been explored, such as features for pronunciation, prosody, and fluency (Cucchiarini et al., 2002; Chen et al., 2009; Cheng, 2011; Higgins et al., 2011), as well as features for vocabulary, grammar, and content (Yoon et al., 2012; Chen and Zechner, 2011; Yoon and Bhat, 2012; Chen and Zechner, 2011; Xie et al., 2012; Qian et al., 2016).

Discourse coherence, which refers to how well a text or speech is organized to convey information, is an important aspect of communicative competence, as is reflected in human scoring rubrics for assessments of non-native English (ETS, 2012). However, discourse-level features have rarely been investigated in the context of automated speech scoring. In order to address this deficiency, this study aims to explore effective means to automate the analysis of discourse and the measurement of coherence in non-native spoken responses, thereby improving the validity of an automated scoring system.

Rhetorical Structure Theory (RST) (Mann and Thompson, 1988) is one of the most influential approaches for document-level discourse analysis. It can represent a document's discourse structure using a hierarchical tree in which nodes are recursively linked with rhetorical relations and labeled with *nucleus* or *satellite* tags to depict the importance of the child nodes in a relation. In our previous study (Wang et al., 2017a), RST-based discourse annotations were obtained on a corpus of 600 spontaneous spoken responses provided by non-native English speakers in the context of an English speaking proficiency assessment. In this paper, we continued this line of research, and made further contributions as follows:

- A larger annotated corpus consisting of 1440 non-native spontaneous spoken responses was obtained using an annotation scheme based on the RST framework. In addition to the previously annotated 600 responses (Wang et al., 2017a), annotations on additional 840 responses were obtained to enlarge the data set that can be used to train

Proceedings of Discourse Relation Parsing and Treebanking (DISRPT2019), pages 153–162
Minneapolis, MN, June 6, 2019. ©2019 Association for Computational Linguistics

an automatic RST parser. When comparing the annotations from two independent human experts on 120 responses, the resulting micro-averaged F1 scores on the three different levels of span, nuclearity, and relation[1] are 86.8%, 72.2%, and 58.2%, respectively.

- Based on all these manual annotations, automatic RST parsers were trained and evaluated. When comparing the automatically generated trees with double annotations from each of the two human experts separately, the F1 scores on the three levels of span, nuclearity, and relation are 76.1%/77.0%, 57.6%/59.7%, and 42.6%/44.4%, respectively.

- A set of RST-based features were introduced to measure the discourse structure of non-native spontaneous speech, where 1) an automatic speech recognizer (ASR) was used to transcribe the speech into text; 2) the aforementioned automatic parsers were applied to build RST trees based on the ASR output; 3) a set of features extracted from the automatic trees were explored, and the results show that these discourse features can predict holistic proficiency scores with an accuracy of 55.9%. Finally, these features were used in combination with other types of features to enhance the validity of an automated speech scoring system.

2 Previous Work

RST is a descriptive framework that has been widely used in the analysis of the discourse organization of written texts (Taboada and Mann, 2006b) and has also been applied to various natural language processing tasks, including language generation, text summarization, and machine translation (Taboada and Mann, 2006a). In particular, the availability of the RST Discourse Treebank (Carlson et al., 2001), with annotations on a selection of 385 Wall Street Journal articles from the Penn Treebank[2], has facilitated RST-based discourse analysis of written texts, since it provides a standard benchmark for comparing the performance of different parsers. A wide range of techniques have

been applied to this task, and document-level discourse parsers are available (Marcu, 2000a; Sagae, 2009; Hernault et al., 2010; Joty et al., 2013; Feng and Hirst, 2014; Li et al., 2014; Ji and Eisenstein, 2014; Li et al., 2016; Liu and Lapata, 2017; Braud et al., 2017; Wang et al., 2017c). Morey et al. (2017) replicated the same evaluation procedure on 9 recent parsers, and indicated that the recent gains in discourse parsing can be attributed to the distributed representations.

Another important application of RST closely related to our research is the automated evaluation of discourse in student essays. For example, one study used features for each sentence in an essay to reflect the status of its parent node as well as its rhetorical relation based on automatically parsed RST trees, with the goal of providing feedback to students about the discourse structure in their essay (Burstein et al., 2003). Another study compared features derived from deep hierarchical discourse relations based on RST trees with features derived from shallow discourse relations based on Penn Discourse Treebank (PDTB) annotations (Prasad et al., 2008) and demonstrated the positive impact of using deep discourse structures to evaluate text coherence (Feng et al., 2014).

Related work has also been conducted to analyze discourse relations in spoken language, which is produced and processed differently from written texts (Rehbein et al., 2016), and often lacks explicit discourse connectives that are more frequent in written language. For example, RST has been used to analyze the semi-structured interviews of Alzheimer's patients (Paulino and Sierra, 2017; Paulino et al., 2018).

However, the annotation scheme with shallow discourse structure and relations from the PDTB (Prasad et al., 2008) has been generally used for spoken language (Demirsahin and Zeyrek, 2014; Stoyanchev and Bangalore, 2015) instead of the rooted-tree structure that is employed in RST. For example, Tonelli et al. (2010) adapted the PDTB annotation scheme to annotate discourse relations in spontaneous conversations in Italian, and Rehbein et al. (2016) compared two frameworks, PDTB and Cognitive approach to Coherence Relations (CCR) (Sanders et al., 1992), for the annotation of discourse relations in spoken language.

Regarding the measurement of discourse coherence in the automated assessment of spoken language, our previous work (Wang et al., 2013,

---

[1] In this paper, all the reported results on the relation level use the full labels of both nuclearity and relation for evaluation.

[2] https://catalog.ldc.upenn.edu/ LDC2002T07

2017b) obtained an annotated corpus of non-native spontaneous speech in which each response was assigned a coherence score on a scale of 1 to 3, and several surface-based features were used to count the use of nouns, pronouns, conjunctions, and discourse connectives. However, that research did not investigate features that can actually represent the hierarchical discourse structure of spoken responses as described in the RST framework.

In contrast to previous studies, this study focuses on monologic spoken responses produced by non-native speakers within the context of a language proficiency assessment and aims to identify the discourse structure of spoken responses. The RST framework was selected due to the fact that it can effectively demonstrate the deep hierarchical discourse structure across an entire response, rather than focusing on the local coherence of adjacent units.

3 Data and Annotation

3.1 Data

This study obtained manual RST annotations on a corpus of 1440 spoken responses, where 600 of them were obtained in our previous work (Wang et al., 2017a), and the additional 840 responses were annotated more recently. All the responses were drawn from a large-scale, high-stakes standardized assessment of English for non-native speakers, the TOEFL® Internet-based Test (TOEFL® iBT), which assesses English communication skills for academic purposes (ETS, 2012). The speaking section of the TOEFL iBT assessment contains six tasks, each of which requires the test taker to provide an unscripted spoken response, 45 or 60 seconds in duration. The corpus used in this study includes 240 responses from each of six different test questions that comprise two different speaking tasks: 1) Independent questions, in which test takers provide an opinion based on personal experience (N = 480 responses) and 2) Integrated questions, in which test takers summarize or discuss material provided in a reading and/or listening passage (N = 960 responses). The spoken responses were all manually transcribed using standard punctuation and capitalization.

Responses were all provided with holistic English proficiency scores on a scale of 1 to 4 (weak to good) by expert human raters in the context of operational, high-stakes scoring for the spoken language assessment. The scoring rubrics address the following three main aspects of speaking proficiency: delivery (pronunciation, fluency, prosody), language use (grammar and lexical choice), and topic development (content and coherence). Responses were balanced for proficiency levels, i.e., 60 responses were included from each of the 4 score points from each of the 6 test questions.

In addition to the holistic proficiency scores, the transcription of each spoken response in this corpus was also provided with a global discourse coherence score by two expert annotators (not drawn from the pool of expert human raters who provided the holistic scores) in our previous study (Wang et al., 2013). The score scale for these coherence scores was from 1 to 3, and the three score points were defined as follows: 3 = highly coherent (contains no instances of confusing arguments or examples), 2 = somewhat coherent (contains some awkward points in which the speaker's line of argument is unclear), 1 = barely coherent (the entire response was confusing and hard to follow). A subset of 600 responses were double annotated, and the inter-annotator agreement for these coherence scores was with a quadratic weighted kappa of 0.68.

3.2 Annotation Guidelines

This study used the same annotation guidelines as in our previous work Wang et al. (2017a), which is a modified version of the tagging reference manual from the RST Discourse Treebank (Carlson and Marcu, 2001). According to these guidelines, annotators segment a transcribed spoken response into Elementary Discourse Unit (EDU) spans of text (corresponding to clauses or clause-like units), and indicate rhetorical relations between non-overlapping spans which typically consist of a nucleus (the most essential information in the rhetorical relation) and a satellite (supporting or background information).

In contrast to well-formed written text, non-native spontaneous speech frequently contains ungrammatical sentences, disfluencies, fillers, hesitations, false starts, and unfinished utterances. In some cases, these spoken responses do not constitute coherent, well-formed discourse. In order to account for these differences, we created an addendum to the RST Discourse Treebank manual introducing the following additional relations:

disfluency relations (in which the disfluent span is the satellite and the corresponding fluent span is the nucleus), **awkward relations** (corresponding to portions of the response where the speaker's discourse structure is infelicitous; awkward relations are based on pre-existing relations, such as *awkward-Reason*, if the intended relation is clear but is expressed incoherently, or *awkward-Other* if there is no clear relation between the awkward EDU and the surrounding discourse), **unfinished utterance relations** (representing EDUs at the end of a response that are incomplete because the test taker ran out of time, in which the incomplete span is the satellite and the root node of the discourse tree is the nucleus), and **discourse particle relations** (such as *you know* and *right*, which are satellites of adjacent spans).

The discourse annotation tool used in the RST Discourse Treebank[3] was also adopted for this study. Using this tool, annotators incrementally build hierarchical discourse trees, in which the leaves are the EDUs and the internal nodes correspond to contiguous spans of text. When the annotators assign the rhetorical relation for a node of the tree, they provide the relation's label (drawn from the pre-defined set of relations in the annotation guidelines) and also indicate whether the spans that comprise the relation are nuclei or satellites. Figure 1 shows an example of an annotated RST tree for a response with a proficiency score of 1. This response includes three disfluencies (EDUs 3, 6, and 9), which are satellites of the corresponding repair nuclei. In addition, the response also includes an awkward Comment-Topic relation between EDU 2 and the node combining EDUs 3-11, indicated by *awkward-Comment-Topic-2*; in this multinuclear relation, the annotator judged that the second branch of the relation was awkward, which is indicated by the 2 that was appended to the relation label.

3.3 Human Annotations

Among the 600 annotations obtained in Wang et al. (2017a), 120 responses from 6 test questions (5 responses from each score level for each question) were double annotated. The standard evaluation method of F1 scores on three levels (span, nuclearity, and relation) (Marcu, 2000b) was used to evaluate the human agreement, where the F1 scores were calculated globally by comparing the two annotators' labels from all samples, i.e., a micro-averaged F1 score. The human agreement results are 86.8%, 72.2%, and 58.2%, according to the span, nuclearity, and relation levels respectively. This level of agreement is similar to the inter-annotator agreement rates on the RST Discourse Treebank, i.e., 88.3% on span, 77.3% on nuclearity, and 64.7% on relation, respectively (Joty et al., 2015; Morey et al., 2017).

The human agreement results also indicate that two annotators tend to agree better on responses from speakers with higher speaking proficiency levels, which is demonstrated by positive correlations (Pearson correlation coefficients) between the F1 agreement scores (F1 scores from each of the double annotated samples) and the human proficiency ratings, approximately 0.2 on all three levels. Meanwhile, the correlations between F1 agreement scores and the human coherence scores are even higher, reaching 0.358 on the fully labeled relation level, which means that human raters agreed better with each other on responses receiving higher coherence scores, as expected. In addition, annotators also provided feedback that this data set posed some unique challenges compared to the data set used to create the RST Discourse Treebank. While the Wall Street Journal articles are written and edited by professionals, our data set consisted of human transcriptions of non-native spontaneous speech, which were at times unintelligible due to the lack of proficiency and transcription inaccuracy.

4 Automatic Parsing

4.1 Parser Training

There has been a variety of research on document-level discourse parsing based on the RST Discourse Treebank, and multiple RST parsers are available as open source tools. In this study, since the focus of our research is not to investigate advanced techniques to improve the state-of-art in parsing, we employed a pre-existing open-source parser from Heilman and Sagae (2015)[4], which was implemented following the work of Sagae (2009) and Ji and Eisenstein (2014). It is a fast, transition-based parser and can process short documents such as news articles or essays in less

Figure 1: Example of an annotated RST tree on a response with a proficiency score of 1.

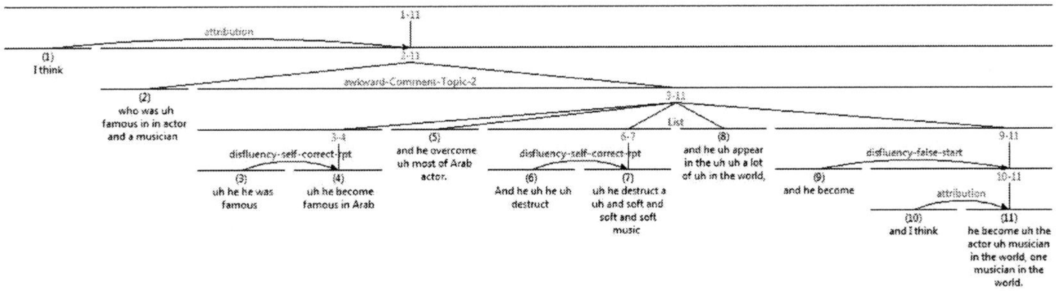

than a second. Since the ultimate goal is to introduce the discourse parser into an automated speech scoring system consisting of many interdependent downstream components, reducing the amount of time required for extracting discourse features is an advantage. We first examined the performance of this selected parser by re-training and re-evaluating it on the RST Discourse Treebank with the standard data partition as in Heilman and Sagae (2015), i.e., 347 samples as the training set, 40 of them were used as the development set, and 38 samples as the test set. In this paper, all the parsers we built were evaluated with the micro F1 score. When using the gold standard syntax trees and EDU segmentations, the F1 scores on three levels of span, nuclearity, and relation can reach 84.1%, 69.6%, and 56.5% respectively, which are close to state-of-the-art accuracy, as reported in Morey et al. (2017).

In this work, the annotated data obtained as described in Section 3 was used for parser building and evaluation. Among the 1440 annotated responses, the data was split into a training set with 1271 single-annotated responses, a development set with 49 single-annotated responses, and a test set with 120 double-annotated responses. Afterwards, the 49 responses in the development set were further double annotated, which allowed us to tune the parser on annotations from both human experts. In contrast to the Wall Street Journal articles in the RST Discourse Treebank (RST_DT), the responses in the corpus of non-native spontaneous speech (RST_SS) are much shorter. Table 1 compares the RST_DT and the RST_SS data sets in terms of the means and standard deviations of the number of EDUs and word tokens. It shows that the RST_SS corpus has more samples (1271 vs. 347 in the training set), but the total numbers of EDUs and words in RST_SS are similar to

Table 1: Average numbers of EDUs and word tokens (and their standard deviations) appearing in the RST Discourse Treebank (RST_DT) and the annotated corpus of non-native spontaneous speech (RST_SS).

	# Samples	# EDUs Mean (std)	# Words Mean (std)
RST_DT			
Train	347	56.0 (51.5)	531.3 (464.0)
Test	38	61.7 (63.4)	570.2 (549.0)
RST_SS			
Train	1271	14.3 (4.7)	122.9 (36.0)
Dev	49	13.0 (4.7)	112.7 (35.7)
Test	120	14.8 (4.4)	127.4 (33.5)

the RST_DT corpus (18,171 vs. 19,443 EDUs and 156,254 vs. 184,352 words in the training set).

In addition, Table 2 shows the most common relations that appear in the training sets of RST_SS and lists their percentages, taken according to their frequency. The percentage of these relations appearing in the RST_DT are also included for comparison. The top five most common relations overlap, but the other five relations that frequently appear in RST_SS are relatively rare in RST_DT, especially the disfluency-self-correct-rpt and disfluency-false-start relations, which is unique to the spoken responses and will not appear in the written texts. In addition, the proportions of each relation appearing in RST_SS and RST_DT are quite different.

4.2 Parser Evaluation

For comparison, we trained three different parsers on both RST_DT and RST_SS: (a) **RST_SS:** using the training set from the corpus of non-native spontaneous speech, where 49 double-annotated responses were used as the development set; (b) **RST_DT:** using the training set from the RST Dis-

Table 2: Top 10 relations appearing in the training set of the annotated corpus of spontaneous speech (RST_SS). The percentages of each relation appearing in both RST_SS and the RST Discourse Treebank (RST_DT) are listed for comparison.

	RST_SS	RST_DT
list	18.2%	13.3%
elaboration -object-attribute-e	7.8%	10.4%
same-unit	7.1%	11.1%
attribution	5.5%	11.3%
elaboration-additional	4.7%	13.2%
reason	3.3%	0.8%
disfluency -self-correct-rpt	2.8%	–
evidence	2.4%	0.7%
disfluency-false-start	2.3%	–
conclusion	2.2%	0.02%

Table 3: Discourse parsing performance in terms of F1 scores (%) on three levels of Span, Nuclearity, and Relation. Human agreements are also listed for comparison. Within each cell, two micro F1 scores according to the gold standards from each of two human annotators are both reported.

	Span	Nucleus	Relation
RST_SS	75.5	56.4	41.2
	76.2	58.6	43.1
RST_DT	73.0	53.0	35.0
	73.8	54.8	36.5
RST_SS +	76.1	57.6	42.6
RST_DT	77.0	59.7	44.4
Human	86.8	72.2	58.2

course Treebank, where 40 samples from the training set were separated as the development set; and (c) **RST_SS + RST_DT:** using the training sets from both RST_SS and RST_DT, where the development set is the same one used in (a). These three parsers were evaluated on the same test set from RST_SS, where the gold standard EDU segmentations were used. As shown in Table 3, the parser trained on RST_SS outperformed the one trained on RST_DT, especially on the relation level, i.e., 41.2%/43.1% vs. 35.0%/36.5%. By combining both data corpora, the F1 scores can further be improved.

Furthermore, besides using gold standard EDU segmentations, we also applied the automatic EDU segmenter within the parser to generate seg-

mentations and then build the RST trees upon them. The evaluation results showed that F1 scores of all three parsers were greatly reduced through this transition. For example, they were decreased to 53.0%/53.6% on span, 40.4%/41.9% on nuclearity, and 29.3%/31.1% on relation for parser (a) trained on **RST_SS**. Therefore, the improvement of EDU segmentations is also a research focus of our future work. In the following section on discourse modeling for spontaneous speech, parser (a), which was trained on RST_SS and using automatic EDU segmentations, was employed for discourse modeling.

5   Discouse Features

The ultimate goal of this line of research is to investigate which features are effective for automatically assessing discourse structure in non-native spontaneous speech. We previously used RST trees for this purpose and proposed several features based on the distribution of relations and the structure of trees (Wang et al., 2017a), including the number of EDUs (n_edu), the number of relations (n_rel), the number of awkward relations (n_awk_rel), the number of rhetorical relations, i.e., relations that were neither classified as awkward nor as disfluencies (n_rhe_rel), the number of different types of rhetorical relations (n_rhe_rel_types), the percentage of rhetorical relations (perc_rhe_rel) out of all relations, the depth of the RST trees (tree_depth), and the ratio between n_edu and tree_depth (ratio_nedu_depth).

In this work, we first examined these eight features on the 1271 single-annotated responses, i.e., the RST_SS training set used to build the automatic parser as described in Section 4.1. Features were extracted from the manually annotated trees, and then the Pearson correlation coefficients of these features with both the holistic proficiency scores as well as the discourse coherence scores are reported in Table 4, which demonstrates the effectiveness of these features. The n_rhe_rel feature achieves the highest correlation with the holistic proficiency scores at 0.719, and the normalized feature perc_rhe_rel achieves the highest correlation with the coherence scores at 0.609. There are six features that receive higher correlations with the proficiency scores, whereas the other two features (n_awk_rel and perc_rhe_rel) receive higher absolute correlations with the coherence scores. This is consistent with our previous obser-

Table 4: Pearson correlation coefficients (r) of discourse features with both the holistic proficiency scores as well as the discourse coherence scores.

Features	Proficiency	Coherence
n_edu	0.612	0.366
n_rel	0.624	0.391
n_awk_rel	-0.425	-0.533
n_rhe_rel	0.719	0.536
n_rhe_relTypes	0.675	0.547
perc_rhe_rel	0.586	0.609
tree_depth	0.402	0.249
ratio_nedu_depth	0.536	0.308

vations, where RST-based discourse features generally have higher correlations with the holistic speaking proficiency scores than with the more specific discourse coherence scores (Wang et al., 2017a). One potential explanation could be the difference in score range: 1-3 for the discourse scores vs. 1-4 for the more fine-grained holistic proficiency scores.

6 Automated Scoring

Besides examining the discourse features based on the manually annotated trees as above, this study also conducted an experiment to examine them on automatically generated trees to measure the discourse structure of non-native spontaneous speech, and then further employ them in an automated spoken English assessment system, SpeechRater^{TM} (Zechner et al., 2007, 2009).

6.1 Experimental Setup

The task is to build effective classification models, referred to as "scoring models", which can automatically predict the holistic proficiency scores by measuring the different aspects of non-native speaking proficiency, including pronunciation, prosody, fluency, vocabulary, grammar, and, in particular, discourse in spontaneous speech. In order to obtain credible evaluation results, this study collected a large data set from the operational TOEFL iBT assessment to conduct this experiment, which includes 17,194 speakers who responded to all the six test questions as described in Section 3.1. The holistic proficiency scores were provided during the operational test, but more specific discourse coherence scores were not available for this large data set. The whole data set was partitioned into two sets: one containing 12,194

speakers (73,164 responses) as the training set to build the scoring models, and the other one containing 5,000 speakers (30,000 responses) to test the model performance.

The baseline scoring model was built with approximately 130 automatic features extracted from the SpeechRater system, which can measure the pronunciation, prosody, fluency, rhythm, vocabulary, and grammar of spontaneous speech. All SpeechRater features were extracted either directly from the speech signal or from the output of a Kaldi-based automatic speech recognizer (Qian et al., 2016) with a word error rate of 20.9% on an independent evaluation set with non-native spontaneous speech from the TOEFL iBT speaking test.

Based on the automatic speech recognition output (without punctuations and capitalization) generated by SpeechRater, the automatic parsers developed in section 4.1 were applied to extract RST trees. Afterwards, the RST-based features were automatically obtained. Therefore, in this process, no manual transcriptions or manual annotations were involved. Furthermore, the RST-based discourse features can be combined with the baseline features to extend the ability of SpeechRater to assess the discourse structure of non-native spontaneous speech.

6.2 Results and Discussion

The automatically generated discourse features were first examined on the scoring model training partition, where Pearson correlation coefficients between automatic features and proficiency scores were calculated. There were two sets of features extracted and examined, based on two different parsers: one was trained with RST_SS and the other one was trained with both RST_SS and RST_DT as shown in Section 4.1.

Table 5 presents the Pearson correlation coefficients of these two sets of features with the proficiency scores. For the five features n_edu, n_rel, n_awk_rel, n_rhe_rel, and tree_depth, the difference is limited, i.e., smaller than 0.004. In contrast, the other three features, n_rhe_rel_types, perc_rhe_rel, and ratio_nedu_depth, achieve better correlations with features based on the RST_SS parser. This indicates the effectiveness of our annotations in capturing discourse in spoken language. Therefore, in the following experiments on scoring models, the features were obtained using the parser

Table 5: Pearson correlation coefficients (r) of discourse features with both the holistic proficiency scores. RST_SS indicates using the parser trained with the annotations on speech data during the feature generation, and RST_SS + RST_DT indicates using the parser trained with both the annotations on speech data and the RST Discourse Treebank.

Features	RST_SS	RST_SS + RST_DT
n_edu	0.424	0.427
n_rel	0.401	0.405
n_awk_rel	-0.096	-0.096
n_rhe_rel	0.418	0.42
n_rhe_rel_types	0.314	0.308
perc_rhe_rel	0.225	0.211
tree_depth	0.329	0.328
ratio_nedu_depth	0.316	0.289

trained with the RST_SS data. Even though all these features were extracted with the automatic speech recognition output and with the automatic parser, they can still achieve moderate correlations with the proficiency scores in a range of 0.2-0.5, except for the feature based on count of awkward relations. The absolute correlation of n_awk_rel feature is less than 0.1, which was caused by the failure of the automatic parser to identify awkward relations.

Furthermore, scoring models were built with SpeechRater features and RST-based discourse features to automatically predict the holistic proficiency scores using the machine learning tool of scikit-learn[5] (Pedregosa et al., 2011). For this experiment, we used the Random Forest classification method to build the scoring models.

Table 6 shows that the baseline system with 131 SpeechRater features can reach an accuracy of 65.3%. By introducing the eight RST-based features, there is a very slight improvement on the accuracy to 65.4% and no improvement in terms of the Pearson correlation coefficient between the automatic and human scores. A scoring system only using eight RST-based features can achieve an accuracy of 55.9%. These results indicate that the proposed features can be used to measure the discourse coherence of non-native spontaneous spoken responses. Due to the fact that these

Table 6: Performance of the automatic scoring models to predict holistic proficiency scores. The baseline system was built with 131 SpeechRater features, and the automatically generated 8 RST-based features were appended to measure the discourse structure.

	Accuracy (%)	r
RST	55.9	0.371
SpeechRater	65.3	0.587
SpeechRater + RST	65.4	0.587

131 SpeechRater features are powerful in measuring various aspects of non-native spontaneous speech, the improvement by introducing discourse features to predict the holistic proficiency scores is limited. But on the other hand, by employing the proposed discourse-level features, the validity of an automatic system for English language proficiency assessment can be improved, because it enables the measurement of an important aspect of speech that appears in the human scoring rubrics.

7 Conclusion

The goal of this research effort is to model discourse structure in non-native spontaneous speech to facilitate the automatic assessment of English language proficiency. In order to achieve this goal, we first obtained an annotated corpus of 1440 spoken responses produced by non-native speakers of English in the context of an English speaking proficiency assessment using Rhetorical Structure Theory and then trained automatic discourse parsers based on the human annotations. Subsequently, discourse features were extracted from the speech signal using automatic speech recognition output and automatically parsed RST trees; these features mostly achieved moderate correlations with human holistic proficiency scores ranging between 0.2 and 0.5. Finally, a scoring model trained using the eight proposed discourse features can predict the proficiency scores with an accuracy of 55.9%, and by introducing them into an automatic speech scoring system, the validity of the system can be improved.

References

Chloé Braud, Maximin Coavoux, and Anders Søgaard. 2017. Cross-lingual RST discourse parsing. In *Proceedings of the EACL conference*.

Jill Burstein, Daniel Marcu, and Kevin Knight. 2003. Finding the WRITE stuff: Automatic identification

---

[5]SKLL, a python tool making the running of scikit-learn experiments simpler, was used. Downloaded from `https://github.com/EducationalTestingService/skll`.

of discourse structure in student essays. *IEEE Intelligent Systems*, 18(1):32–39.

Lynn Carlson and Daniel Marcu. 2001. Discourse tagging reference manual. Technical Report ISI-TR-545, ISI Technical Report.

Lynn Carlson, Daniel Marcu, and Mary Ellen Okurows. 2001. Building a discourse-tagged corpus in the framework of rhetorical structure theory. In *Proceedings of the 2nd SIGDIAL Workshop on Discourse and Dialogue*, pages 1–10.

Lei Chen, Klaus Zechner, and Xiaoming Xi. 2009. Improved pronunciation features for construct-driven assessment of non-native spontaneous speech. In *Proceedings of Human Language Technologies: The 2009 Annual Conference of the North American Chapter of the Association for Computational Linguistics*, pages 442–449.

Miao Chen and Klaus Zechner. 2011. Computing and evaluating syntactic complexity features for automated scoring of spontaneous non-native speech. In *Proceedings of the 49th Annual Meeting of the Association for Computational Linguistics: Human Language Technologies*, pages 722–731, Portland, Oregon, USA.

Jian Cheng. 2011. Automatic assessment of prosody in high-stakes English tests. In *Proceedings of Interspeech*, pages 27–31.

Catia Cucchiarini, Helmer Strik, and Lou Boves. 2002. Quantitative assessment of second language learners' fluency: Comparisons between read and spontaneous speech. *Journal of the Acoustical Society of America*, 111(6):2862–2873.

Isin Demirsahin and Deniz Zeyrek. 2014. Annotating discourse connectives in spoken Turkish. In *Proceedings of LAW VIII - The 8th Linguistic Annotation Workshop*, pages 105–109.

ETS. 2012. The official guide to the TOEFL® test. *Fourth Edition, McGraw-Hill*.

Vanessa Wei Feng and Graeme Hirst. 2014. A linear-time bottom-up discourse parser with constraints and post-editing. In *Proceedings of the 52nd Annual Meeting of the Association for Computational Linguistics (Volume 1: Long Papers)*, pages 511–521.

Vanessa Wei Feng, Ziheng Lin, and Graeme Hirst. 2014. The impact of deep hierarchical discourse structures in the evaluation of text coherence. In *Proceedings of COLING 2014, The 25th International Conference on Computational Linguistics: Technical Papers*, pages 940–949.

Michael Heilman and Kenji Sagae. 2015. Fast rhetorical structure theory discourse parsing. *CoRR*, abs/1505.02425.

Hugo Hernault, Helmut Prendinger, David A. duVerle, and Mitsuru Ishizuka. 2010. HILDA: A discourse parser using support vector machine classification. *Dialogue & Discourse*, 1(3):1–33.

Derrick Higgins, Xiaoming Xi, Klaus Zechner, and David Williamson. 2011. A three-stage approach to the automated scoring of spontaneous spoken responses. *Computer Speech and Language*, 25:282–306.

Yangfeng Ji and Jacob Eisenstein. 2014. Representation learning for text-level discourse parsing. In *Proceedings of the 52nd Annual Meeting of the Association for Computational Linguistics (Volume 1: Long Papers)*, pages 13–24.

Shafiq Joty, Giuseppe Carenini, Raymond Ng, and Yashar Mehdad. 2013. Combining intra- and multi-sentential rhetorical parsing for document-level discourse analysis. In *Proceedings of the 51st Annual Meeting of the Association for Computational Linguistics (Volume 1: Long Papers)*, pages 486–496, Sofia, Bulgaria.

Shafiq Joty, Giuseppe Carenini, and Raymond T Ng. 2015. Codra: A novel discriminative framework for rhetorical analysis. *Computational Linguistics*, 41(3):385–435.

Qi Li, Tianshi Li, and Baobao Chang. 2016. Discourse parsing with attention-based hierarchical neural networks. In *Proceedings of the EMNLP conference*, pages 362–371.

Sujian Li, Liang Wang, Ziqiang Cao, and Wenjie Li. 2014. Text-level discourse dependency parsing. In *Proceedings of the 52nd Annual Meeting of the Association for Computational Linguistics (Volume 1: Long Papers)*, pages 25–35.

Yang Liu and Mirella Lapata. 2017. Learning contextually informed representations for linear-time discourse parsing. In *Proceedings of the EMNLP conference*, pages 1289–1298.

William C. Mann and Sandra A. Thompson. 1988. Rhetorical structure theory: Toward a functional theory of text organization. *Text - Interdisciplinary Journal for the Study of Discourse (Text)*, 8(3):243–281.

Daniel Marcu. 2000a. The rhetorical parsing of unrestricted texts: A surface-based approach. *Computational Linguistics*, 26:395–448.

Daniel Marcu. 2000b. *The Theory and Practice of Discourse Parsing and Summarization*. MIT Press.

Mathieu Morey, Philippe Muller, and Nicholas Asher. 2017. How much progress have we made on RST discourse parsing? a replication study of recent results on the RST-DT. In *Proceedings of the EMNLP conference*, pages 1319–1324.

A Paulino, Gerardo Sierra, Laura Hernandez-Dominguez, Iria da Cunha, and Gemma Bel-Enguix. 2018. Rhetorical relations in the speech of alzheimer's patients and healthy elderly subjects: An approach from the rst. *Computacion y Sistemas*, 22:895–905.

Anayeli Paulino and Gerardo Sierra. 2017. Applying the rhetorical structure theory in alzheimer patients' speech. In *Proceedings of the 6th Workshop on Recent Advances in RST and Related Formalisms*, page 34–38.

Fabian Pedregosa, Gaël Varoquaux, Alexandre Gramfort, Vincent Michel, Bertrand Thirion, Olivier Grisel, Mathieu Blondel, Peter Prettenhofer, Ron Weiss, Vincent Dubourg, et al. 2011. Scikit-learn: Machine learning in python. *Journal of machine learning research*, 12(Oct):2825–2830.

Rashmi Prasad, Nikhil Dinesh, Alan Lee, Eleni Miltsakaki, and Livio Robaldo. 2008. The Penn Discourse TreeBank 2.0. In *The 6th International Conference on Language Resources and Evaluation (LREC)*, pages 2961–2968.

Yao Qian, Xinhao Wang, Keelan Evanini, and David Suendermann-Oeft. 2016. Self-adaptive DNN for improving spoken language proficiency assessment. In *Proceedings of Interspeech 2016*, pages 3122–3126.

Ines Rehbein, Merel Scholman, and Vera Demberg. 2016. Annotating discourse relations in spoken language: A comparison of the PDTB and CCR frameworks. In *The Tenth International Conference on Language Resources and Evaluation (LREC 2016)*, pages 1039–1046.

Kenji Sagae. 2009. Analysis of discourse structure with syntactic dependencies and data-driven shift-reduce parsing. In *Proceedings of the 11th International Conference on Parsing Technologies*, pages 81–84.

Ted J. M. Sanders, Wilbert P. M. Spooren, and Leo G. M. Noordman. 1992. Toward a taxonomy of coherence relations. *Discourse Processes*, 15(1):1–35.

Svetlana Stoyanchev and Srinivas Bangalore. 2015. Discourse in customer care dialogues. Poster presented at the Workshop of Identification and Annotation of Discourse Relations in Spoken Language. Saarbrücken, Germany.

Maite Taboada and William C. Mann. 2006a. Applications of Rhetorical Structure Theory. *Discourse Studies*, 8(4):567–588.

Maite Taboada and William C. Mann. 2006b. Rhetorical Structure Theory: Looking back and moving ahead. *Discourse Studies*, 8(3):423–459.

Sara Tonelli, Giuseppe Riccardi, Rashmi Prasad, and Aravind Joshi. 2010. Annotation of discourse relations for conversational spoken dialogs. In *The Seventh International Conference on Language Resources and Evaluation (LREC'10)*, pages 2084–2090.

Xinhao Wang, James Bruno, Hillary Molloy, Keelan Evanini, and Klaus Zechner. 2017a. Discourse annotation of non-native spontaneous spoken responses using the rhetorical structure theory framework. In *Proceedings of the 55th Annual Meeting of the Association for Computational Linguistics (Volume 2: Short Papers)*, pages 263–268.

Xinhao Wang, Keelan Evanini, and Klaus Zechner. 2013. Coherence modeling for the automated assessment of spontaneous spoken responses. In *Human Language Technologies: Conference of the North American Chapter of the Association of Computational Linguistics, Proceedings*, pages 814–819, Atlanta, Georgia.

Xinhao Wang, Keelan Evanini, Klaus Zechner, and Matthew Mulholland. 2017b. Modeling discourse coherence for the automated scoring of spontaneous spoken responses. In *Proceedings of the Seventh ISCA workshop on Speech and Language Technology in Education 2017, SLaTE, August 25–26, Djurö, Stockholm, Sweden*.

Yizhong Wang, Sujian Li, and Houfeng Wang. 2017c. A two-stage parsing method for text-level discourse analysis. In *Proceedings of the 55th Annual Meeting of the Association for Computational Linguistics (Volume 2: Short Papers)*, pages 184–188.

Shasha Xie, Keelan Evanini, and Klaus Zechner. 2012. Exploring content features for automated speech scoring. In *Proceedings of the 2012 Conference of the North American Chapter of the Association for Computational Linguistics: Human Language Technologies*, pages 103–111.

Su-Youn Yoon and Suma Bhat. 2012. Assessment of ESL learners' syntactic competence based on similarity measures. In *Proceedings of the 2012 Conference on Empirical Methods in Natural Language Processing (EMNLP)*, pages 600–608.

Su-Youn Yoon, Suma Bhat, and Klaus Zechner. 2012. Vocabulary profile as a measure of vocabulary sophistication. In *Proceedings of the 7th Workshop on the Innovative Use of NLP for Building Educational Applications*, pages 180–189.

Klaus Zechner, Derrick Higgins, and Xiaoming Xi. 2007. Speechrater[SM]: A construct-driven approach to scoring spontaneous non-native speech. In *Proceedings of the International Speech Communication Association Special Interest Group on Speech and Language Technology in Education*, pages 128–131.

Klaus Zechner, Derrick Higgins, Xiaoming Xi, and David M. Williamson. 2009. Automatic scoring of non-native spontaneous speech in tests of spoken English. *Speech Communication*, 51(10):883–895.

Applying Rhetorical Structure Theory to Student Essays for Providing Automated Writing Feedback

Shiyan Jiang, Kexin Yang, Chandrakumari Suvarna,
Pooja Casula, Mingtong Zhang, Carolyn Penstein Rosé
School of Computer Science
Carnegie Mellon University
Pittsburgh, PA
{shiyanj,kexiny, csuvarna,
pcasula, mingtonz, cprose,}@andrew.cmu.edu

Abstract

We present a package of annotation resources, including annotation guideline, flowchart, and an Intelligent Tutoring System for training human annotators. These resources can be used to apply Rhetorical Structure Theory (RST) to essays written by students in K-12 schools. Furthermore, we highlight the great potential of using RST to provide automated feedback for improving writing quality across genres.

1 Introduction

Recent work in automated essay scoring focuses on local features of writing, often simply to predict grades, though sometimes to offer feedback (Burstein et al., 2003; Wilson et al., 2017). Our focus is specifically at the rhetorical structure level. Structural writing feedback is designed for helping writers to develop a clear structure in which sentences and paragraphs are well-organized (Huang et al., 2017). Researchers have made much progress in providing feedback for enhancing writing structure with the development of intelligent writing systems, such as Writing Mentor (Madnani et al., 2018) and Writing Pal (Roscoe and McNamara, 2013). However, structural writing feedback generated from existing systems is either locally situated in individual sentences or not specific enough for students to take actions. This paper presents how RST can be used to provide global structural feedback for improving writing quality and discusses future work about providing automated writing feedback with deep learning technology. Our contributions are 1) presenting RST annotation resources that can be used to annotate student essays and 2) highlighting the huge potential of using RST annotation for providing automated writing feedback in K-12 education.

2 Creating an Annotated RST Corpus of Student Writing

Though there is an existing data source annotated with RST (Carlson et al., 2002), for our effort we required a corpus of student writing that was annotated with RST. We obtained a student writing corpus through our partnership with TurnItIn.com. Here we describe the data we received, our effort to develop a coding manual for RST applied to this data for our purposes, and the resulting coded corpus.

2.1 Source data

Our data is drawn from a set of 137 student essays from Revision Assistant (Woods et al., 2017), which is an automated writing feedback system developed by TurnItIn.com. Of the 137 essays, 58 are from two genres (i.e., analysis and argumentative writing) and were the primary focus of our effort to design and develop resources to support our annotation effort, including a fine-grained annotation flowchart, guideline, and an intelligent tutoring system (ITS) for training human annotators. As a test of generality, we analyzed the remaining 79 essays, which were randomly sampled from four genres (i.e., analysis, argumentative, historical analysis, and informative writing).

2.2 Goal of annotation

The goal of annotation is to represent an essay in a rhetorical structure tree whose leaves are Elementary Discourse Units (EDUs) (Stede et al., 2017). In the tree, EDUs and spans of text are connected with rhetorical relations (explained in section 2.3). We assume a well-structured essay will have meaningful relations connecting the portions. When meaningful relations connecting EDUs or spans cannot be identified, the assumption is that a revision of structure is needed. The goal of

163

our envisioned automatically generated feedback is to point out these opportunities for improvement through restructuring to students.

More specifically, a span is formed by EDUs connected with rhetorical relations and usually includes multiple EDUs. For example, Figure 1 represents a tree that includes six EDUs (28-33) and four spans (span 29-31, 28-31, 32-33, and 28-33). In some cases, a single EDU is a span when there are no EDUs connecting with it.

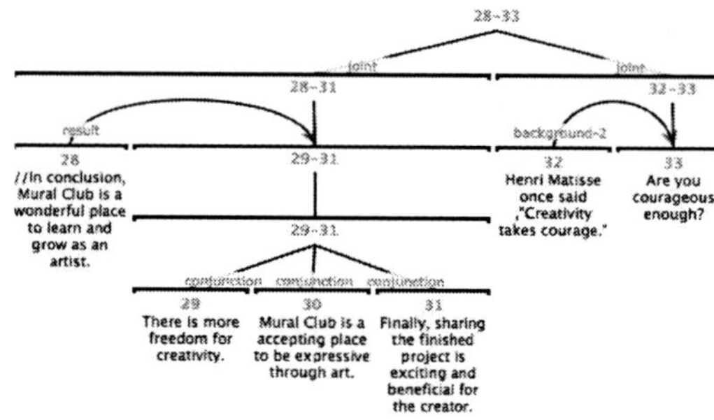

Figure 1: Example of RST annotation with rstWeb

Notice that the EDUs of text at the leaf nodes are mostly single sentences. We segment essays with sentences to represent essays with higher level structure and trigger structural feedback. We used individual sentences as EDUs to provide writing feedback between sentences and paragraphs. Namely, each EDU is a complete sentence, which could be indicated by a full stop, exclamation, or question mark. However, students might use several sentences in prompt sources or punctuation in the wrong way. In these two scenarios, the criteria of punctuation cannot be used to segment essays into EDUs. Instead, we treated continuous sentences in prompt sources as one EDU and segmented essays based on correct punctuation.

2.3 Adaptation of RST for our Data

Though our goal was to retain as much of the spirit of RST as possible, we adjusted its definitions and scope in order to tailor it for our data. We could not share the dataset due to privacy issues. Instead, we clearly demonstrate how to adapt RST for annotating student essays in this section. Annotators need to identify rhetorical relations between three kinds of units: EDUs, spans, and paragraphs. These relations can be divided into two categories: Nucleus-Satellite (N-S) relation and multi-nuclear relation. N-S relation represents the relation between units that are not equally important while multi-nuclear relation represents the relation between equally important units. We developed a guideline for annotators to understand the definition and examples of these relations.

Combine	Eliminate	Change
Conjunction	Condition	Background
Sequence	Unless	Justify
List	Purpose	Preparation
	Disjunction	Summary

Table 1: Adaptation of RST relations.

Mann and Thompson (1987) defined 23 rhetorical relations and the set of relations has been augmented with eight more relations. We combined, eliminated, and made minor changes (e.g., dividing one relation into multiple ones) to some relations for the purpose of providing meaningful writing feedback (see Table 1).

Specifically, we use Conjunction to represent the relations of Conjunction, Sequence, and List. These three relations all represent sentences being conjoined to serve a common purpose, we combined them because it is doubtful that distinguishing the nuance between these homogeneous relations will have much benefit for triggering writing feedback. In addition, we eliminated the relations of Condition, Unless, Purpose, and Disjunction as they rarely occurred between sentences.

Furthermore, based on the characteristics of student essays, we made minor changes to the relations of Background, Justify, Preparation, and Summary. We divided the relation of Background into two relations, namely the relations of Background-1 and Background-2. Background-1 refers to the relation that describes two closely connected units in which one of them includes pronouns (e.g., it or them) pointing at something mentioned in the other one. This makes it necessary to present one unit for readers to understand the other unit. Background-2 refers to the relation that describes two loosely related units in which one unit increases the reader's ability to understand the other one. We made this distinction because these two relations are very frequently seen in students' essays, yet they can potentially prompt for different writing feedback.

In terms of the relation of Justify, we used the common scenario of two units being inseparable (i.e., one unit is a question and the other unit is the answer) to identify it. This differs from the relation of Solutionhood as it refers to a pair of answer and question, instead of problem and solution.

In addition, we extended the definition of the relation of Preparation. Our definition of Preparation includes the common scenario of one unit being the generic description and the other unit being the detailed description. For instance, one unit is: "I have three reasons to be vegetarian", and the other unit is: "First, it is healthier, second, it protects animals, and the third is that it saves the earth from global warming." This type of sentence pairs fit the definition of Preparation which describes that the reader's comprehending the Satellite increases the reader's readiness to accept the writer's right to present the Nucleus.

For the relation of Summary, we only looked at the paragraph level granularity. One unit being the summary of parts of a paragraph is not useful for providing feedback and not much different from the relation of Restatement, while one unit summarizing all other units in a paragraph could indicate a high-quality student writing. Therefore, we only considered cases where one unit summarizes a whole paragraph for providing feedback.

While these changes may seem arbitrary, we find it necessary to make these changes during our annotation process to reduce confusion, increase inter-rater reliability and identify relations that can reveal the structure of student essays and trigger meaningful writing feedback. Specifically, the first and second author independently annotated all essays. Any inconsistencies were discussed and resolved resulting in 100% agreement.

2.4 Annotation process

The structure of the coding manual is driven by the process we advocate to human annotators and we followed a top-down annotation strategy (Iruskieta et al., 2014). Overall, the annotation process is meant to consist of five steps:

First step: Segment an essay into EDUs. This step is explained in subsection 2.2.

Second step: Identify central claims in each paragraph. In this step, annotators should first read the whole essay and understand its line of argumentation. Then annotators should identify EDUs that are central claims in each paragraph. Identifying central claims is useful for deciding whether two units are equally important in the third step.

Third step: Identify rhetorical relations between EDUs. In this step, annotators can use rstWeb, a tool for RST annotation developed by Zeldes (2016), to decide the relations between adjacent EDUs in each paragraph from left to right. Specifically, annotators should first determine whether two adjacent EDUs are equally important. The more important EDU is a Nucleus while the other EDU is a Satellite. To identify whether two EDUs are equally important, annotators can use the flowchart in Figure 2. Then annotators should follow a flowchart (Jiang et al., 2019) to identify the relation. The order of relations in the flowchart is based on the ease they can be excluded. Namely, the easier it is to decide whether one relation applies or not, the earlier it appears in the flowchart. If no relation can be used to describe the relation, then the left EDU is the end of a span. A span is formed by EDUs connected with rhetorical relations, as described in subsection 2.2.

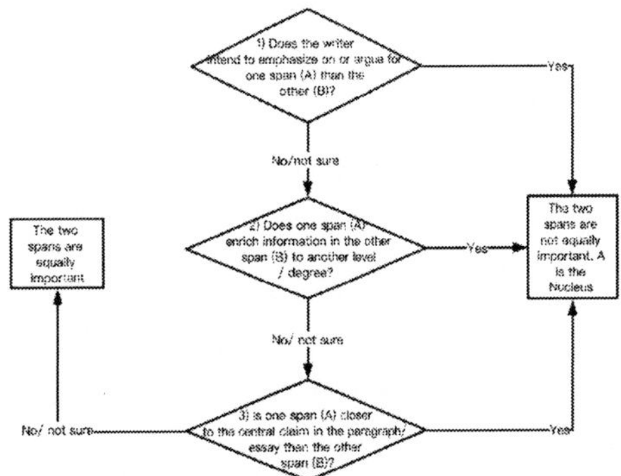

Figure 2: Flowchart for identifying importance

Fourth step: Identify rhetorical relations between spans. In this step, annotators should identify relations between spans within each paragraph from left to right. When identifying relations between two spans, annotators should use the same flowchart in the third step to determine relations between the Nucleus of two spans. If no relation exists between spans, annotators should use Joint to build the paragraph into a tree.

Fifth step: Identify rhetorical relations between paragraphs. Annotators should identify relations between paragraphs from left to right. Similar to the fourth step, annotators should determine the relation between the Nucleus of two paragraphs. If any of the two paragraphs contain the relation of Joint, it indicates that spans in the paragraph do

165

not have strong relations. In this case, the relation of Joint should be used to connect two paragraphs.

2.5 Practical RST Intelligent Tutor

Based on the flowchart and guideline that make up our coding manual, we developed an Intelligent Tutoring System (ITS) to help novice annotators learn RST annotation efficiently. We built the Practical RST Intelligent Tutor using Cognitive Tutor Authoring Tools (CTAT), an authoring tool for ITS (Aleven et al., 2009). This tutor (Figure 3, access upon request) is hosted on an open platform TutorShop that provides free access for research or public use. As shown in Figure 3, annotators are first presented with three RST relations including their definitions, examples of sentence pairs, conjunction phrases, and groups. Conjunction phrases refer to connection words or phrases that can naturally conjoin two spans. For example, "because" can be used to connect two spans that indicate the relation of Cause. Groups refer to the categories of relations: progressive, supplementary, conjunct, repeating, contrast or no relation. These categories represent a higher level of RST relations. Annotators are then guided to identify the relation of a given sentence pair, and are scaffolded with step by step procedures and hints to complete the task.

To develop the system, we conducted two rounds of cognitive task analysis (Crandall et al., 2006), respectively with five subjects who had no prior experience in RST and three subjects with experience in RST. After analyzing think-aloud data from the first round, we found that novice annotators regularly referred back to the definition of RST relations, compared given sentence pairs with provided examples, and inserted conjunction phrases between annotation units to see whether it made sense logically. Based on these findings, we developed an initial intelligent tutoring system. We further ran a pilot study involving target users with background or experience in RST. These users further provided feedback on both the interface and instructional design. We refined our tutor accordingly with additional features of arranging problems from easy to hard, adjusted granularity of step-loop, and used more harmonious visual design. This intelligent tutor also takes advantage of the Bayesian Knowledge Tracing algorithm (Baker et al., 2008) developed at Carnegie Mellon University to provide adap-

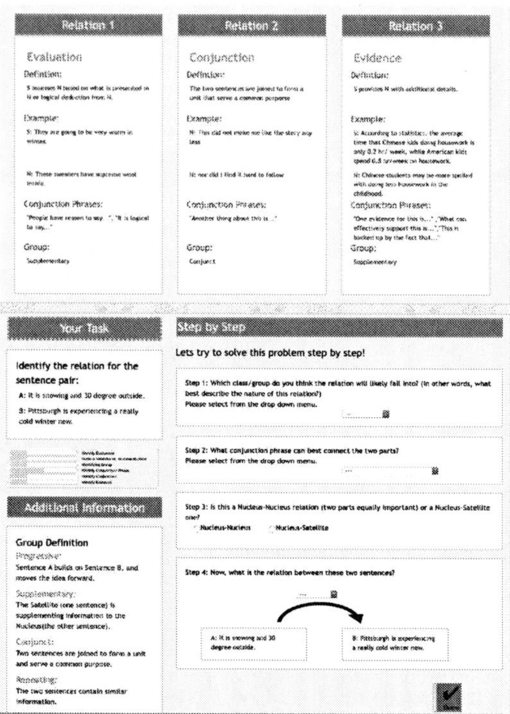

Figure 3: Interface of Practical RST Intelligent Tutor

tive problem selection, which can assist learners to achieve mastery in four knowledge components (i.e. identifying groups, conjunction phrases, nuclearity, and relations) about identifying RST relations (Koedinger et al., 2012).

3 From RST Analysis to Writing Feedback

Here we explain the potential of using RST for providing structural writing feedback across genres and for specific genres.

RST can be used to provide writing feedback for enhancing coherence across genres. Coherence refers to how sentences in an essay are connected and how an essay is organized. RST could be used to provide actionable writing feedback for increasing the level of coherence that traditional automated coherence scores were deemed insufficient to realize. Specifically, the relation of Joint indicates a low level of coherence. As an example, Figure 1 is an annotation of one paragraph from student writing. This paragraph includes two spans (i.e., span 28-31 and span 32-33) that are not connected clearly. In span 28-31, the writer listed three benefits of joining a club. In span 32-33, the writer might intend to encourage people to join the club while the intention is not clear as there is no mention of joining the club. The RST tree had the potential of giving more concrete context for low-level coherence and in this way, students could identify where they can make revisions for clearer structure.

In terms of providing feedback in specific genres, the combination of relations can indicate high-quality writing. For example, presenting and analyzing evidence is an indication of high-quality argumentative writing (Gleason, 1999). Researchers have made much effort in predicting whether there is evidence in student writing and pointed out the need for future studies in examining how evidence was used to show the soundness and strength of arguments. RST can be used to meet the need with predicting the combination of relations, such as the combination of evidence and interpretation or the combination of evidence and evaluation.

Furthermore, RST is valuable to provide writing feedback in analysis writing. Making comparisons is a common structure of well-organized analysis writing. It's easy to identify sentences involving comparison locally. However, identifying the whole structure of making comparisons in an essay remains to be a challenging automation task. RST has the potential to address the challenge by illustrating a global comparative structure with the relation of Contrast, Antithesis, or Concession.

4   Conclusion

We take full advantage of RST in providing structural feedback for enhancing writing quality across genres. Currently, based on the work from Li et al. (2014), we are building an RST parser that can generate RST trees to represent student essays automatically with deep learning techniques. In the future, we plan to build the work from Fiacco et al. (2019) to generate RST trees more accurately and efficiently. Our long term goal is to embed these techniques in a writing tutor like Revision Assistant and conduct large-scale classroom studies to evaluate the effect of RST trees in writing instruction.

Acknowledgments

This work was funded in part by NSF grant #1443068 and a Schmidt foundation postdoc fellowship. We thank our collaborators at TurnItIn.com for providing student essays. We also thank Vincent Aleven and Jonathan Sewall for design suggestions and guidance in building the practical RST intelligent tutor.

References

Vincent Aleven, Bruce McLaren, Jonathan Sewall, and Kenneth R. Koedinger. 2009. Example-tracing tutors: A new paradigm for intelligent tutoring systems. *International Journal of Artificial Intelligence in Education*, 19(2):105.

Ryan S. Baker, Albert T. Corbett, and Vincent Aleven. 2008. More accurate student modeling through contextual estimation of slip and guess probabilities in Bayesian Knowledge Tracing. In *International conference on intelligent tutoring systems*, pages 406–415.

Jill Burstein, Daniel Marcu, and Kevin Knight. 2003. Finding the write stuff: automatic identification of discourse structure in student essays. *IEEE Intelligent Systems*, 18:32–39.

Lynn Carlson, Daniel Marcu, and Mary Ellen Okurowski. 2002. *RST Discourse Treebank*. Linguistic Data Consortium, University of Pennsylvania.

Beth Crandall, Gary Klein, and Robert R. Hoffman. 2006. *Working Minds: A Practitioner's Guide to Cognitive Task Analysis*. A Bradford Book.

James Fiacco, Elena Cotos, and Carolyn Rose. 2019. Towards enabling feedback on rhetorical structure with neural sequence models. In *Proceedings of the 9th International Conference on Learning Analytics and Knowledge*, pages 301–319.

Mary M . Gleason. 1999. The role of evidence in argumentative writing. *Reading and Writing Quarterly*, 15(1):81–106.

Yi-Ching Huang, Jiunn-Chia Huang, Hao-Chuan Wang, and Jane Yung jen Hsu. 2017. Supporting ESL writing by prompting crowdsourced structural feedback. In *Proceedings of the Fifth AAAI Conference on Human Computation and Crowdsourcing*, pages 71–78.

Mikel Iruskieta, Arantza Daz de Ilarraza, and Mikel Lersundi. 2014. The annotation of the central unit in rhetorical structure trees: A key step in annotating rhetorical relations. In *Proceedings of COLING 2014, the 25th International Conference on Computational Linguistics: Technical Papers*, pages 466–475.

Shiyan Jiang, Kexin Yang, Chandrakumari Suvarna, and Carolyn Ros. 2019. Guideline and Flowchart for Rhetorical Structure Theory Annotation. Technical report, Carnegie Mellon University, School of Computer Science.

Kenneth R. Koedinger, Albert T. Corbett, and Charles Perfetti. 2012. The Knowledge-Learning-Instruction framework: Bridging the science-practice chasm to enhance robust student learning. *Cognitive Science*, 36:757–798.

Jiwei Li, Rumeng Li, and Eduard Hovy. 2014. Recursive deep models for discourse parsing. In *Proceedings of the 2014 Conference on Empirical Methods in Natural Language Processing (EMNLP)*, pages 2061–2069.

Nitin Madnani, Jill Burstein, Norbert Elliot, Beata Beigman Klebanov, Diane Napolitano, Slava Andreyev, and Maxwell Schwartz. 2018. Writing mentor: Self-regulated writing feedback for struggling writers. In *Proceedings of the 27th International Conference on Computational Linguistics: System Demonstrations*, pages 113–117.

William C. Mann and Sandra A. Thompson. 1987. *Rhetorical Structure Theory: A Theory of Text Organization*. University of Southern California, Information Sciences Institute.

Rod Roscoe and Danielle McNamara. 2013. Writing pal: Feasibility of an intelligent writing strategy tutor in the high school classroom. *Journal of Educational Psychology*, 105(4):1010–1025.

Manfred Stede, Maite Taboada, and Debopam Das. 2017. Annotation guidelines for rhetorical structure. Version 1.0.

Joshua Wilson, Rod Roscoe, and Yusra Ahmed. 2017. Automated formative writing assessment using a levels of language framework. *Assessing Writing*, 34:16–36.

Bronwyn Woods, David Adamson, Shayne Miel, and Elijah Mayfield. 2017. Formative essay feedback using predictive scoring models. In *Proceedings of the 23rd ACM SIGKDD International Conference on Knowledge Discovery and Data Mining*, pages 2071–2080.

Amir Zeldes. 2016. rstWeb-a browser-based annotation interface for Rhetorical Structure Theory and discourse relations. In *Proceedings of the 2016 Conference of the North American Chapter of the Association for Computational Linguistics: Demonstrations*, pages 1–5.

Author Index

Association for Computational Linguistics
209 N. Eighth Street
Stroudsburg, Pennsylvania 18360

ISBN 978-1-5108-8781-7